INTERPRETIVE ETHNOGRAPHY

Dedicated to Kenneth F. Denzin
1920-1995
Friend and Father

INTERPRETIVE ETHNOGRAPHY

Ethnographic Practices for the 21st Century

Norman K. Denzin

SAGE Publications
International Educational and Professional Publisher
Thousand Oaks   London   New Delhi

For information address:

 SAGE Publications, Inc.
2455 Teller Road
Thousand Oaks, California 91320
E-mail: order@sagepub.com

SAGE Publications Ltd.
6 Bonhill Street
London EC2A 4PU
United Kingdom

SAGE Publications India Pvt. Ltd.
M-32 Market
Greater Kailash I
New Delhi 110 048 India

Printed in the United States of America

Library of Congress Cataloging-in-Publication Data

Denzin, Norman K.
  Interpretive ethnography: ethnographic practices for the 21st century /
author Norman K. Denzin.
     p. cm.
  Includes bibliographical references.
  ISBN 0-8039-7298-9 (cloth: acid-free paper).—ISBN 0-8039-7299-7 (pbk.:
acid-free paper)
     1. Ethnology—Philosophy. 2. Ethnology—Authorship. 3. Ethnology—
Methodology. I. Title.
  GN345.D46 1996   96-25245
  305.8'001—dc20

         00 01 02 03 10 9 8 7 6 5 4

Acquiring Editor:	Peter Labella
Editorial Assistant:	Frances Borghi
Production Editor:	Michèle Lingre
Production Assistant:	Sherrise Purdum
Typesetter/Designer:	Marion Warren
Indexer:	Paul Benson
Cover Designer:	Lesa Valdez
Print Buyer:	Anna Chin

Every morning brings us news of the globe, and yet we are poor in noteworthy stories. This is because no event any longer comes to us without already being shot through with explanation. In other words, by now almost nothing that happens benefits storytelling: Almost everything benefits information. Actually, it is half the art of storytelling to keep a story free from explanation as one reproduces it.

—Benjamin (1968, p. 89)

Writers are always selling somebody out.

—Didion (1968, p. xiv)

Contents

PART 3:
Whose Truth?

Introduction

It is a question, rather, of producing a new concept of writing.
                                                    —Derrida (1981, p. 26)

The anthropologist, as we already know, does not find things; s/he makes them. And makes them up.
                                                    —Trinh (1989, p. 141)

Ethnography is that form of inquiry and writing that produces descriptions and accounts about the ways of life of the writer and those written about. This is a book about ethnographic writing in the twilight years of the twentieth century—ethnography's sixth moment. In the twentieth century, ethnography has passed through five historical moments: the traditional (1900 to World War II), modernist (World War II to the mid-1970s), blurred genres (1970-1986), crisis of representation (1986 to present), and the fifth moment (now)(see Denzin & Lincoln, 1994; Lincoln & Denzin, 1994).[1]

Interpretive ethnography faces a crossroad. It is time to take stock, to review where ethnography has come, and to examine the experimental work of the past decade and the critiques it has produced and confronted (Clough, 1992, 1994; Conquergood, 1991; Jackson, 1989; Marcus, 1994, p. 567; Tyler, 1986).

A single, nine-part thesis organizes my reading of this situation. First, I read ethnography through Derrida (1981), who argues, as Clough (1994, p. 171) reminds us, that a theory of the social is also a theory of writing. A theory of writing is also a theory of interpretive (ethnographic) work. Theory, writing, and ethnography are inseparable material practices. Together they create the conditions that locate the social inside the text. Hence, those who write culture also write theory. Also, those who write theory write culture. Paraphrasing Clough (1994), there is a need for a reflexive form of writing that turns ethnographic and theoretical texts back "onto each other" (p. 62).

Second, American ethnography is deeply embedded in American and world culture. As that culture has gone postmodern and multinational, so too has ethnography. The ethnographic project has changed because the world that ethnography confronts has changed. Disjuncture and difference define this global, postmodern cultural economy we all live in (Appadurai, 1990, 1993). National boundaries and identities blur. Everyone is a tourist, an immigrant, a refugee, an exile, or a guest worker, moving from one part of the world to another. The new global cultural economy is shaped by new technologies, shifting systems of money, and media images that flow across old national borders. Cultural narratives still entangled in the Enlightenment worldview circulate between the First and Third Worlds (Fischer, 1994; see Geertz, 1995, pp. 128-131). The periphery has been electronically transported into the center of these First World stories. Old master images and values, from freedom to welfare, human rights, sovereignty, representation, and "the master-term 'democracy' " (Appadurai, 1990, p. 10), are part of this global discursive system.

This is a postcolonial world, and it is necessary to think beyond the nation (Appadurai, 1993, p. 411), or the local group, as the focus of inquiry. This is the age of electronic capitalism, diaspora, and instant democracy in the media. Postnational social formations compete for resources to serve the needs of refugees, exiles, and the victims of ethnic and cultural genocide. America has become "a federation of diasporas, American-Indians, American-Haitians, American-Irish, American-Africans. . . . The hyphenated American might have to be twice hyphenated (Asian-American-Japanese, or . . . Hispanic-American-Bolivian)" (Appadurai, 1993, p. 424).

Third, this is the world that ethnography is mapped into and grows out of—the world in which ethnographic texts circulate like other commodities in the electronic world economy. It may be, as Tyler (1986, p. 123) argues, that ethnography is "the discourse of the post-modern world." If this is so, however, it is no longer possible to take for granted what is meant by ethnography.[2] The classic realist ethnographic text is now under attack. It is time to teach readers and writers how to engage, produce, and understand the new ethnographic text.[3] Global and local legal processes have problematicized and erased the personal and institutional distance between the ethnographer and those he or she writes about (Lee & Ackerman, 1994, p. 350). We do not own the field notes we make about those we study. We do not have an undisputed warrant to study anyone or anything. Subjects now challenge how they have been written about and some ethnographers have been taken to court (Lee & Ackerman, 1994, p. 343).

Fourth, accordingly, self-reflexivity in ethnography is no longer a luxury, a "privileged understanding done at one's leisure" (Lee & Ackerman, 1994, p. 351). The writer can no longer presume to be able to present an objective, noncontested account of the other's experiences. Those we study have their own understandings of how they want to be represented.

Furthermore, the worlds we study are created, in part, through the texts that we write and perform about them. These texts take four forms: ordinary talk and speech, inscriptions of that speech in the form of transcriptions, written interpretations based on talk and its inscriptions, and performances of those texts. Ethnographic texts are the primary texts given for the interpretive, ethnographic project. These texts are always dialogical—the site at which the voices of the other, alongside the voices of the author, come alive and interact with one another. Thus, the voices that are seen and heard (if only imaginatively) in the text are themselves textual, performative accomplishments. These accomplishments have a prior life in the context of where they were produced. Texts, as I discuss in Chapter 2, are easily reproduced; contexts are not.

Fifth, ethnography is a gendered project. Feminist, postcolonial, and queer theory question the Oedipal logic of the heterosexual, narrative ethnographic text that reflexively positions the ethnographer's

gender-neutral (or masculine) self within a realist story about the
"other" (see Anzaldua, 1987; Chow, 1993; Clough, 1994; Spivak, 1990;
Trinh, 1989). It is now understood that reflexivity does not produce a
solidified ethnographic identity. The ethnographer works within a "hybrid" reality (Trinh, 1992, p. 140). Experience, discourse, and self-under-
standings collide against larger cultural assumptions concerning race,
ethnicity, nationality, gender, class, and age. A certain identity is never
possible; the ethnographer must always ask, "Not *Who* Am I?," but
"*When, where, how* am I (so and so)?" (Trinh, 1992, p. 157; also quoted in
Clough, 1994, p. 116).

Sixth, following from the third and fourth assumptions, ethnography is a moral, allegorical, and therapeutic project. Ethnography is more
than the record of human experience. The ethnographer writes tiny
moral tales—tales that do more than celebrate cultural difference or
bring another culture alive. The ethnographer's story is written as a
prop, a pillar, that, to paraphrase William Faulkner (1967, p. 724), and
C. Wright Mills (1959, p. 225), will help men and women endure and
prevail in the frightening twilight years of the twentieth century. These
tales record the agonies, pains, successes, and tragedies of human
experience. They record the deeply felt emotions of love, dignity, pride,
honor, and respect.

A feminist, communitarian moral ethic structures these tales (see
Ryan, 1995). Following Christians, Ferre, and Fackler (1993, pp. 12-17,
194-195), this ethic presumes a dialogical view of the self.[4] It seeks to
produce narratives that ennoble human experience while facilitating
civic transformations in the public (and private) spheres. This ethic
promotes universal human solidarity. It ratifies the dignity of the self
and the value of human life. It is committed to human justice and the
empowerment of groups of interacting individuals (Christians et al.,
1993, pp. 193-194).

The feminist, communitarian ethical model produces a series of
norms for ethnographic writing.[5] The ethnographer's moral tales are
not written to produce harm for others. The ethnographer's tale is
always allegorical—a symbolic tale that is not just a record of human
experience. This tale is a means of experience for the reader. It is a
vehicle for readers to discover moral truths about themselves. More
deeply, the ethnographic tale is a utopian tale of self and social redemp-

tion, a tale that brings a moral compass back into the readers (and the writer's) life. The ethnographer discovers the multiple "truths" that operate in the social world—the stories people tell one another about the things that matter to them (see Straley, 1992, p. 9). These stories move people to action, and they rest on a distinction between fact and truth. Truth and facts are socially constructed, and people build stories around the meanings of facts. Ethnographers collect and tell these multiple versions of the truth.[6]

Seventh, although the field of qualitative research is defined by constant breaks and ruptures, there is a shifting center to the project: the avowed humanistic commitment to study the social world from the perspective of the interacting individual (Lincoln & Denzin, 1994, p. 575). From this principle flow the liberal and radical politics of action that are held by feminist, clinical, ethnic, critical, and cultural studies researchers. Although multiple interpretive communities now circulate within the field of qualitative research, they are all united on this single point.

Eighth, ethnography's sixth moment will be defined by the work that ethnographers do as they implement the previously discussed assumptions. Endless self-reflections and self-referential criticisms will produce few texts anchored in the worlds of concrete human experience (Ashley, Gilmore, & Peters, 1994; Lincoln & Denzin, 1994, p. 577). Although I will add my own self-reflections to this project, my aim is always to keep my text anchored in the worlds of lived experience.

Ninth, the experimental versions of ethnography that have appeared since *Writing Culture* (Clifford & Marcus, 1986) have been vehemently criticized for being narcissistic, overly reflexive, and not scientific; some even call the new ethnographers ethnographs (e.g., see Dawson & Prus, 1993, 1995; Farberman, 1991, p. 475, 1992; Kleinman, 1993; Kunda, 1993; Lofland, 1993; Nader, 1993; Prus, 1996, p. 218; Sanders, 1995; Snow & Morrill, 1993, 1995a, 1995b). These criticisms serve to police the boundaries of ethnography, inscribing a proper version of how this form of scientific work should be done. These criticisms reproduce a traditional bias that argues that ethnographers study real people in the real world. The ethnographer's task is clear. Malinowski (1922/1961), a founding father, was quite clear on this: "Find out the typical ways of thinking and feeling, corresponding to the institutions and culture of a given community and formulate the results in the most convincing way" (p. 3; also quoted in Van Maanen, 1995b, p. 6). This injunction dictated that the analyst show how culture and social structure were mapped into the mental structures of the persons studied. A cultural transmission model was thereby directly translated into realist ethnography. Ethnographers connect meanings (culture) to observable action in the real world.

I will argue repeatedly in the chapters that follow that this is a flawed and inadequate model. C. Wright Mills (1963) and Stuart Hall (1985) remind us that humans live in a secondhand world of meanings. They have no direct access to reality. Reality as it is known is mediated by symbolic representation, by narrative texts, and by cinematic and televisual structures that stand between the person and the so-called real world. In critically reading these texts, the new ethnographers radically subvert the realist agenda because the real world is no longer the referent for analysis. Ethnographies of group life are now directed to this world of televisual and cinematic narrativity and its place in the dreams, fantasies, and interactions of everyday people. Malinowski's (1922/1961) definition of ethnography is no longer workable.

These nine situations set the stage for ethnography's transformation in the twenty-first century. If the postmodern ethnography is the moral discourse of the contemporary world, then this writing form must be changed. Several interconnected lines of action are suggested. The ethnographer can act as a scribe for the other, writing "messy" texts (see below; Marcus, 1994). The writer can become a coauthor with the other, producing a joint document, which has long been the tradition in critical, participatory research (see Kincheloe & McLaren, 1994; Reason, 1994). The writer can produce a purely autoethnographic text based on his or her personal experiences (see Ellis, 1994, 1995a, 1995b; Richardson, 1993, 1995; Ronai, 1995). A performance text (Chapter 4) can be constructed; the writer can experiment with the writing styles created by the new journalists, even those pursuing mystery fiction.

These are some of the many options available to us. They are explored in detail in the chapters that follow. In every instance, the ethnographer attempts to write in a way that adheres to the norms and values of the feminist, communitarian ethic.

Background

This, then, is a book about the prospects, problems, and forms of ethnographic, interpretive writing in the twenty-first century. Since 1986, ethnographers have been writing their way out of Clifford and Marcus's (1986) *Writing Culture*. Ethnographers are now in the "sixth moment" of inquiry. This is a period of intense reflection, "messy texts" (Marcus, 1994, p. 567), experiments in autoethnography (Okely & Callaway, 1992), ethnographic poetics (Marcus & Fischer, 1986, p. 74), anthropological and sociological poetry (Benson, 1993; Brady, 1991a, 1991b, 1991c; Diamond, 1982, 1985a, 1985b, 1986a, 1986b; Hymes, 1985; Prattis, 1985a, 1985b, 1985c; Richardson, 1993, 1992; Rose, 1991), evocative and layered accounts (Ellis, 1994; Ronai, 1995), short stories (Ellis, 1993), the "New Journalism" (Marcus & Fischer, 1986, pp. 75-76; Wolfe & Johnson, 1973), performance texts (McCall & Becker, 1990; Paget, 1990a, 1990b; Richardson, 1993, 1994a, 1994b), plays (Grindal & Shephard, 1993; Richardson & Lockridge, 1991), ethnographic fictions and ethnographic novels (Marcus & Fischer, 1986, p. 75), and narratives of the self (Ellis, 1995a, 1995b; Ellis & Flaherty, 1992b; Van Maanen, 1995a).

These messy texts are often grounded in the study of epiphanal moments in people's lives: the birth of a child (Prattis, 1985c), a sudden death (Ellis, 1993), and the field experience itself (Gottlieb & Graham, 1993). The focus is on those events, narratives, and stories people tell one another as they attempt to make sense of the epiphanies or existential turning-point moments in their lives.[7] Messy texts are many sited, open ended, they refuse theoretical closure, and they do not indulge in abstract, analytic theorizing. They make the writer a part of the writing project. These texts, however, are not just subjective accounts of experience; they attempt to reflexively map multiple discourses that occur in a given social space. Hence, they are always multivoiced, and no given interpretation is privileged. They reject the principles of the realist ethnographic narrative that makes claims to textual autonomy and to offering authoritative accounts of the processes being examined (Bruner, 1993, p. 1; Clough, 1992, p. 10; Lee & Ackerman, 1994, p. 350).

The epiphanic, messy text redefines the ethnographic project. The writer-as-scribe for the other also becomes a cultural critic, a person who voices interpretations about the events recorded and observed. At the same time, as the scribe of a messy text the writer shapes the representations that are brought to the people studied. We study those biographical moments that connect us and our private troubles (our epiphanies) to the larger public culture and its social institutions (Mills, 1959, p. 8). There are many risks here and they are explored in Chapter 7 (see Hymes, 1985).

These experiments in genre, voice, narrative, and interpretive style challenge, while they belie a commitment to a visual, ocular epistemology—an epistemology that privileges sight, sound, and vision (Chapter 8; Denzin, 1995a; Jay, 1993; Tyler, 1986, p. 136). There are other ways of knowing, other ways of feeling our way into the experiences of self and other (see Ong, 1977). An ethnographic epistemology that goes beyond vision and mimesis is required (see Tyler, 1986, p. 130). This will be an evocative epistemology that performs, rather than represents, the world (Tyler, 1986, p. 136; see also Bochner and Ellis, 1996).

The dividing lines between a secular science of the social world and sacred understandings of that world are now being challenged and, in some cases, erased (Lincoln & Denzin, 1994, p. 576; Nelson, 1983, 1989). Interpretive ethnographic writing in the twenty-first century will move closer to a sacred and critically informed discourse about the moral, human universe (Clough, 1992, 1994). The chapters in this book speak to this new discourse, a new ethics of inquiry.

This Book

This book begins where *The Cinematic Society: The Voyeur's Gaze* (Denzin, 1995a) ended—with the call for a postpragmatist, ethnographic, ethical model fitted to the cinematic, video age.[8] In that book, I used the voyeur's cinematic text as a backdrop for criticizing current interpretive practices in the social sciences, especially the practices of ethnography and cultural studies. I argued that the cultural logics of the postvideo, cinematic culture define the lived experiences that a critical cultural studies project takes as its subject matter.

Television, cinema, ethnography, and the panoptic gaze of the cultural voyeur are the keys to the production of these authentic, realistic accounts of lived experience. In these texts, there is a subtle and sudden switching of surveillance codes from Foucault's panopticon to a system of deterrence (Baudrillard, 1983, p. 53), in which the person gazed upon is the person doing the gazing—the voyeur-as-newsmaker, tourist, traveling ethnographer, or the writer of messy texts.

The cultural voyeur moves back and forth between both forms of textuality—the cinematic, televisual representation of reality and the new ethnographic text. The unstable relationship between the ethnographer, the cultural subject, the ethnographic text, and cinematic and video representations cannot be avoided. Current cultural critics of ethnography, and cultural studies, however, have yet to seriously interrogate and question their own license to gaze, let alone write about what they gaze upon (see Clough, 1994, p. 117; see also Anzaldua, 1987, p. 23; Chow, 1993; Sharpe, 1993; Spivak, 1990, p. 51; Trinh, 1989, p. 22). That is, many appear to justify the gazing eye of the voyeuristic cultural critic by appealing to the politics of resistance that they attempt to write (see Drotner, 1994; Schwarz, 1994, p. 389). They remain, accordingly, under the protective umbrella the surveillance society has traditionally and always made available to the voyeur disguised as ethnographer or field-worker.

In *The Cinematic Society* (Denzin, 1995a), I sought to unmask this voyeur. In the nine chapters that follow, I seek to put into place a new mask for this individual.

The first chapter in Part I, "The Lessons James Joyce Teaches Us," outlines the representation and legitimation crises now confronting the social sciences and the ethnographic project more broadly defined. I use the work of James Joyce as a model for the kind of writing I will develop in later chapters. In this chapter, I struggle to name this project, offering the unsatisfactory term, critical poststructuralism. Chapter 2, "Visual Truth and the Ethnographic Project," elaborates the representational crisis, focusing on a critique of the cinematic apparatus and the visual regimes of truth that apparatus has produced. I attempt to expose the limits of the gaze and the new technologies that have been deployed to better capture and reveal reality in its fullest. I assess the part the social sciences have played in this project, critiquing the investigative, ethnographic, qualitative gaze that the social sciences have used throughout the twentieth century. I call, after Martin Jay (1993), for a new epistemology of truth. This is an epistemology that goes beyond the ocular-based systems of knowing, emphasizing the other senses, especially hearing (the acoustical eye).

The five chapters in Part II turn to the new experiential texts that ethnographers are now producing. Chapter 3, "Standpoint Epistemologies," examines the works of Dorothy Smith, Patricia Hill Collins, Gloria Anzaldua, and Trinh T. Min-Ha. I show how the standpoint text reproduces certain misunderstandings concerning lived experience and its representation in the ethnographic text. Chapter 4, "Performance Texts," examines performance-based texts and offers a framework for producing this kind of work in ethnography's sixth moment.

Chapter 5, "The New Journalists," takes up the work of the literary or new journalists (Wolfe, Didion, Malcom, Capote, and Mailer), arguing that ethnographers have much to learn from this body of work, which I return to in Chapter 9 when I discuss civic journalism. Chapter 6 suggests that the modernist ethnographic model of textuality must be replaced by a new form of fiction that draws on the postmodern detective and his or her search for a moral truth about self. The postmodern detective, unlike his or her modernist counterpart, is no longer an objective observer of the world. In this chapter, I challenge the privileged place Tyler (1986, p. 123) assigns the postmodern ethnography. I call for a form of detective fiction that answers to moral and not scientific or aesthetic norms of accountability. Chapter 7 offers an interpretation of ethnopoetics and personal narratives of the self, creating a space for this kind of work within the framework of the messy text.

The two chapters in Part III bring this work to conclusion. Chapter 8 analyzes the recent embracement of narrative analysis by the social sciences (see Brown, 1987; Clandinin & Connelly, 1994; Clough, 1992, 1994; Manning & Cullum-Swan, 1994; Polkinghorne, 1988, 1995; Reissman, 1993; Rorty, 1989; Tyler, 1986; Vidich & Lyman, 1994; Wolcott, 1994). This narrative turn has produced an embarrassment of riches because multiple narrative strategies now exist (semiotic, rhetorical, topological, structural, feminist, content based, micro level, dramaturgical, thematic, and functional). These strategies falter at the moment when the recorded or analyzed text is taken to be an accurate (visual) representation of the worlds and voices studied.

Chapter 9, "The Sixth Moment," charts ethnography's future, beginning with the criticisms of the new writing that have been produced since *Writing Culture* (Clifford & Marcus, 1986). This leads to a treatment of new models of truth—the ethics and epistemologies of a postprag- matist social criticism. A feminist, communitarian ethics is outlined and connected to the radical democratic project of the new, civic journalism (Charity, 1995; Fallows, 1996). The norms for writing the new ethnog- raphy are discussed as I attempt to bring ethnography closer to a set of critical, journalistic practices. A text must do more then awaken moral sensibilities. It must move the other and the self to action. Ethnogra- phy's future can only be written against the history of a radical demo- cratic project that intends humane transformations in the public sphere.

Notes

1. Elsewhere (Denzin & Lincoln, 1994; Lincoln & Denzin, 1994), five moments of ethnographic inquiry are identified: the traditional, modernist, blurred genres, crisis of representation, and the present or fifth moment. The sixth moment (Lincoln, 1995a, p. 40) charts the future.
2. As Tyler (1986, pp. 127-128) notes, the metaphors and allegories that organize the ethnographic text have changed: the eighteenth century's noble savage, the nineteenth century's primordial primitive, the twentieth century's primitive turned into data and evidence, on occasion pure difference, and most recently the postcolonial hybrid writer (Chow, 1993).
3. The realist text, Jameson (1990) argues, constructed its version of the world by "programming . . . readers; by training them in new habits and practices. . . . Such narratives must ultimately produce that very category of Reality . . . of the real, of the 'objective' or 'external' world, which itself historical, may undergo decisive modification in other modes of production, if not in later stages of this one" (p. 166). The new ethnographic text is producing its versions of reality and teaching readers how to engage this view of the social world.
4. Following Clifford Christians's (personal communication, January 8, 1996) com- munitarianism is understood here to be a social philosophy developed by Charles Taylor, Michael Sandel, Carole Pateman, and others as an alternative to equalitarian democracy (such as Richard Rorty's version). When Amitai Etzioni uses the term for a political movement, it bears the same discontinuity with communitarian political theory as the democratic party does with the term "democracy."
5. These are extensions of the norms Christians et al. (1993, pp. 55-57) see as operating for journalists.
6. Cecil Younger, Straley's (1992, p. 9) fictional private investigator, puts it this way, "If cops collect the oral history of a crime, I gather folklore."
7. Each of these moments operates in the present. Elsewhere (Denzin, 1989b, p. 17), I distinguish four types of epiphanies, or turning-point moments in people's lives: the major (an experience shatters a life), cumulative (a series of events build up to a crisis),

minor (underlying problems are revealed in a small event), and relived (a person relives a major, turning-point moment).

8. It also extends the model of inquiry developed in *Interpretive Biography* (Denzin, 1989a) and *Interpretive Interactionism* (Denzin, 1989b).

Acknowledgments

I thank Mitch Allen for his quick and early support of this project and Peter Labella for helping see it through to conclusion. Interactions in the Unit for Criticism and Interpretive Theory at the University of Illinois and conversations with Katherine Ryan, Cliff Christians, Yvonna Lincoln, Patricia Clough, Laurel Richardson, Carolyn Ellis, Art Bochner, John Straley, Paul Benson, and Carl Couch helped to clarify my arguments. Patricia Clough, in particular, gave the entire manuscript an important, critical evaluation. Karin Admiral was an outstanding research assistant. I thank Frances Borghi for her careful assistance during production, Dan Hays for copyediting, Michèle Lingre, production editor, for patience and assistance throughout, Paul Benson for his meticulous reading of the page proofs and the production of the index. Johanna Bradley, Sara Connell, and Sylvia Allegretto also assisted with proofreading. I also thank the students at the University of Illinois who patiently sat through formal and informal seminars, listening to earlier versions of my arguments about ethnography and writing. Finally, I gratefully acknowledge the moral, intellectual, and financial support given this project by Dean Kim Rotzoll of the College of Communication and Clifford Christians, the director of the Institute of Communication Research, my new home at the University of Illinois.

Portions of the material in Chapter 1 appeared in Norman K. Denzin's "Evaluating Qualitative Research in the Poststructural Moment: The Lessons James Joyce Teaches Us" (1994b); portions of the material in Chapter 2 appeared in Norman K. Denzin, "On Hearing the Voices of Educational Research: Review Essay" (1995c) and Norman K. Denzin, "The Experiential Text and the Limits of Visual Understanding" (1995d); portions of the material in Chapter 3 appeared in Norman K. Denzin, "The Standpoint Epistemologies and Social Theory" (in press-a); an earlier version of Chapter 4 appears in *Re-Privileging Voice: The Poststructural Turn in Qualitative Research.* (in press-b); portions of Chapter 5 appeared in *American Cultural Studies* (1996a); portions of Chapter 9 appeared in Norman K. Denzin, "Institutional Perspectives on Sociology" (1996b).

PART 1

Reading the Crisis

CHAPTER 1

Lessons James Joyce Teaches Us[1]

A triple crisis of representation, legitimation, and praxis confronts qualitative researchers in the human disciplines. Embedded in the discourses of poststructuralism and postmodernism (Derrida, 1978; Lather, 1991, 1993; Martin, 1992; Richardson, 1992, 1994a, 1994b), these three crises are, as Lather (1993) notes, coded in multiple terms variously called and associated with the "critical, interpretive, linguistic, feminist, and rhetorical turns" in social theory.[2] These new turns make problematic two key assumptions of qualitative research. The first assumption presumes that qualitative researchers can no longer directly capture lived experience. Such experience, it is argued, is created in the social text written by the researcher. This is the representational crisis. It confronts the inescapable problem of representation but does so within a framework that makes the direct link between experience and text problematic (Denzin, 1991a, 1991b).

The second assumption makes problematic the traditional criteria for evaluating and interpreting qualitative research. This is the legitimation crisis. It involves a serious rethinking of such terms as validity, generalizability, and reliability—terms already retheorized in postpositivist (Hammersley, 1992), constructionist and naturalistic (Guba &

3

Lincoln, 1989, pp. 163-83), feminist (Fonow & Cook, 1991, pp. 1-13; Smith, 1992), interpretive (Denzin, 1991c, 1994a), poststructural (Lather, 1993), and critical discourses (Fay, 1987; Kincheloe & McLaren, 1994). The question from this crisis is, "How are qualitative studies to be evaluated in the contemporary, poststructural moment?" The first two crises shape the third, which questions, "Is it possible to effect change in the world, if society is only and always a text?" Clearly, these crises intersect and blur, as do the answers to the questions they generate.

In this chapter, I examine these three crises and locate them within the history of qualitative, ethnographic research and social theory in the United States (for other histories both in the United States and in Europe, see Atkinson, 1992; Guba, 1990; Lincoln & Guba, 1985; Quantz, 1992; Spindler & Spindler, 1992a; Wolcott, 1992). James Joyce's four pivotal literary works, *Dubliners* (1914/1964a), *A Portrait of the Artist as a Young Man* (1916/1964b), *Ulysses* (1922/1968a), and *Finnegan's Wake* (1939/1968b), will be used as vehicles to illustrate how the representation and legitimation crises have been resolved in earlier historical moments.[3] Drawing on Joyce's texts (and the stories in Chapters 1 and 2), I outline new directions for research and theory in qualitative research, a discussion that will be taken up again in Chapters 4 through 8.

The Representational Crisis

A single but complex issue defines the representational crisis. It involves the assumption that much, if not all, qualitative and ethnographic writing is a narrative production, structured by a logic that "separates writer, text, and subject matter" (Denzin, 1991c, p. 278; see also Richardson, 1994a). Any social text can be analyzed in terms of its treatment of four paired terms: (a) the "real" and its representation in the text, (b) the text and the author, (c) lived experience and its textual representations, and (d) the subject and his or her intentional meanings. The text presumes that there is a world out there (the real) that can be captured by a "knowing" author through the careful transcription (and analysis) of field materials (interviews, notes, etc.). The author becomes the mirror to the world under analysis. This reflected world then represents the subject's experiences through a complex textual apparatus. The subject is a textual construction because the real flesh and blood person is always translated into either an analytic subject as a social type or a textual subject who speaks from the author's pages.

Several questions follow from this interpretation (see Denzin, 1991b, p. 61). Who is the subject? Does the subject have direct access to his or her lived experiences (see Fuss, 1989, p. 25)? Is there a layer of lived experience that is authentic and real? Is any representation of an experience as good as any other? Are the subject's formulations always the most accurate? Traditional ethnographers have historically assumed that their methods probe and reveal lived experience. They have also assumed that the subject's word is always final, and that talk directly reflects subjective and lived experience. The literal translation of talk thus equals lived experience and its representation.[4]

Critical poststructuralism challenges these assumptions. Language and speech do not mirror experience: They create experience and in the process of creation constantly transform and defer that which is being described. The meanings of a subject's statements are, therefore, always in motion. There are, as Bruner (1986) argues, inevitable "gaps between reality, experience, and [the] expressions [of that experience]" (p. 7). Ethnographers deal, then, with performed texts, "structured units of experience, such as stories, or dramas . . . socially constructed units of meaning" (Bruner, 1986, p. 7). There can never be a final, accurate representation of what was meant or said—only different textual representations of different experiences. As Lather (1993, p. 3) observes, these arguments do not put an end to representation, but rather they signal the end of pure presence. Description becomes inscription. Inscription becomes evocative representation (see Tyler, 1986, p. 130). That is, in the written (and performed) text the writer textually presents the subject's experiences (as I did in Chapter 2)—for example, the telling of a story, recounting a conversation, or describing the performance of a ritual. Accordingly, the task is to understand what textually constructed presence means because there is only the text, as Derrida (1976) argues.[5] This leads to the question of a text's authority.

The Legitimation Crisis

A poststructural, critical, social science challenges traditional post-positivist arguments concerning the text and its validity.[6] Poststructuralism interprets the postpositivist's validity as a text's call to authority.[7] It understands postpositivisms's validity to be a plea for epistemological certainty and calls this version of validity or legitimation epistemological. A text's authority, for the postpositivist, is established through recourse to a set of rules that refer to a reality outside the text. These rules reference knowledge, its production, and representation. These rules, as Scheurich (1992, p. 1) notes, if properly followed establish validity. Without validity (authority) there is no truth, and without truth there can be no trust in a text's claims to validity (legitimation). With validity (legitimation) comes power (Cherryholmes, 1988). Validity as legitimation becomes a boundary line "which divides good research from bad, separates acceptable (to a particular research community) research from unacceptable research. . . . It is the name for inclusion and exclusion" (Scheurich, 1992, p. 5).

Critical poststructuralism reads the discussions of logical, construct, internal, ethnographic, and external validity, text-based data, triangulation, trustworthiness, credibility, grounding, naturalistic indicators, fit, coherence, comprehensiveness (see Eisenhart & How, 1992, pp. 657-669), plausibility, truth, and relevance (Atkinson, 1992, pp. 68-72) as attempts to reauthorize a text's authority in the postpositivist moment. Such moves cling to the conception of a "world-out-there" that is truthfully and accurately captured by the researcher's methods. Radway (1988), describing the ethnographies of communication, phrases this as a struggle to be overcome

> No matter how extensive the effort to dissolve the boundaries of the textual object or the audience, the most recent studies of reception . . . begin with the 'factual' existence of a particular text which is understood to be received by some set of individuals. (p. 363)

The methodological strategies that lie behind such words as credibility, grounding, and the epistemological status of data represent attempts to thicken and contextualize a work's grounding in the external empirical world (e.g., postpositivism's critical realism). They designate efforts to develop a set of transcendent rules and procedures that lie outside any specific research project. These rules, when successfully followed, permit a text to bear witness to its own validity (authority). Hence, a text is valid (legitimate) if it is sufficiently grounded, triangulated, based on naturalistic indicators, respondent validation, carefully fitted to a theory, comprehensive in scope, credible in terms of member checks, and so on (see Silverman, 1993, p. 159). The text's author then announces these validity claims to the reader. Such claims now become the text's warrant to its own authoritative representation of the experience and social world under investigation.

Epistemological validity (authority) can now be interpreted as the desire of the postpositivist's text to assert its own power over the reader. Validity as legitimacy, however, represents the always just-out-of reach-but-answerable claim a text makes for its authority. After all, the research could have always been better grounded, the subjects more representative, the researcher more knowledgeable, the research instruments better formulated, and more member checks could have been conducted. A fertile obsession, validity is the researcher's mask of authority (Lather, 1993, p. 674) that allows a particular regime of truth within a particular text (and community of scholars) to work its way on the reader.

Responses to the Legitimation Crisis

Within the social science community, there have been four responses to the legitimation crisis. First, there are those, the positivists, who see no basic difference between qualitative and quantitative research. Here, there is the belief that one set of criteria should be applied to all scientific research; that is, there is nothing special about qualitative research that demands a special set of criteria. The positivists apply four standard criteria to disciplined inquiry: internal validity, external validity, reliability, and objectivity. A normative epistemology organizes work within this paradigm. It is assumed that the normal is what is most representative in a larger population, and it is to that "normal" population that generalizations are directed. Less attention is thereby given to the "nonrepresentative," marginal formations that can exist in any social structure (Fiske, 1994, p. 196).

The second position, postpositivist, argues that a set of criteria unique to qualitative research needs to be developed. This is so because qualitative research represents "an alternative paradigm to quantitative social research" (Hammersley, 1992, p. 57). Although there is considerable disagreement over what these criteria should be, there is agreement that they should be different (see Lincoln & Guba, 1985). In practice, as discussed previously, this position has often led to the development of a set of criteria that are in agreement with the positivist criteria; they are merely fitted to a naturalistic research context (see Kirk & Miller, 1986; Lofland & Lofland, 1995; Silverman, 1993, pp. 156-169).

Hammersley (1992, p. 64) summarizes the postpositivist criteria in the following way: Such researchers assess a work in terms of its ability to (a) generate generic and formal theory, (b) be empirically grounded and scientifically credible, (c) produce findings that can be generalized or transferred to other settings, (d) be internally reflexive in terms of taking account of the effects of the researcher and the research strategy on the findings that have been produced.[8]

The third position, which may be termed postmodernism, argues that "the character of qualitative research implies that there can be no criteria for judging its products" (Hammersley, 1992, p. 58). This argument contends that the very idea of assessing qualitative research is antithetical to the nature of this research and the world it attempts to study (see Smith, 1984, p. 383). This position doubts all criteria and privileges none, although those who work within it favor criteria such as those adopted by some poststructuralists (see below).

For postmodernism, ethnographic practices are ways of acting in the world. These ways of acting (interviewing and observing) produce particular, situated understandings. The validity, or authority, of a given observation is determined by the nature of the critical understandings it produces. These understandings are based on glimpses and slices of the culture in action. Any given practice that is studied is significant because it is an instance of a cultural practice that happened in a particular time and place. This practice cannot be generalized to other practices; its importance lies in the fact that it instantiates a cultural practice, a cultural performance (story telling), and a set of shifting, conflicting cultural meanings (Fiske, 1994, p. 195).[9] Messy texts are based on these kinds of empirical materials—for example, the death from AIDS described in Chapter 2. Postpositivist concerns for representativeness, generalizability, and scientific credibility do not operate in this paradigm.

The fourth position, critical poststructuralism, contends that an entirely new set of criteria, divorced from the positivist and postpositivist traditions, need to be constructed. Such criteria would flow from the qualitative project, stressing subjectivity, emotionality, feeling, and other antifoundational criteria (see Ellis & Flaherty, 1992a, pp. 5-6; Richardson, 1994a; Seidman, 1991). It is to this position that I now turn.

Poststructural Forms of Legitimation

Paraphrasing Lather (1993) and invoking Derrida (1974/1976), it is now necessary to ask, "What do we do with validity and the legitimation question once we've met critical, poststructuralism?" The following answers, all political, are suggested. Each is predicated on the assumption that the term validity has been replaced with the words authority and legitimation.

Politics

The first answer is explicitly political. If there is a center to critical poststructural thought, it lies in the recurring commitment to strip any text of its external claims to authority. Every text must be taken on its own terms. The desire to produce a valid and authoritative text is renounced. The unmasking of validity as authority now exposes the heart of the argument. If validity is gone, values and politics, not objective epistemology, govern science (see Lather, 1986).[10] This is familiar territory. The answer is equally familiar. It is given in Foucault's concept of a subversive genealogy, a strategy that refuses to accept those "systems of discourse (economic, political, scientific, narrative)" (Denzin, 1991c, p. 32) that "ignore who we are collectively and individually" (Racevskis, 1983, p. 20). This is a politically informed, antifoundational position. An antifoundational, critical social science project seeks its external grounding not in science, in any of its revisionist, postpositivist forms, but rather in a commitment to post-Marxism and feminism with hope but no guarantees (Hall, 1986, p. 58). It seeks to understand how power and ideology operate through systems of discourse, asking always how words and texts and their meanings play a pivotal part in "those decisive performances of race, class [and] gender . . . [that] shape the emergent political conditions . . . we refer to as the postmodern world" (Downing, 1987, p. 80). A good text is one that invokes these commitments. A good text exposes how race, class, and gender work their ways into the concrete lives of interacting individuals. Lather (1986, p. 67) calls this catalytic validity, the degree to which a given research project empowers and emancipates a research community.[11]

Verisimilitude

The second solution dispenses with the quest for validity and seeks to examine instead a text's verisimilitude, or ability to reproduce (simulate) and map the real. Verisimilitude has been the most important criterion of traditional validity. It rests on the assumption that reality can be truthfully, faithfully, and accurately captured. There are three essential levels of verisimilitude: (a) a collection of laws set by convention, (b) a mask that presents these laws as evidence of a text's submission to the rules of a particular genre (Todorov, 1977, p. 84), and (c) the production of a text that "feels" truthful and real for the reader. In its most naive form, verisimilitude describes a text's relationship to reality. It asks, "Are the representations in a text consistent with the real? Is the text telling the truth?" Certain actions, for example, are said to lack verisimilitude "when they seem unable to occur in reality" (Todorov, 1977, p. 82). A second meaning of verisimilitude refers to the relationship of a particular text to some agreed-on opinion—for example, epistemological validity, or what Mishler (1990, p. 417) calls valid exemplars accepted by a relevant community of scientists. Here, it is understood that separate interpretive communities (Fish, 1980) have distinctively different standards or versions of verisimilitude as proof, truth, or validity. The third level, or meaning, of verisimilitude refers, in Stake's (1994, p. 240) words, to a text's ability to permit naturalistic generalization. A text with high verisimilitude provides the opportunity for vicarious experience, the reader "comes to know some things told, as if he or she had experienced them" (Stake, 1994, p. 240). In this case, the reader submits to the laws of verisimilitude that govern a given genre, willingly suspending for the moment the laws of disbelief that otherwise operate in everyday life (Coleridge, 1817/1973, p. 516). As Todorov (1977, p. 83) notes, there are as many verisimilitudes as there are genres (i.e., comedy, detective fiction, tragedy, etc.). In the social sciences, there are multiple genres, or writing forms: book reviews, presidential addresses to scholarly societies, research notes, critical essays, grant proposals, research reports, committee reports, and so on (see Agger, 1989; Richardson, 1994a). Each form has its own laws of genre, its own verisimilitude. The validity of a statistical table is different from the so-called validity of a thick description in an ethnographer's report (Geertz, 1973). Two separate genres are operating in these two contexts. A work's narrative (textual) freedom is limited by the requirements of the genre itself (Todorov, 1977, p. 83). Verisimilitude can be described as the mask a text assumes as it convinces the reader it has conformed to the laws of its genre; in so doing, it has reproduced reality in accordance with those rules. Every text enters into a relationship with verisimilitude and its laws, including taking verisimilitude or validity as its theme (e.g., Mishler, 1990). In this case, the text must establish an antiverisimilitude; that is, a subtext that appears to lack truth, validity, or verisimilitude. Such moves allow a text to make a separation between truth and verisimilitude because what appears to be true is false, and what appears to be false is true.

Verisimilitude, of course, is the theme of the murder mystery. "Its law is the antagonism between truth and verisimilitude" (Todorov, 1977, p. 86). In a murder mystery, the murderer must appear to be innocent, and the innocent person must be made to appear guilty. "The truth has no verisimilitude, and the verisimilitude has no truth" (Todorov, 1977, p. 86). The end of the narrative must, of course, resolve this tension or contradiction. It must show the apparently innocent person to be guilty and the apparently guilty party to be innocent. The skilled detective-as-ethnographer unravels this situation for the reader.[12] Only in the end, as Todorov (1977) notes, do truth and verisimilitude coincide. Thus, truth is only and always a "distanced and postponed verisimilitude" (Todorov, 1977, p. 88).

The same law, with an important twist, structures qualitative, ethnographic research. The truth of a text must always be aligned with the verisimilitude it establishes, but this verisimilitude will always be deferred because the text's grounding in the "real" (the site of the true) can always be contested. At the same time, in the qualitative research article structural and causal variables accepted by positivist researchers must be shown to have an antiverisimilitude for the case under analysis. A goal of the qualitative researcher will be to contest, contrast, and challenge these two forms of verisimilitude, the qualitative and the quantitative, while at the same time showing how they supplement and compliment one another. The better the researcher succeeds, however, the more powerfully is established the verisimilitude of the genre championed; hence the impossibility of ever escaping verisimilitude. "The more it is condemned, the more we are enslaved by it" (Todorov, 1977, p. 87). Two questions now emerge. The first doubles back on itself and asks, "Can a text have verisimilitude and not be true;" conversely, "can a text be true but lack verisimilitude?" The controversy ("Special Issue," 1992; Whyte, 1992) surrounding William Foote Whyte's (1943, 1955, 1981, 1993) classic work, *Street Corner Society*, illuminates this question, which turns on the status of a text's grounding in the real world. Whyte's work, historically accepted as a truthful text with high verisimilitude, was challenged by another researcher (Boelen, 1992, p. 49) who claimed that his study, although having some degree of verisimilitude, lacked truth. He had, the researcher argued, misrepresented the real structure of Italian street corner life and perpetuated false truths about that life. Whyte (1992, 1993) replied that his study was based on member checks and, hence, had both verisimilitude and truth. His critic, he asserted, had misunderstood his original text and had not penetrated the real fabrics of street corner life in the Italian community. The implications of this exchange are clear. The truth of a text cannot be established by its verisimilitude. Verisimilitude can always be challenged. Hence, a text can be believed to be true while lacking verisimilitude. (The opposite case holds as well.) Challenges to verisimilitude in qualitative research rest on the simple observation that a text is always a site of political struggle over the real and its meanings. Truth is political, and verisimilitude is textual. The meaning of each of these terms is not in the text but rather brought to it by the reader. Here is the dilemma. Ethnographers can only produce messy texts that have some degree of verisimilitude; that is, texts that allow readers to imaginatively feel their way into the experiences that are being described by the author. If these texts permit a version of Stake's (1994) naturalistic generalization (the production of vicarious experience), then the writer has succeeded in bringing "felt" news from one world to another. Little more can be sought.[13]

The second question following from this discussion of verisimilitude becomes, "Whose verisimilitude?," because it is the researcher's goal to contest multiple verisimilitudes, multiple versions of reality, and the perceived truths that structure these realities. A text must embody multiple masks as it seeks to unmask the regimes of truth that structure experience in any given situation. With Baudrillard (1983), it is understood that in the postmodern, contemporary moment

> the real is no longer what it used to be. . . . There is an escalation of the true, of the lived experience; a panic-stricken production of the real and the referential . . . a strategy of the real, neo-real and hypperreal. . . . The very definition of the real becomes: that of which it is possible to give an equivalent reproduction. (pp. 12-13, 146)

In any situation, the researcher can only produce a text that reproduces these multiple versions of the real, showing how each version impinges on and shapes the phenomenon being studied. A text's verisimilitude is given in its ability to reproduce and deconstruct the reproductions and simulations that structure the real. I call this deconstructive verisimilitude. Baudrillard's (1988) *America* is an attempt in this direction.

Other Forms of Validity and Legitimation

The third answer entertains alternative forms of validity and legitimation poststructurally conceived. Lather (1993) suggests four new forms of validity that can only be briefly discussed: ironic, paralogical, rhizomatic, and voluptuous. (Following the previous discussion, I will term Lather's forms of validity forms of legitimation, or authority.) Ironic legitimation, like deconstructive verisimilitude, proliferates multiple representations and simulations of the real, showing the strengths and limitations of each, arguing that no single representation is superior to another. Lather cites Agee and Evans (1944/1988), *Let Us Now Praise Famous Men*, as an example of a text that deploys this form of validity-as-legitimation. The authors refuse to endorse the authority of any single representation (or interpretation) of the Great Depression on the lives of the three white tenant farm families that were studied. Paralogical legitimation foregrounds dissensus, heterogeneity, and multiple discourses that destabilize the researcher's position as the master of truth and knowledge. Lyotard (1984) articulates the logic of this position in *The Postmodern Condition*. Rhizomatic legitimation represents attempts to present nonlinear texts with multiple centers in which multiple voices speak and articulate their definitions of the situation. Deleuze and Guattari's (1980/1987), *A Thousand Plateaus*, is an example of a text that enacts this form of validity. (The work associated with the Bakhtin Circle [Bakhtin, Volosinov, & Medvedev] invokes this multivoiced form of textual legitimation.) Voluptuous legitimation imagines a feminine authority opposed to the dominant male voice that excludes women in their multiplicities—their bodies, their emotions, and the maternal world (Lather, 1993, p. 682). Richardson's (1992, 1993) poetic representations of a transcribed interview with an unwed mother situate authority and legitimacy in the intersection of the researcher's and the subject's voices. As these voices cross paths, multiple feminine versions of sexuality, marriage, motherhood, and family are created.

Into History[14]

None of the previously discussed measures are completely satisfactory. They are all reflexive and messy. That is how it should be because the world we encounter is neither neat nor easy to make sense of. Where do we go next? If the previous arguments are allowed, we find ourselves, perhaps like the listener to the song by Bob Seger (paraphrasing), not wanting to know now what we did not know before.

Turn back and look at where we started and where we have come. The history of interpretive theory and inquiry in the twentieth century is coterminous with the history and the cultural logics of capitalism and the economic formations that have been connected to these apparatuses (Table 1.1). "Into History" (Denzin, 1995b; Denzin & Lincoln, 1994) charts this history.

Following Jameson (1991, pp. 400-412), Table 1.1 connects the three major phases of capitalism with ethnography's major moments (see

Table 1.1 Into History

Ethnography's Phases	*Capitalism's Phases and Cinema's Voyeur*		
	Market (1900-World War II) to Blatant (1900-1920)	*Monopoly (World War II-1960) to Voyeurism Repressed (1930-1960)*	*Multinational (1960-Present) to Transgressive (1960-Present)*
Realism	Objective ethnographies		
Modernism/high modernism		Golden age	
Postmodernism-present			Blurred genres Writing culture

below) and shows how these moments overlap with the history of cinematic voyeurism in the twentieth century as well as with the dominant aesthetic theories of this century (realism, modernism, and postmodernism).[15]

A major thesis organizes this reading of history (see Denzin, 1995a). The twentieth-century democratic capitalist societies required information from and about their citizens.[16] The social sciences provided this information in the form of social surveys, community studies, and ethnographic, qualitative studies of modern urban life. The introduction of cinema and the cinematic apparatus into American (and European) culture corresponded with this need for surveillance. Cinema introduced new ways of looking and gazing into everyday life. The cinema's voyeur came in several forms, including the journalist, the psychologist and psychoanalyst, the sociologist, the anthropologist, and the detective. Cinema's voyeur, like the social science ethnographer, gathered information about society for others and kept alive the central idea of private and public spaces in this culture. Consider the three major moments and formations of capitalism's twentieth-century history (see Jameson, 1991, pp. 400-412): market or local (1900 to World War II), monopoly (World War II to 1960), and multinational (1960 to present).[17] Connect these formations to the three dominant aesthetic moments of the twentieth century: realism (a commitment to faithfully reproduce reality), modernism (a self-consciousness that draws on realism), and postmodernism ("which ransacks all the preceding moments for its new forms of 'cultural credit' " [Jameson, 1990, p. 157]). These aesthetic regimes correspond to capitalism's three major formations. This correspondence is not symmetrical. It is, as Jameson (1990, p. 157) argues, dialectical. The latter stages of each formation build on the accumulated capital of the first stages, rearranging the meanings and formations in the former as they solidify their own representational practices. These formations, in turn, correspond to the major periods in qualitative inquiry and interpretive theory: realism with ethnographic and case study objectivity (Whyte, 1943, 1955, 1981, 1992, 1993), modernism with the mixed and qualitative-quantitative strategies of grounded theory (Glaser & Strauss, 1967), and postmodernism with the writing culture project (Clifford & Marcus, 1986). Each of these transformations retains a commitment to a realist epistemology. The early realist moment in qualitative research, like the nineteenth-century realist novel, carried the ideological task of creating a factual realist narrative about the social world (see Clough, 1992, p. 6). Modernist qualitative research (*Boys in White* [Becker, Geer, Hughes, & Strauss, 1961] and *The Discovery of Grounded Theory* [Glaser & Strauss, 1967]) self-consciously enacted and drew its abstractions and generalizations from the older realism of the case studies of the early Chicago school of sociology (see Becker, 1966). The postmodernist project continues to produce realist and modernist ethnographies because these works are now being criticized from the poststructural perspective (see Atkinson, 1992; Clough, 1992; Hammersley, 1992).

Another History

Interpretive inquiry divides into five moments (see Vidich & Lyman, 1994).

The Traditional Period

The first or traditional period begins in the early 1900s and continues until World War II. In it, qualitative researchers wrote "objective," colonializing accounts of field experiences reflective of the positivistic science paradigm. They were concerned with offering valid, reliable, and objective interpretations in their writings. The other who was studied was alien, foreign, and strange (see Rosaldo, 1989, for a critique of this moment in anthropology).

Modernist Phase

The modernist phase builds on the canonical works from the traditional period. It extended through the postwar years to the 1970s and is still present in the work of many (see Geertz, 1988). In this period, many texts attempted to formalize qualitative methods (see, for example, Glaser & Strauss, 1967).[18] The modernist ethnographer and sociological participant observer attempted rigorous, qualitative studies of important social processes, including deviance, and social control in the classroom and society. Work in this period clothed itself in the language and rhetoric of positivist and postpositivist discourse.

Blurred Genres

By the beginning of the third stage (1970-1986), "Blurred Genres," qualitative researchers had a full complement of paradigms, methods, and strategies to employ in their research. Theories ranged from symbolic interactionism to constructivism, naturalistic inquiry, positivism and postpositivism, phenomenology, ethnomethodology, critical (Marxist), semiotics, hermeneutics, psychoanalysis, structuralism, feminism, and various ethnic paradigms.[19] Geertz's two books, *The Interpretation of Culture* (1973) and *Local Knowledge* (1983), shaped the beginning and end of this moment. In these two works, he argued that the old functional, positivist, behavioral, and totalizing approaches to the human disciplines was giving way to a more pluralistic, interpretive, open-ended perspective. Geertz suggested that all anthropological writings were interpretations of interpretations. The observer had no privileged voice in the interpretations that were written. The central task of theory was to make sense out of a local situation.

Crisis of Representation

A profound rupture occurred in the mid-1980s. What I call the fourth moment, or the crisis of representation, appeared with *Anthropology as Cultural Critique* (Marcus & Fisher, 1986), *The Anthropology of Experience* (Turner & Bruner, 1986), *Writing Culture* (Clifford & Marcus, 1986), *Words and Lives* (Geertz, 1988), and *The Predicament of Culture* (Clifford, 1988). These works made research and writing more reflexive and called into question the issues of gender, class, and race. They articulated the consequences of Geertz's (1988) blurred genres interpretation of the field in the early 1980s.

New models of truth and method were sought (Rosaldo, 1989). The erosion of classic norms in anthropology (objectivism, complicity with colonialism, social life structured by fixed rituals and customs, and ethnographies as monuments to a culture) was complete (Rosaldo, 1989, pp. 44-45). Critical, feminist, and epistemologies of color now compete for attention in this arena (see Clough, 1994).

Clough (1992, p. 136) elaborates this crisis and criticizes those who would argue that new forms of writing represent a way out of the crisis. She argues that in writing the field-worker makes a claim to moral and scientific authority. These claims allow the realist and experimental ethnographic text to function as sources of validation for an empirical science. They show that the world of real lived experience can still be captured, if only in the writer's memoirs, fictional experimentations, or dramatic readings. These works have the danger of perpetuating "empirical science's hegemony" (Clough, 1992, p. 8) because such experiments come up against, and then back away from, the difference between empirical science and social criticism. Too often, they fail to fully engage a new politics of textuality that would "refuse the identity of empirical science" (Clough, 1992, p. 135), while openly engaging social criticism as the form of preferred discourse.

The Fifth Moment

The fifth moment is the present, defined and shaped by the crises described previously. We are writing our way out of writing culture and into the still undefined Sixth Moment (Lincoln, 1995a; Lincoln & Denzin, 1994).

One More History

A third look at history yields an additional sequence of images (Table 1.1). Here, I borrow from the history of narrative cinema and cinema's voyeur in the twentieth century (e.g., Burch, 1990; Denzin, 1995a). Cinema's voyeur has passed through three basic stages: the blatant voyeurism of early, primitive cinema (1900-1920), the repressed, anxious, displaced voyeurism of moderni (1930-1960, as in Hitchcock's *Rear Window*), and the openly aggressive, transgressive, yet confused voyeurism of postmodernism (*Sex, Lies and Videotape, Blue Velvet,* and *Sliver*). The cinematic, surveillance society systematically introduced the voyeur into everyday life. This figure maintained the fiction of a private, sacred space that he or she protected. The progressive insertion of this fire into every corner of life systematically opened up the private to the public gaze. The history of qualitative (and positivist) research in the twentieth century follows the previous trajectory. Like cinema's voyeur, we began as blatant observers during market capitalism under the regime aesthetic realism. Then we became anxious and furtive in our looking (the repressed voyeurism of mid-century capitalism). Today we are once again blatant, openly acknowledging our own place in the voyeuristic looking and gazing project. Our epistemological aesthetic has moved from realism to modernism, and now to postmodernism. Today, we seek a multinational, multicultural gaze that probes, yet goes beyond local markets while it remains always anchored in the interactional experiences of the reflexive ethnographer.

Reading History

Several conclusions can be drawn from this brief history—noting that it is, like all histories, somewhat arbitrary. Each of the earlier historical moments is still operating in the present, either as legacy or as a set of practices that researchers still follow or argue against. The multiple and fractured histories of qualitative research now make it possible for any given research to attach a project to a canonical text from any of the previously discussed historical moments. Multiple criteria of evaluation now compete for attention in this field. There have never been so many paradigms, strategies of inquiry, or methods of analysis to draw on. We are in a moment of discovery and rediscovery as new ways of looking, interpreting, arguing, and writing are debated and discussed. The qualitative research act can no longer be viewed from within a neutral or objective positivist perspective. Class, race, gender, and ethnicity shape the process of inquiry, thereby making research a multicultural process.

Hybrid texts of several varieties are emerging. There are pro-postmodernist works that challenge the realist tenets of modernism and openly engage poetic, literary forms of representation (Richardson, 1994a). There are also pro-postmodernist works that accept modernism, addressing postmodern themes from within the earlier modernist and realist traditions (see Smith, 1992). Some refuse the postmodern turn (Geertz, 1988) while rejecting the assumptions of modernism. Still others embrace modernism while dismissing postmodernism (see Whyte, 1992).

A new set of textual aesthetics associated with each of these hybrid types of textuality is taking shape. New canons of evaluation for qualitative research are on the horizon. Promodernist and anti-postmodern canons continue to reflect a commitment to a realist epistemology. This developing canon is sensitive to the textual and contextual effects of research settings, the relationship between the observer and the observed, the issue of perspective or point of view, the place of the (reader) audience in the interpretation of texts, and the issue of rhetorical or authorial style used by writers in the production of the text (Altheide & Johnson, 1994). The unfolding pro-postmodernist, anti-modernist canon envelops the concerns of the promodernist text while erasing the distinction between fact and fiction and exploring in detail (as outlined previously) multiple forms of verisimilitude and poststructural validity.

As these canons solidify and take shape, they dialectically affect one another, creating modernist texts that look postmodern and postmodern texts that espouse modernist concerns. As Jameson (1990, p. 166) implies, each aesthetic (research) form constructs its own world of meaning and programs readers to understand and accept that world. Thus, realism (promoderism) teaches readers how to accept the versions of "reality" it produces, whereas postmodernism does the same. The clash between these canons appears on the surface to be incommensurable. In fact, this clash represents a site at which the practitioners of these forms are afforded the opportunity to sharpen and clarify the terms of their respective positions. A new hybrid form of textuality is likely to emerge out of this encounter between the pro- and antimodernist and the pro- and anti-postmoderist positions. This can be observed in attempts to make postmodern texts modernist (Dawson & Prus, 1993; Schmitt, 1993) and modernist texts postmodern (Clough, 1992; Denzin, 1992b). Until consensus about this new form of textuality occurs, each position is obliged to clarify the standards and programs that organize its practices. That is, each form of textuality should be read from multiple perspectives, the canon it is embedded in (modernist or postmodernist), and the canon that it opposes. This duality of evaluative perspective can only serve to sharpen and clarify the tensions between these competing (but not entirely incompatible) points of view.

Where has this history gotten us? The question is rhetorical. The current poststructural crisis in the human disciplines articulates the history, contradictions, and cultural logics of capitalism. A product of this history, the social sciences have embodied capitalism's contradictions in each historical moment providing, at all times, the kinds of interpretive texts, practices, methodology, and theories this complex social formational has demanded.

James Joyce's Writing Project

I now turn to James Joyce's writing project (see Levin, 1978; McHale, 1992; Chapter 2), focusing on his four key works: *Dubliners* (1914/1964a), *A Portrait of the Artist as a Young Man* (1916/1964b), *Ulysses* (1922/1968a), and *Finnegans Wake* (1939/1968b). In a writing career spanning 36 years (1905-1941), Joyce (1882-1941) traversed ethnography's five moments[20] while charting new ground within literary modernism, even broaching the outer limits of postmodernism.[21] *Dubliners* is hard-core, traditional-realist ethnography. The lives of ordinary men and women are presented in detailed, realistic fashion as they grapple, from childhood to death, with epiphanic moments in their lives. *A Portrait of the Artist as a Young Man* is a subjective, autoethnography. It is the story of a struggle, an attempt to find a voice, and a series of epiphanic moments: The artist questions which way he should turn. In the end, he leaves the world of the *Dubliners* and sets off to write the history of his country and its racist, religious, sexist, political, and economic repressions.

Dubliners and *A Portrait of the Artist as a Young Man* deploy two of the most familiar and most important modernist textual strategies: mobile consciousness and parallax, or multiple points of view (McHale, 1992, p. 44).[22] These two works are repeatedly marked by a variety of interior monologues (first-person, third-person, autonomous, and free indirect) that secure a "finer-grained interaction between consciousness and the world outside consciousness" (McHale, 1992, p. 45). Joyce presumes a stable world outside a mobile consciousness. This interior, always-moving consciousness constantly reflects on and describes the exterior world. This consciousness may be unreliable, shifting, and digressive, but the world itself is stable. Joyce's characters are always obliged to return to this world, as with Gabriel in *The Dead* (Joyce, 1978, pp. 240, 242), "A few light taps upon the pane made him turn to the window. . . . The time had come for him to set out on his journey westward," and Stephen Dedalus, "3 April: Met Davin at the cigar shop opposite Findlater's church. . . . Asked me why I did not join a rowing club. I pretended to think it over. . . . More mud, more crocodiles" (Joyce, 1978, p. 523). In these lines, an external observer (Joyce) puts words and descriptions in the mouth of a character while connecting those words to a world outside the character's consciousness. This is classic, modernist ethnographic writing. An objective account of a state of affairs is given by the writer.[23]

From these rather conventional works, Joyce leaps into *Ulysses*, an interpretive, high-modernist, stream of consciousness, first-person experimental text. A text that insults, provokes anger, and mocks the writer and his sexuality; it is the story of an ordinary man, one day in his life. It is a text that turns against everything that has come before, including the major myths that circulate in Western culture. *Ulysses* takes interior dialogue to new levels. Joyce repeatedly experiments with parallax, or point of view. The first half of this book, McHale (1992, p. 48) argues, is defined by a mobile consciousness fitted to a stable, external world. Joyce incessantly juxtaposes "two or more characters' different constructions of the same world" (McHale, 1992, p. 46). For example, in the "Ithaca" section of *Ulysses*, both Stephen and Bloom reflect on the same cloud in the sky. The chain of associations produced by this experience is different for each man. Bloom thinks of Jewish diaspora. Stephen remembers his dead mother (McHale, 1992, p. 47). In the first half of *Ulysses*, "the parallax of subjectivities helps to confer solidity and stability on the world outside consciousness" (McHale, 1992, p. 51). In contrast, the second half of the book becomes more avant-garde. It proliferates interior dialogues and connects moving, mobile minds with a shifting, external world. The effect is to create a parallax of discourses in which nothing is stable. The world dissolves into "a plurality of incommensurable worlds" (McHale, 1992, p. 51). Here, discourse on discourse, discourse on perspective, point of view, and language itself predominates. For example, consider the dog that Stephen observes on Sandymount. The dog "metamorphoses from hare to buck to bear to wolf to calf and back to dog again—but all in metaphor: like a bounding hare, bearish fawning, at a calf's gallop" (McHale, 1992, p. 50). The dog Bloom encountered in Nighttown changes breed "from retriever to wolfdog to setter to mastiff to spaniel to bulldog to boarhound . . . not in metaphor . . . but evidently in 'reality' " (McHale, 1992, p. 50). Many dogs in the same text, metaphor, hallucination, or reality? What breed of dog did Bloom encounter? The reader cannot say. Such texts disrupt the relationship between reality and its perceptions. Here, there are only multiple worlds and multiple representations of it. Nothing is stable or certain.

Ulysses is followed by *Finnegans Wake*—an unreadable journey into language and its mysteries. ("In the name of the former and of the latter and of their holocaust, Allmen" [Joyce, 1978, p. 759]; "Can't hear with the waters of. The chittering waters of. Flittering bats, fieldmice bawk talk. Ho!" [Joyce, 1978, p. 744]). This book was another new text, postmodern and poststructural, reflexive in new ways, always an experiment in and through language—an attempt to create a new language for Ireland, a new radical way to start afresh, free of the categories, tongues, and voices of the past; hence its unreadability, for how can we read what has not been written before? Joyce's scandalous texts (and the reactions to them) enact the representational and legitimation crises outlined previously. *Dubliners* purported to reach out and grab lived experience and bring it into the text. *Portrait* turned the ethnographer's gaze inward and sought its validation and authority on the strength of Joyce's ability to evoke the subjective struggle undertaken by his protagonist. *Ulysses* displays multiple verisimilitudes and each of Lather's forms of textual legitimation. Reflexively, the text continually turns in on itself, as it proliferates, in ironic, paralogical, rhizomatic, and voluptuous ways, multiple paths through its own structure. It even dares to capture a feminine validity that becomes a central topic of *Finnegans Wake*.[24]

In these multiple textual moves, Joyce displays a deconstructive verisimilitude and antiverisimilitude. His texts, taken as a totality, mock the real and its representations. Joyce's journey is to fashion a text that creates a new poststructural genre. His lessons need to be applied to the history and practices of qualitative research and ethnographic writing.

The Lessons James Joyce Teaches Us

In 1800, Friedrich Schlegel, the early German romantic student of language and history, contended "that modern literature lacked a centre, such as mythology was for the ancients" (Kiberd, 1992, p. 4). Schlegel went on to predict the emergence of a new mythology that "would be less a radical act of creation than a 'collaboration' between old and new" (Kiberd, 1992, p. 4). He continued, "Why should not what has already been emerge anew, and why not in a newer and finer, grander manner?" (Kiberd, 1992, p. 4). This is how we can read *Ulysses* (Joyce, 1922/1968a), Eliot's (1952) *The Wasteland*, and Picasso's *Guernica* (Kiberd, 1992, p. 4). They are new mythologies, finer and grander mergers of the new with the old. Thus, Joyce gave to modern literature a new center, a new language wrestled out of lived experience. Joyce created a new mythology. His new forms of textuality were given authority to the extent that they revealed his ability to break from the past and work outward from self-experience to the world as a whole. Joyce created a new form of reflexive and transgressive verisimilitude. A text's authority was now self-referential.

Joyce's Referential Project: Seeing, Hearing, Knowing, and Understanding

Joyce's irreverent works were a parody of modernist texts. They mocked and ridiculed modernist textual assumptions. He unhinged from within the concept of a stable world out there. He did this through the use of ontological parallax and the parallax of discourses. In these moves, he argued that language could no longer mirror reality. Nor could reality be reflected from within a single linguistic system. More deeply, he argued that language could no longer function as a visual mirror of reality. He understood that under the modernist regime visual perception had been invested with the power of truth. Thus, the careful writer could construct a visual picture (for the reader) of the world that would tell the truth about this world. Joyce also understood, however, that human understanding had been (and was) excluded from the epistemological equation that converted human knowledge into visual perception. He knew that understanding was not seeing; it was more than visual knowledge. The fully interpretive text plunges the reader (and writer) into the interior, feeling, hearing, tasting, smelling, and touching worlds of subjective human experience (Ong, 1977, p. 137).

Joyce's journey constantly moves away from the objective, visual text—the text that maps interior and exterior realities. His texts become increasingly more acoustic, stressing the sounds of words—the voice in the acoustic mirror that hears itself speak and hears the sound of its own voice (Silverman, 1988, p. 80). Joyce's journey is thus away from the gaze in the looking-glass text to the voice, to the sound of the text in the reader's mind, and to the sounds in the acoustic mirror when the text is read. Joyce sought a text that would produce embodied, subjective understanding; such a text that would bring the reader more directly into the contradictory, shifting, and fragile worlds of experience that connected his subjects to the many worlds they inhabited. To understand this world, you had to hear it spoken. This was a carnavalesque world filled with sights and sounds, given to a collage-like structure, where parody was everywhere (see McHale, 1992, p. 55).

Into the Future

In 1996, interpretive inquiry lacks a center. We confront Joyce's situation anew. We seem to no longer know who the subject is let alone how to write his or her experiences. We have no agreed-upon method, no new text that points the way forward. We have lost our myths, those larger-than-life paradigms we did battle with during our earlier historical moments. We seek today a new mythology, perhaps not a radical collaboration with the old myths but a redoing of the old, in light of where we have traveled.

The following are Joyce's lessons: We should not take ourselves too seriously. We should have fun doing what we are doing. We need to understand that writing is inscription, an evocative act of creation and of representation. We can invent a new language, as other avant-gardes have done. This should be done playfully, however, with a sense of parody, knowing always that any new form of writing that goes beyond autoethnography, "teletheory," or "mystories" (Ulmer, 1989) can always be undone. Any new language, of course, will be the language of a new sensibility, a new reflexivity. This will be a language that refuses the old categories, that reflexively and parasitically, in a rhizomatic manner (Deleuze & Guattari, 1987, Chapter 1), charts its own course against Joyce's repressive structures of history, economy, religion, race, class, and gender. This new language, poststructural to the core, will be personal, emotional, biographically specific, and minimalist in its use of theoretical terms. It will allow ordinary people to speak out and to articulate the interpretive theories that they use to make sense of their lives. Beyond *Dubliners* (Joyce, 1914/1964a) and learning from *Portrait* (Joyce, 1916/1964b), this new language will express the personal struggles of each writer as he or she breaks free of the bonds that connect to the past. This language will always be interactive as it moves back and forth between lived experience and the cultural texts that shape and write that experience.

With Joyce, we move forward by moving inward. Finding our lost center in ourselves, we seek to create new forms of verisimilitude and new forms of truth—a truth from experience. This will require extensive experimentation with the use of multiple centers or points of view in a text (mobile consciousness and parallax), multiple forms of narration and narrative structure, as well as antirealist, antimodernist emotional texts. The avant-garde, postmodern writing sensibility introduced by Joyce suggests new writing forms and formats, including those evocative representations enumerated by Laurel Richardson (1994a): narratives of the self, fiction, poetry, drama, performance science, polyvocal texts, responsive readings, aphorisms, comedy and satire, visual presentations, and mixed genres (e.g., hypertexts).

Performance texts (Chapter 4), including responsive readings that incorporate audiences, may well be one wave of the future (see Richardson, 1993). This will also involve works that key on the aural, melodic, rhythmic, and acoustical side of the multivoiced, experimental text. Joyce's new language was aural, not visual. He sought a textual format that would wed visual knowledge with visceral, subjective understandings. Hence, his emphasis on the sounds of words as they are spoken and heard in the acoustical mirror.

At the same time, there may well be a search for forms of writing that shamelessly and playfully transgress the personal while making public that which modernism kept hidden and repressed (see Ellis & Bochner, 1992; Ronai, 1992, 1995). Writing our way out of *Writing Culture* (Clifford & Marcus, 1986), qualitative research in the fifth (and now sixth) moment discovers what has always been known: We are our own subjects. How our subjectivity becomes entangled in the lives of others is and has always been our topic. These are the lessons James Joyce teaches us. They will be explored in greater detail in the next chapter in which I turn to visual truth and the ethnographic project.

Notes

1. This is a revised version of Denzin (1994b).
2. With Kincheloe and McLaren (1994), I seek an impossible generic term that refers to several schools of thought at the same time, including the neo-Marxist tradition of critical theory; the genealogical writings of Foucault; the poststructural, deconstructionism of Derrida, Foucault, and others; the postmodernist discourse of Lyotard, Baudrillard, and Jameson; the recent antifoundational turn in social theory (Rorty, 1991, pp. 1-20; Seidman, 1991); poststructural and postmodern feminist discourse (Clough, 1992; Lather, 1993; Olesen, 1994; Richardson, 1993); the critical Marxism of cultural studies (Grossberg, 1992; Hall, 1986); the interpretive and postmodern turn in anthropological theory and ethnography (Clifford & Marcus, 1986; Geertz, 1973, 1988); and materialist, critical ethnography (see Kincheloe & McLaren, 1994, for a review of this tradition). A reviewer suggests the term poststructural critical social science. Whatever term is used, the intent here is to point to a series of new theoretical formations that contain antifoundational and poststructural elements merged with a commitment to an emancipatory project shaped by feminist, cultural studies, postmodern ethnographic, and interpretive perspectives. This new terrain is complex and contradictory, enfolding within its borders multiple paradigms and epistemologies (see Denzin, 1994a).
3. I am mindful of Joyce's notoriously paternal view of women (see Note 24). I select his texts because they conveniently map the history of realist, ethnographic writing in the twentieth century.
4. Critical ethnographers, of course (see Kincheloe & McLaren, 1994, for a review; Fay, 1987; Chapter 2) have never made these assumptions.
5. A fieldwork axiom can be offered. The realities that human groups pay attention to are given meaning in oral and textual performances, and there are always gaps between the text of a performance and its oral meanings.

6. Postpositivism, following Guba (1990, p. 23), differs only slightly from positivism. Its practitioners adhere to a critical realist ontology, a modified objectivist epistemology, and a naturalistic, grounded theory methodology.

7. In which case the term validity should be dispensed with and replaced by a term such as legitimacy or authority, both of which more clearly designate what validity has traditionally referenced. Henceforth, I will use legitimacy or authority in place of validity.

8. Hammersley's (1992, pp. 67-72) version of these criteria for validity rests on a subtle realism: "An account is valid or true if it represents accurately some feature of the phenomena that is intended to describe, explain or theorise" (p. 69). True or valid accounts are plausible, credible, and relevant. The constructivists (e.g., Lincoln and Guba) offer an important departure from the postpositivists. They argue for quality criteria that translate internal and external validity, reliability, and objectivity into trustworthiness and authenticity. These criteria are different from those employed by critical theorists, who stress action, praxis, and the historical situatedness of findings. In contrast, feminist scholarship, in the three traditions outlined by Olesen (empiricist, standpoint, and cultural studies), works, respectively, within the traditional positivist, postpositivist, postmodern (and poststructural) models of evaluation. Ethnic, critical theory, and cultural studies models of inquiry are similarly aligned. As one moves from the postpositivist to the postmodern and poststructural positions, increased importance is attached to such antifoundational criteria as emotionality, caring, subjective understanding, dialogic texts, and the formation of long-term trusting relationships with those studied.

9. An analogy may help. In discourse analysis, "no utterance is representative of other utterances, though it shares structural features with them; a discourse analyst studies utterances in order to understand how the potential of the linguistic system can be activated when it intersects at its moment of use with a social system" (Fiske, 1994, p. 195). Psathas (1995, p. 50) offers a parallel argument for what he terms the method of instances, which is used in conversation analysis. This method takes each instance as an occurrence that evidences the operation of a set of cultural understandings currently available for use by cultural members. The analyst's task is to understand how this instance works; whether it occurs again is irrelevant, and the question of sampling from a population is also not an issue because it is never possible to say in advance what an instance is a sample of (Psathas, 1995, p. 50).

10. Of course, this has always been the case.

11. Clearly, antifoundational projects, as a reviewer notes, problematicize empowerment. The same reviewer labels Lather's (1993) concept of catalytic validity prepoststructural (but see Quantz, 1992, p. 470). Much of the tensions in recent post-Marxist theory revolve around the intersections of poststructuralism and the emancipatory projects (see Anderson, 1989; Fay, 1987; Quantz, 1992, p. 473). Habermas's notion of "emancipatory interest" is critical to this discourse (see Quantz, 1992, p. 473).

12. How this works for the postmodern detective is examined in detail in Chapter 6.

13. I will return to this problem in Chapter 9.

14. This is another telling of the history offered in Denzin and Lincoln (1994) and Denzin (1995b).

15. Space prohibits the development of these themes, which can only be sketched here (see Denzin, 1995a, pp. 8-9, 191-195).

16. Richard Harvey Brown (personal communication, June 6, 1995) notes that such information gathering has been central to the rise of the modern nation state. William the

Conqueror, for example, ordered a census of land, people, animals, and so on for tax and military purposes soon after 1066.

17. As Richard Harvey Brown (and others) have noted, Jameson's storied version of capitalism's twentieth-century history is quite idiosyncratic. For example, some histories of the U.S. economy suggest a local, market capitalism prior to the Civil War, the monopolization and nationalization of the economy from about 1880 forward, and in increasing internationalization of capital in spurts since World War I, especially during and after World War II, and since 1975. Jameson's periodization is tempting because it enables the other correlations I want to establish, but I am mindful of these problems in his story.

18. See Lincoln and Guba (1985) for an extension and elaboration of this tradition in the mid-1980s.

19. Edward M. Bruner (personal communication, January 24, 26, 1995) clarifies this and the next period. Bruner, Barbara Myerhoff, James Fernandez, Renato Rosaldo, and Victor Turner (and others) were involved in a series of conferences and sessions at the American Anthropological Association Meetings (1980, 1983, and 1985) focused on what would be called the anthropology of experience (Bruner, 1984, p. 4). These conferences produced three edited collections (see Bruner, 1984; Lavie, Narayan, & Rosaldo, 1993; Turner & Bruner, 1986). During this same period, Clifford and Marcus organized the Sante Fe Conference (1984) (see Clifford & Marcus, 1986). Parallel to these two movements, but not overlapping with them, was the development of the field of ethnopoetics and an anthropological humanism in anthropology. This movement began in the early 1970s, and gained momentum in the early 1980s, with sessions on poetry at the American Anthropological Association meetings in 1982, 1983, and 1984 (see Brady, 1991c; see also Prattis, 1985a). The poetry movement did not, until recently, intersect with the writing culture movement and the other branches of contemporary anthropology. When the Tedlocks (leaders from the poetry branch) became editors of the *American Anthropologist,* a collision occurred (see McMillen, 1994; Riley, 1995). Today, the *Anthropology and Humanism Quarterly* regularly publishes poems and short stories written by anthropologists. These works are read at the business meetings of the Society for Humanistic Anthropology, which are held in conjunction with the annual meetings of the American Anthropological Association. An annual prize (the Victor Turner Award) for the best literary work is given. In 1993, it was won by Gottlieb and Graham (1993). Sociology has yet to experience or bring value to this kind of work, although it has gained some currency within the Society for the Study of Symbolic Interaction (see Ellis & Flaherty, 1992a, 1992b; Richardson, 1993).

20. He also moved through cinema's three versions of the voyeur.

21. McHale (1992, pp. 42-43) locates Joyce's early works within early modernism and finds in *Ulysses* (Joyce, 1922/1968a) and *Finnegans Wake* (Joyce, 1939/1968b) the avant-garde of high modernism fitted to a postmodernist project.

22. Following Booth (1983), five basic modernist textual principles can be enumerated. Texts should be realistic, authors reliable and objective, readers should not be swayed by emotions, the author's voice should only provide facts, and impersonal narration is to be avoided. The use of mobile consciousness and parallax both implement and destabilize these modernist principles.

23. This account, however, presumed the fallibility of perception because the relations between things (their truth) can only be given in the act of perception (see Shi, 1995). Meanings are made. Here, modernism implements its version of pragmatic literary

realism—that is, the commitment to reveal the ills of the social world through a textual form that presents interior psychological consciousness and the social circumstances surrounding that inner world (Shi, 1995).

24. Although, as Ernest Lockridge (L. Richardson, personal communication, April 26, 1995) observes, Joyce held reactionary views of women, apparently believing that Irish women should have more children, especially sons.

CHAPTER 2

Visual Truth and the Ethnographic Project[1]

We shall be interested . . . in the problem of verbal [and visual] texts, which are the initial givens of the corresponding human sciences.
—Bakhtin (1986, p. 104)

As discussed in Chapter 1, a questionable pragmatic epistemology organizes current qualitative inquiry in the human disciplines (see Lincoln & Denzin, 1994). Much contemporary inquiry is organized under modernist, postpositivist ethnographic assumptions (Lather, 1993). Like the modernist novel (see McHale, 1992, p. 44), the modernist ethnographic text presumes a stable external social reality that can be recorded by a stable, objective, scientific observer.[2] Although this external reality may yield to multiple interpretations, the interpretive, mobile consciousness of the researcher-as-observer is able to form certain and conclusive observations about it (see Wolcott, 1994, p. 408).

The modernist qualitative, ethnographic text records the many voices heard in the field setting as indicators of how this stable reality is socially constructed and given meaning. The modernist observer-writer, apparently even the nomadic ethnographer (see Grossberg, 1988), then mediates those voices and assembles them into a text that reorders reality according to a particular interpretive logic. Unlike its postmodern counterpart, this traditional text does not attempt to connect mobile, moving, shifting minds (and their representations) to a shifting, external world. There is no attempt to create a parallax of discourses where nothing is stable. If this were the case, there would be discourse on discourse and discourse on perspective, point of view, and language itself (see Lather, 1993; McHale, 1992; Richardson, 1994b; see also Grossberg, 1988).

Seeking to create a space for the voices of those studied, qualitative researchers attempt to capture and re-present, through photographs, transcribed interviews, and audiotapes, the authentic, original voices heard, seen, and felt in the field setting. It is understood that this re-presentation of the voice and experiences of the other requires special skills, a special way of seeing—what Eisner (1991, pp. 1-7) calls the enlightened eye, a form of connoisseurship that goes beyond looking, allowing the scholar to then make public, in a critical way, what has been seen.

In this chapter, extending the discussion in Chapter 1, I offer a critical interpretation of this epistemological bias in recent ethnographic research and writing. My intentions are fourfold. I will examine the qualitative research text as a cultural form, a form of writing and representation. I will then analyze the concepts of voice, hearing, listening, reading, and text as these terms are represented in the qualitative text, drawing on the works of Bakhtin (1968, 1981, 1986), Barthes (1957/1972, 1975, 1982, 1985), and Derrida (1967/1978, 1974/1976). This will lead to a critical appraisal of recent attempts to recover and represent the "voice" of the other in the qualitative research text (see Hertz, 1996, pp. 6-8). I will conclude with a series of proposals concerning how the voice and the presence of the other can be used in such research, anticipating a postmodern, feminist epistemology for qualitative inquiry that will be elaborated in Chapters 3 through 7.

Qualitative Research Text as a Cultural Form

The qualitative research text is a distinct form of cultural representation, a genre in its own right (see Van Maanen, 1988, 1995a, 1995b).[3] The qualitative researcher reproduces experiences that embody cultural meanings and cultural understandings that operate in the "real" world. These texts, to repeat Raymond Carver's (1989a) injunction, carry news from one world to another. This news is based (as suggested in the Preface) on three types of discourse: ordinary talk and speech, inscriptions of that speech in the form of transcriptions, and written interpretations based on talk and its inscriptions (see Clandinin & Connelly, 1994; Duranti & Goodwin, 1992).

Lived Experience, Lived Textuality

This discourse is based on the modernist commitment to study lived experience in the real world. Those who honor lived experience ground their work on the study of flesh-and-blood individuals. This experience, and its materiality, as given on the videotape, the picture, or the transcribed text, is taken as the final court of appeal for such researchers. This emphasis on lived presence falters on the following points.

First, as discussed in Chapter 1, the worlds we study are created through the texts that we write—for example, Steve dying of AIDS or Al not doing the first step. We do not study lived experience; rather, we examine lived textuality (Frow & Morris, 1993, p. xvii). Lived texts are representations that are themselves embodied representations of experience. The direct link between experience and text (as discussed in Chapter 1) can no longer be presumed. Lived textuality transforms lived experience. Real-life experiences are shaped by prior textual representations. These experiences are in turn shaped by understandings gained from participating in the performances of others—performances turned into texts.

These understandings, in turn, are reinscribed in the transcribed voice and dialogue of the other. They are created in the social text. These texts are dialogical, the site at which multiple voices comingle. In them, the voices of the other, and the voices of the researcher, come alive and interact with one another. These accomplishments have a prior life in the context in which they were produced—a life and a form that can never be fully recovered.

Second, the modernist project privileges visual representation. This representation is a stand-in for real interaction. It is one level removed from the actual experiences studied. Accordingly, scholars find themselves in the position of reading videotapes and transcriptions as cultural texts that represent experience.

This ocular epistemology presumes the primacy of visual perception as the dominant form of knowing. Perception, however, is never pure. It is clouded by the structures of language that refuse to be anchored in the present—the site of so-called pure presence. Presence in its plenitude can never be grasped. Consequently, presence on a tape or in real life is always elusive, shifting, and indeterminate, and its meanings are never final or clear-cut. Visual representations can only be understood as textual constructions. Furthermore, the specularity of the visual image is always problematic because the image is never a pure copy. Even when two images appear identical, there is always a surplus of meaning—an invisible otherness that disrupts "specular unity" (Jay, 1993, p. 505). The image always splits what it doubles and is always more than itself.

As I have discussed elsewhere (Denzin, 1995b, pp. 27, 211-212), human understanding is excluded from the epistemological equation that converts human knowledge into visual perception. Lonergan (1963/1977; also quoted in Springer, 1991, pp. 177-178) exposes this inconsistency:

> Now if human knowing is conceived exclusively . . . as similar to ocular vision, it follows . . . that human understanding must be excluded from human knowledge. For understanding is not like seeing. Understanding grows with time: you understand one point, then another, and a third, a fourth . . . and your understanding changes several times until you have things right. Seeing is not like that, so that to say that knowing is like seeing is to disregard understanding as a constitutive element in human knowledge. (pp. 121-122)

Using this formula, the conscious subject is excluded from the knowing process. Lonergan (1963/1977) elaborates:

> A further consequence of conceiving knowledge on the analogy of the popular notion of vision, is the exclusion of the conscious subject. Objects are paraded before spectators, and if the spectator wants to know him [her] self, he [she] must get out in the parade and be looked at. There are no subjects anywhere; for being a subject is not being something that is being looked at, it is being the one who is looking. (pp. 121-122)

The knowing, conscious subject now becomes someone who is looked at, but being looked at, or looking itself, does not constitute understanding. The ethnographer who wishes to understand another has to build up an understanding based on a deep involvement in the subject's worlds of experience. This means the subject is transformed into a person who is no longer the object of an external voyeuristic gaze.

The interpreter-observer, however, is not a neutral spectator. As Springer (1991, p. 178) observes, what is suppressed in the seeing-knowing equation is the fact "that interpretations are produced in cultural, historical, and personal contexts and are always shaped by the interpreter's values." As ethnographers invested the records of visual perception with the power of truth, truth itself became an unstable phenomenon, dependent on the viewer's interpretive framework for its empirical grounding. The very processes that joined truth and perception undermined from within the observer's ability to point with certainty to what was seen and, hence, known about the visual world and the subjects who inhabited that world. Thus, a special type of viewer was born: the ethnographer voyeur who looked repeatedly to know.

Consider two of cinema's classic voyeurs, Hitchcock's L. B. Jeffries in *Rear Window* (1954) and Francis Ford Coppola's Harry Caul in *The Conversation* (1974). Both men, as ethnographic voyeurs, had multiple sightings and recordings of their subjects actions (and speech, for Harry). Neither man could prevent evil (a murder) from occurring, and neither understood the motives of the murderers. Their visual and ocular epistemologies rendered them impotent. They were men obsessed with the technological gaze that turned their subjects into objects.

Third, modernist qualitative researchers place considerable faith in the primacy of voice over writing. Perhaps this is the case because they believe that hearing their own voice defines their presence in a situation. Speech is seen as the window into experience and its meanings. Speech is not transparent, however, as Harry Caul, Coppola's wiretap expert, comes to understand. To privilege the ear as the central communicative organ is to misunderstand hearing and listening as interactional activities. Paraphrasing the singer Willie Nelson, I hear the sound of your voice in my mind, and I hear what I want to hear. The ear is an impediment to common understanding; the acoustical mirror always distorts (Silverman, 1988, pp. 79-80).

Therefore, qualitative researchers' two main methods of inquiry, voyeuristic looking and hearing, on inspection turn into self-fulfilling methods that privilege the theatrical spectacles of sight and sound. These technologies of representation crumble precisely at that moment when the representation is taken to be a measure of pure presence, pure interaction, and a window into human intentionality and meaning. There are no such measures; they are all textual constructions.

Thus the mystery of experience. There is no secret key that will unlock its meanings. It is a labyrinth with no fixed origins and no firm center, structure, or set of recurring meanings. All that can be sought is a more fully grounded, multisensual, multiperspectival epistemology that does not privilege sight (vision) over the other senses, including sound, touch, and taste.

The Text as a Parallax of Discourses

Bakhtin (1986) anticipates the postmodernist text—a text based on a parallax of discourses in which nothing is ever stable or capable of firm and certain representation. His is a multiperspectival epistemology that thickens and makes more complex the very processes that qualitative researchers wish to capture and represent in their reflective texts.

For Bakhtin (1986), all discourse (everyday speech, poetry, drama, novels, music, and scientific articles) is contextual, immediate, and grounded in the concrete specifics of the interactional situation. Discourse is dialogical; it joins people in tiny, little worlds of concrete experience. In every situation, there are three parties (Bakhtin, 1986, p. 126): the speaker, the addressee (the person who hears), and the superaddressee, a third party who is presumed to understand what is being spoken. The dialogues that occur in these thickly peopled worlds cannot be repeated. They are always first-time occurrences; each attempt at repetition creates a new experience. (Each time Harry Caul replays the tape of the two speakers in Union Square he hears something new, and this new experience produces a new set of actions for him.)

No text or utterance can be repeated without a change in meaning and in context. The reproduction of the text is a new, unrepeatable event in the life of the text (Bakhtin, 1986, p. 106)—a new link to the historical moment that produced it. This life always exists between two subjects—the self and the other. The basic, underlying structure of the text lies in its connectedness to the boundaries that join two consciousnesses, two selves (Bakhtin, 1986, p. 106). Two speakers (or a reader confronting a text) create a context for meaning that cannot be easily transferred to another context. This life is thoroughly contextual, grounded in the moment of its existence.

Consider the following Russian parable analyzed by Bakhtin (Clark & Holquist, 1984, p. 203): "Two people are sitting in a room. They are both silent. Then one of them says, 'Well!' The other does not respond." For an outsider, this exchange is without meaning. For Bakhtin, four crucial elements are absent in this text: the intonation of the speaker—how the word "Well" was pronounced; the visible, concrete, historical situation the two speakers shared; their shared knowledge of the situation; and their shared interpretation of it (Clark & Holquist, 1984, p. 203).

Bakhtin (1986) fills in this discourse.[4] The two Russian speakers were looking out the window in a railway station and saw that it had begun to snow. Both knew that it was time for spring to finally come, and "*both* were *sick* and *tired* of the protracted winter, *were looking forward* to spring, and were *bitterly disappointed* by the late snowfall" (Clark & Holquist, 1984, p. 204). All these assumptions were unstated; they were glossed, indexical to the situation. The word well contains many meanings. "The snowflakes remain outside the window; the date, on the page of the calendar; the evaluation in the psyche of the speaker; and nevertheless all this is *assumed* in the word well" (Clark & Holquist, 1984, p. 204). The meaning of the word well can only be understood by "analyzing the relationship between what is said and what is unsaid" (Clark & Holquist, 1984, p. 204).

A discourse is always more than what is said or seen. It never reflects an extraverbal situation "in the way that a mirror reflects an object" (Clark & Holquist, 1984, p. 204). Discourse is always productive: It brings a situation into play, enunciates evaluations of the situation, and extends action into the future. "Discourse does not reflect a situation; it is a situation" (Clark & Holquist, 1984, p. 204).

This context of the utterance encompasses the visible (what is seen), the auditory (what is heard), and the sensory (what is felt). This context rests on shared knowledge and taken-for-granted assumptions that are unique to the moment. The unsaid, the assumed, and the silences in any discourse provide the flesh and bone—the backdrop against which meaning is established. Intonation is the bridge between the speaker, the word, and the listener. The way a word or utterance is inflected and given bodily and facial expression (surprise, incomprehension, doubting, affirmation, refutation, or admiration) is critical. Intonation creates the double voicedness of talk. It mediates and connects a speaker's meanings with the text of their talk. Discourse is thus always both specular and productive. It is not a mirrored reflection of what is seen or heard, but an emergent, unpredictable occurrence—a specular production.

Comprehension (understanding) is made possible when two speakers enter into a dialogic relationship with one another. In this relationship, each person becomes a party to the utterances of the other. Together, the two speakers create a small, dialogical world of unique meaning and experience. This universe cannot be reduced to mere transcripts. It cannot be captured in logical structures nor in the relationship between linguistic units. It must be treated as a whole, as a slice of experience unique to itself. An outside observer has no place in this dialogue. Only by entering into the dialogue can understanding be gained. Even then, understanding will be problematic. The best that can be hoped for is a version of Stake's (1994) naturalistic generalization, vicarious emotional experience, and naturalistic verisimilitude.

In discourse, cultural values are enacted and social structures come alive. The self, a constantly shifting process, is always the incomplete sum of its discursive practices. In speaking, I hear myself being created. I hear myself, not as the other hears me (and sees me) but as I want them to hear me. In this cracked acoustical mirror (Silverman, 1988, p. 80), I hear the sound of my own thoughts, knowing that you will never hear me as I hear myself. I am a constant acoustical production. These sounds, and their meanings to me, anchor my inner (and outer) meanings in this specific act of speaking and hearing. My voice creates the public context for my articulated thought.

The other, always embodied, moving, and shifting, inhabits this space. They fill it with the sounds of their voice, their eyes meet mine, and glance off my shoulders and my head. I talk to and at them, and they talk at me. They hear my thoughts against the sound of their own voice, which reverberates in the spaces that lie between us. Inner and outer dialogues merge, interact, shape, and inform one another. Punctuated by silences, dramatic pauses, and gestures, these two dialogical orders are the said and the unsaid, the heard and the unheard of everyday life. Together, we create a historical situation, a social structure, a moment of experience, and enlivened culture.

On occasion, this enlivened culture can become problematic, especially when the spoken word is printed. The printed text allows an inspection of what was spoken, and inspection may produce interpretations that are at odds with the speaker's intent. Disavowals are often created. Dick Armey, a member of the United States House of Representatives, called it a slip of the tongue—a mispronunciation—when he was quoted as having referred to his colleague Barney Frank as Barney Fag (Bauman, 1995). Similarly, when the tapes from a question-and-answer session with faculty members were published, Frank L. Lawrence, the current president of Rutgers University, denied that he meant anything racist when he was quoted as having said three words, "genetic, hereditary background." (These words were uttered as Lawrence was making reference to scores on Scholastic Assessment Tests.) He later claimed that they slipped into his conversation because he had been reading reviews about *The Bell Curve* (Herrnstein & Murray, 1994), a book that "examines the links between genetics and intellectual achievement" (Carvajal, 1995).

Any account of this byzantine social world must, then, address this complex event that two or more speakers (and then readers) have shared and created. The person who wishes to understand (comprehend) the text must be given a way to enter into the parts and spaces of listener and speaker. Only in this way will it be possible for interlocutors to bring to (and take from) this text the same depth of understanding and sympathy that is brought to their own experience. This is Bakhtin's moral and epistemological imperative: an ethical aesthetic that demands that texts be written and read in ways that morally move readers and viewers.

Ethics and the Minimalist Text

This ethical, moral, and ecological approach to the text places two demands on the writer (Clark & Holquist, 1984, p. 210). Written texts are moral, cultural productions; they enact culture as they pass judgment on it. This means that every speaker-as-writer has an obligation to develop a personal style that brings meaning and morality into discourse. This will be done through intonation, inflection, pacing, and word choice.[5] This style is political and conflictual. It refers to how something is morally expressed. A text should show, not tell. Talk about what something means to the other should be kept to a minimum. A minimalist text is saturated with theoretical understandings, but it does not announce or parade its theory. Of course, conflict will always be present. Meanings are misunderstood, and values and ideology clash. Power always comes into play because one party nearly always wishes to dominate the style, meanings, and forms of discourse of another.

This is how Bakhtin (1986) informs the project of qualitative researchers who seek to recover and represent the voice of the other. Photographs, videotapes, transcribed field notes, and interviews do not constitute texts that conform to Bakhtin's concept of the moral, dialogical text. Reproductions of the other's voice are doomed to leave us in the situation of the person reading Bakhtin's parable. What does "Well!" mean? We are left with "What does voice mean?"

The Many Sounds (and Meanings) of Voice

Voice, any dictionary reminds us, is a complex matter. It refers to many things at the same time: utterances that announce or report; sounds made through the mouth—for example, talking or singing; a quality of vocal sound—for example, an angry voice; a characteristic speech sound connected to a particular person—for example, Hillary's voice; a right to express one's opinion; the expression of a wish or opinion; the person or agency by which something is expressed—for example, the press being the voice of the people; the quality of being voiceful or voiceless—having no voice; and silence. One who has voice is vocal—articulate in various ways: clamorous, eloquent, expressive, forthright, frank, free-spoken, noisy, outspoken, plainspoken, shrill, strident, vociferous, inarticulate, and quiet.

What is voiced or given a voice is also heard. To hear is to perceive, to be aware of sound—the sound of the other's voice; to acknowledge, to attend to, to ascertain, catch, discover, eavesdrop, examine, find, gather, heed, harken, investigate, judge, learn, overhear, try to understand, listen; and to seek a hearing of one's voice or one's opinion. Hearing requires that one give careful attention to what is heard and said. Hearing presumes listening—the conscious effort to hear; to attend closely so as to hear; to give or lend an ear; to keep one's ears open; to prick up one's ears; and to hang on someone's words. Listen can also mean to heed; to give heed to; to take advice; to obey; to take notice; and to observe. One can hear and not listen. A listener is one who listens and hears.

A reader-as-viewer is one who is ready to hear, see, and listen to the voices, images, and sounds of a text. In so doing, the reader renders the text intelligible and meaningful. A written text becomes a montage (and a mise-en-scène)—a meeting place where "original" voices, their inscriptions (as transcribed texts), and the writer's interpretations come together.

The Text as Experiential Cinema[6]

The written text is a continuous field of cinematic experiences: emotional, visceral, sensory, visual, and auditory—an Altman film. This field is a constantly moving horizon that draws the near and the distant to the reader-as-viewer. It enfolds within itself spoken speech and the continuous play of visual images and symbols. This moving horizon of meaning contextually anchors, unhinges, locates, and relocates ongoing experience. The viewer-as-reader becomes an active, participating voyeur—a detective who hears and sees the sounds and consequences of the other's voice and actions.

This cinematic field carries the sounds and sights of everyday life. Its natural soundtrack reproduces the source and background sounds of the surrounding world. It is filled with music, the hum of air conditioners, the clanging of bells, automobile horns, sirens, birds chirping, multiple conversations going on elsewhere, footsteps in the hallway, doors slamming, dogs barking, the sounds of a cane tapping on the floor, laughter, and screams in the distance.

Embalmed transcribed speech is alien talk. The trap of "scription" (Barthes's [1985, p. 3] term for written speech) is threefold. Everyday, natural talk is visual, theatrical, inflective, and rhetorical. Barthes (1985) observes,

> Speech is fresh, innocent, immediately theatrical, always tactical. . . .
> When we speak we 'expose' our thoughts as they are put into words.
> . . . We express aloud the inflections of our search. . . . When we speak,
> we want our interlocutor to listen to us; we revive his (her) attention
> with meaningless interpellations (of the type 'Hello'). . . . Unassuming
> as they are, these words and expressions are . . . discreetly dramatic.
> (pp. 3-5)

Talk's theatrical elements, along with its immediate innocence, are lost in the transcribed conversation (see Reissman, 1993, for a review of transcription practices). The transcribed text changes the receiver of the message as well as the subject and the other (Barthes, 1985, p. 5). The new text takes on a hierarchical order and logic. The body, along with the self-image and speaking repertoire of the speaker, are gone. The "tiny liaisons speech uses to fill up silences" (Barthes, 1985, p. 5) are absent. The printed text follows the laws of grammar, which are alien to speech.

Embracing Inscribed Speech

Like the photograph, the inscribed text is a form of mimesis. It copies what has already been (see Barthes, 1985, p. 355). Therefore, its wonder, as Taussig (1993, p. xiii) argues, lies in that moment when the copy, the representation, assumes the power of the original—more real than the real. The printed text replaces the spoken word; it is more accurate then what was spoken. In this moment, however, a confusion occurs. The original "original" changes each time it is spoken. It cannot be copied. Mimesis is a fraud.

The inscribed text, like all copies, is caught between three dangers. Its copies are originals. It cannot copy as well as the cinematic text (which contextualizes the social). Also, the referent of what is copied is no longer the subject being quoted or copied. Rather, the subject of the new text, as with the photograph, is the viewer-as-reader. Still, the seductiveness of the transcribed text is given in its illusive naturalness. On the surface, its referent points to the lived experiences of a real person. This reality, however, is one-dimensional. It is a construction, one of many possible slices or images of reality selected by the scribe. Its naturalness is a masquerade.

The original voices of individuals in a field setting, and the intentions behind those voices, can never be recovered. There are no original voices because every instance of a voice being heard is an original, a new hearing, and a new voice speaking (and hearing) its mind. Every transcription is a retelling—a new telling of a previously heard, now newly heard voice. Similarly, each telling by a speaker is a new telling, a new event in the history of the event being recounted.

On Hearing (and Seeing) the Voices
in Ethnographic Research

Consider the following sampling of transcribed voices reported in Michael Schratz's (1993a, 1993b, 1993c) seminal edited collection, *Qualitative Voices in Educational Research*. This valuable collection is filled with the transcripted talk of interviewers, teachers, and students. Teachers are speaking: "Group work? Colleagues might think the lesson is getting out of hand" (Ruddick quoted in Schratz, 1993c, p. 17).

Interviewers talking to students:

Interviewer: How do you know the teacher agrees with what these documents say?

Student (looking very surprised at the interviewer because of this stupid question): The teacher wouldn't give you these documents in the first place if he didn't agree with them, would he? (Altrichter, 1993, p. 46)

Interviewer: It's remarkable that the children work on their own as they do. How do you prepare them to do this?

Teacher: I'm not sure I do prepare them. They have to trust me. We try to develop a relationship, that has to happen first. (Spindler & Spindler, 1992b quoted in Schratz, 1993c, p. 113)

A field document (written letter by a male union secretary): "I am surprised at your decision to write to our representative concerning her letter of 15 November. I met you informally concerning her letter . . . and offered to withdraw the letter" (Burgess quoted in Schratz, 1993c, p. 33).

These uses of voice are not focused on hearing or listening. The scholars quoted here are representing the voices of others. Their texts function as the agency that is the voice of the people. When the text becomes the agency that represents the voices of the other, the other becomes an object spoken for. A doubling of agency occurs behind the text because the agent is the author of the text doing the interpreting. The other becomes an extension of the author's voice.

Representations, such as those given previously, do not conform to the guidelines set by Bakhtin (1986) and Barthes (1985). These guidelines focus (to repeat) on four dialogical structures: talk's immediate context; talk's extraverbal features, including the drama of talk; and the moral imperatives of discourse. To these four guidelines, a fifth can be added: The researcher's place inside the text must be clearly identified.

Revisioning the Qualitative Text

The modernist ethnographic text must be read as a photograph. It offers up fixed representations of things that have happened in a stable, external world. As with the photograph, such texts have multiple uses. They can be looked at and read, over and over again, each looking or reading being a new encounter with the text. Six uses can be noted:

- The transcribed text records (in distorted form) a moment of history. This history, textually reconstructed, provides a window into what was thought and expressed by a particular subject in a particular time and place. Like a photo, it is a glimpse of the past. This use of the text produces a situated telling, a narrative from the field that reflects the researcher's telling of what has been studied.
- The transcribed text can affirm what is (or was) already known about the topic at hand. It supplements existing knowledge.
- The text can affirm new discoveries, bearing witness to understandings not previously known or understood. It reveals new ways of looking, seeing, and hearing.
- The text can represent a minority voice or position within the site studied; a position that runs counter to the dominant views in the setting. Here, researchers use other voices to supplement or contrast with their own.
- The text can function as an exemplar of a style or form of discourse.

■ The text can function as a context for other voices to be heard. The researcher groups or clusters multiple transcripts together, montage-like, creating a multitude of transcribed voices, each providing context for the other.

Used in any of these ways, the transcribed voice functions as a nondialogical vehicle for the text-as-agency. Qualitative research, however, is back where it started—seeking to find a space and a voice for those studied. That space will never be found as long as stable observers insist on producing stable pictures of reality.

Back to the Beginning

Today, the modernist, pragmatic method of knowing is under assault. The very methods of knowing are themselves no longer certain. Modernism's pragmatism falters at that precise moment when the phobia for truth confronts the truth of Baudrillard's (1983) simulacrum; the truth that says there is no truth. Suppose, then, that nothing is no longer certain except uncertainty. If this is so, then science and ethnography are no longer certain; they are only two among many discourses about reality.

Hollywood has taken the lead in this discourse. Since mid-century, reflexive voyeuristic cinema has systematically attacked the belief that reality can be faithfully recorded (Denzin, 1995a). Starting with films such as *Blowup* and *The Conversation*, and continuing to the present, with texts such as *Sex, Lies, and Videotape* and *JFK*, Hollywood has systematically attacked the assertion that reality can be unquestionably captured with the camera. This attack undermines the modern pragmatist's epistemology because consequences can no longer be firmly established. Dead bodies disappear, pictures are destroyed, and reality, as it was previously known, is erased.

The postpragmatist's project in the postmodern period confronts an epistemological crisis. Firm claims about truth, knowledge, consequences, causes, and effects can no longer be made. A new epistemological framework is sought, and a pragmatism fitted to the globalizing cyberspaces of the cinematic, television age.

As discussed in the Chapter 1, a return to the beginning is required; a new form of textuality is needed. A way of writing that embodies a fundamental accuracy of statement about what is heard and felt will be cultivated (Carver, 1989a, p. 23). This writing will be organized by the principle that even if something did not happen, it could have happened. This criterion for truth means that what could have happened will happen in this text.[7]

This new text implements Bakhtin's (1986) fundamental insight that the social world is best described as a parallax of discourses. This text will move forward with the understanding that although the modernist regime invested visual perception and the cinematic text with the power of truth, this investment was not without loss. Human understanding, as discussed previously, is excluded from any epistemological equation that equates human knowledge with visual perception. Seeing is not understanding. Understanding is more than visual knowledge. Understanding is visceral. The fully interpretive text plunges the reader into the interior, feeling, hearing, tasting, smelling, and touching worlds of subjective human perception (Ong, 1977, p. 137).

The new text will move away from the objective, visual mimesis of modernism. It will turn to a form of textuality that is caught in the grip of a mobile consciousness recording its relationship to an ever-changing external world. This text will become increasingly acoustic and performance-based, stressing the sound and feel of worlds, the voices in the acoustic mirrors that hear themselves speak, hearing the sounds of their own voices. This will be a move away from the reflective, looking-glass text to the acoustic text, with its fractured, overlaid, multiple sound-tracks.[8] These will be works that key on the aural, melodic, rhythmic, and acoustical side of the multivoiced text envisioned by Bakhtin. This means that a new form of looking, hearing, and feeling must be cultivated—a form that goes beyond the male way of seeing.

Here, recent feminist scholarship becomes relevant. Irigaray (1985) has argued that the feminine gaze (unlike the male look) is multiperspectival or multisensual. It transcends pure vision and specularity to privilege the other senses, including touch, hearing, and taste. On the other side of the masculine looking glass, on the "other side of the mirror, behind the screen of male representations, is an underground world" (Jay, 1993, p. 533). This is the "dark night of [the feminine] soul" (Irigaray, 1985, p. 103; also quoted in Jay, 1993, p. 533). If women only identify with the narcissistic subject created by the masculine, flat mirror, "they are imprisoned in a male specular economy in which they are always devalued as inferior versions of the male subject, as mere objects of exchange, dead commodities" (Jay, 1993, p. 533).

This dark side of the feminine soul calls into question the power of the masculine gaze. This harkening exposes and illuminates the need for an empowering, multisensual feminine subjectivity. This subjectivity embraces a field of experience that is more than just visual. When released into society, this multisensual field of experience threatens the status quo. This is an unstable threat, however, because the feminine gaze must always fight to resist the masculine pull, which is the pull of science, objectivity, law and order, and family.

Ethnographic researchers, borrowing a metaphor from Mayne (1990, p. 8), must learn to look at themselves from both sides of the voyeur's keyhole, seeing themselves looking at themselves through the eyes of the modernist gaze. Reversing the logic of the traditional, masculine, investigative project, this new female look will shift and take on multiple forms, making it impossible to clearly define who is subject and who is object.

As new ways of capturing voice are sought, it may be necessary for qualitative researchers to momentarily suspend their preoccupation with the field interview and the carefully transcribed voice of the other. If there is a warrant to the narrative turn in the human disciplines (see Chapter 5), then this warrant directs researchers to the study and collection of the personal experience and self stories people tell one another about the important events in their lives (Denzin, 1989b, p. 43). These narratives will work outward from the researcher's biography, entangling his or her tales of the self with the stories told by others. As lived textualities, these personal experience narratives and "mystories" recover the dialogical context of meaning, placing the observer on both sides of the "keyhole." As an emergent cultural form, these fragmented, moral texts mediate and connect persons to culture, history, and ongoing group life. Their production and interpretation requires a new version of the enlightened eye, a new form of cultural connoisseurship. They represent the preferred path for implementing the critical, post-structural project.

Taking narrative and a parallax of discourses seriously, the interpretive scholar will hopefully find in these practices and performances fruitful strategies for creating the much needed dialogical text. This uncertain discursive field will open to a parallax of discordant voices, visions, and feelings. It will be read from the vantage point of a radical democratic ethos, a new (but old) form of social criticism that celebrates diversity and multiplicity. This discursive field will yield to a cacophony of voices demanding to be heard (and seen). From the vantage point of this new beginning, qualitative researchers will launch attacks on those structures of science, political economy, and ideology that threaten to take away our most basic freedoms always in the modernist name of objectivity truth and civility.

This chapter concludes Part I, my interpretations of the representation and legitimation crises in current qualitative research. In the next three chapters, I turn to a discussion of experiential and experimental texts that attempt to move ethnographic writing in new directions. In the next chapter, I examine texts based on the standpoint epistemologies.

Notes

1. Earlier versions of portions of this chapter appeared in Denzin (1995c, 1995d).

2. As discussed in Chapter 1, McHale (1992) argues that the modernist text is marked by two key textual strategies: mobile consciousness and parallax or multiple points of view. Such texts attempt to secure a fine-grained interaction between "consciousness and the world outside consciousness" (McHale, 1992, p. 45). This internal consciousness may be unreliable, unstable, shifting, and digressive, but the world itself is stable. A new cultural studies journal, *Parallax*, attempts to critically exploit this concept of multiple perspectives and multiple realities to reinvigorate theory and praxis.

3. There are many variations on the ethnographic writing form, including those labeled realist, confessional, and impressionistic (Van Maanen, 1988); I-witnessing, us-not us, and being here (Geertz, 1988); oedipal (Clough, 1992); feminist (Wolfe, 1992); cultural studies (Drotner, 1994; Grossberg, 1988; Radway, 1988); generic (Lofland & Lofland, 1995); naturalistic and constructionist (Lincoln & Guba, 1985); grounded theory (Strauss & Corbin, 1990); and postmodern (Wolfe, 1992).

4. This can be read as a violation of his framework because he presumes an external, all-knowing position in this situation.

5. This becomes even more critical in the performed text (see Chapter 4).

6. I use the phrase experiential cinema to reference a subjective cinema (see Kawin, 1978) that uses a mobile camera and attempts to capture the moving, fluid, multiple perspectives, dialogues, and actions that occur in daily life. Woody Allen (on occasion), Robert Altman, and John Cassavetes deploy this style.

7. With the caveat that the writer is writing ethnographic fiction (see Eason, 1986).

8. The films of Robert Altman (e.g., *Nashville, The Player,* and *Short Cuts*) are excellent examples of this approach to the acoustical mirror.

PART 2

Experiential Texts

CHAPTER 3

Standpoint Epistemologies

The master's tools will never dismantle the master's house.
—Lorde (1984, p. 112; also quoted in Collins, 1992, p. 79)

Ethnography's sixth moment is defined, in part, by a proliferation of interpretive epistemologies grounded in the lived experiences of previously excluded groups in the global, postmodern world. Working outward from feminist critiques of positivism (Collins, 1991, p. 205), these frameworks have moved in several directions at the same time, producing many different feminisms, including gynocriticism, materialist, standpoint, psychoanalytic, poststructural, African American, empiricist, postmodern, cultural studies, and those defined as postcolonial (see Clough, 1993a, 1994; Collins, 1991; Harding, 1991).

United in their criticisms of "Eurocentric masculinist approaches" (Collins, 1991, p. 205) to reading, writing, and inquiry, these works propose to make women's experiences instead of men's experiences the point of departure (Clough, 1994, p. 62) for interpretive work.[1] Loosely based on the concept of a standpoint epistemology (Clough, 1992, 1994; Collins, 1991; Harding, 1991; Hartsock, 1983; Krieger, 1991; Lather, 1991, 1993; Olesen, 1994; Smith, 1992), epistemologies of color building on Afrocentric (Collins, 1991; hooks, 1990), Chicana(os) (Anzaldua, 1987; Rosaldo, 1989), Native American, Asian (Chow, 1993; Trinh, 1989, 1992),

Third World, postcolonial (Chow, 1993; Clough, 1994; Spivak, 1990), and other minority group experiences now circulate in the ethnographic literature.

More elaborated epistemologies of gender (and class) are also appearing, including various feminist materialist approaches to theory and ethnography (Clough, 1994; Hartsock, 1983; Roman, 1992), and recent queer embodiments of feminist theorizing (Butler, 1990; Fuss, 1989; Krieger, 1991, 1983; Sedgwick, 1990; Seidman, 1994; Terry, 1991; see also Clough, 1994, pp. 142-165).[2] Members of each of these interpretive communities draw on their marginalized group and individual experiences as the basis for the texts they write as they seek texts that speak to the logic and cultures of these communities.

In this chapter, these new interpretive styles that privilege lived experience and the standpoints that experience brings to the ethnographic text are examined. Taking liberties with the concept of standpoint, I begin with the shared assumptions that organize the standpoint epistemologies.[3] Then, the works of three key authors in this tradition, representative texts of Patricia Hill Collins (1991), Trinh T. Minh-ha (1989, 1991, 1992), and Gloria Anzaldua (1981a, 1981b, 1987) are critically examined.[4]

The following arguments organize my reading of these texts. First, although these authors argue against positivism and postpositivism, these writers maintain (in varying degrees) a connection to the ocular, visual epistemology that defines the realist, positivist project. That is, they emphasize sight, vision, and a textual form that, as discussed in Chapter 4, turns the knowing subject into someone who is looked at, made a spectacle of, and the subject of the gazing ethnographer's eye.[5] Second, the standpoint authors stress lived experience but do not show the reader how the experience of the other is brought into the texts they write. Hence, the connections between texts and lived experience remain unexamined. In many cases, lived experience disappears entirely from the theorist's texts. Third, the writer's place in the text is seldom clarified. The standpoint theorist presumes a privileged but problematic place in her own textuality. Fourth, a romantic, utopian impulse organizes this work: the belief that if lived experience is recovered, somehow something good will happen in the world. A politics of action or praxis, however, is seldom offered (see Collins, 1992, p. 79; Connell, 1992, p. 87; Smith, 1992, pp. 96-97). Finally, a version of the standpoint text is required if ethnography is to continue to connect itself to the worlds of everyday life. Such works contain the seeds of a new textuality that leads naturally to the performance texts to be taken up in the next chapter.

Logic of the Standpoint Text

Standpoint texts are organized in terms of the following assumptions. First, the starting point is experience—the experiences of women, persons of color, postcolonial writers, gay and lesbians, and persons who have been excluded form the dominant discourses in the human disciplines (Smith, 1993, p. 184). This argument is foundational. It challenges the very "notion of a single standpoint from which a final overriding version of the world can be written" (Smith, 1989, p. 58; see also Harding, 1991, pp. 119-121). Each of the standpoint epistemologies questions the standpoint from which traditional, patriarchal social science has been constructed (Smith, 1989, p. 57). This masculine standpoint presumed a universal sociological subject, the white male. It presumed a view outside society and argued that society could be written about from the position of an objective observer (Smith, 1989, p. 44). This observer-as-a-social-theorist created a discourse that suspended the presence of a real subject in the world. It made social experience irrelevant to the topic at hand. It created an interpretive structure that said social phenomena should be interpreted as social facts (Smith, 1989, p. 45). It shifted arguments about agency, purpose, meaning, and intention from the subject to the phenomena being studied. It then transformed those phenomena into texts about society, giving the phenomena a presence that rested in the textual description (Smith, 1989, p. 45). Real live people then entered the text as a figment of discourse in the form of excerpts from field notes, the casual observations of the theorist, or as "ideal types" (Smith, 1989, p. 51).

The feminist standpoint theorists wish to overturn this picture of social science. They begin from the perspective of women's experiences—experiences shaped by a gender-based division of labor that has excluded women from the public sphere. A feminist standpoint is thus constructed, building, as Clough (1994, p. 74) states, on women's identities in the private sphere (housewife, homemaker, mother, and daughter), working outward to her identities in the public sphere (secretary, administrative assistant, Marxist-feminist social scientist, filmmaker, and writer). Not only do women know different then men but women's experiences should be the starting point for a more accurate representation of reality (Clough, 1994, p. 74). This starting point will erase the public and private distinction in everyday life. It will lead to the production of local, gendered knowledge about the workings of the world. It will show how the patriarchal apparatus structures this daily life through the reproduction of text-mediated discourses (Smith, 1993).

Second, a nonessentializing stance toward the categories that classify people is taken. In Harding's (1991, p. 179) words, "race, class, gender, and culture are interlocking" producing concrete situations in which race, class, age, and gender intersect in the actual lives of real people. Trinh (1992) states,

> The question of ethnic identity and the question of female identity are one to me . . . as if identity could be separated from oneself . . . with respect to truth, to ethnicity and feminity: I can't take hold of it nor lose it/When I am silent it projects/When I project, it is silent. (p. 240)

Smith (1992) contextualizes the argument,

> The categories that identify diversity (race, gender, class, age, and so forth) . . . are categories of . . . discourse. . . . To begin with the categories are to begin in discourse. Experiencing as a woman of color . . . does not break down into experience as a women and experience as a person of color.[6] (p. 240)

Dorothy Smith (1993) describes her feminist standpoint epistemology: "There are indeed matters to be spoken and spoken of that discourse does not yet encompass." She elaborates, "we had no language in which our experience could be spoken among women by women" (pp. 183-184). Thus, an insider sociology is sought that uses the "outsider within" status (Collins, 1986, pp. 14-15) of women to create a discourse situated in the "everyday/everynight world of her actual lived experience" (Smith, 1989, p. 34). This sociology will not necessarily reproduce the lived experiences of women; it is only necessary to show how women's actual experiences activate the apparatuses and relations of ruling in the larger patriarchal social order (Smith, 1987, pp. 154-155). Smith calls this doing institutional ethnography (see discussion below).

Collins (1986) speaks of the Afro-American woman as an outsider to white society,

> Afro-American women have long been privy to some of the most intimate secrets of white society . . . but . . . black women knew they could never belong to 'white' families. In spite of their involvement, they remained 'outsiders.' This 'outsider within' status has provided a special standpoint on self, family and society for Afro-American women. (p. 14)

This standpoint means that "African-American women as a group experience a world different from those who are not Black and female. . . . These concrete experiences can stimulate a distinctive Black feminist consciousness concerning that material reality" (Collins, 1991, p. 24). Sedgwick (1990, pp. 1-2) argues that the dominant epistemology of experience in the human disciplines has been heterosexual, creating an epistemology of the closet. This framework required an opposition between homosexuality and heterosexuality and between secrecy and privacy, private and public, masculine and feminine, and health and illness. This epistemology of the closet presumed a universal sexual subject—the male heterosexual. It created, as with the case of Afro-Americans, subjugated knowledges, knowledges those in power could afford to ignore (Clough, 1994, p. 145).

Spivak (1988) drives the argument even deeper: Disciplinary anthropology has made it impossible for the subaltern subject to even speak, for it has presumed a unified "?'naturally articulate' subject" (p. 289). There is no single standpoint for the subaltern subject who lives a series of hybrid identities on the borderlands between home, America, Mexico, India, China, and elsewhere (Anzaldua, 1987; Chow, 1993).

Third, this discourse often begins from the painful autobiographical experiences of the writer. Thus, Smith (1989) locates her work within her personal, family, and professional history:

> When my children were small I was working at the University of California at Berkeley. I went back and forth between doing the work of mothering in all its particularities and demands, and the sociolocal-

world-in-texts that I taught. . . . It was . . . a search for a consciousness in myself that had been present (in the anxieties, the tensions, the feelings of nausea accompanying my work, departmental meetings, trying to write sociology, and so forth) but impotent. (pp. 36-37)

Patricia Hill Collins (1991, p. 1) begins with her childhood: "When I was five years old, I was chosen to play Spring in my preschool pageant." Sedgwick (1987, p. 111) also returns to her childhood: "When I was a little child the two most rhythmic things that happened to me were spanking and poetry." Anzaldua (1987, p. 16) speaks of leaving home: "I was the first in six generations to leave the alley, the only one in my family to ever leave home." hooks (1989) is less than sanguine about her childhood:

To me, telling the story of my growing up years was intimately connected with the longing to kill the self. . . . I wanted to be rid of the girl who was always wrong, always punished, always subjected to some humiliation or other, always crying, the girl who was to end up in a mental institution because she could not be anything but crazy or so they told her. (p. 155)

Trinh (1989) resists this pull: "The image is of a mirror capturing only the reflections of other mirrors. . . . I . . . am alluding to . . . the play of mirrors that defers to infinity the real subject and subverts the notion of an original 'I' " (p. 22).

Fourth, from the autobiographical arises a desire (as discussed previously) to recover a self that has been subjugated by the dominant structures of racism, sexism, and colonialism in everyday life. A utopian impulse is at work. If the previously suppressed self can be recovered, liberation, freedom, and dignity will be experienced.[7] The scientific project is thereby redefined; the personal defines theolitical, which transforms science into a politics of experience. This means that the standpoint epistemologies move in two directions at the same time. The first direction is toward the discovery of knowledge about the social world as that world works its way into the lives of oppressed people. Second, there is an attempt to recover and bring value to knowledge that has been suppressed by the existing epistemologies in the social sciences. Thus, Collins (1991, p. 208) places great value on the riddles, proverbs, and stories that are central to the Afro-American woman's family experiences.

Knowing Experience: The Materialist Challenge

Feminist standpoint theorists begin with the subject who knows the "world directly through experience" (Clough, 1994, p. 73), arguing that that experience is the starting point for social change—the site for a politics of empowerment. The link, however, as discussed previously, between experience, text, knowledge, and praxis is problematic. Feminist materialists (Clough, 1994, p. 77) argue that "an individual's knowledge of the world and of self are always constructed in unconscious desire. . . . There is . . . no direct knowledge of the world of experience." There is no "agentic subject who directly knows reality through experience" (Clough, 1994, p. 74). Reality is lived through ideology and through the workings of the subject's unconscious desire (Clough, 1994, p. 75). Therefore, experience is already defined by ideology and unconscious desire and by the apparatuses of the state, culture, the media, and the popular. The subject is constructed by these apparatuses. Reality is the effect of these constructions. There is no direct access to lived experience, and there "is no subject outside of unconscious desire and, therefore, discourse" (Clough, 1994, p. 77).

Smith (1992) disagrees: "Are we really stuck with Althusser's . . . condemnation of the subject to lasting dependency on being interpellated by 'ideological state apparatuses'? . . . from discourse to subjectivity. . . . I want to go another way" (p. 91). Smith's concept of standpoint does not privilege a knower; it begins with the knower located in the world, caught up in a web of invisible social relations that shape her experiences (Smith, 1992, p. 91). This figure of woman is positioned in the social relations of discourse as an active, knowing agent of her own experience (Smith, 1993, p. 185).

Two meanings of discourse are operating. The materialist perspective sees the subject defined in and through discourse at the unconscious level of desire. Smith's position examines the systems of text-mediated discourse that organize the relations between people in the world. Smith reads Clough as saying that there is no subject outside the text, "hence no speaking of or from actual experience" (Smith, 1993, p. 186). Clough (1993b) challenges this interpretation:

> Experience is [not] purely an epiphenomen of discourse. . . . Uncon-
> scious desire is productive in the construction of the subject's experi-
> ence and . . . this understanding is critical for political and social
> criticism. . . . Discourse and experience . . . are [not] distinct. . . . They
> are enjoined in unconscious desire. (pp. 193-194)

The issue turns on the status of lived experience and the unconscious and their place in the standpoint epistemologies. The materialist,
psychoanalytic model calls for the serious interrogation of those cultural texts that shape and define desire, sexuality, and identity. Lived
experience is always mediated by unconscious desire. Smith (1993)
examines those discourses that articulate the structures of experience
women confront and live at the actual, everyday level. In both models,
lived experience disappears from the text.

Grossberg (1988, 1993) partially mediates these two positions;
drawing on his reading of Gramsci, he is closer to Smith than to Clough.
Experience in any situation is always shaped by the hegemonic cultural
practices that individuals use, including the texts they call on. These
practices and the texts they interact with produce situated, subjective
interpretations based on conflicting meanings and social relationships.
At this level, the politics of culture (Grossberg, 1993),

> Involves the work of placing particular practices into particular rela-
> tions or contexts, and of transforming one set of relations, one context
> into another. The identity and effects of a practice are not given in
> advance; they are not determined by its origin or by some intrinsic
> feature of the practice itself. (p. 90)

Here, lived experience disappears into cultural practices. The ethnographer becomes a traveling nomad who writes of the world so as to
discover the multiple meanings and effects of diverse cultural practices.
Subjectivity dissolves into the signs and road maps that represent the
culture to its members.[8]

The Textual and the Empirical Subject

None of these proposals is entirely satisfactory. In each case, the
experiences and the point of view of the interacting subject in the world
disappear, to reappear in ideology and unconscious desire, in a set of

cultural practices, or in another level of discourse.[9] This situation can be partially resolved by maintaining a distinction between the textual subject and the empirical subject (see Stacey, 1994, pp. 24-31).[10] The textual subject is the subject created in discourse, a figure in a film, or an ethnographic text. The flesh and blood person is the actual person in the world who lives, feels, and thinks and has social relationships with other flesh and blood people. This person interacts with the texts of the culture, often finding their experiences inscribed in these discourses.

Of course, it is not possible to represent a life as it is actually lived or experienced. Bruner (1986, p. 6) explains, clarifying three terms and noting that the link between experience and its expressions is always problematic: "The critical distinction here is between reality (what is really out there) . . . experience (how that reality presents itself to consciousness), and expressions (how individual experience is framed and articulated)." Experiences constitute the flux and flow of consciousness. Experiences are constantly out of reach of language and discourse and on the borderlines of consciousness and awareness. On the other hand, as Bruner (1986, p. 6) notes, it is possible to represent a life (or its meanings) as it is told in a narrative, a proverb, a story, a slice of a conversation, or a folktale. Spoken, performed, told, and retold in the narrative form, this is the realm of lived experience that is recoverable. As discussed in Chapters 3 and 4, however, the original meaning of a told experience can never be recovered. There are only retellings— performed texts evocatively re-presented in the ethnographer's text. These, of course, become new expressions of the experience. These tellings, told by the writer, now become the writer's versions of the subject's lived experiences. In this retold form, the subject is understood to be constantly caught up in the webs of discourse Clough and Smith describe.

The performed text opens another window into the world of lived experience. The writer collects and reproduces the texts and stories that circulate in the subject's world. These stories and tales are understood to be repositories of wisdom and knowledge (Collins, 1991, p. 208) that "reflect the standpoint of their creators" (Collins, 1991, p. 201). As such, they enter into the meanings that are brought to experience at the everyday level of existence. They become stand-ins for lived experience.

Critical Theory

Each of the standpoint epistemologies is connected (even if indirectly) to the critical and empancipatory styles of interpretation (see Kincheloe & McLaren, 1994). All begin from Marx's notion of the relations of ruling in a capitalist society that has structured the production of knowledge about the world. There are ruling ideas in any society, and these involve ideas about race, class, gender, and nation. These ideas "penetrate social consciousness . . . in ways that deny expression to the actual experience people have in their working relations to their everyday world" (Smith, 1987, p. 55). A fault line is created—a line between the world directly experienced and the ideas about the world embedded in the ideas and images the society constructs and fabricates about itself (Clough, 1994, p. 70; Smith, 1987, p. 55).

All share a critical realist ontology (a world out there) and a dialogic, transformative, ethnographic methodology (Guba, 1990, p. 25).[11] This frequently produces a criticism of traditional, naturalistic ethnographies (Roman, 1992, p. 558) and an affinity for neo-Marxist and cultural studies models of the race, class, and gendered structures of contemporary societies (Carspecken & Apple, 1992, pp. 541-542). It may produce, however, an alignment with conventional ethnographic practices. That is, the knower is positioned in an objective relationship to the world studied (Grossberg, 1988; Radway, 1988), even in the institutional ethnographies endorsed by D. E. Smith (1987) and G. W. Smith (1990).

An emancipatory principle drives such research, which is committed to engaging oppressed groups in collective, democratic theorizing about "what is common and different in their experiences of oppression and privilege" (Roman, 1992, p. 557). A constant focus is given to the material and cultural practices that create structures of oppression.

A critical standpoint text is judged by its ability to reflexively reveal these structures of oppression as they operate in the worlds of lived experience (Smith, 1990). A critical text thus creates a space for multiple voices to speak or be represented; those who are oppressed are asked to articulate their definitions of their situations. For some, but necessarily the standpoint theorists, critical theory must be testable, falsifiable, dialogical, and collaborative (Carspecken & Apple, 1992, pp. 547-548). Others reject the more positivist features of this formulation (Roman, 1992, p. 558). Dorothy Smith (1992, p. 96), for example, evaluates a text by its ability to reveal the invisible structures of oppression in women's worlds (see G. Smith, 1990).[12]

Criticisms

A good critical, emancipatory, standpoint text is one that is local, multivocal, collaborative, naturalistically grounded in the worlds of lived experience, and organized by a critical, interpretive theory. Such formulations have been criticized on many grounds, including their tendency to ignore the writer's place in the text while privileging an ocular epistemology; confusing problems of capturing "real" experience with its representation (Ganguly, 1992, pp. 62-63); ignoring the partial, situated nature of feminist knowledge (Haraway, 1988) while pursuing the impossible quest of objectivity, and risking the reinscription of "humanist and masculine myths of power and certitude" (Ganguly, 1992, p. 61; Haraway, 1988); imposing their voices and values on the groups studied (Quantz, 1992, p. 471); presuming a unified or essentialized subject; arguing from a null point of experience while not being sufficiently self-reflexive (Lemert, 1992, p. 69); not developing local knowledge that could be used for political change (Collins, 1992, p. 77); using the language of those in the inner circle of power (Collins, 1992); producing extralocal abstractions that are not locally grounded (Connell, 1992, p. 83); focusing on the experiences of white women (Connell, 1992, p. 83); not actively engaging the arguments of participatory action research (Connell, 1992); lacking a utopian impulse (Connell, 1992); being too theoretical (top-down theory) and too preoccupied with theory verification (Roman, 1992, p. 571); and not being sufficiently aware of materialist feminist sensibilities concerning the political unconscious, sexual desire, the text, and its social construction (Clough, 1992, p. 137, 1994; see Smith, 1992, 1993). Finally, the terrain of lived experience remains problematic, as the previous discussion indicates.

These critical approaches, with their action criteria, politicize qualitative research. They set the background for the specific standpoint epistemology texts analyzed here. They foreground praxis, yet often leave unclear the methodological side of the interpretive process that is so central to my concerns in this book.

Patricia Hill Collins:
An Afrocentric, Feminist Epistemology

In *Black Feminist Thought* (Collins, 1991), Collins is Gramsci's organic intellectual (Collins, 1991, pp. 14, 18)—the outsider within white society who reclaims the everyday world of the black woman as her topic. The starting place is lived experience and its representations in the voices, images, sayings, songs, fictions, and autobiographies of bloodmothers, othermothers, and sisters. This world of everyday action and experience, the world of the commonplace and the taken for granted, is the place where a self-defined black woman's standpoint is anchored. From this standpoint emerges Collins's Afrocentric feminist epistemology (Collins, 1991, p. 219).

This epistemology challenges positivism and extreme relativism (Collins, 1991, p. 235), stressing, instead, the value of her standpoint as a partial perspective on the "truths" it discovers (Collins, 1991, p. 236). Collins states,

> Those ideas that are validated as true by African-American women, African-American men, Latina lesbians, Asian-American women . . . and other groups with distinctive standpoints . . . thus become the most 'objective' truths. Each group speaks from its standpoint and shares its own truth as partial, its knowledge as unfinished. (p. 236)

Collins's (1991) text is grounded in the study in the texts of black women intellectuals, activists, musicians, poets, and fiction writers, including Aretha Franklin, Toni Morrison, Gwendolyn Brooks, Billi Holliday, Alberta Hunter, Zora Neale Hurston, Bessie Jackson, Audre Lorde, Ma Rainey, Nina Simone, Bessie Smith, Sojourner Truth, and Alice Walker. These standpoint texts contain the kernels of her standpoint epistemology.

I read *Black Feminist Thought* (Collins, 1991) as a standpoint, textual ethnography—a study in the representations of lived experience that stand at the core of black women's experiences in late twentieth-century America. As a textual ethnography, the work establishes and achieves its verisimilitude and authority through the use of the voices that Collins quotes and draws on. These voices come from the so-called world of lived experience. Thus, the text, *Black Feminist Thought*, invokes a world that is never directly present, only heard and seen in the texts that Collins quotes. The authority granted this text turns, then, on the authority granted the observers of the real world who are brought into Collins's argument. These observers, black female blues singers, poets, and novelists, stand in a canonical relationship to African American culture. They have articulated a story and a standpoint about racism and sexism that has been suppressed by positivist and Marxist social scientists (Collins, 1991, p. 235). In using these sources, Collins erases the dividing line between science, literature, and fiction, "drawing without distinction on literature, art [and] music" (Clough, 1994, p. 89) for the claims she makes. This is critical because the writers Collins quotes write fiction, so the fictional world (and its characters) now become stand-ins for that real world real black women inhabit.[13] How does Collins do this?

The answer lies in her last two chapters, Chapters 10 and 11 ("Toward an Afrocentric Feminist Epistemology" and "Knowledge, Consciousness, and the Politics of Empowerment"). Here, Collins (1991) articulates her Afrocentric feminist epistemology offering four criteria for interpreting the truth and knowledge claims of a social science or cultural text. These criteria focus on the primacy of concrete lived experience, the use of dialogue in assessing knowledge claims, the ethic of caring, and the ethic of personal accountability. The works she quotes presumably embody these criteria. They all arise out of the shared experiences of being black and female in American culture, experiences grounded in racism, sexism, sexual violence, economic exploitation, and cultural denigration (Collins, 1991, pp. 22-23).

Experience as a criterion of meaning directs attention to black sisterhood and to the stories, narratives, and Bible principles embodied in black church and community life. Concrete, black feminine wisdom is contrasted to knowledge without wisdom: "A heap see, but a few know" (Collins, 1991, p. 208). Wisdom is experiential, cultural, and shared in the black feminine community. Dialogue, bell hooks (1989) argues, is humanizing speech. Black feminists assess knowledge claims through discourse, storytelling, connected to dialogue in a group context. This emphasis on dialogue is directly translated into the black feminist text. Zora Neale Hurston, for example, located herself inside the folktales she collected and carried on extensive dialogues with them, thus creating a multivocal text (Collins, 1991, p. 214).

Dialogue extends to the ethic of caring, which suggests that "personal expressiveness, emotions and empathy are central to the knowledge validation process" (Collins, 1991, p. 215). A feminist ethic, not unlike the feminist, communitarian moral ethic discussed in the Preface, is presented. Collins's ethical system values the black woman's individual uniqueness, her invisible dignity, quiet grace, and unstated courage (p. 107), the mothering mind (p. 131), love, community, and justice (p. 197), and the expression of emotionality in the text. It seeks writers who can create emotional texts that others can enter into. The ethic of personal accountability makes individuals accountable for their values and the political consequences of their actions.

These four criteria embody a "self-defined Black women's standpoint using an Afrocentric epistemology" (Collins, 1991, p. 219). This epistemology creates the conditions for an existential politics of empowerment that will allow African American women to actively confront racial, gender, and class oppression in their daily lives (p. 237). Collins is faithful to her standpoint, materialist epistemology on this point (p. 26). Material conditions of oppression produce "varying types of [individual] consciousness" (p. 26). By "aggregating and articulating these individual expressions of consciousness, a collective, focused group consciousness becomes possible" (p. 26). The articulation of this consciousness at the group level is "key to Black women's survival" (p. 26). This consciousness then works back into the lives of individual women, creating the conditions for new, empowering self-definitions in which consciousness becomes a "sphere of freedom" (p. 227). Black feminist thinkers like Collins thereby offer "individual African-American women the conceptual tools to resist oppression" (p. 228).

Each author Collins (1991) quotes has this form of group and individual consciousness. These writers embody Collins's Afrocentic feminist epistemology. Their works structure her analysis of the black feminist experience in America. Thus, these works do double duty in her text. They define a previously repressed standpoint, a subjugated knowledge, while embodying the Afrocentric feminist epistemology she puts forth. She is aware of this situation, quoting Alice Walker who observes, "to write the books one wants to read is both to point the direction of vision and at the same time, to follow it (Collins, 1991, p. 17; Walker, 1983, p. 8).

Reclaiming Voice

Recall the earlier quote from Collins (1991): "When I was five years old, I was chosen to play Spring in my preschool pageant" (p. xi). She goes on,

> All the grown-ups told me how vital my part was and congratulated me. . . . As my world expanded, I learned that not everyone agreed with them. . . . I tried to disappear into myself in order to deflect the painful, daily assaults designed to teach me that being an African-American, working-class woman made me lesser than those who are not. . . . I became quieter and eventually was virtually silenced. This book reflects one stage in my ongoing struggle to regain my voice. (p. xi)

The voice that Collins (1991) finds is apocalyptically located in that utopian moment, in the beginning, before young African American women and their mothers confronted racism, slavery, and sexism. Spring resides in this space, in those "Afrocentric ideas of classical African civilizations" (p. 10)—a loving, black feminist ethic of mothering, love, community, caring, and justice. In this prior moment, black women did not confront racism, sexism, and sexual violence. Therefore, Collins finds her voice in this subjugated black feminist ethic, an ethic that embodies these classical African ideals as they were dialectically shaped by the structures of oppression in American culture (p. 10). Finding her voice (pp. 97-98), Collins thereby creates a voice (and a space) for all of those black women who have come before her and who will follow in her steps.

A paradox operates, however, because the voice she finds, which becomes hers, is already entangled in the very structures of oppression and discrimination she opposes. Thus, this voice is a voice of survival, a voice of self-respect, ground out of the "iron that enters Black women's souls" (Collins, 1991, p. 34). It is not a pure voice; it is a voice that has had to make do with those few resources the culture has made available to its members. Already shaped by what it opposes, there is no spring to which this voice and its speaker can return.

Therefore, not surprisingly, it is primarily the voice of fiction, the voice of the female blues singers that Collins (1991) appropriates. Here, as a sample of her selections, Lorraine Hansberry describes the African features of black feminine beauty: "Sometimes in this country . . . you will see it—*Beauty* . . . stark and full . . . Africa, simply Africa . . . without negation or apology. A *classical people demand a classical art*" (Hansberry, 1969, p. 106; quoted in Collins, 1991, p. 88).

Bessie Smith (as quoted in Collins, 1991) gives advice to black women about their men:

> *I've had a man for fifteen years, give him his room and his board.*
> *Once he was like a Cadillac, now he's like an old worn-out Ford.*
> *He never brought me a lousy dime, and put it in my hand.*
> *Oh, there'll be some changes from now on, according to my plan.*
> (p. 101)

Aretha Franklin (as quoted in Collins, 1991) sings about respect:

> *What you want? Baby I got it.*
> *What you need? You know I got it.*
> *All I'm asking for is a little respect when you come home.*
> (p. 108)

Billie Holiday (as quoted in Collins, 1991) on self-reliance and independence:

> *The strong gets more, while the weak ones fade,*
> *Empty pockets don't ever make the grade;*
> *Mama may have, Papa may have,*
> *But God bless the child that got his own.*
> (p. 109)

Motherhood, and a mother's gift to her daughter, as defined by a traditional blues song (Collins, 1991):

> *I ain't good lookin' and ain't got waist-long hair.*
> *I say I ain't good lookin' and I ain't got waist-long hair.*
> *But my mama gave me something that'll take me anywhere.*
> (p. 126)

On mother's love, from Toni Morrison's *Sula* (1974, pp. 67, 69; Collins, 1991, p. 127):

Eva's daughter, Hanna, asks: Mamma, did you ever love us?
Eva replies: What you talkin' bout did I love you girl I stayed alive for you.

These are powerful texts—tales of struggle, survival, oppression, dignity torn out of the tarnished, and the ugly soul of racism. These lyrics, lines, and short stories carry the weight of emotion. Eyes closed, stereo turned up, the listener can literally feel the presence of these female blues singers. These are evocative texts, poetic, direct, personal, and biographical. They are, at the same time, cultural performances. They reinscribe lived experience within a valued cultural tradition—the blues.

These are Collins's (1991) concrete experiences. They are used as her criterion of meaning. Her logic is clear: If a lived experience has been inscribed in a powerful cultural text, then that text applies "to the lived experiences of African-Americans" (p. 210). These texts, selected because they apply to these experiences, now "become symbolic representations of a whole wealth of experience" (p. 210). These texts contain wisdom and truth about experience in which truth now turns on the meaning of the experience as defined by wisdom. Collins states, "Bible tales are often told for the wisdom they express about everyday life, so their interpretation involves no need for scientific historical verification. . . . Concrete experiences are used as a criterion of meaning" (p. 210).

Thus, we learn the wisdom concerning the meaning of a mother's suicide by reading the following lines from June Jordan's (1985) essay on her mother's death:

I am not sure my mother's suicide was something extraordinary. Perhaps most women must deal with a similar inheritance, the legacy of a women whose death you cannot pinpoint because she died so many, many times and because, even before she became your mother, the life of that woman was taken. (p. 26; quoted in Collins, 1991, p. 210)

Therefore, this black feminist standpoint epistemology never really returns to the site of lived experience. Lived experience serves as a proxy for the theory, an ideological commitment to enter, study, and talk about the real world of repression and racism. On inspection, however, that real world appears only in the form of a standpoint, textual ethnography: a rewriting of the world of lived experience through the canonical black feminist representations of that world— tales from survivors.

Struggles with an Ocular Epistemology

Collins (1991) struggles with the epistemological metaphors that organize her text. Rejecting the visual metaphors (illumination, equating knowing with seeing, and truth with light) that structure realist discourses on epistemology, she calls for a set of epistemological metaphors that emphasize "finding a voice, speaking, and listening" (p. 214). (This call is folded into her discussions concerning the central place of dialogue and sharing in the black feminist community.) Throughout, however, her standpoint epistemology privileges vision, even as it struggles to find an alternative starting point for itself. She repeatedly calls for a new angle of vision (pp. 11, 26, 39, 207) that builds on what black women see from their outsider-within perspective (p. 12), a perspective that has turned them into media spectacles (mammies, matriarchs, welfare recipients, and hot mommas [p. 67]), the voyeuristic object of the white man's sexual gaze (pp. 168, 172).

Understanding that no single group has a monopoly on knowledge, a privileged, "clear angle of vision" (Collins, 1991, p. 234), Collins wishes to transcend the visual and to invoke a form of dialogical textuality that is empathetic (p. 205) and allows one group to enter into (and feel) the experiences of another (p. 236). When this occurs, as in her use of the blues singers, "groups can come to better understand other group's standpoints, without relinquishing the uniqueness of its own standpoint or suppressing other groups' partial perspectives" (p. 236). Collins draws on Elsa Barkley Brown (1989, p. 922) for support: "all people can learn to center in another experience, validate it, and judge it by its own standards without need or comparison or need to adopt that framework as their own" (quoted in Collins, 1991, p. 236).

Three events must occur for this to happen. Members of groups must desire to understand and feel their way into the experiences of another group. This process must be structured by the kind of sharing, loving, communitarian feminist ethic Collins (1991) connects to black feminist thought. Also, texts and experiences must be produced that allow members from one group to vicariously enter into, and then emotionally understand, the experiences of another group. Ideally, members from each group would enter into a common field of shared experience (Denzin, 1984, p. 145). If this does not occur, spurious understanding is produced (Denzin, 1984, pp. 153-156). If these three conditions are not met, there is no assurance that one group will understand or desire to understand the perspectives of another group. This will be case even if members of both groups have experienced repression, exploitation, racism, and sexism.

Collins (1991) does not address these three conditions because they speak to persons who are not part of the interpretive community she has created. Many can only spuriously enter into her discourse, even as they share her ethics. Also, to the extent that this is the case, such readers can only cognitively and spuriously understand the experiences of racism and sexism that black women have experienced in America.

Still, this most powerful of contemporary standpoint epistemologies succeeds because it opens the door for others to follow. It charts an ethical path that challenges others to question their own standpoints and the taken for granted knowledge they use to support their actions in the world, including their actions toward all African Americans. On still another level, Collins (1991) opens the door for the re-entry of lived experiences into the "new" ethnographic text. Her work asks others to articulate the connections between lived experiences and their inscriptions in powerful cultural texts. Also, in calling attention to the performed text, the blues that are sung, and the poems that are read, she suggests that a work's most powerful effects occur when it is performed in front of an audience because in that moment the evocative text comes alive and creates that necessarily shared space from which understandings can be forged.

Trinh T. Minh-Ha:
Framer Framed

In this postmodern society of the male-centered spectacle (Trinh, 1991, p. 104), ethnography has traditionally functioned as that method that allows the writer to "grasp the native's point of view, to realize his vision of the world" (Trinh, 1991, p. 65) and to present that vision to the world of the reader. Such texts, written from the standpoint of the male anthropologist, the anthropologist as bricoleur (Trinh, 1989, pp. 62-63), never question where the anthropologist stands vis-à-vis his interpretive community and the natives he writes about (Trinh, 1991, p. 72). In this certain interpretive, scientific world, experience near and experience distant concepts are married. The anthropologist's objectivity merges with the native's subjective view of the world, producing a text that allows the observer to get inside the other's skin (Trinh, 1991, pp. 67-68). Lived experience is captured and reproduced in the writer's text.

In three major texts, *Woman, Native, Other* (Trinh, 1989), *When the Moon Waxes Red* (Trinh, 1991), and *Framer Framed* (Trinh, 1992), and four films, *Reassemblage* (1982), *Naked Spaces—Living Is Round* (1985), *Surname Viet Given Name Nam* (1989), and *Shoot for the Contents* (1991), Trinh T. Minh-Ha unravels this worldview, contesting the masculine standpoint that organizes mainstream, and postmodern, interpretive anthropology, from Levi-Strauss to Clifford Geertz, George Marcus, and James Clifford (Trinh, 1989, pp. 20, 43-44, 49, 56-63, 67-73, 84, 103; 1991, pp. 44-45, 65-68, 73-75, 113-114; 1992, pp. 116, 229). Trinh challenges the very foundations of this project, where science (anthropological knowledge) becomes institutional gossip, the native's world is never penetrated, and the anthropologist re-enacts a version of the " 'Pet' Negro System" (Trinh, 1991, p. 68-69), bringing his version of the foreign "Other" in front of the reader.[14]

Trinh's (1991, p. 157) standpoint is fragile, illusive, and plural. The figure of postcolonial woman always writes from a position of triple jeopardy: "as a writer, as a woman, and as a woman of color" (Trinh, 1989, p. 28). She is always crossing borders, moving through in-between spaces, a hyphen, a hybrid, Asian American woman, African American feminist (Trinh, 1991, p. 157), constantly negotiating "the difference not merely between cultures, between First and Third World, but more importantly within culture . . . a plural singularity . . . [that problemati-cizes] the insider-outsider position" (Trinh, 1992, p. 144). This space is fluid, infinite, unnamable, and the space of becoming (Trinh, 1991, p. 157): the site of feminist consciousness (Trinh, 1991, p. 112).

This, however, is not a state of consciousness arrived at after a new body of knowledge has been acquired. It is not a personal or group consciousness. It is a process, "a dialectical understanding and practice of identity and difference . . . [where] the ethnic me and the female me [become] political" (Trinh, 1991, p. 113). From this space, culture is rewritten from within, on the borders and silences of the body (p. 129), where women bring their stories to bear on the stories they tell (p. 131), where the metaphysics of presence is challenged (p. 135), and where writing becomes a launching of the self into the world (p. 140).

In this space that is a process, in which silences are heard, she is not the subaltern other, nor can she assume the place of the insider or enter the standpoint of the outsider because these spaces also do not exist, except as processes (Trinh, 1991, p. 74). She is I and not I, different and the same (Trinh, 1991):

> She knows she is different while at the same time being Him. Not quite the Same, not quite the Other, she stands in that undetermined thresh-old place where she constantly drifts in and out. Undercutting the inside/outside opposition, her intervention is necessarily that of both the deceptive insider an the deceptive outsider. (p. 74)

Thus, Collins (1991) is undone because there is no outsider within, no firmly defined outside position from which the outsider can view the inside. Invoking bell hooks (1989), Trinh declares that what is needed is a new revisioning, the need to

> Examine the self from a new critical standpoint. Such a perspective, while it must insist on the self as the site for politicization, would equally insist that simply describing one's experience of exploitation or oppression is not to become politicized. It is not sufficient to know the personal but to know—to speak in a different way. (p. 107; quoted in Trinh, 1991, pp. 163-164)

Subjectivity and lived experience cannot be reduced to personal expres-sions of the self (Trinh, 1991, p. 113). These expressions must be connected to the individual's experiences. This must be done in a way that is then linked to the systems of difference and domination (race, class, gender, sexuality, nation, geography, and ethnicity) that seek to impose an essential identity on the person and her experiences (p. 113).

Texts must be produced that allow women to experience and assert their difference in relation to others and to assume the position of active speakers, listeners, readers, writers, and viewers. Such works issue a challenge to the individual (and to their producers) (Trinh, 1991, p. 113). In their textual spaces, the personal is politicized, and the political is personalized. This is an in-between ground where the text "materializes itself and resists its status as mere object of consumption" (p. 113).

More is operating here, however. Trinh (1991) seeks to undo the entire realist ethnographic project that is connected to such terms as lived experience, authenticity, verisimilitude, truth, knowledge, facts, and fictions. She borrows from Barthes (1975): There is no real—reality is something already classified by men, a ready-made code (Trinh, 1991, p. 136). This code allows writers and filmmakers to produce texts that look real because they conform to the rules concerning what the real looks like. Under this regime, authenticity becomes a textual accomplishment, and factual truth becomes the "dominant criterion for evaluation . . . [and] the more the representation leans on verisimilitude, the more it is subject to normative verification" (Trinh, 1991, p. 76). Also, reality always runs away (Trinh, 1991, p. 40).

Truth becomes a realist construct (Trinh, 1991, p. 12): something "produced, induced, and extended according to the regime of power" (p. 30). A statement is true if it accurately accounts for and explains events that occur in the real world. The real world, however, is a construction—a product of a set of images that conform to prior images of what the real looks like (p. 38). Trinh is quite forceful on this point:

> The belief that there can exist such a thing as an outside foreign to the inside, an objective, unmediated reality about which one can have knowledge once and for all, has been repeatedly challenged by feminist critics. . . . The fight against 'realism' is . . . not a denial of reality and of meaning, but rather a determination to keep meaning creative, hence to challenge the fixity of realism as a style and an arrested form of representation. . . . Realism as one form of representation defined by a specific attitude toward reality is widely validated to perpetuate the illusion of a stable world. (p. 164)

Therefore, reality is a historical fiction (Trinh, 1991, p. 41), and in this world the criterion of authenticity "no longer proves pertinent. It is like asking an atheist: 'How faithful to the words of God are yours?' " (p. 76). Trinh's writer knows that she cannot speak of the other "without speaking of herself, of history without involving her story . . . [and she] also knows that she cannot make a gesture without activating the to-and-fro-movement of life" (p. 76). In this textual world, the concepts of subjectivity and objectivity disappear. These terms, which produce sciences of the subject, no longer operate because subjectivity is always intersubjective, unstable, and embodied in the concrete situations of life (p. 76).

Cinema Meets Ethnography: Ethnography in the Sixth Moment

Trinh is a filmmaker first, and her critique of the ethnographic project is based on her analysis of the cinematic apparatus. Her cinematic texts must be read as postmodern ethnographies—ethnography in the sixth moment. She begins by deconstructing the classic documentary film, the ethnographic film that enters the native's world and brings news from that world to the world of the Western observer. Like ethnography, which separated itself from fiction (Clough, 1992, pp. 26-27), the documentary film defines itself against mainstream, Hollywood cinema. Not tangled up in or complicitous with the star and studio system, documentary (Trinh, 1991)

> Takes real people and real problems from the real world and *deals* with them. It sets a value on intimate observation, and *assesses its worth* according to how well it succeeds in capturing reality on the run . . . powerful living stories, infinite authentic situations. (p. 33)

Documentary, like ethnography, starts with the real world: It uses an aesthetic of objectivity and a technological apparatus that produces truthful statements (images) about the world (Trinh, 1991, p. 33). The following elements are central to this apparatus (pp. 33-36):

- The relentless pursuit of naturalism, which requires a connection between the moving image and the spoken word, must be incorporated.
- The use of the directional microphone and the portable tape recorder must be incorporated.
- Lip-synchronous sound must be used.
- Authenticity—real people in real situations—must be incorporated.
- Real time is more truthful than film time; hence, the long-take.
- Minimal editing must be made, with no use of montage.
- Few close-ups should used, with emphasis on wide-angle shots.
- Use of the hand-held, unobtrusive camera to "provoke people into uttering the 'truth' that they would not otherwise unveil in ordinary situations" (Trinh, 1991, p. 34) should be incorporated.
- The filmmaker is an observer, not a person who creates what is photographed.
- Only events unaffected by the recording eye should be captured.
- The film must capture objective reality.
- Truth must be dramatized.
- Actual facts should be presented in a credible way, with people telling them.
- The film must convince the spectator that they should have confidence in the truth of what they see.
- There should be a focus on common experience by which the 'social' is defined.
- The presence of the filmmaker should be masked, hidden.
- The use of various persuasive techniques, including personal testimony, and the talk of plain folks should be incorporated.
- The film is made for the common, silent people; they are the film's referent.
- The film is shot with three cameras: the camera in the technical sense; the filmmaker's mind; and the generic patterns of documentary film. The film's facts are a product of these three cameras (Trinh, 1991, p. 39).

These aesthetic strategies define the documentary style, allowing the filmmaker to create a text that gives the viewer the illusion of having "unmediated access to reality" (Trinh, 1991, p. 40). Thus naturalized, the documentary style has become part of the larger cinematic apparatus in American culture, including a pervasive presence in TV commercials and news (p. 40).

Trinh (1991) brings a reflexive reading to these features of the documentary film, citing her own texts as examples of documentaries that are aware of their own artifice, sensitive to the flow of fact and fiction, to nuances, and to meanings as political constructions (p. 41). Such texts reflexively understand that reality is never neutral or objective; that it is always socially constructed. Filmmaking thus becomes a question of "framing" reality. Self-reflexivity does not translate into personal style or a preoccupation with method. It rather centers on the reflexive interval that defines representation (Trinh, 1991):

> The place in which the play within the textual frame is a play on this very frame, hence on the borderlines of the textual and the extra-textual. . . . A work that reflects back on itself offers itself infinitely as nothing else but work . . . and void. (p. 48)

In such works, meaning is not imposed. The film becomes a site for multiple experiences.

A responsible, reflexive text embodies the following characteristics (Trinh, 1991, p. 188):

- It announces its own politics and evidences a political consciousness.
- It interrogates the realities it represents.
- It invokes the teller's story in the history that is told.
- It makes the audience responsible for interpretation.
- It resists the temptation to become an object of consumption.
- It resists all dichotomies (male-female, etc.).
- It foregrounds difference, not conflict.
- It uses multiple voices, emphasizing language as silence, the grain of the voice, tone, inflection, pauses, silences, and repetitions.
- Silence is presented as a form of resistance.

Reflexive films seek the truth of life's fictions, the spirit of truth that resides in life experiences, in fables, and in proverbs in which nothing is explained, but everything is evoked (Trinh, 1991, p. 162). This is Collins's (1991) world, in which "A heap see, but a few know" and knowledge does not equal wisdom. Meaning is not confused with truth.

Trinh's Ocular Epistemology

Trinh (1991) creates the space for a new ocular epistemology, a version of the cinematic apparatus that challenges mainstream film and traditional ethnography.[15] Reflexive film questions the very notion of a stable, unbiased, middle-class gaze (Trinh, 1991, pp. 97-98, 115). It focuses on the pensive image—on representations that do not turn women into versions of the exotic, erotic, feminine ethnic minority other (p. 115). The pensive image "unsettles the male apparatus of the gaze, in which men own, articulate, and create the look of woman as either being looked at . . . [or as one who] holds the [male] look to signify the master's desire" (p. 115). This look makes the camera's gaze visible. It destabilizes any sense of verisimilitude that can be brought to this visual world. In so doing, it disrupts the spectator's gaze, itself a creation of the unnoticed camera—the camera that invokes the image of a perfect, natural world, a world with verisimilitude (p. 115).

This ocular epistemology creates the space for a subversive cinema—a cinema that creates new ways of encountering reality and its representations. Thus, in *Surname Viet Given Name Nam* (Trinh, 1989), Trinh deconstructs the interview and its basis in the documentary film. (The film is a study of Vietnamese women whose names change and remain constant depending on whether they marry a foreigner or a Vietnamese.) Trinh (1992, p. 49) has Vietnamese women speak from five places (representing lineage, gender and age status, leadership position, and historical period). This creates a complex picture of Vietnamese culture (Trinh, 1992, p. 144). The film is multitextual, layered with pensive images of women in various situations. Historical moments overlap with age periods (childhood, youth, adulthood, and old age), ritual ceremonies (weddings, funerals, war, the market, and dance), and daily household work (cooking) while interviewees talk to off-screen interviewers. There are two voice-overs in English, and a third voice sings sayings, proverbs, and poetry in Vietnamese (with translations as texts on the screen). There are also interviews with Vietnamese subtitled in English and interviews in English synchronized with the on-screen image (Trinh, 1992, p. 49).

The interviews were originally published in 1983 (Mai, 1983). They are re-enacted in Trinh's (1992, p. 146) film by Vietnamese women who are then interviewed at the end of the film—asked about their experiences of being performers in the film. One woman comments on the reactions of her friends when they heard she was going to be in a film: "They all laugh and tease me, saying that I'll become a movie star and will earn enough money so I can quit my job in the future" (Trinh, 1992, p. 87). Another woman: "Once I worked on my part, I wanted to give my best because I don't think it is an individual matter but one that concerns a whole community" (Trinh, 1992, p. 86).

In undoing the interview as a form of gathering information about reality, Trinh (1992, p. 145) takes up the question of truth. Whose truth is she presenting: that of the original interviewer (Mai Thu Van), that given in the on-screen interview situation, or that of the women-as-actresses who are interviewed at the end of the film? The film (*Surname Viet Given Name Nam*) allows the practice of doing interviews to enter into the construction of the text itself, thus the true and the false (the actresses are not the women interviewed by Mai Thu Van) and the real and the staged intermingle; indeed, the early sections of the film unfold like a traditional, realist documentary film (p. 145). The viewer does not know these are actresses re-enacting interviews. Nor does the viewer know that the interviews were conducted in the United States, not Vietnam. (This only becomes apparent near the end of the film.)

By using both types of interviews, Trinh examines the politics of interviewing as a mode of gathering information about the other. This is done, in part, by creating a distance between the written and the performed text; the women doing the interviews and the women reflecting on the interviews. In so doing, she creates the space for the viewer to critically appraise the politics of representation that structure the documentary film. This strategy makes the practice of "reading" and interpreting the film a constant process of discovery and re-evaluation (Trinh, 1992, p. 146). At the same time, and at a perhaps even deeper level of understanding, Trinh explodes the notion of a unified Vietnamese feminine subject. The idea of a unified national identity is also challenged because such an identity can only be sustained when one uncritically joins patriarchy, imperialism, and colonialism (Clough, 1994, p. 127).

Writing and the Storytelling Self

Trinh's project turns on the redefinition of three intertwined activities: filmmaking, writing, and the storytelling self. A major portion of *Surname Viet Given Name Nam* consists of women engaged in storytelling and the telling of proverbs and poetry. There is no equivocation here; these are not fictional materials. They are the materials that contain the cultural truths about women and their lived experiences. They are stories that must be told and retold. The burden of the story truth cannot be escaped; there must be no lies, only the truth (Trinh, 1989, p. 149), even if the truth appears to be a lie or an impossibility.[16] There is always a difference between the truth and the facts, and Trinh's storytellers know this. Truth does not need to make sense; it exceeds meaning (p. 123). Women's stories are told in defiance "of a whole system of white man's lies" (p. 150). Each telling allows the truth to live on.

Thus, Trinh's (1989, p. 119) women enter into the ongoing telling (and retelling) of Grandma's Story, that story passed on from generation to generation, grandmother to granddaughter, mother to daughter, and daughter to her children. It is the story of women's lives and women's stories, not men's histories (p. 119); Zora Neale Hurston's stories about lies and lovin' (p. 129). These are stories that heal, that carry love, solidarity, community, the fire and desire of the feminine soul, and that re-create life (p. 138). They cannot be reduced to structural categories or subsumed under narrative terms and functions (pp. 142-143). They are not just stories; they arouse forces, create their own momentum when set in motion, they circulate, humanize, "they are about what happened and what *is happening* . . . mother talking-stories" (p. 133). Therefore, *Surname Viet Given Name Nam* tells these stories.

Trinh's (1989) writing self is caught in several dilemmas at the same time; she seeks to create a new form of writing, a new writing style, and a new but old way of telling women's stories and of hearing (seeing and feeling) the voices of women. Women writers must overcome the "Quiller-Couch" or the "Lady Painter syndrome" (Trinh, 1989, p. 27).[17] Otherwise, they can be accused of producing personal, subjective, narcissistic, neurotic, confessional texts (the Quiller-Couch syndrome) or texts that sound like what a man would write (the Lady Painter syndrome). There are dangers here. Women who write like men may be called "scribblers. . . . [Their] technique is indistinguishable from masculine writing" (Trinh, 1991, p. 124). If they indulge the personal, emphasizing the intimate, and the domestic, focusing only on their own experiences, reflections of themselves (Trinh, 1989, p.29), and ornate texts, they risk being trapped in the personal and losing sight of the political (Trinh, 1989, p. 35).

Still, although the diary form may be liberating, it is also confining if it is the only means of self-expression available for women (Trinh, 1989, p. 35). This personal form, however, when combined with the autobiographical, may allow the personal to become communal, shared, liberating, and political—a way for a collectivity to make history and rewrite culture (Trinh, 1991, pp. 191-192). Such writing can defy the masculine norms of objectivity and subjectivity, creating new ways of presenting the "subjectivity of a non-I/plural I" (Trinh, 1991, p. 192). In this way, an opening is created, as in *Surname Viet Given Name Nam* in which many different women speak from many different positions, undermining from within, even as they tell their own stories. This writing style is at once masculine and feminine, writing the woman's body against the masculine norms of objectivity. Recognizing the masculine inside the language she uses, Trinh's writer seeks to become the first female-male reader of her text. She ignores the male eye that gazes over her shoulder (Trinh, 1991, pp. 124-125). The language she writes cannot be gender neutral (Trinh, 1991, p. 125).

African writers and their novels offer suggestions for this writing self (Trinh, 1991, p. 192). These writers produce texts that are to be read out loud. They produce a spoken form of writing (p. 170) that emphasizes repetitions, cliches, stereotypes in dialogue, the sounds of words, the use of proverbs, hollow language, and "hackneyed words which no longer mean much and whose voicing transmits nothing but sound" (p. 172). The writer's text circulates these "truth-sounds" (p. 170), locating them in multiple contexts, giving them to diverse speakers, and showing how their meaning is always contextual in relationship to a "verbal surrounding" (p. 170). This oral style allows the writer to openly address the reader, to make the reader a part of the text, raising the question "who is speaking here?" (pp. 173- 174).

Trinh's writer (and filmmaker) writes not to free the masses because who can speak for the other (Trinh, 1989, p. 13). She writes and makes films to create spaces for the retelling of the stories that the science of ethnography has stolen, reduced to history, categorized as fiction and subaltern literature. In these spaces, she works to create texts that bring out the "plural, sliding relationship between ear and eye and to leave room for the spectators to decide what they want to make out of a statement or a sequence of images" (Trinh, 1991, p. 206). She uses silences, gaps, repetitions, cuts, and holes in the text as vehicles for producing an "ever-changing verbal and visual context" (Trinh, 1991, p. 206) of meaning. She resists those textual strategies (verbatim transcriptions, sound tracks with music, sound effects, and voice-overs) that help spectators (and readers) assimilate a narrative as a realist text (Trinh, 1991, pp. 203-204). She cultivates a form of writing, filmmaking, and storytelling that embodies satori—"that Zen event defined as loss of meaning . . . a speech-void" (Trinh, 1991, p. 209), a sudden awakening, in which new meanings are revealed. In works of this kind, truth and certainty are constantly displaced, deferred, and postponed. The text resists easy classification or location within an interpretive system (Trinh, 1991, p. 218). Criticisms based on verisimilitude are "declared non-pertinent" (Trinh, 1991, p. 218).

Therefore, a new history is being written: A plural, unstable, multicultural history in which borders and boundaries are constantly questioned and crossed (Trinh, 1991, p. 232). A new aesthetics of the text is sought—one that rejects old categories and binary oppositions—a new discourse, a new way of writing, looking, reading, and relating to ourselves and others (p. 232).

Gloria Anzaldua:
The Borderlands of the Textual Self

If Trinh's texts fill gaps and exposes holes in Collins' standpoint epistemology, leading to a deconstruction of such terms as reality, realism, lived experience, and the self, Gloria Anzaldua returns to the self, writing from a dark, deep place. For example, the following is an excerpt from her poem, "A Creature of the Dark" (Anzaldua, 1987):

> *Three weeks I've wallowed*
> *in this deep place*
> *   this underplace*

this grieving place
getting heavier and heavier
sleeping by day creeping out at night

Nothing I can do
nothing I want to do
but stay small and still in the dark. . . .

Three weeks I rocked . . .
    refusing to move
    barely daring to breathe
sinking deeper
growing great with mouth
    a creature afraid of the dark
    a creature at home in the dark.
(pp. 186-187)

A self that seeks its inner depths; a self with *La facultad*, "the capacity to see in surface phenomena the meaning of deeper realities, to see the deep structure below the surface" (Anzaldua, 1987, p. 38). A voice for the dark-skinned woman, the lesbian of color (Anzaldua, 1987, p. 19), the new Mestiza, and the queer (Anzaldua, 1987, p. 85); an accounting of white, Mexican, and Indian cultures, her own feminist architecture (Anzaldua, 1987, p. 22). A writing self that creates itself through its writing, in which the personal is fused with the everyday, and nothing is too trivial to write about because everything relates back to her soul. "24 mayo 80: It is dark and damp and has been raining all day. I love days like this. As I lie in bed and I am able to delve inward. Perhaps today I will write from that deep core" (Anzaldua, 1981a, p. 169); and, "With terror as my companion, I dip into my life and begin work on myself. Where did it begin, the pain, the images that haunt me?" (Anzaldua, 1981b, p. 199). Anzaldua (1981a) states that to

write is to confront one's demons, look them in the face and live to write about them. . . . Writing is dangerous because we are afraid of what the writing reveals: the fears, the angers, the strengths of a woman under a triple or quadruple oppression. Yet . . . a woman who writes has power. And a woman with power is feared. (p. 171)

She begins from her unstable location at the intersection of four interconnected borderlands: the actual physical borderland between Texas, the U.S. southwest, and the Mexican border; the psychological borderlands (her inner- and outer-self, a Tejana Chicana poet, and fiction writer); the sexual borderlands (lesbian and feminist); and the spiritual borderlands, which knows no boundaries (Anzaldua, 1987, p. vii). Anzaldua writes of her preoccupations with the "inner life of the Self, and with the struggles of that Self (p. vii), a self that knows itself in at least eight languages: standard English, working-class and slang English, standard Spanish, standard Mexican Spanish, North Mexican Spanish dialect, Chicano Spanish, Tex-Mex, and Pachuco (p. 55). This is a new and old language of the borderlands—Chicano Texas Spanish, Tex-Mex (p. 59)—a language of sexuality, desire, and struggle.

This is cinematic, visual writing. She writes to return to the beginning, to recover, wrestle with, and live her way through the Coatlicue state (Anzaldua, 1987, p. 42).[18] In the Coatlicue state, she experiences a crossing over to a new form of consciousness, everything rushes "to a center, a nucleus. "All the lost pieces of myself come flying from the deserts and the mountains and the valleys, magnetized toward that center" (p. 51). In this state, she sees herself seeing herself, being seen through, and the mirror's gaze, that mirror made of volcanic glass, reveals this deep psychic formation to her (p. 42).

Anzaldua (1987, p. 42) writes and performs her stories and poetry from this moving place, the site of the gaze that allows her to possess the world. She thinks cinematically, a picture language, voices and scenes projected on the inner screen of her mind (pp. 69-70). Eyes closed, she produces her own soundtracks and becomes a participant in the dramas she creates. Inside and outside her own "picture" frame, she is the male and female actor, the film director, screenwriter, and camera operator. She has been making up these stories her entire life: "Nudge a Mexican and she or he will break out with a story" (p. 65). Her stories are performances (p. 67).

The stories all return, somehow, in one form or another, to the beginning: "I see the four of us kids getting off the school bus, changing into our work clothes, walking into the field with Papi and Mami, all six of us bending to the ground. Below our feet lie the watermelon seeds" (Anzaldua, 1987, p. 91). The seeds grow into green shoots, and the family hoes, waters, and harvests them. The vines die and rot and are plowed into the earth (Anzaldua, 1987):

Growth, death, decay, birth. . . . A constant changing of forms. . . .
This land was Mexican once
was Indian always
and is.
And will be again. (p. 91)

Ancient stories.

Standpoints and Traveling Texts

There are three versions of the standpoint text and its transformations: Collin's outsider within, Trinh's woman in the hyphens who has neither an inside place nor an outside position to occupy, and Anzaldua's new Mestiza and the queer. Shared conceptions of the borderland, all three writers cross and recross borderlands, boundaries, and new and old frontiers. Each engages in textual transgressions, challenging while reaffirming certain and old truths, and validating meanings embedded in oral texts that inscribe and interpret experience—the recovery of subjugated knowledges.

Each locates the writer at the center of her text, the writer who has access to her own lived experiences. Lived experience, however, means something different in each theory. Although Collins uses personal pronouns to join herself with other black feminists, she seldom draws on her own experiences. Trinh understands lived experience to be a fragile site of multiple, unstable meanings. There is no direct access to lived experience. As a textual form, lived experience is a fiction, a realist construction. The writer cannot write from experience itself. Writing (and filmmaking) are built on the representations of experiences.

Anzaldua will have none of this. She writes her stories and her poems out of her lived history. Lived experience is her subject matter. On this point, she "outs" the heterosexism of the classic white ethnographers of experience. She also undoes (like Trinh) the very framework that reduces Indian and Mexican thought and experience to so-called primitive, pagan categories and forms of consciousness (Anzaldua, 1987, pp. 36-37, 94-95). Thus, she joins, at this level, one form of queer theory with her particular version of a standpoint epistemology.

The three writers also differ on the identity of the writer. Trinh challenges any scheme that would fit her into a framework, such as post-colonial, Asian-American feminist. These terms are only given meaning in the spaces that surround the hyphen. Although she will seek to intertwine the masculine and the feminine in a new feminine writing style, she understands that each woman writes from a unique place. Collins has no trouble identifying her black feminist standpoint theorist, and she only occasionally troubles these categories. Anzaldua knows who she is, and although she does not take up the language of the hyphen, it is clear her writer is caught in multiple spaces at the same time; hence her emphasis on writing out of her own experiences.

Finally, there are two directions to take, both starting from Marx and the concept of standpoint. Marx provided a wedge, "a way to get to our own versions of standpoint theories" (Haraway, 1988, p. 578). With Marx come many problems, including those discussed earlier: the romantic, utopian text, a visual epistemology, lived experience and its representations, the writer's place in the text, partial, subjugated knowledges, objectivity, relativism, a feminist, successor science, and whose standpoint and whose experiences will be written.

One direction (Collins, Haraway, Smith, and Harding) moves to retain a commitment to some version of science. The "scientific" standpoint epistemologies falter at the moment when they aspire to be successor sciences—subjugated standpoints providing "more adequate, sustained, objective, transforming accounts of the world" (Haraway, 1988, p. 584). This stance hopelessly entangles the project in the dominant patriarchal discourse on science, leaving practioners to always answer how their science can be objective and partial, critical, embodied, and situated at the same time.[19]

The other stance, which is in a sense nonstandpoint, turns its back on science (and ethnography). This is the path of Trinh and Anzaluda: the direction of experimental, reflexive, cinematic texts. For these writers, the science questions no longer operate. Nor is there any break between empirical activity (gathering empirical materials or reading social texts), theorizing, and social criticism.

This is the space the new ethnography will enter. As it does, however, it will encounter criticisms from those who hold to the successor science image of ethnographic work. As this occurs, standpoint epistemologies of race, class, nation, gender, and sexuality will continue to develop. These race, ethnic, and gender-specific interpretive communities will fashion interpretive criteria out of their interactions with the postpositivist, critical theory, and poststructural sensibilities. These criteria will continue to push the personal to the forefront of the political, where the social text becomes the vehicle for the expression of politics.

Underneath the complexities and contradictions that define this field of the standpoint epistemology rest three common commitments. The world of human experience must be studied from the point of view of the historically and culturally situated individual.[20] Ethnographers will continue to work outward from their own biographies to the worlds of experience that surround them. Scholars will continue to value and seek to produce works that speak clearly and powerfully about these worlds. Therefore, the stories ethnographers tell one another will change and the criteria for reading stories will also change.

Here, the romantic, utopian impulse is once again confronted. Collins would change the world by creating a new form of group consciousness, forged out of centuries of racial oppression and injustice. Trinh wonders if group consciousness works this way, whereas Anzaluda writes a text of personal and group liberation, hoping to return home. There is no space of pure innocence to return to, however. Nostalgia will not work. The new ethnographic text can only hope to change that world already marred by the loss of innocence. Utopias founded on mythical constructs are no longer appropriate. In the next chapter, I examine what happens when these stories are turned into performance texts.

Notes

1. Marx hovers in the background as the original standpoint theorist, having written from the standpoint of the proletariat, while asserting that human activity or material life structures human consciousness and arguing that what we do shapes what we know (Harding, 1991, p. 120).

2. A disclaimer is in order. Clough (1994) reads queer theory as challenging the "heterosexism . . . which is constitutive of the [standpoint] epistemolog[ies] of experience. . . . Queer theory refuses to be a standpoint epistemology" (pp. 142, 145). Queer theory argues that the subjugated knowledges uncovered by the standpoint epistemologies reproduces the identity categories contained in heterosexism. Grounding an epistemology in experience reproduces these ideological categories (Clough, 1994, p. 144). Queer theory examines the practices that create these categories in the first place (see Terry, 1991).

3. That is, certain writers explicitly announce a connection to the standpoint perspective (Collins, 1991, p. 201; Harding, 1991; Hartsock, 1983; Smith, 1992, pp. 88-89), whereas others do not (see Anzaldua, 1987; Krieger, 1991; Trinh, 1991). Some (Trinh, 1989, p. 6) even go so far as to suggest that there is no "there" from which a standpoint can be launched (see Clough, 1994, p. 115; Haraway, 1988). Each begins, however, from the experiences of the previously silenced person in the dominant discourses of the human disciplines.

4. I will also briefly discuss the works of Dorothy Smith (1987, 1989, 1990a, 1990b, 1992, 1993). Each of these authors has produced works that have achieved near canonical status in the discourses of white feminist, Marxist standpoint epistemology (Smith), African American feminist standpoint epistemology (Collins), and lesbian, postcolonial, and Third World feminist writings (Anzaldua and Trinh).

5. Haraway's (1988) call for a subjugated standpoint epistemology, which produces partial, situated knowledges, attempts a subversion of this visual epistemology (pp. 581-589), asking women to take back the male gaze and its apparatuses.

6. Smith (1992, p. 93) elaborates the functions of these text-mediated discourses: "in contemporary societies, the functions of organization and control are increasingly vested in distinct, specialized, (and to some extent) autonomic forms of organization and relations mediated by texts. I've called these the 'relations of ruling.' " Power is located in these relations of ruling, which are constituted as texts. These texts exist outside lived time and the actualities that define people's experiences in the real world (p. 93).

7. I will return to this theme, which carries romantic, psychoanalytic overtones (see Clough, 1994, pp. 104-105).

8. Grossberg (1988) distinguishes four ethnographic writing models: the poststructural ethnographer who makes the familiar world strange; the cultural critic who examines the strange, the marginal, and the deviant; the ethnographer as tourist; and the materialist ethnographer who examines the signs and cultural practices of a group. Grossberg's materialist ethnographer is not the same as Clough's materialist, psychoanalytic ethnographer because there is no unconscious in his model.

9. Recall Marx's distinction between two forms of representation: to speak for and to make present (Ganguly, 1992, p. 62). Speaking for the other risks intervening on their behalf (becoming their voice), whereas making the other present encounters all of the problems discussed in Chapters 3 and 4 concerning the creation of a concrete subject in the world and putting ideas in their head.

10. In the cinematic context, Stacey fits female spectatorship to the actual moviegoing experience, identifying a gap between textual studies of the spectator and empirical studies of real people watching movies.

11. This produces aversions to both relativism and objectivism (Haraway, 1988, p. 584), a call for a successor science project that rests on an embodied subjectivity that generates situated knowledges (p. 577).

12. Lived experience, however, is not the site of Smith's studies. Although she begins with lived actualities, her concern focuses on how those experience are inscribed in official

texts, texts that "produce a formally warranted factual account" (Smith, 1990a, p. 148) of the activity. This textual account reinterprets the experience, connecting it to larger cultural codes and systems of power (see also her analysis of "K Is Mentally Ill" (Smith, 1990b).

13. Although Collins (1991, pp. xiv, 17) argues that she inserts herself into her text through the use of the pronouns "I," "we," "us," and "our," only rarely (pp. 97-98, 218) do her lived experiences constitute the materials she draws upon, and when this occurs she announces some discomfort: "I run the risk of being discredited as being too subjective and hence less scholarly. But by being an advocate for my material I validate the epistemological stance that I claim is fundamental for Black feminist thought" (p. 17).

14. This is Zora Neale Hurston's term (Trinh, 1991, pp. 68-69).

15. Here, there are parallels with Haraway's (1988, p. 593) call for a feminist visual epistemology, feminist visualizations of the world.

16. Here, Trinh (1989, pp. 144, 149) discusses the story told by a woman who kills (in her story) the storeman who lied to her grandmother. Charged with this murder (which she did not commit), the woman is given the opportunity to correct herself, which she refuses. Her attorney corrects her story to the judge, stating, "her mind is confused" (p. 148).

17. The Quiller-Couch syndrome refers to masculine and feminine types of writing. The Lady Painter syndrome "refers to a statement by a male painter, who . . . postulates, 'When she's good, we call her a painter; when she's bad, we call her a lady painter' " (Trinh, 1989, p. 27).

18. The Coatlicue state describes a powerful set of images that pass through her psyche: "a consuming internal whirlwind, the symbol of the underground aspects of the psyche. Coatlicue is the mountain, the Earth Mother . . . Goddess of birth and death . . . the incarnation of the cosmic processes (Anzaldua, 1987, p. 46).

19. Harding (1991, pp. 149-163), after Haraway (1988), wrestles with these issues, rejecting both extreme relativism and the objectivism of positivism. She advocates a strong objectivity and a strong reflexivity that allows the researcher to identify and reflexively engage in causal analyses of the social causes of good and bad beliefs.

20. Where the middle-class, heterosexual, privileged white male stands in all of this remains problematic and will be discussed in Chapter 8.

CHAPTER 4

Performance Texts

In anthropology there has been a noticeable shift in theoretical emphasis in recent years from structure to process, from competence to performance.

—V. Turner (1986b, p. 21)

This rethinking of ethnography is primarily about speaking and listening, instead of observing. . . . [This] shifts the emphasis from space to time, from sight and vision to sound and voice, from text to performance, from authority to vulnerability.

—Conquergood (1991, p. 183)

An oracle and a bringer of joy, the storyteller is the living memory of her time, her people. She composes on life.

—Trinh (1989, p. 125)

We must reinvent our cultural topographies and engage in collaborative intercultural art, media and research projects. And in view of a 'postmodern theatre,' we need to accommodate the sudden impact of women's perfor- mances, both on the stage and on feminist critical practices seeking to analyze cultural productions in regard to their constructions of identity, gender, race, and sexual preference.

—Birringer (1993, pp. xi-xii)

Borrowing from Turner (1986b), Turner and Turner (1982), and Conquergood (1991), and extending Trinh (1991), my topic is performing ethnography, the performance text. I examine ethnographic and cultural texts turned into poems, scripts, short stories, and dramas that are read and performed before audiences (see Bauman, 1986; Becker, McCall, & Morris, 1989; Bochner, 1994; Bruner, 1986; Conquergood, 1985a, 1986, 1989, 1991, 1992; Hilbert, 1990; Kapferer, 1986; Loseke, 1995; McCall & Becker, 1990; Mienczakowski, 1992, 1994, 1995; Mienczakowski & Morgan, 1993; Paget, 1993, pp. 24-25; Richardson, 1995; Schechner, 1986; Stern & Henderson, 1993; Tedlock, 1983; Turner, 1982, 1986a, 1986b). Performed texts have narrators, drama, action, and shifting points of view. Performance texts make experience concrete, anchoring it in the here and now (Paget, 1993, p. 40). They are dramaturgical, and they create spaces for the merger of multiple voices and experiences (Conquergood, 1985a, p. 10).

The performance text is a genre within ethnography, what Paget (1993, p. 42) calls ethnoperformance, Mienczakowski (1994) labels ethnodrama, and Turner (1982, p. 40) terms performance and reflexive anthropology, the rendering "of ethnography in a kind of instructional theater" (Turner, 1982, p. 41).[1] I connect this textual form to the narrative turn in the human disciplines (Bochner, 1994, p. 30; Maines, 1993; Mitchell, 1981; Rorty, 1980), the move that sees culture as a performance—as theater (Bruner, 1984; Burke, 1989; Geertz, 1973, 1995; Goffman, 1959; Turner, 1981, 1982, 1986a, 1986b). Performance texts are messy; they exist in what Conquergood (1992) calls "the borderlands" (p. 80), the spaces where rhetoric, performance, ethnography, and cultural studies come together (Conquergood, 1992, p. 80).

I will critically read this genre, offering a vocabulary of performance text terms, while tracing the genre's genealogy in sociology and anthropology, locating it within the field of performance studies (Stern & Henderson, 1993, pp. 3-32; Strine, Long, & Hopkins, 1990). I will give special attention to performance science texts (Becker et al., 1989; McCall & Becker, 1990) while discussing the main strengths and weaknesses of other contemporary performance approaches. Guidelines for constructing these texts will be addressed.

I will privilege those performance texts that focus on the construction and coaudience performance of critical, improvised "mystories" (Ulmer, 1989, p. 209). Mystories are reflexive, critical, multimedia tales and tellings. They begin with the writer's biography and body, epiphanic moments, turning point experiences, and times of personal trouble and turmoil—Turner's (1986b, pp. 34-35) liminal experiences.[2] Performed mystories move from epiphanic moments to those larger cultural and scientific texts that purport to interpret and make sense of such personal experience and public explanations of private troubles (Mills, 1959). When performed, mystories critique these larger systems of personal, popular, and expert knowledge (Ulmer, 1989, pp. 209-211). I conclude with a discussion of politics and ethics and their place in performative cultural studies.

Interpretive Assumptions

The following assumptions and arguments organize my readings of this textual form. In the beginning is the field—arenas of ongoing dramatic experience entered by the field-worker. This arena may be known and already familiar or it may be foreign and strange. The interpretive ethnographer enters those strange and familiar situations that connect critical biographical experiences (epiphanies) with culture, history, and social structure. He or she seeks out those narratives and stories people tell one another as they attempt to make sense of the epiphanies or existential turning-point moments in their lives.

The postmodern world stages existential crises. Following Victor Turner (1986b, p. 34), the ethnographer gravitates to these narratively structured, liminal, existential spaces in the culture. At these dramaturgical sites, people take sides, forcing, threatening, inducing, seducing, cajoling, nudging, loving, living, abusing, and killing one another (see Turner, 1986b, p. 34). At these sites, ongoing social dramas occur. These dramas have a temporal or chronological order (Turner, 1986b, p. 35), multiple beginnings, middles, and ends. They are also storied events, narratives that rearrange chronology into multiple and differing forms of meaningful experience (Turner, 1986b, p. 35). The storied nature of these experiences continually raises the following questions: Whose story is being told (and made) here? Who is doing the telling? Who has the authority to make their telling stick? (Smith, 1990a). As soon as a chronological event is told in the form of a story, it enters a text-mediated system of discourse in which larger issues of power and control come into play (Smith, 1990a). In this text-mediated system, new tellings occur. The interpretations of original experience are now fitted to this larger interpretive structure (Smith, 1990b).

This larger, text-based interpretive system reproduces the cultural logics of Western naturalism. This is realism writ large—the attempt to accurately reproduce a real, external world of objects and to accurately map and represent that world with a high degree of verisimilitude. This is a socially constructed world, however, with multiple points of view operating. Kurosawa's (1950) *Rashomon*'s effects are always present. This is the space entered by the performance text because it attempts to expose and challenge these larger systems of realistic interpretation and meaning.

Performance ethnography enters a postmodern culture "with nearly invisible boundaries separating theatre performance from dance, music, film, television, video, and the various performance art 'disciplines' " (Birringer, 1993, p. 182). This means that the performance text is situated in a complex system of discourse in which traditional and avant-garde meanings of theater, film, video, ethnography, performance, text, and audience all circulate and inform one another. Aesthetic theories (naturalism, realism, modernism, and postmodernism) collide with positivist, postpositivist, and poststructural epistemologies, and hypertexts interact with traditional print and performance forms of representation.

The reflexive performance text must contest the pull of traditional "realist" theater, "method" acting, (and ethnography) wherein performers, performances, and texts solely or primarily re-enact and re-create a "recognizable verisimilitude of setting, character and dialogue" (Cohn, 1988, p. 815), in which dramatic action reproduces a linear sequence, a "mimetic representation of cause and effect" (Birringer, 1993, p. 196). A postmodern performance aesthetic and evocative epistemology must be developed—an aesthetic that goes beyond "the already-seen and already-heard" (Birringer, 1993, p. 186). This aesthetic will venture into those undefined, taboo spaces in which the unpresentable in the culture is felt and made visible, seeking a performance sublime for postmodernism (Birringer, 1993, p. 197).

This means that there will be a continual rediscovery of the body; that is, the performance text always works outward from the body. The body's theatrical presence is "a site and pretext for . . . debates about representation and gender, about history and postmodern culture, and about theory and its vanishing point or referent" (Birringer, 1993, p. 203; see also Conquergood, 1991, p. 180). The postmodern body, and the discourses that surround it, must be presented, including the AIDS body, the oversized body, the undersized anorexic body, the porno-graphic or the sporting body, Haraway's (1985) cyborg, and the bombed, mutilated bodies of little children. Accordingly, performance texts should be dialogical, critical of the structures of experience they enact (see Conquergood, 1985a, p. 4). They should not be mere com-modified extensions of a theater (and ethnography) that reproduces the ideological and technological requirements of late-capitalist social real-ism and hyperrealism (Birringer, 1993, p. 175).

These texts-as-performances will challenge the meanings of lived experience as simulated performance. They will interrogate the con-cepts of specularity, reconceptualizing the framing features that define the visual apparatus of the stage, including sound and lighting. Tradi-tional understandings of costume, directors, actors, performers, the spectator, spectatorship and the audience, voyeurism, and performance space will also be questioned, as will conventional notions of the theater and what goes on in a performance—in a night at the opera—to invoke the Marx Brother's film (see Birringer, 1993, p. 186).

The performance text enters that world opened by the standpoint epistemologies. These works potentially answer to Trinh's (1991, p. 162) call for the production of texts that seek the truth of life's fictions in which experiences are evoked, not explained. As dramatic theater, with connections back to Brecht (Epic Theater) and Artaud (Theater of Cru-elty), they turn tales of suffering, loss, pain, and victory into evocative performances that have the ability to move audiences to reflective, critical action, and not just emotional catharsis (see Coger & White, 1973, pp. 29-31; Maclay, 1971, pp. 37-38).

In the moment of performance, these texts have the potential of overcoming the biases of an ocular, visual epistemology. They can undo the voyeuristic, gazing eye of the ethnographer, bringing audiences and performers into a jointly felt and shared field of experience. These works also unsettle the writer's place in the text, freeing the text and the writer to become interactional productions. The performance text is the single, most powerful way for ethnography to recover yet interrogate the meanings of lived experience. The performed text is a lived experience in two senses. The performance doubles back on the experiences previously represented in the ethnographer's text. It then re-presents those experiences as embodied performance to the audience. It thus privileges experience—the evocative moment when another's experiences come alive for the self. There are many ways, however, to present lived experience. If performance is interpretation, then performance texts have the ability to criticize and deconstruct taken for granted understandings concerning how lived experience is to be represented.

As ethnographic stagings, performances are always "enmeshed in moral matters. . . . [They] enact a moral stance" (Conquergood, 1985a, pp. 2, 4), asking the audience to take a stand on the performance and its meanings. In these productions, the performer becomes a cultural critic (Bowman, 1988, p. 4). If culture is an ongoing performance (Bruner, 1986), then performers critically bring the spaces, meanings, ambiguities, and contradictions of culture alive in their performances (Conquergood, 1986, p. 56). The performed text is one of the last frontiers for ethnography to enter Victor Turner's (1986b, p. 25) liminal space—a new but old border to be crossed.[3] When fully embraced, this crossing will forever transform ethnography and cultural studies. It will serve, at the same time, to redefine the meanings of ethnography in its other moments and formations.

Performance Text Vocabulary

A family of contested concepts and terms (see Table 4.1), including theater, dramatic script, editing reality, interpretation, performance syntax, performance, performer, performance text, and audience, define the ethnographic performance perspective (see Strine et al., 1990). These terms blur into one another.

Dramatic performances occur within the spaces of ethnographic theater, an aesthetic place and space where texts, performers, performances, and audiences come together. The theater may be a stage organized for performances, or it may be an improvised space, such as a classroom or a lecture hall. A performance is marked as theater when a dramatic script with delineated characters in plotted dramatic action

Table 4.1   A Performance Text Vocabulary

Concept	Variations
Audience	Interactive structure; types: professional, participatory-interactional, coparticipants, lay, aesthetic, electronic, cinematic, and postmodern
Dramatic script	Evocative text, "delineated characters in a plotted dramatic action capable of stirring the imagination/and or emotions of an audience, bringing it to a state of awareness" (Coger & White, 1973, p. 6); fragmentary, composite, messy, natural, and autobiographical
Editing reality	Turning a field text into a dramatic, reflexive script performance syntax (McCall & Becker, 1990, p. 118) that is then rehearsed, staged, and performed
Interpretation	As performance, text versus performance centered
Performer	Types: solo, group, natural, professional, ensemble, reader chamber, and interactional theater
Performance	As interpretive event; meanings: aesthetic, intellectual, emotional, participatory, political, and commemorative; types: natural, dramatic, and improvised
Performance syntax	A text's theoretical, interpretive vocabulary that is embedded in the script, giving a connection and shape to the field text (Jackson, 1993, p. 29); directions for performing and presenting, including publication
Performance text	Types: dramatic, natural, performance science, ethnodrama, staged readings, realist, and postmodern
Theater	An aesthetic place and space where text, performers, performances, and audiences come together to participate in an embodied, evocative, reflective experience. Contemporary types: readers, chamber, of the mind, community, regional, Cruelty, absurd, Epic, forum or oppressed (Boal), realist, postmodern, Third World, feminist, and ethnographic (see also types of performance texts)

is performed. Dramatic scripts are crafted from field notes—what McCall and Becker (1990, p. 118) call editing reality. They have a performance syntax—a theoretical, interpretive vocabulary that articulates the drama of the field situation (see below). Scripts can be based on composite experiences and characters and be fragmentary, personal, autobiographical, and incomplete. Good ethnographic theater stirs the critical, emotional imagination of the audience.

A performance is an interpretive event, a rehearsed or improvised creative set of activities, with a beginning, middle, and end, performed for the benefit of an audience and the performers. Performance is interpretation. A performance is simultaneously a text and an interpretive process (see Strine et al., 1990, p. 184). Performance events always occur in a context—those immediate and historical social, political, biographical, and aesthetic factors that shape the understandings persons bring to and experience during the performance (Stern & Henderson, 1993, pp. 17, 19).

Three types of performances can be distinguished. A natural performance is the reperformance of ordinary interaction—a staged version of a recorded conversation (Stucky, 1993, p. 168). A dramatic performance is organized in terms of the aesthetics of performance or oral interpretation theory (see Bacon, 1980). Traditionally, dramatic performances have been text based, drawing on existing drama or literature for the text that is performed (i.e., chamber or reader's theater; see Maclay, 1971). Recently (Conquergood, 1992), ethnographers have performed rituals and stories drawn from fieldwork sites. An improvised performance seeks its own organization and structure in the process of performance.

A performance is a public act, a way of knowing, and a form of embodied interpretation. Performances are contextual, situated productions that mediate and define ongoing relationships between texts, readers, interpreters, performers, and audiences (Loxley, 1983, p. 42). Any given performance event is shaped by an aesthetics of experience (theories of performance and audience expectations) and by the social experience of bearing witness to the performance itself (p. 42).

Two generic performance aesthetics can be identified: presentational and representational theater (see Donmoyer & Yennie-Donmoyer, 1995). Representational theater enacts the logics of naturalistic realism. It re-creates an on-stage verisimilitude. Through realistic, method acting, a faithful rendering of everyday interaction and conversation is produced, complete with slurred speech, mumbles, hesitations, repetitions, scratches, slouches, and other personal mannerisms. In representational theater, method actors bring their inner experiences to the character, action, and emotion being portrayed, submerging themselves in the character—for example, Marlon Brando in *Street Car Named Desire*. Thus, the audience does not see the performer playing a character; they see only the character.

In contrast, presentational theater is the stylized and individual display of the part and character in question: there is no attempt to dissolve the performer into the role—the emphasis is on stylization, not realism. Performers might read from scripts, "assume a variety of roles. . . . interact with imaginary characters, and manipulate non-existent or partial props in the process of presenting literary works" (Donmoyer & Yennie-Donmoyer, 1995, p. 7). Presentational theater asks the audience to create meaning from "what is suggested, rather than from what is literally shown" (p. 7). Representational theater employs a performance-based aesthetic, whereas presentational theater creates the spaces for an audience-based aesthetic that works to uncut the logic of strict realistic theater. This aesthetic allows audience members to separate their emotional reactions to a performance from the text (and the performance).[4]

Following Stern and Henderson (1993, pp. 14-15), performances can be arrayed along a continuum, moving from the individual performance (a solo performer, the Rap artist, or a party hostess) to increasingly more complex, collective performances, including performance artists, children playing on the sidewalk, theatrical events, and other public ceremonies such as Mardi Gras. Performances can be focused on ordinary everyday, cultural experiences—for example, children's games. Other performances mix the cultural and the aesthetic (performance art), whereas some are primarily aesthetic (staged plays), and others focus on out of the ordinary, collective cultural event (Mardi Gras).

The performed text interacts with a prior text, field notes, interviews, or a literary work.[5] This interaction produces the performance—the interpretive event. Multiple meanings and pleasures can be brought to the performance site, including those that are aesthetic, intellectual, emotional, participatory, political, and commemorative of various forms of cultural memory (Strine et al., 1990, pp. 185-188). The performance text reports on (brings news from), dramatizes, and critiques some segment of ongoing cultural life (pp. 188-189).

The performance text can take one of five forms: dramatic texts, such as rituals, poems, and plays meant to be performed (see Bacon, 1980; Turner, 1986b); natural texts—transcriptions of everyday conversations turned into natural performances (see Stucky, 1993); performance science texts—fieldwork notes and interviews turned into performance texts (see Becker et al., 1989; McCall & Becker, 1990; Paget, 1993); and improvisational, critical ethnodramas that merge natural script dialogues with dramatized scenes and the use of composite characters (see Mienczakowski, 1992, 1994, 1995; Mienczakowski & Morgan, 1993).

These five dramatic forms must be distinguished from "staged readings" in which one or more persons holds a script, the text, and reads from it (see Paget, 1993, p. 27). Staged readings are text-centered productions and may involve rehearsals by readers-as-performers. Improvised staged readings call for the stage director (the author of the paper) to hand out parts of the script to members of the audience, who then read on cue. Performance texts attempt to move away from the written text, although some may preserve "its content on stage" (p. 27). Finally, these five forms have different performance syntaxes and semantic structures.[6]

Nondramatic, natural performance scripts recount events, tellings, and interpretations from the field. They do not necessarily move the audience through a dramatic structure of events, such as is found in the many variations (absurd, German Epic, and cruelty) on the traditional (Elizabethan, Stuart, restoration, realism, neoclassical, romanticism, comedy, etc.) theater model (see Turner, 1986b, p. 27-31). They may have only a few speaking parts. They use a scholarly performance syntax, invoking terms and theories that resonate within the intended scholarly community.

Dramatic natural performance texts, in contrast, conform, in some fashion, to this traditional theater model and its variations (as well as those found in Chamber, Story, and Readers and Peoples Theater; see discussion below). They have multiple speakers, protagonists, and antagonists, and they move action through to a dramatic resolution. Audience-centered, dramatic performances make the audience part of the performance, attempting to break down the wall between performer and audience. A scholarly performance syntax is often woven into the script (see Jackson, 1993, p. 29).

Improvisational and critical ethnodramas draw on field texts (interviews and conversations) while combining multiple narratives within a single performance that may have many dramatic beginnings, middles, and endings (see Mienczakowski, 1995). Audiences may be coperformers in these productions. If the postproduction method of forum theater (Boal, 1979/1985, 1995) is used, discussions with audience members and performers will occur, and scripts and performances will be modified, on the basis of these conversations. The text's syntax draws primarily from the worlds studied, with a minimum emphasis on scholarly, theoretical terms. Each of these performance variations (which of course blur) may focus respectively on reporting, dramatizing, or critiquing that which is being presented. However, critical, ethnodrama explicitly focuses on cultural critique (Mienczakowski, 1994, p.48).

Dramatic and nondramatic texts, based on the performance science model, will utilize scripts taken from the literal translation of field notes and field texts. These scripts can be turned into dramatic performances—for example, Stucky's (1993) natural performances or Jackson's (1993) and Paget's (1993) plays. They can also be nondramatic readings—for example, Becker et al.'s (1989) scripts with speaking parts for researchers and informants. Dramatic, improvisational ethnodrama alters and changes the field text, producing composite characters, emphasizing multiple tellings of the same event, and shifting concern away from verisimilitude toward dramatic reinterpretation and cultural critique (but see Mienczakowski, 1994, pp. 50-51).

Varying degrees of text centeredness define these three styles. Although the performance is a transformative process for each, those that emphasize natural performances are more text centered, keying on the actual words that were spoken and transcribed. The closer the text moves to an audience-centered production, the less text centered and more improvisational it becomes. Of course, all performances are based on texts. The issue here is the status of the text as it refers back to the field experience and the field text. Improvisational, ethnodrama texts fundamentally transform that experience. Dramatic and nondramatic natural performances maintain a deeper commitment to that site and its "original" meanings.

Audiences are neither pure voyeurs of nor passive recipients of performance events (Peterson, 1983, p. 33). Audiences are organized around performance events, witnesses to an oral interpretation of a text (Langellier, 1983, p. 36). Audiences interpret and live through performances—they are performers of their own interpretations and witnesses of the performed text (Dufrene, 1973; Iser, 1978; Langellier, 1983, p. 34). Audiences complete performances by being there for the performance, they participate in mute dialogue, and they also offer "a background of pure silence that allows other voices to emerge" (Langellier, 1983, p. 34). They also clap, laugh, cough, weep, perceive, listen, appreciate, respond, evaluate, and perform (Loxley, 1983, p. 43).

The audience is an interactive structure. Although members bring their own interpretive frameworks as audience members to a performance, the audience-as-a-performer can also enact its own performance aesthetic. In this way, the audience is both inside the performance text and observer of its performance (Langellier, 1983, p. 36). The audience both creates a text and is created by the text as a performance. Hence, the audience "may be more or less competent, equal to or unqualified" (p. 37) to interpret the performance in question.

Every audience, like any performance, is different. Any audience "simultaneously participates in an unrepeatable creation as well as within a history of performances that precede and succeed it" (Langellier, 1983, p. 37). Unable to see the text as a totality, the audience is an ongoing witness to the text as it is performed. This moving viewpoint means that audiences (and their members) are always in interpretive motion, continually moving in and out of the performed text as performer, witness, and interpreter (p. 38).

There are four types of ethnographic performance audiences: professional, participatory, lay, and aesthetic. A professional audience is a group of scholars at a professional meeting hearing a text performed rather than read (Becker et al., 1989). A participatory audience is an audience involved as coperformers or critics (in the postperformance phase) of the performance. Participatory audiences are often lay groups whose experiences are being performed by fellow performers (see Mienczakowski, 1992, 1994, 1995; Mienczakowski & Morgan, 1993). A lay audience is distinct from the aesthetic audience, which is an audience who comes to enjoy a work for its performance values—its ability to re-create experiences and interpretations connected to a performance tradition (i.e., classic Shakespearean theater).

Performers may be solo performers or members of a theater, ensemble, readers, peoples, or chamber performance group (Bacon, 1980). Performers may be natural actors, scholars, or persons from everyday life performing their own or other's texts. Performers use props, including manuscripts, lecterns, lighting, and music, for their performances (p. 5). Performers interpret texts, bringing them alive. A performer creates a living space for a text, locating the performance in some form of direct or indirect contact with the audience (p. 4).

Performers or actors may perform their own or someone else's work. In the first instance, they are writers who are also performers— artists doing a narrative text. In this case, they are in doing an interpretation of a text they have produced. In the second case, they are interpreters of another's text. In both performative contexts, performers bring their interpretations to bear on this work, connecting a performative self to a performance that brings the work alive (see Van Oosting, 1981, p. 68). Method actors work from the outer edges of a work, the printed text, moving into its inner meanings, fitting those meanings to their own interpretations of the event or character in question (p. 68). They attempt a realistic rendering of the text and character in question, folding themselves into the character. Such performers move through three interpretive stages in their performance work. They begin as readers of the text, moving to interpreters who become translators able to move from print to performance, "from imaginative vision to structured articulation" (p. 74). In contrast, non-method actors are more concerned with presentation and not representation. They draw, accordingly, on their noncharacter experiences as they improvise an interpretation of the situation and part in question.

Genealogy of the Performance Text

The origins of the alliance between ethnography and performance can be traced to many sources and told in many different ways (Conquergood, 1992, p. 80; Jackson, 1993; Stern & Henderson, 1993, pp. 9-16). In 1959, Erving Goffman proposed to read society dramaturgically, to look at those parts of daily life that were staged, and to place an emphasis on the difference between reality and appearance. In 1969, Kenneth Burke (1969, p. 43) suggested that anthropologists examine the rhetorical nature of their own field and that anthropology be imported (in part) into rhetoric. Victor Turner (1986b) called for an anthropology of performance. At the same time, Richard Bauman (1986) was formulating a model for connecting narrative texts and oral performances, and Dennis Tedlock (1983, pp. 300, 304) examined the problems involved in joining the spoken word with the printed text, situating the anthropoplogist in the center of the performances being recorded. Richard Harvey Brown (1987) contented that society be read rhetorically, and Stanford Lyman (1990, p. 221) suggested that the metaphor of a dramaturigcal society had become an interactional reality in America. Today, Debord's (1983) society of the spectacle has been realized: We understand everyday life through the mass-mediated performances that make the hyperreal more real than the real (Baudrillard, 1983; see also Denzin, 1992a, p. 138).

Turner's (1986b) call to perform ethnographic narratives is anticipated by Paget's (1987) concept of "verbatim theater," which Mienczakowski (1995, p. 5) connects to the British Broadcasting Company's documentary radio ballads of the 1950s that culminated in Joan Littlewood's "Oh What a Lovely Way," a musical play that used verbatim accounts and "documentary evidence as a basis for its depiction of class-attitudes towards the First World War" (Mienczakowski, 1995, p. 5). Chessman (1971) extended this approach using oral history techniques to develop realistic narratives then presented on stage (Mienczakowski, 1995, p. 5). The concept of performance science—scholars performing ethnogaphic texts—was introduced by Becker et al. in 1989 and elaborated by McCall and Becker in 1990. In 1991, Laurel Richardson and Ernest Lockridge presented "The Sea Monster: An Ethnographic Novel," a further extension of this form, now using the dramatic form to deconstruct the traditional ethnography (see Richardson, 1993). In a parallel vein, Mienczakowski (1992, 1994, 1995; Mienczakowski & Morgan, 1993) has been experimenting with Boal's (1979/1985, 1995) forum theater techniques using postperformance discussions with informants and audience members as a way of modifying scripts and performances. Mienczakowski's performance scripts (see discussion below) are based on verbatim accounts of field materials gathered via grounded theory, case study, and ethnographic methods of inquiry.

During the past decade, Conquergood and his students have continued to rethink ethnography in terms of a performance rhetoric, doing fieldwork to have new texts to perform (see Conquergood, 1985a, 1986, 1989, 1991, 1992; see also Jackson, 1993).[7] In this framework, building on Goffman, Burke, Geertz, Turner, and Bakhtin, the world is understood to be a performance, culture is a verb, not a noun, fieldwork is a collaborative process—a performance—and knowledge is performative, not informative (Conquergood, 1991, p. 190). This model assesses the ethics and politics of the performed text, arguing that it should exist alongside the published text as a scholarly work in its own right (Conquergood, 1991, p. 190). The performance text thus complements the narrative, storytelling approach to ethnographic practice, that approach that problematizes the place of the other in the messy, layered text (Marcus, 1994; Ronai, 1995), while encouraging the reflexive, autobiographical voice that is aware of its own historical contingencies (Bochner, 1994, pp. 32-33).

Conquergood's arguments for the performance text are embedded in a deep history connected to theater, rhetoric, and oral interpretation (see Bacon, 1979, 1980; Sayre, 1990; Strine et al., 1990, pp. 181-183).[8] This history revolves around the meanings brought to the terms discussed previously (texts, performers, and performances). From the 1950s to the 1970s, the field of performance studies was text centered, viewing texts as repositories of latent meaning and focusing on performances and oral interpretations as the methods for making these latent meanings manifest (Strine et al., 1990, p. 182).

Chamber and Readers Theater

Text-centered performance studies extended the traditional dramatic theater model (in which plays were performed by a group of actors), to chamber and readers theater. Chamber theater was defined as a "technique for staging prose fiction, retaining the text of the story or novel being performed, but locating the scenes of the story onstage" (Bacon, 1979, p. 466). Chamber theater often used a narrator. Readers theater embodies the same elements as chamber theater but may not use a narrator, and the locus of the drama is not onstage with the readers (as it is for chamber theater), but offstage in the imagination of the audience (Bacon, 1979, p. 457). Readers theater is a technique for staging literary texts in such a way that the text is featured in the performance (Maclay, 1971, p. 7). Chamber theater is representational, attempting to reproduce the illusion of reality on stage. Readers theater is presentational: The emphasis is less on realism and more on action that occurs in the audience's critical imagination (see Donmoyer & Yennie-Donmoyer, 1995).

Chamber and readers theater (also called theater of the mind or the theater of the imagination) used a grammar of practice that modified the traditional theater model while giving special meanings to scripts, casting, rehearsals, directing, stage design (the arrangement of readers on stage), props (lecterns, stools, and chairs), costumes (ordinary clothes), lighting, dialogue, performance standards, and specific guidelines for relating performances to texts (see Coger & White, 1973, p. 31; Maclay, 1971; Pickering, 1975).

Readers theater has three essential elements. First, it must have a script with delineated characters in a plotted dramatic, often conflictual action. The materials in the script may be a collation of materials (poems, diary entries, and excerpts from short stories), but they must interact, functioning as a gestalt—a dramatic whole (Coger & White, 1973, p. 6)—producing a sense of drama for the audience. Thus, a reading of a poem or a group reading of a text is not readers theater. Second, readers theater must be embodied through vocal intonations and bodily tensions (and movements), and characters must be evoked and brought alive: "Effective performance is the second essential element in Readers Theatre" (p. 7). Third, a willing and participatory audience must be present. In readers and chamber theater, the audience is asked to imagine their way into the characters and story that is being staged and to ignore the fact that the actors are readers and not characters in a play. This is called double vision (p. 7). The audience is asked to give itself over to the performance and to suspend literary analysis and literary criticism. These criticisms may come later, after the performance, but if present during the performance they interfere with the audience member's "contribution to the work, and lacking [this] participation, the performance will be incomplete" (p. 7).

In certain versions (Coger & White, 1973, pp. 29-31; Maclay, 1971, pp. 37, 99), readers theater attempted to break from traditional staging procedures to develop new relationships with the audience. Many readers theater directors drew upon Bertolt Brecht's concept of epic theater, which used the method of actor alienation to make the audience aware of the "simultaneous presence of actor and actor" (Maclay, 1971, p. 37). Brecht's alienating devices included direct speeches to the audience, avoidance of the concept of the fourth wall, actors shifting roles and playing more than one character or more than one actor playing the same character, actors singing to the audience in a way that commented on ongoing action, the projection of pictures and printed comments on background screens, bare stage walls, minimal props, successions of independent scenes and segments, and the use of narrators who tied sequences together (Coger & White, 1973, pp. 29-31).

Although readers theater seeks emotional involvement on the part of the audience, Brecht's experiments were intended to create a thinking audience, an audience with detachment, an audience who could think and act critically. Brecht's was not a theater of emotional catharsis; rather, "it was to be a stimulus for social action and social criticism" (Maclay, 1971, p. 37). In contrast to conventional readers theater, which is representational and realistic, Brecht's epic, or dialectical theater, is deliberately disruptive and political and thus anticipates the more radical forms of contemporary postmodern, political theater that has connections back to Artaud's concepts of a pure theater (Birringer, 1993, p. 217).

Third World popular theater, "theatre used by oppressed Third World people to achieve justice and development for themselves" (Etherton, 1988, p. 991), extends these critical views of what theater (and ethnography) can do politically. The International Popular Theatre Alliance, organized in the 1980s, uses existing forms of cultural expression to fashion improvised dramatic productions that analyze situations of poverty and oppression. This grass-roots approach uses agit-prop and sloganizing theater (theater pieces devised to ferment political action) to create collective awareness and collective action at the local level. This form of theater has been popular in Latin America, in Africa, in parts of Asia, in India, and among Native populations in the Americas (p. 992).

The crisis of representation in ethnography's fourth and fifth moments (see Chapter 3) challenged the text-centered approach of chamber and readers theater. The work to be performed could no longer be viewed as a stable entity with inherent meanings that a performance would reveal (Strine et al., 1990, p. 182). The performance of a text was now redefined, no longer confined to the single performance of a "repeatable and preexistent text" (Sayre, 1990, p. 91). Texts were now understood to be subject to multiple interpretations and meanings.[9] Thus, a text could neither authorize nor transcend its own performance (Sayre, 1990, p. 91). This is the space that Conquergood and Turner's work enters and defines.

Performance Art

Thus emerged performance art, a movement that predates, while running alongside, the crisis of representation in the human disciplines. It is traced (Sayre, 1990, pp. 92-93) to the futurists in the 1910s, the dada cabaret movement of the 1920s, surrealism (1924 to mid-1930s), Brecht's experiments with a theater of the mind (Capo, 1983, p. 35), and culminating in the mid-1960s in an "interdisciplinary, often multimedia kind of production which has come to be labeled 'performance art' " (Sayre, 1990, p. 93; Stern & Henderson, 1993, p. 383).[10] Transformations of this movement focused on the gendered body, dissolving, fragmenting, blurring, and displacing its centered presence in performance (Birringer, 1993, pp. 220-221). The literal body was challenged, replaced by a gendered, autobiographical, confessional body text, cries and whispers on stage, gyrations and repetitions, and a body in motion working against itself and its culture (Birringer, 1993, p. 221). This body was soon supplemented by a globalizing, electronic, postmodern video technology. Laurie Anderson's multitrack, audiovisual choreographies are key here. Her electronic body represents a "kind of electronic closed-circuit transvestism" (Birringer, 1993, p. 222), awaiting only on-line movement into cyberspace, her own hypermedia site on the World Wide Webb—video theater on the computer. Montage and mise-en-scène will never be the same again.

In performance art, a performance becomes a dialogical, often improvisational work that takes authority away from the text; the emphasis is on the performance, not the work per se.[11] The concept of an original, against which the performance can be measured, is questioned (Sayre, 1990, p. 94). The world outside the text, including the audience, is brought into the performance. The performance becomes a transformative process in which performers are no longer locked into fixed characters in a text. Audiences may become active participants or coperformers in the performance. The performer creates a field or aesthetic situation in which audience and performer together "face, as a group, a common dilemma" (Sayre, 1990, p. 101); together, audience members and performers coproduce a shared text, participatory theater (Capo, 1983, p. 33; see also Dufrenne, 1973; Iser, 1978; Langellier, 1983, p. 34). At the same time, performance artists maintain their own identities and "distinguish themselves from actors and actresses . . . because the latter 'pretend' to be someone else in a time different from the real time of the event" (Sayre, 1990, p. 96).[12]

Enter the Social Sciences: Performance Science Texts

Becker, McCall, and Morris (1989) introduced the concept of performance science, a play on performance art (McCall & Becker, 1990, p. 119). Instead of reading scientific papers aloud at professional meetings, they began performing them, first writing and then reading scripts in which they played themselves, while also reading the parts given to their informants. A quasi-storytelling format, unlike the argumentative structure of the scientific article, was adopted. This format allowed them to present their work as a collaborative project without privileging a single authorial voice. The script format permitted the presentation of emotion and mood. Through the use of intonation and pacing, they could alter the meanings of their text, thereby highlighting, and openly acknowledging, the constructed nature of their social science data (Becker et al., 1989, pp. 94-95).[13] As performers, they felt as if they were having the experiences they were describing. Performances made the research process more visible and alive to outsiders; voices became real people.

The following is a sample text—it is from the prologue of their play, "Theatres and Communities: Three Scenes (Becker et al., 1989, p. 100):

(A meeting room at an academic conference. On a raised platform at the front of the room are three circles in a semicircle. Three sociologists enter, carrying scripts).

Lori: Everyone says Chicago is so hot now. Well, it's because of the Non-Equity Theatres.

Michal: Minneapolis/St. Paul was a very fat theater town in 1978. There was a good crowd for everything.

Howie: San Francisco has a problem that we share with a lot of smaller centers, smaller cities, which is that we have a lot of talented, really fine actors.

These script fragments define the problem analyzed in the play: the interconnection between theaters, workers, groups, communities, plays, and productions and a shrinking national theater scene.

The performance science script, as analyzed by Becker et al. (1989), presents certain problems of formatting and syntax, including how to mark speakers, how to indicate shifts in headings, how to indent quotes, what to leave in and what to leave out, and whether to give stage directions or not (Becker et al., 1989, pp. 95-96; McCall & Becker, 1990, pp. 122-123; see also Jackson, 1993, pp. 26-31).[14] These scripts represent a mixed genre, part theater and part social science, and standards for reading them are yet to be fully developed (see Hilbert, 1990).[15]

Jackson (1993, p. 28) addresses some of the problems identified by Hilbert (1990) in the McCall and Becker project—namely, the absence of a theoretical framework for understanding the quotes from the field. Drawing on Strine et al. (1990, p. 189), Jackson's script (and performance) combined three types of performance scholarship: reporting, dramatizing, and critiquing. She simultaneously reported on and dramatized the world of the audition by evoking that world and its tensions. Within her script, she inserted critiques of the structures of domination that impinge on actors and actresses in these arenas, using in several places lines from the works of Michel Foucault (Jackson, 1993, p. 30). Her performance text became an ideological critique of objectivist ethnography and that brand of objectivism that is reified in the audition process (Jackson, 1993, p. 21).

In the following lines, Jackson (1993, p. 30) offers a critique (using Foucault) of the auditioning process:

Theorist: Each subject finds himself caught in a punishable, punishing university.

Actor 1: Don't give a big introduction to your piece.

> **Director:** Act like you want to be there.
> **Actor 1:** But don't brown-nose.
> **Actor 2:** Be real.

Jackson (1993, p. 31) describes her efforts with this script segment: "I was representing more than information gleaned from the interviews. The attempt was to dramatize the actor's dilemma within the audition structure." Jackson (1993) elaborates:

> During the editing process, decisions about what to include and exclude, how many characters to have, in what order to place the accounts, how to stage the piece—all were made . . . and remade in tandem. . . . Eventually, I would decide on a cast of two actors, two actresses, one director, and a director's assistant. The words of each character were not the words of a single respondent. . . . I clustered the words of several individuals around each figure. (p. 126)

Jackson's text dramatizes action and moves it forward, in contrast to the nondramatic, Becker et al. script.

Stucky (1993) takes the performance science project to another level—what he terms the aesthetics of natural performances. Natural performances are reperformances of "something which was, at first performance, an ordinary event" (p. 168)—for example, natural conversational interaction. Stucky distinguishes two types of natural performances: staged natural performances, which resemble dramatic monologues (personal narratives of a single speaker), and those natural performances that are drawn from conversational settings (interviews and telephone talk). These performances resemble dramatic dialogue (p. 169).

The following is a fragment from a longer scene in a fully staged theatrical production called "Naturally Speaking" (Stucky, 1993, p. 169). The words are taken from a recorded conversation between a counselor (Pat) and a client (Liz):

> **Liz:** And when, uh: the abuse started it didn't start like he would just come in and beat me up or something it was
> **Pat:** Um hmmm . . .
> **Liz:** like a slap in the face . . .

Pat: . . . started slow

Liz: Uh . . . b'cause I remember that slap in the face real hh w(h)ell

Stucky's performers listen to tapes of texts like this, gleaning an understanding of paralinguistic details such as intonation and voice quality (Stucky 1993, p. 170).

The texts for natural performances, which include interviews, stories, and personal narratives, are based on audiovisual recordings of "real" conversations, which are rich in "first-order performance details" (Stucky, 1993, p. 170). Performances then draw on these texts; a second body does what a "prior body has already done" (p. 171). The goal is a mix of mimesis and verisimilitude, understanding that there is no "original" against which the performance is to be judged. Performers use natural speech to create the impression that they are re-enacting the experiences and actions of ordinary people in the world.[16]

This natural world is, however, privileged; it describes what Stucky (1993) calls the first-order performance source of the text (p. 173). It is different from the world of fiction: Recordings of speeches, stories, and conversations reference how things actually happened. Performers base their performances on these texts, taking them in, learning them, and modifying them, making the performance a theatrical event (p. 173). A distinction is maintained between the original source, or text, and the performance, the real and its fictional representation. An example would be Dana Carvey, formerly of the TV show *Saturday Night Live*, imitating former President Bush (see Stucky, 1993, p. 174).

Paget (1993) clarifies this distinction between the real text from the performed text by referring back to her play, "The Work of Talk." The real text, the written version of the performed text, was "a version of a series of conversations/encounters/exchanges on the problems of a woman seeking medical care. The 'real' text was the text from life. . . . The performed text was another version of the text" (p. 32), but in the performed text Paget was no longer the narrator of her story. Paget's real text was moved directly to the stage, it was a "a piece of science on stage" (p. 25); hence the use of words like discourse, microparadigm, and speaking practices (p. 25). The play had seven characters: the narrator, the doctor, the patient, and a panel of four experts (p. 25). The doctor and the patient enacted the dialogue taken from her transcribed interviews.

Finally, an excerpt from Mienczakowski and Morgan's (1993) "Busting: The Challenge of the Drought Spirit," a two-act, 10-scene play with 18 characters is discussed. Part of a larger project, the play is set in a detoxification unit and is intended to present "audiences with validated experiential ideas in regard to alcohol and drug use and abuse" (Mienczakowski & Morgan, 1993, p. 1). After each performance, audience members are invited to critically reflect on the play and to inspect their understandings of the issues involved. The dialogue in the script is based on verbatim interview transcriptions, and the characters are composite figures—symbolic persons drawn from the field setting. The text is dramatically performed by nursing and theater students who take a Stanislavskian (method acting) approach to their performances, including being paired with staff members who acted as their mentors (Mienczakowski, 1995). The play opens this way:

> A teenage girl, Maria, lit by a solitary spot light, stands center stage. She has a half bottle of bourbon in her hand. . . . the cyclorama (a curved background on the stage set) is suddenly littered with several slide images of the girl. . . . Gradually the slides change to Maria in a variety of 'street drinking' situations.

The play quickly moves to an exchange between Maria and two nurses:

> **Nurse 1:** Can you tell me your name?
> **Maria:** Maria.
> **Nurse 1:** How old were you when you began drinking?
> **Nurse 2:** When did drinking first become a problem for you?

Mienczakowski (1995) calls this ethnodrama, turning ethnographic narratives into a dramatized form. Ethnodrama methodology, based on interviews and participant observation, attempts to create texts with a high degree of verisimilitude; that is, texts that are plausible and realistic, containing validated accounts that evoke commonly understood perceptions and beliefs about the phenomenon in question (p. 6). A complex interpretive process occurs wherein informants, audience members, and health care professionals engage the drama and its performance in a reflective discourse, struggling to create and share meaning, coming to agreement on the authentic nature of the language in the text.

This form of writing and performance brings a new, public voice to science, placing it in the hands of consumers who validate its authenticity as well as its potential for practical, political, therapeutic, and pedagogical purposes. Ethnodramas are written, then, for public consumption and are often distributed to audiences prior to performances (Mienczakowski, 1995, p. 9).

Reading Performance Science and Ethnodrama Texts

These several examples of the performance science, ethnodrama text open the spaces where I want to go. To repeat, I seek a critical postmodern, performance aesthetic for a performative cultural studies. This aesthetic will work against the realist impulse that organizes the logic of the natural performance text, an impulse not unlike the one that can be found in *America's Funniest Home Videos* and *Court Television* (Stucky, 1993, p. 177). This impulse valorizes real, lived experience, ordinary life, arguing that the recent emphasis on performance in anthropology (Turner, 1986b) requires serious consideration of "the ways people perform their everyday lives" (Stucky, 1993, p. 177). The reproduction of realist texts, however, often fails to untangle and expose the very structures that make any situated version of reality a historical fiction.

Trinh's (1991, p. 39) criticisms (Chapter 5) of the documentary film style are discussed. Like documentary film, natural science performance texts seek to re-create the circumstances and authentic experiences of real people in real-life situations. Natural science texts invoke real time and its passage. They attempt to capture objective reality, to dramatize the truth, and to always maintain a naturalistic connection between the moving image and the spoken word. They relentlessly remind the spectator that actual facts are being presented in a truthful way, and that the words spoken and heard here are ones spoken by common, ordinary people.

Thus, despite their many virtues, natural performance texts remain dangerously close to those forms of ethnography that dominated ethnography in its golden age, that moment when the ethnographer remained committed to coming back from the field with an authorized telling of what had been found.[17] Authentic tales, with high verisimilitude, reproduce the pull of realism and run the risk of not criticizing what they reproduce. They remain confined within the spaces of a modernist aesthetic and a postpositivist (at best) epistemology. There is, accordingly, a tension between representational and presentational theater (Donmoyer & Yennie-Donmoyer, 1995). The field is caught between those who produce ethnographic performances that report on and reproduce reality on stage and those who critique reality and its representations. Preoccupations with the syntax of the text, recordings, transcriptions, analysis, and rehearsals, and the structure of the printed text and its directions to the reader, reveal an unwillingness to fully enter the improvisational spaces created by postmodern, performance studies.

These texts do not always contest the body as a site of resistance. They thereby fail to make problematic how identity, gender, race, and sexual preference are socially constructed on the postmodern cultural terrain. By emphasizing the recovery of lived experience, these works falter at that moment when they could interrogate those cultural apparatuses that valorize specularity and simulated, hyperreal reproductions of the real. This means that they do not exploit the insights of the standpoint epistemologies, especially the arguments of Collins and Trinh that explore the facades of realism and examine the truth of fictional texts. With the exception of the work of Richardson and Mienczakowski, there are few attempts to explore a form of theater that moves an audience to critical, reflective action. Finally, there is a tendency either to remain within the confines of a traditional readers theater model or to produce solo, dramatized, text-centered readings. These readings entangle the performance with its text. In their celebration of performance, readers may fail to critique the autoethnographic text being performed.

Although performance science and ethnodrama texts dramatize field notes and destablize the teller's place in the story that is told, they do not take the next step, which is entry into that space where full improvisation, audience coparticipation, and cultural critique operate. It is this space that I explore next. I return to the mystory and the study and performance of those cultural moments that leave indelible marks on people, their bodies, and their biographies. Aesthetics and epistemology will be discussed first.

Mystory Text and Its Performance

A critical, performative cultural studies attempts to put in place subversive performance texts that carry forward Trinh's agenda for the retelling of stories that the sciences of the human disciplines have reduced to fiction and minor literature or have marginalized, stigmatized, and paternalized as politically correct multicultural performances. These works, as discussed in Chapter 5 and the Preface, interrogate the realities they represent, locate the teller's story in the history that is presented, make the audience responsible for their own interpretations, foreground difference and not conflict, oppose dichotomies, and use multiple voices in their tellings. These texts resist the temptation to turn actors into objects of the voyeuristic gaze, destablizing common methods of establishing verisimilitude. Performance texts are messy productions, and they presume an evocative epistemology that performs rather than represents the world (see Introduction).

These texts invoke and then criticize standard social science methods of research, including doing parodies of the interview as a tool for gathering objective data about the world of the other. The scientific article as a vehicle for presenting knowledge about the world is also mocked, and the objective ethnographer is criticized for his or her so-called objective methods of truth seeking. Following Trinh, there is an attempt to create a distance between the written and the performed text. Critiques of the notion of any kind of unified subject are offered. These works open a space for the audience as coperformers to constantly create new understandings of the experiences being described and interpreted.

Writers and performers attempt to avoid Trinh's Lady Painter and Quiller-Couch syndromes, neither scribbling masculine texts nor overindulging the personal, confessional style of presentation. A form of writing and performing that opens new ways of presenting the plural self in its multiple situations is sought. The goal is to create texts that produce a sudden awakening on the part of the viewer, who as audience member is also a performer. This means that the performed text will be ever changing. It will constantly work against those textual strategies (verbatim transcriptions, etc.) that would allow readers and listeners to assimilate the performance as a realist text. These are the aesthetic and epistemological features that partially define a postmodern performance sublime.

Mystory as Montage

The mystory is simultaneously a personal mythology, a public story, and a performance that critiques. It is an interactive, dramatic performance. It is a variation on readers theater, a participatory theater of the mind, a version of one of Brecht's learning plays (Ulmer, 1989, p. 210), and a presentational, not representational theater (Donmoyer & Yennie-Donmoyer, 1995). A mystory performance has parallels with a staged reading. These, however, are performance, not text-centered interpretive events. The emphasis is on performance, presentation, and improvisation and not just a reading of the fixed text.

The mystory is a montage text, cinematic and multimedia in shape, filled with sounds, music, and images taken from the writer's personal history. This personal text (script) is grafted into discourses from popular culture and locates itself against the specialized knowledges that circulate in the larger society. The audience coperforms the text, and the writer, as narrator, functions as a guide—a commentator on what is occurring.

The mystory performance event is improvised; each member of the audience brings his or her biography and voice to the lines that are read and spoken. A stage, per se, is not used; the wall between performers and audience disappears because all parties to the performance are also performers. The script is fashioned from the imagined and put into action words, words that were or could have been and will be spoken here. The script brings this world and its ethnodramas alive (Rose, 1995), reports on it, in some fashion, and then criticizes the structures of power that operate therein. It delineates specific characters and these characters are caught up in dramatic conflict, which moves to some degree of resolution at the end of the script. Simplistic characterizations based on traditional oppositions (male-female, etc.), however, are avoided; difference, not conflict, is privileged (Trinh, 1991, p. 188). There can be as many characters as there are readers available to do readings. The same reader can read the parts of the same and different characters. Every performance is different—different readers, different lines, and different meanings and interpretations; in every instance, however, a story is told and performed.

Of course, the mystory text is not easily constructed. It involves the hard interpretive work of editing personal, biographical reality (Jackson, 1993, p. 26; McCall & Becker, 1990, p. 118). Editing biographical reality produces a dramatic reinterpretation of what has been felt and lived by the person—moments of crisis and pain. What will be edited is determined by what has been remembered, collected, and written down: notes to the self, the "Rashomon" effect turned inside out. From the several layers and versions of the biographical field text, the writer aims to tell a story with some degree of dramatic power. Editing, or crafting, the text will involve many decisions. These include what words to put in the mouths of which characters, who the characters will be, and how many readers there will be. This story may well tell itself—for example, Steve's death in Chapter 2. The focus is always on showing, not telling. Minimal interpretation is favored.

The mystory text begins with those moments that define the crisis in question—a turning point in the person's life. Ulmer (1989, pp. xii, 139) suggests the following starting point:

> Write a mystory bringing into relation your experience with three levels of discourse—personal (autobiography), popular (community stories, oral history or popular culture), [and] expert (disciplines of knowledge). In each case use the punctum or sting of memory to locate items significant to you. (p. 209)

The sting of memory locates the moment, the beginning; once located, this moment is dramatically described and fashioned into a text to be performed. This moment is then surrounded by those cultural representations and voices that define the experience in question.

The following is an excerpt from a poetic mystory play (Sanmiguel, 1995) titled "Re-Defining Endometriosis/Re-Defining Me." The play has parts for Dad, Lisa, family-society, the voices of physicians, medicine, psychiatry, self-help, first love, lasting love, Mom, Grandma, and the popular media. The text is meant to be read, not staged, and has been performed several times by and to classes of communication graduate students at the University of Illinois.

Dad: My daughter doesn't worry about boys and all that shit.

Lisa: She was supposed to be a boy. That's what her daddy always said. . . . Her Aunt said, 'You're a woman now.' A woman at age 10?

Family-Society: It's just a woman's lot. . . . It's just a female thing.

Physicians: So what have you been up to? Good girls don't come to see me this young. Who've you been having sex with?

Lisa: I'm a good girl. . . . I haven't even kissed a boy!

Physicians: They all say that.

Mom: When a doctor finally did exploratory surgery and told us she had endometriosis, I was so relieved and happy to know what was wrong.

Medicine: Endometriosis is . . . the presence of endometrial glands and stroma outside the endometrial cavity.

Lisa: Endometriosis is defined as the thief that stole my life.

The play continues. Sanmiguel has psychiatrists, self-help groups, first loves, and members of her family comment on her condition. The play ends with the following lines:

Lisa: A new definition for endometriosis: A condition that empowers as it strengthens character and makes one re-evaluate the gendered self as constructed by society. Individual solutions become collective action. No more victims of categorization. No more labels. No more good girls.

Family-Society: She's never been like the other girls.

This text, when performed, powerfully and critically moves the audience into the position of cocreating a female subject defined as having endometriosis. The text unsettles and criticizes medicine, psychiatry, and those popular culture texts that urge women to accept this condition as their fate.

Sanmiguel's play gives the audience lines to perform, and an alternative textual form allows the audience to create its own response to a prior text. Allan Northcott's (1995) "New Woman" is a song written as a critical and participatory performance text about women's magazines and their discourses. The audience is asked to compare the lines of this song to the words found in *Playboy* or *Penthouse:*[18]

The magazines at the check-out stand made a
thousand things go running thru my head
the cover the cover girl was as cute as can be

Lye Lovett can do it so why not me.
So take your Glamour and your Vanity Fair
take your silicone parts and your perfect hair
pack your magazines and say good-bye
you're Cosmo baby but you're not my style.

On hearing the song performed by Northcott and Martin Srajek, with a moderate blues shuffle in the key of G, audience members were asked to write their own lines for the song. Individuals responded to "New Woman" with the following sample verses:

What to tell your psychiatrist
15 days to sexual bliss
natural perfumes and aphrodisiacs
silk dresses to enhance your bare back
A New Man is who I'd like to be
Sensitive, aware and fancy-free
So me and my New-Age spiritual pals
Could make it with all those feminist gals.

These verses were then incorporated into the original song, which became a new song when it was performed again. Thus, the audience as coparticipants and co-songwriters created their version of the new woman.

Finally, a natural performance text assembled out of multiple posts from the Internet is discussed; in this case, the text is from a newsgroup for persons with eating disorders (Walstrom, 1996). The performance text is guided by the author's personal experience with an eating disorder and a desire to use this experience of her "self" to analyze and critique the limits of social understandings of those disorders (Foucault, 1984; Rabinow, 1984). The researcher fills the performance text with excerpts from postings to the newsgroup along with experiences stemming from her own experience of anorexia. This juxtapostion of the newsgroup excerpts and the researcher's mystories (Ulmer, 1989) aims to offer "shocks of recognition" (Probyn, 1993) of the experience of eating disorders to the audience members. The performance begins with audience members' reading of introductions as women post for the first time on the newsgroup:

I hope it is okay that I have come here. One thing that many of us have in common is that to a greater or lesser extent our bodies, how we deal with them, and how we feed them are the expression of how we feel in relation to the world. . . . Thanks, and I wish you all peace and healing.

An introduction of the author to the newsgroup is read by the author as well. The following are text fragments given to audience members to be read:

One: I always hate my body. It never looks good enough to me. I don't think it ever will.

Two: I think if I could stop hating my body, it would be a good step.

Three: Can you ever get over hating your body? I look at pictures of models, and wish I looked like them. I remember a lot of people commenting on how horrible Kate Moss looked. Part of me agreed, but another part would whisper "Why can't I look like that?"

The performed electronic text restores a voice and new embodied emotion to the silent screen. This text offers a view of women who are struggling to find a mystory that will help them make sense of the new troubling situations they find themselves in. These writers conceivably react to the new woman described in Northcott's song and could add their lines to his, just as their words could exist alongside those written by Sanmiguel.

The previous three performance texts take up Birringer's (1993, pp. xi-xii) challenge to accommodate and integrate the impact of women's experiences into a postmodern, performance cultural studies.[19] The texts work back and forth between private troubles and public discourse, trouble the body and its meanings, and take the truth of fiction as a starting point for social criticism.

Ethics for a Performative Cultural Studies

Every time a text is performed, a performance ethics is enacted. Performers, as Stucky (1993, p. 176) argues, need to take responsibility for their interpretations of another's life experiences. These interpretations will be shaped by a variety of factors, including who the audience is, rehearsal histories, what is selected to be performed, whose point of view is represented, what is revealed about the other in the performance, and the ranges of actions that are attributed to another individual (pp. 176-177).

In each of these texts, there remains a tension between the writers' and the performers' identity and their ability to recognize and understand the differences that define another person's world. In every instance, the researcher must ask and answer the question raised by Prattis (1985b, p. 277): "Just what are we doing in other people's culture?" This question (and its answer) are doubly problematic in performance work. As Conquergood (1985a, p. 2) observes, the performer is unable to maintain aesthetic distance from the experiences being performed and interpreted. Empathetic performances intensify the participatory nature of fieldwork. They challenge attempts to create intellectual or epistemological barriers that would separate the writer from those studied (Conquergood, 1985a, p. 2). Performances do not "proceed in ideological innocence and axiological purity (Conquergood, 1985a, p. 2).

Performers must avoid four ethical pitfalls, morally problematic stances toward the representation of the other's experiences (Conquergood, 1985a, p. 4). Conquergood (p. 4) gives the following labels to these four pitfalls: "The Custodian's Rip-Off," "The Enthusiast's Infatuation," "The Curator's Exhibitionism," and "The Skeptic's Cop-Out." Cultural custodians, or cultural imperialists, enter the field looking for good texts to perform and then perform them for a fee, often denigrating the cultural group that regards its texts as sacred.[20] The enthusiast, or superficial stance, occurs when the writer (and the performer) fail to become deeply involved in the cultural setting that they reperform. Conquergood (p. 6) says this trivializes the other. The skeptic, or cynic, values detachment and cultural differences, taking the position, for example, that "only blacks can understand and perform black literature [and] only white males [can perform] John Cheever's short stories" (p. 8). This position refuses to to face up to the "ethical tensions and moral ambiguities of performing culturally sensitive materials" (p. 8). Finally, the curator, or sensationalist, is a performer who sensationalizes the cultural differences that supposedly define the world of the other. He or she stages performances for the tourist's gaze. This is "the Wild Kingdom approach to performance that grows out of a fascination with the exotic, primitive, culturally remote. . . . the Noble Savage" (p. 7).

These four stances make problematic the following questions: How far into the other's world can the performer and the audience go? Can the differences that define the other's world be respected? Is their a null point in the moral universe? (Conquergood, 1985a, pp. 8-9). Does the other, however, always exist, as Trinh would argue, in the spaces on each side of the hyphen (p. 9)? If so, the performance text can only ever be dialogic—a text that does not speak about or for the other but that "speaks to and with them" (p. 10). The dialogic text attempts to keep the dialogue, the conversation, between text, performer, and audience ongoing and open-ended (p. 9). This text does more than invoke empathy: It interrogates, criticizes, and empowers. This is dialogical criticism. The dialogical performance is the means for "honest intercultural understanding" (p. 10).

If this understanding is to be created, the following elements need to be present. Scholars must have the energy, imagination, courage, and commitment to create these texts (see Conquergood, 1985a, p. 10). Audiences must be drawn to the sites at which these performances take place, and they must be willing to suspend normal aesthetic frameworks so that coparticipatory performances can be produced. At these sites, a shared field of emotional experience is created, and in these moments of sharing, critical, cultural awareness is awakened.

The coperformed cultural studies text aims to enact the feminist, communitarian moral ethic discussed in the Preface. As discussed in the Preface, this ethic presumes a dialogical view of the self and its performances. It seeks narratives that ennoble human experience and performances that facilitate civic transformations in the public and private spheres. This ethic ratifies the dignities of the self and honors personal struggle. It understands cultural criticism to be a form of empowerment, arguing that empowerment begins in that ethical moment when individuals are lead into the troubling spaces occupied by others. In the moment of coperformance, lives are joined and struggle beings anew.

Conclusions

Of course there are more ways to do a text then to just read it to an audience. The text can be performed—for example, the writer reads a poem. The written text can be supplemented by other devices. The author can use pictures, slides, photographs, show a film, use audiovisual aides, bring in music and a sound track, lip sync words set to a musical text, or create a scholarly version of a Merle Haggard MTV text. The author can even bring the audience into the performance, do a sing-along, hand out a script, give audience members speaking parts, or make a communal performance out of the scholarly text. Within the performance, the author can assume multiple places and be the ethnographer, the subject in the field, the audience member, or a representative from a scholarly community who asks, "What is going on here?"

This chapter has attempted to answer this question. What is going here is something new; ethnography has crossed that liminal space that separates the scholarly text from its performance. The text is now given back to those to whom it has always belonged—the reader, the other, who finds in these texts parts of themselves and parts of others just like them. We are all coperformers in our own and others' lives. This is what the performance text does. A fear lingers, however. Ethnographers of performance must produce texts that are accessible and performable. If they cannot do this, to paraphrase Conquergood (1985a, p. 11), the "performance movement in cultural studies will die."

Notes

1. A performance and conception of oral literature (and folklore), with an emphasis on the performance event (the telling of a story or myth) is also an important part of this tradition (see Bauman 1986, p. 3; Tedlock, 1983, pp. 3-6).

2. Turner's (1986b, pp. 34-35) liminal experience is always part of a larger, processually structured social drama. They are bracketed by public action on both sides, beginning with a breach of an everyday code of conduct, moving to a crisis (in which the liminal experience occurs), with people taking sides, applying redressive or remedial pressures on the person, culminating in the social reintegration or exclusion of the person from the social group. (See Note 6 and Introduction for a discussion of the four main types

of epiphanies and Stern & Henderson, 1993, pp. 45-46, for the connection between personal narratives and liminal moments of experience).

3. Recall the discussion in the Preface on the long history of performance texts (poetry and short story readings) within anthropology.

4. A confusion in such response is often termed the affective fallacy (Bacon, 1979, p. 196), being taken in by the performance, neglecting to critique the text on which the performance is based. Of course, this relationship is always dialectical (see Tedlock, 1983, p. 236).

5. There are at least five texts embedded in every performed text: notes from the field, research texts, and interpretive documents (memos), which become public texts (drafts of articles). These public texts are then transformed into a performance text. Then, fifth, there is the performance, the mis-en-scène itself (Paget, 1993, p. 27), the live event. Behind all of this stands the dramatic field experience, which the performance aims to re-create or relate back to in an evocative fashion. These textual forms stand in a complex relationship to one another.

6. These two terms refer to the ways in which the text uses everyday and scientific language as well as how it articulates that language for the printed, as opposed to the performed, text (see Becker et al., 1989). In the following section, I omit a discussion of staged readings and the performance of preexisting dramatic texts. They appear to have less relevance for performance ethnography at this stage of its development.

7. Conquergood's work is located on the boundaries between speech communications, communication and performance studies, and urban ethnography. See also his two documentary films (Conquergood, 1985b, 1990).

8. Of course, there is a large literature on performance texts, especially in the field of speech communication, in which the oral and performance interpretation of classic, folk, and native literatures has a long history (see Hamera, 1986; Strine, 1988). The interpretive move in anthropology opened the way for these practioners to take an ethnographic turn, producing texts that could then be performed (see Conquergood, 1985a, 1986, 1991, 1992). This led to interactions with Bakhtin, Geertz, Victor Turner, poststructuralism, the Frankfurt school, feminism, postmodernism, language poetry, and performance art (see Bowman, 1988; Capo, 1988; Conquergood, 1992; Hamera, 1986; Pace, 1987; Park-Fuller, 1986; Pollock, 1988; Strine, 1988; Tallant, 1988; for a synthesis of these movements in this field, see Stern & Henderson, 1993).

9. A case in point is Richardson (1993, p. 699), who skipped a line when she read a poem that was based on a transcribed interview. Audience members charged her with changing the poem's meaning, violating the original text, and endangering its reliability and validity. Some said her findings were no longer accurate. One audience member even asked if it was all fiction: "Did you actually do an interview?" (p. 700).

10. The rise of performance art corresponds to the politicization of art and culture associated with the Vietnam War and Watergate as well as with the women's movement (Sayre, 1990, p. 98). It would be co-opted in the 1980s with the New Wave movement (see Birringer, 1993, p. 173).

11. Stern and Henderson (1993, pp. 382-383, 546) define performance art as a hybrid, improvisatory, antiestablishment, multimedia, interventionist, open-ended form of performance that is opposed to the commodification of art. Performance art uses the principles of juxtaposition, incongruence, simultaneity, collage, and assemblage, "drawing for its materials not only upon the live bodies of the performers but upon media images, television monitors, projected images, visual images, film, poetry, autobiographical material, narrative, dance, architecture, and music" (pp. 382-383). A number of

contemporary performance artists (Holly Hughes, Karen Finley, Tim Miller, and John Fleck) have come into conflict with the National Endowment for the Arts. Their work (as well as that of Robert Mapplethorpe and Andres Serrano) has been judged to be offensive to the public taste, "read *homoerotic*" (p. 433).

12. The concept of a group (ensemble) of performers who performed the same dramatic work over and over again was also challenged ("traditional" theater). Peoples' theater also emerged in which (in some versions) members of the local community, previously denied power, including the elderly, ethnic minorities, women, the handicapped, and the imprisoned (Capo, 1983, p. 34), become performers of their own stories of oppression (see also Bacon, 1979; Boal, 1979/1985, 1995; Liggett, 1970; Pickering, 1975).

13. They called this "editing reality" (McCall & Becker, 1990, pp. 117-118), contending that the script method created spaces for the inclusion of large chunks of verbatim quotes while letting many different voices be heard.

14. They offer a series of rules: If the performance is to be documented, then stage directions should be included in the published script; if not, they can be left out. If the script is formatted for publication, when sociologists speak they can be treated like a theater chorus, giving the audience interpretations of what is going on. When members of the audience speak, their speeches are indented and their characters are given names. When the sociologist speaks to other characters, the dialogue format is used, and the names of real people are not used in the script (Becker et al., 1989, p. 86).

15. Hilbert (1990, p. 134) argued that McCall and Becker had not given sufficient reasons to support their new form of reporting social science data. He suggested that that there is no inherent advantage in presenting large chunks of verbatim quotations and wondered what happened to the sociologist's goal of analyzing ethnographic materials, fearing that McCall and Becker leave the analyst with no guidelines for what to do with their scripts and performances.

16. Stucky (1993, p. 178) argues that the staging of natural performances involves five steps: recording, transcribing, analyzing, rehearsing, and performing.

17. Mienczakowski's project is less subject to these criticisms.

18. The song's title "refers not only to a magazine but also to a feminine ideal from the 1920s that glamorized women by making them equal in position to men" (Northcott, 1995, p. 3).

19. Limitations of space prohibit the presentation and discussion of another coperformance text that uses quilting and the arrangement of fabric squares with text fragments that are held and spoken by audience members (see Page, 1995).

20. Conquergood (1985a, p. 5) cites a cultural preservation group that performed (over the objections of Hopi elders) the sacred Hopi Snake Dance and sold trinkets for $7.50, all in the name of preserving a dying culture.

CHAPTER **5**

The New Journalism

There is no longer any such thing as fiction or nonfiction, there is only narrative.

—E. L. Doctorow (as quoted in Fishkin, 1985, p. 207)

None of this was made up.

—John Hersey (1980, p. 2)

Reality is not what it is. It consists of the many realities which it can be made into.

—Wallace Stevens (as quoted in John Updike, 1995, p. 21)

My topics are facts, fictions, and the New (and old) Journalism (Frus, 1994; Wolfe, 1973), the nonfiction novel (Zavarzadeh, 1976), the new and old ethnography (Webster, 1982), the facts of fiction, fictionalized facts, and the narrative turn in the human disciplines (Bochner, 1994; Maines, 1993), and what this turn means for writing ethnography in the sixth moment.[1] My argument moves in two directions at the same time.

Experimental ethnographic writing,[2] the doing of poems, stories, plays, and performances, requires that the ethnographic project simultaneously question and establish the credibility of its use of facts and fictions in the stories that are told and performed (see Marcus & Fischer, 1986, pp. 40, 76, 183-184).

Ethnographers have much to learn from journalists in this regard because it is in the field of journalism that the arguments over factually accurate literary and nonliterary texts have been most hotly debated (see Carey, 1986; Christians, Ferre, & Fackler, 1993, pp. 32-58, 113-122; Condit & Selzer, 1985; Glasser & Ettema, 1989; Reese, 1990; Wolfe, 1973; Zelizer, 1992, pp. 8-9, 19-20, 1993).[3] I will, accordingly, discuss the history of the New Journalism (Eason, 1984; Fishkin, 1985; Frus, 1994; Hollowell, 1977; Pauly, 1990; Sims, 1984, 1990; Wolfe, 1973)[4] while examining select celebrated journalistic cases in which the accuracy of the journalist's text has been challenged (see Christians et al., 1993; Eason, 1986; Fishkin, 1985, pp. 209-217).

I have no desire to reproduce arguments that maintain distinctions between fictional (literary) and nonfictional (journalism and ethnography) texts (Frus, 1994, p. xi; see also Zavarzadeh, 1976, pp. 50-67).[5] Such efforts inevitably resort to canon pointing and the use of essentializing categories.[6] With Frus (1994, p. xi), I oppose all hierarchical categories including those that distinguish literary and nonliterary and fictional and nonfictional textual forms. These categories, which are socially and politically constructed, work against the creation of an expansive, complex public discourse wherein multiple narrative forms circulate and inform one another (see Frus, 1994, p. xi; see also Ellis, 1995a, p. 317). If all is narrative, then it can be argued that narrative techniques are neither fictional or factual; they are merely formal "methods used in making sense of all kinds of situations" (Eason, 1982, p. 143). Invoking and paraphrasing Tyler (1986, p. 123), the discourses of the postmodern world involve the constant comingling of literary, journalistic, fictional, factual, and ethnographic writing.[7] No form is privileged over another. Truth is socially established by the norms that operate for each form or genre.[8]

As ethnographers engage experimental writing forms, a parallel movement has occurred—namely, the full-scale embracement of methods of narrative analysis (for reviews, see Feldman, 1995; Manning & Cullum-Swan, 1994; Polkinghorne, 1988; Reisman, 1993). This move by the social sciences has produced an embarrassment of riches. Multiple strategies for analyzing narrative texts now exist, including semiotic, rhetorical, topological, structural, feminist, content-based, microlevel,

dramaturgical, thematic, and functional-based models of interpretation. Of course, these strategies falter at the moment (analyzed in
Chapter 2) when the recorded or analyzed text is taken to be an accurate
(visual) representation of the worlds and voices studied.

These models are pivotal because they authorize the turn to narrative, offering methods that ensure the truth and accuracy of a text and
its interpretation (see Trinh, 1989, pp. 142-143). Unlike the "traditional"
journalistic text, whose factual accuracy and meaning is presumably
self-evident and guaranteed in advance, the social science narrative text
requires serious, interpretive analysis. This analysis often divides the
text into structural units or reads it in terms of various narrative functions. The story is thereby lost. These methods of interpretation will be
reviewed and assessed in Chapter 8.

The previously discussed issues frame the story I tell in this chapter
and the next: another chapter in the story about the narrative turn in the
human disciplines (Bochner, 1994; Maines, 1993)—the story about facts,
fictions, and how fictions become facts. I ask, how do we read storytelling in ethnography's sixth moment?[9] I begin with the facts of fiction.

From Fact to Fiction

In his epilogue to *From Fact to Fiction: Journalism and Imaginative
Writing in America,* Fishkin (1985, p. 207) observes that "during the last
two decades the line between fact and fiction has grown more and more
blurred." A decade later, Mitchell and Charmaz (1995) argue that "ethnographers and fiction writers rely on similar writing practices to tell
their tales" (p. 1). William Foote Whyte, referring to an earlier age when
these distinctions were not blurred, notes, in the fourth edition to *Street
Corner Society* (Whyte, 1993, pp. 366, 371), that

> When I began my *SCS* research [1936], I wanted to contribute to
> building a science of society.... I based my own framework on a basic
> distinction between the objective (what is out there to be observed),
> and the subjective (how the observer or others interpret the observed
> phenomena). . . . [If social realism is but one narrative strategy for
> telling stories] then the critic can only depend on the persuasive power

of the author. Scientific arguments are thus transformed into literary criticism. (p. 371)[10]

For Whyte, there is a clear difference between fact and fiction. The differences are not to be minimized because, when they are, we are left with only rhetoric. This argument, of course, ignores the fact that science writing is a form of rhetorical persuasion (Agger, 1989; Brown, 1989).

Fact and fiction have not always been so confused. Fishkin (1985, p. 207) argues that from the middle of the nineteenth century to the 1920s the journalist and the imaginative writer were held to different standards. Journalists worked with verifiable facts, and readers could expect stories to be factually accurate. Imaginative writers, novelists, told truths that were not necessarily factually accurate, but they ad- hered to aesthetic standards of good storytelling. Ethnography enters this same terrain, and ethnographers like William Foote Whyte learned how to objectively report the facts of the social situations they studied. Like good journalism, good ethnography reported the facts of life to a scientific and, at times, public community.

Robert E. Park, a founder of the Chicago School of Ethnographic Research (Vidich & Lyman, 1994, pp. 32-33), clarifies this relationship between journalism and social science writing (Park, 1950):

> After leaving college, I got a job as a reporter. . . . I wrote about all sorts of things. . . . My interest in the newspaper had grown out of the discovery that a reporter who had the facts was a more effective reformer than an editorial writer. . . . According to my earliest concep- tion of a sociologist he was to be a kind of super-reporter. . . . He was to report a little more accurately, and in a little more detail. (pp. v, vii-ix)

Thus, the duties and practices of sociologists and journalists were separated.

All this held steady from the 1920s through the 1960s. There were three different professional groups (journalists, novelists, and social science ethnographers), each producing different but often parallel tellings about society. Then the lines between journalism, imaginative writing, and ethnography began to blur again (see Connery, 1992; Eason, 1984; Frus, 1994; Sims, 1984, 1990; Wolfe, 1973). Impatient with the rigid conventions of objective journalism, the new journalists "started to borrow technical devices from the novel . . . [and] novelists . . . began to borrow research methods and subjects from journalism" (Fishkin, 1985, p. 207).

Truman Capote would boldly insist, for example, that with *In Cold Blood* he had invented a new literary genre, what he called "the nonfiction novel" (as quoted in Wolfe, 1973, p. 37).[11] Thus did Tom Wolfe and Joan Didion join the terrain now shared by Truman Capote and Norman Mailer. The *Armies of the Night* (Mailer, 1966), *The Executioners Song* (Mailer, 1979), and *In Cold Blood* (Capote, 1966) emerged as imaginative, journalistic accounts, not unlike the journalistic fictions of Wolfe and Didion. By 1980, the novelist Doctorow (as quoted in Fishkin, 1985, p. 207) would speak the lines quoted previously: "There is no longer any such things as fiction or nonfiction, there is only narrative."

By the mid-1970s, this situation had solidified. Tom Wolfe (1973) codified the epistemology of the new journalists and offered a rich sampling of works by representative writers (Gay Talese, Richard Goldstein, Michael Herr, Truman Capote, Hunter S. Thompson, Norman Mailer, John Gregory Dunn, and Joan Didion). In 1976, Zavarzadeh introduced the term nonfiction novel or true life novel to describe the works of Capote, Mailer, and Oscar Lewis. He suggested that there were three generic (exegetical, testimonial, and notational) nonfiction writing forms. David Eason (1981, 1982, 1984) would soon offer paradigmatic readings of the new journalists and the nonfiction novelists, dividing them into two camps—the ethnographic realists (Wolfe and Capote) and the cultural phenomenologists (Mailer and Didion).

This situation held steady until a series of journalistic scandals (see below) rocked the nation's leading newspapers in the 1980s, leading to serious challenges to the so-called New Journalism (Agar, 1990; Christians, Ferre, & Fackler, 1993, p. 118; Eason, 1984, 1986; Van Maanen, 1988, pp. 131-136). At the same time, more and more social scientists were turning to imaginative forms of ethnographic reporting, including poems, short stories, and nonfictional novels (see Marcus & Fischer, 1986, pp. 73-76; Richardson, 1994). Like the attacks against the journalists in the 1980s, a new generation of critics is charging that the new ethnography produces fiction, not scientific truth (see Agar, 1990; Fine,

1993; Kunda, 1993; Lofland, 1995, pp. 48, 63; Snow & Morrill, 1993, 1995a; Whyte, 1993, p. 371).

I now turn to the new journalists and the nonfiction novelists, with the understanding that these two terms refer to the same group of writers. The new journalists and nonfiction novelists are all using narrative in new ways to say new things about people in society. I will then discuss the criticisms brought to this work.

Nonfiction Texts and the New Journalists

Seven understandings shaped this new work. The new writers treated facts as social constructions; blurred writing genres, combining literary and investigative journalism with the realist novel, the confession, the travel report, and the autobiography[12] (Hollowell, 1977, p. 15); used the scenic method to show rather than tell (Agar, 1990, p. 77; Wolfe, 1973, p. 50); wrote about real people and created composite characters[13] (Hollowell, 1977, p. 30); used multiple points of view to establish authorial presence; deployed multiple narrative strategies (flashbacks, foreshadowing, interior monologues, and parallel plots) to build dramatic tension (Agar, 1990, p. 78); and positioned themselves as moral witnesses to the radical changes occurring in American society (Hollowell, 1977, p. 13).

These identifying features of the new writing also define the points of criticism that would be brought to this blurred genre (see the following discussion; Agar, 1990; Hollowell, 1977, pp. 30-33, 44-45; Van Maanen, 1988).

The cinematic society was the point of departure for all these writers.[14] Social life and the report about life were both understood to be social constructions (Eason, 1984, p. 61). Norman Mailer (1966), summarized by Eason (1984, p. 60), captured this position best, arguing that the technology of the media "disengages subjects from their own expressions. . . . Individuals become observers of their own acts. . . . As actions come to be negotiated in terms of a media aesthetic, both actor and spectator live a reality arbitrated by the assumptions of media technicians."

Facts were created by the media, shaped into narrative accounts of newsworthy happenings that could be inserted into predetermined news slots on the evening news or in the evening newspaper. These understandings challenged the epistemology of the totalizing, fictive novel and the objective news account (Zavarzadeh, 1976, p. 26).

Since its origins in the nineteenth century, informational, commercial journalism had operated under two imperatives (Eason, 1981, p. 128). A report should be a valid accounting of the events it describes, and the account should be written in a way that engages the audience. Such accounts were to be written in an objective fashion. The reporter was not a biographically specific person. He or she gathered and reported facts. The report would be written in a concrete fashion, answering to the who, what, when, where, why, and how of the events in question. The account would be emotionally neutral, given to understatement, and written in a straightforward syntax. Like documentary cinema, the narrator and the processes of textual production would be invisible. The production of the text was never at issue; the problem was to explain (and order) the facts at hand. The facts were visible events, taken as givens, objectively known and knowable by the scientific reporter. This unquestioning acceptance of the facts creates, as Dorothy Smith (as quoted in Frus, 1994, p. 113) notes, a situation in which "what ought to be explained is treated as fact or as assumption." In this model, facts are reified (Frus, 1994, p. 112). The validity of the text is self-evident: It is grounded in the objectively reported facts.

Validity thus became, as it was for positivistic social science, the key legitimating device that authorized the journalistic text's claims to truth. Thus conceptualized, validity operated as a marketing device. Newspapers sold to consuming publics valid accounts of newsworthy events. Readers, as an abstract yet concrete market category, could count on their newspapers to print not only all the news that is fit to print but only news that was truthful. The nonfiction writers and the new journalists questioned this equation. Empirical validity was a social construct, and there was no objective news reporting.

By focusing on the tension between the real and its hyperreal, larger than life media representations, nonfiction writers documented Hayden White's (1973) argument that the formal techniques of history and fiction are the same (Eason, 1982, p. 143). In both forms of writing, writers use narrative strategies (characterization, motif repetition, point of view, and different descriptive strategies) to bring coherence to their materials (Eason, 1982, p. 143). The nonfiction writer uses modernist and postmodern narrative strategies (see below) to make sense of real (and imagined) situations. The historian uses narrative to bring meaning to situations perceived to be real (Eason, 1982, p. 143). For both the historian and the fiction and nonfiction writer, facts become symbolic representations to be interpreted. Narrative techniques are interpretive practices that allow the writer to make sense of the world being described (Eason, 1982, p. 143). In this way, the nonfiction writers turned narrative on its head. They erased the distinction between fact and fiction. They produced true-life accounts of real events.

The New Writers

The basic unit of analysis for the new writers was not the fact; rather, they focused on the scene, the situation in which the event in question occurred or would happen (Wolfe, 1973, p. 50). The distinguishing feature of this work is not given by the use of empirical data because the naturalistic and realistic novel also use empirical materials. The new writers refuse to use facts to support a totalizing reading of reality. The nonfiction text "is written not *about* facts, but *in* facts" (Zavarzadeh, 1976, p. 219). These facts are treated as extensions of real life, which has been interpreted (or presented) by the writer. These writers used the methods of journalistic reporting and ethnographic participant observation to gather the facts and meanings of a particular situation or experience (see Mailer, 1979, pp. 1020-1021). They fashioned these details into stories and novels. Some called it reality fiction (Zavarzadeh, 1976, pp. 226-227).

The writer's task was clear: "to stay with whomever you are writing long enough for the scenes to take place before your own eyes" (Wolfe, 1973, p. 50). This point is critical; unlike the traditional journalist, who relies on other's reports of events, for the new journalist "It seemed all-important to *be there* when dramatic scenes took place" (p. 21). The writer attempted to enter a world of complete strangers, to "move in on their lives in some fashion, ask questions you have no natural right to expect answers to, ask to see things you weren't meant to see, and so on" (p. 50). Wolfe stated that the writer believes that

what he is doing is as a writer is as important as what anyone he is
writing about is doing. . . . If he doesn't believe that his own writing
is one of the most important activities going on in contemporary
civilization, then he ought to move on to something else. (p. 51)

The new writers found a writing model, at one level, in the realistic
novels of Balzac and Dickens who had offered detailed, moralistic
accounts of the key social issues of the day.[15] This narrative model was
exploited by the new writers who would write accurate nonfiction
"with techniques usually associated with novels and short stories"
(Wolfe, 1973, p. 15). They discovered that it was possible in nonfiction
and in journalism "to use any literary device, from the traditional
dialogisms of the essay to stream-of-consciousness, and to use many
different kinds simultaneously . . . to excite the reader intellectually and
emotionally" (p. 15). This form of writing allowed the reader to see and
feel ordinary people in unusual situations.

The new journalists attempted to give a full objective description
of the situation they were describing (Wolfe, 1973, p. 21). The novelists, however, wanted to probe and reveal the inner, subjective, emotional life of the characters they were writing about (p. 21). They
provided a depth of information "that had never been demanded in
newspaper work. Only through the most searching forms of reporting
was it possible in nonfiction, to use whole scenes, extended dialogue,
point-of-view, and interior monologue" (p. 21). A new typology of the
printed text was produced: the "lavish use of dots, dashes, exclamation
points, italics, and occasionally punctuation that never existed before
:::::::::: and of interjections, shouts, nonsense words . . . mimesis . . . the
continual use of the historical present and so on" (p. 21).

Four narrative devices, borrowed from the social realist novelists
(Balzac, Gogol, Dickens, and Fielding), were used. The most basic
device "was scene-by-scene construction, telling the story by moving
from scene to scene" (Wolfe, 1973, p. 31). The second device was the use
of extensive, realistic dialogue. Inserted into each scene, this dialogue
defined the key characters. The third device was the use of the third-
person point of view, presenting every scene through the eyes (and
voice) of a particular character (p. 32). This device allowed Wolfe and
others to transcend the problems of the first-person narrative style, a
style that did not allow the writer entry into the minds of others in the
situation (p. 32). They entered other people's minds by interviewing

them (p. 32). The fourth device focused on social manners. The new journalists, especially Wolfe, focused on "everyday gestures, habits, manners, customs, styles of furniture, clothing, decoration, styles of traveling, eating, keeping house . . . symbolic details that might exist in a scene" (p. 32).

Underlying this commitment to social status and its situational specifications rests a moral theory of the text. Wolfe is clear on this. The realist text records history and provides moral instruction (Wolfe, 1973, p. 38). Wolfe equates realism with electricity:

> The introduction of detailed realism into English literature in the eighteenth century was like the introduction of electricity into machine technology. It raised the state of the art to an entirely new magnitude. . . . Abandoning social realism would be like an engineer trying to improve upon machine technology by abandoning electricity. (p. xi)

On the basis of their careful attention to status details, Wolfe and the other new writers developed a theory of life in contemporary America. Fragmented American culture produces subcultures and enclaves (stock cars, Las Vegas, and radical chic). These social worlds have created their own authentic, bizarre lifestyles and status rituals. Generally ignored by American observers, these enclaves deserve careful study. They are the site of the "true" America, the places were we now live, and in them are displayed a basic cultural truth: "Human nature follows the same barbaric patterns regardless of class, region or circumstance" (Bellamy, 1982, p. xiii). The rapid fragmentation of America has produced status confusions, leading to the production of status dropouts and bewildering lifestyle formations (p. xiii).

The new writer chronicles these lifestyles, mocks them, pokes fun at them, and brings them alive, and in so doing suggests that we are not unlike those written about. Thus, history goes on behind people's backs as they continually struggle for social recognition and social domination over one another. By focusing on the symbolism of such events, the new writers attempt to probe and reveal a deeper level of cultural experience. At this deeper level, reality and text have become deeply entangled in one another: Life imitates art and art imitates life (Eason, 1984, p. 52).

Variations in Narrative Style:
The Nonfiction Novel

The new writers were not cut from a single cloth. Some wrote novels or ethnographic and journalistic texts of the exegetical, testimonial, and notational variety. A brief discussion of each of these forms of the nonfiction novel is required.

Paraphrasing Zavarzadeh (1976, p. 93), the exegetical nonfiction novel is an expositional narrative. It focuses on past public and private events, none of which were shaped by the author's presence or participation. This is a universe waiting to be interpreted. It is not fictional. It is not created by the writer; rather, he or she uses various narrative strategies to bring this experiential reality alive (p. 123). Often, the writer will present extensive documentation about the events in question, including news accounts, official documents and announcements, statistics, figures, and bulletins. Zavarzadeh (p. 98) wrote that these materials, supplemented by first-person narratives, individual portraits, general scenes, and discursive passages, form the core of a work's documentation. They provide "evidence that the events in the book are authentic, not figments of the author's imagination" (p. 98). For example, Truman Capote's (1966) *In Cold Blood* opens with a fictional account of the last day in the life of the Clutter family (November 14, 1959). This account is supplemented with actual details from the real lives of each of the family members. Later in the text, Capote turns to the lives of Perry Smith and Richard Hickock, the two murderers, quoting from family letters, Perry's own autobiographical sketch, a psychiatrist's evaluation, the names of hotels, and so on.

This mingling of discursive, factual passages with first-person narratives challenges the modernist aesthetic, which argues against turning life into art. In the nonfiction novel, such passages ground the work in another version of real life (Zavarzadeh, 1976, p. 101). In this fictional use of fact, the nonfiction writer exercises empirical omniscience (Zavarzadeh, 1976, p. 125); the narrative point of view is that of the author who knows everything (or as much as possible) about the subject in question. Thus, Capote (1966, p. 13; also quoted by Zavarzadeh, 1976, p. 125), in speaking of Mr. Clutter, describes him interacting with pheasant hunters: "touching the brim of his cap, he headed home and the day's work, unaware that it would be his last." Capote puts fictional words in Mr. Clutter's mouth, knowing only that he spoke with them on the day he was killed.

In the retelling of the past, the writer uses synchronic narration, stopping the flow of time and presenting multiple interpretations simultaneously (Zavarzadeh, 1976, p. 97). This method contrasts to the usual modernist, fictional (and cinematic) technique that matches and contrasts chronological clock time with interior, phenomenological time (p. 97). The suspense that occurs in the nonfiction novel is inscriptional rather than situational (p. 126). Because the facts are known in advance (everybody knew what happened to the Clutter family), suspense comes from how the story is told.

The testimonial nonfiction novel, in contrast to its exegetical counterpart, makes the writer's voice a central part of the text (Zavarzadeh, 1976, p. 130). This version of the nonfiction novel is the story of the encounter between the writer and the experience being described. Thus, Mailer (1966)in *The Armies of the Night* tells the story of his involvement in the 1967 march on the Pentagon, and Tom Wolfe (1969) in *The Electric Kool-Aid Acid Test* records his experiences with Ken Kesey and his Merry Pranksters as they took a bus trip across the United States in 1964. The writer is a witness to real events. He or she participates in and records these events, acting as a medium who registers the effects and meanings of these events for their various participants.

The writer attempts to inscribe the emotional experiences of the other, depicting their interior life in a way that maps subjective reality. This, however, is an intersubjective, or intertextual, reality—the inner mental life of the other made visible in the writer's text (Zavarzadeh, 1976, p. 142). Wolfe (1969; also quoted in Zavarzadeh, 1976, p. 150) describes Beauty Witch, the girl who went mad on Kesey's bus:

> She keeps coming up to somebody who isn't saying a goddamn thing and looking into his eyes with the all-embracing look of total acid understanding, our brains are one brain, so let's *visit*, you and I, and she says: 'Oooooooh, you really *think* that. I know what you mean, but do you-u-u-u-u-u-ueeeeeeeeeeeeeeeeeeeeeee'—finishing off in a sailing tremolo laugh as if she had just read your brain and it is the weirdest of the weird shit ever, your brain eeeeeeeeeeeeeeeeeeeeeeeeeeeeeeeeeeeeeee. (p. 84)

Wolfe uses iconic typography to describe this layer of reality. Layers of subjective reality are thus placed on top of one another, alternating between the writer's experiences in the world at hand, the actual events occurring in the world, and the meanings of those experiences for those involved.

Mailer (1966) creates a public document with his opening of *Armies of the Night*: "From the outset, let us bring you news of your protagonist. The following is from *Time* magazine, October 27, 1967" (p. 13). Mailer then quotes from the *Time* article that describes Mailer the writer confronting an audience of 600, most of them students.

The notational novel is a minimalist text. The writer stays out of the way and attempts to reproduce lived experience in its total transparency. Aided by the camera and the tape recorder, the writer extensively quotes from the life stories and oral histories of everyday people in ordinary situations. This experience, as it is told, is the subject matter of the text, which has no official author (Zavarzadeh, 1976, p. 177). If the exegetical text recovers experiences, and the testimonial work covers a series of events, the notational work attempts to capture the "there-ness of reality, its absolute literalness" (Zavarzadeh, 1976, p. 180). The following is a description by Oscar Lewis (1966; also quoted in Zavarzadeh, 1976, p. 212) of the home in which the Cruz family lives:

> The room where she was sitting, the main living and sleeping area, was about nine by twelve feet. With only one small shuttered window facing the sea, it was always dark and damp. . . . A dozen colorful pictures of saints and several bright calendars partially relieved the drab color of the room. Finally photographs were tacked on the two-by-fours in the east wall. Below the pictures on a low table were snapshots of Cruz's two children in a handmade wooden frame in the form of two hearts. (pp. 536-538)

Lewis inserts into this setting monologues from the Cruz family, anchoring their days and lives in this drab home. Their stories thus illuminate, in vivid detail, the cultures of poverty Lewis wishes to describe (Lewis, 1966, p. 125).

Thus, the new writers created and reproduced forms of writing that also circulated in ethnography's modernist and blurred genre phases. Those who held to a realist version of the text did not doubt their ability to penetrate reality. Only a few (Didion) were skeptical about their place in the text, and even fewer anticipated the criticisms that would be launched against the realist ethnography in ethnography's fifth and sixth moments (Clough, 1992).

Reading the New Writing

Following Eason (1984), it is useful to distinguish two versions of the new writing: ethnographic realism and cultural phenomenology.[16] Ethnographic realists (or modernists) display a subculture or social world in rich detail, whereas the cultural phenomenologists (the postmodernists) describe what it feels like to be present in such a world. As indicated previously, Eason locates Wolfe and Capote in the first grouping and Joan Didion and Norman Mailer in the second.

This classification complicates Wolfe, who stressed the priority of a shared social realism for all the new journalists. Eason's (1984) two categories, however, have the virtue of establishing the overlap and continuity between the new journalists and the exegetical, testimonial, and notational nonfiction writers. Both groups of writers work from scenes, not facts, locate themselves in their texts (at one level), and cut against the grain of established writing styles. Eason's typology stresses the writer's treatment of the relationship between reality and image— the writer's place in the text, including his or her relationship to the scenes and worlds described.

Image and Reality

Ethnographic realists attempt to penetrate the images and facades that surround a group, hoping to reveal an underlying reality or cultural logic that holds the group together. Wolfe, for example, invokes social types and uses history to show how his subjects embody current cultural stereotypes. The following is a typical description: "She is a socialite in the sense that she lives in a twelve-room apartment on Park Avenue with a wealthy husband" (Wolfe, 1982, p. 103). These terms anchor Wolfe's text in a body of taken for granted meanings.

Cultural phenomenologists refuse such moves, seeing image and reality as basically intertwined and inseparable (Eason, 1984, p. 53) and doubting the interpretive power ability of any a priori scheme. Joan Didion (1968, p. xii; also quoted in Eason, 1984, p. 54) is explicit on this point, noting that she started *Slouching Towards Bethlehem* at a time "when she had been paralyzed by the conviction that writing was an irrelevant act, that the world as I had known it no longer existed. . . . [This report] is an attempt to come to terms with disorder." There is no recourse to preexisting cultural categories in Didion's text.

Observing and Writing

Ethnographic realists place a distance between themselves and those they write about (Eason, 1984, p. 53). Like classical ethnography, reports are written as if the observer is a passive participant in the events described. The reporter is cautioned to not get too close to those observed because a close personal relationship may be formed. Writers may "become stricken with guilt. . . . They may begin to feel like voyeurs. . . . People who become overly sensitive on this score should never take up the new style of journalism" (Wolfe, 1973, p. 51).

Cultural phenomenologists question this ethical relationship, often even mistrusting their right to tell a story or do an interview. Janet Malcom (1990) is quite explicit on this point: "Every journalist who is not too stupid or too full of himself to notice what is going on knows that what he is doing is morally indefensible" (p. 4). Joan Didion (1968) agrees: "People tend to forget that my presence runs counter to their best interest. . . . Writers are always selling somebody out" (p. xiv).

Stories

Ethnographic realists have faith in the reporting process, believing that stories are out there waiting to be told and the storytelling form will accurately reveal what they have learned (Eason, 1984, p. 59). The reporter penetrates an image, a scene, to reveal underlying patterns in American culture. In contrast, cultural phenomenologists "call attention to reporting as a way of joining together writer and reader in the creation of reality" (Eason, 1984, p. 53). These writers doubt their ability to "impose a narrative line on disparate images" (Didion, 1979, p. 11; also quoted in Eason, 1984, p. 60). Stories are not waiting to be told; they are constructed by the writer who attempts to impose order on perceived events. Indeed, when it comes time to write, the writer experiences a crisis. Didion (1979) observes, "I was meant to know the plot but all I knew was what I saw: Flash pictures in variable sequence, images with no 'meaning' beyond their temporary arrangement, not a movie but a cutting room experience" (p. 13; also quoted in Eason, 1984, p. 60).

These two modes of the new writing reflect radically different ways of responding to the cinematic society (Denzin, 1995a). For the ethnographic realist, the diversity "of contemporary society is interesting but not threatening" (Eason, 1984, p. 62). An underlying cultural logic can always be revealed if scenes are penetrated and the reporter digs deep enough. For the cultural phenomenologist, contemporary reality is a "lunar landscape" (Eason, 1984, p. 62): Nothing is fixed, nothing makes sense any longer. The reporter has no privileged position (Eason, 1984, p. 62), and stories are only temporary understandings—nothing holds firm. One can only write stories about these provisional understandings—stories about one's personal relationship to these seemingly disconnected events.

The Legacies of the New Writers

The legacies of these arguments were multiple (see Eason, 1986, pp. 437-444). The new journalists and the nonfiction writers changed the way reality was represented and interpreted. They described scenes, not facts, created composite characters, and manipulated point of view and temporality in the stories they told. They reasserted the primacy of realism as a major literary style and worked from underlying interpretive theories about the postmodern culture. They generated enormous skepticism about the government as a source of trustworthy information and had no hesitation about locating themselves in the stories they told. They were part of the movement that undermined the authority of the white middle-class reporter. In so doing, they were part of the process that opened the door for minority and women reporters. They thrived on the notion of the celebrity journalist—the star literary and investigative reporter. This diminished the cultural authority of the traditional, informational journalist.

These legacies, and their challenges to objective news reporting, persist and reemerge, as will be discussed in the cases of Janet Cooke,

Michael Daly, Christopher Jones, Alastair Reid, and Janet Malcolm (see Fishkin, 1985, pp. 209-216). First, however, a brief summary of the criticisms that were launched against these new writing forms is presented.

The Critics

Five criticisms, connected to the defining features of this genre discussed previously, were directed against the new writers (see Agar, 1990; Eason, 1986, pp. 437-442; Fishkin, 1985, pp. 210-217; Frus, 1994, pp. 155-156; Hollowell, 1977, pp. 13, 33, 38, 53, 73-75, 148; Van Maanen, 1988, pp. 134-136). First, the critics were unanimous on the fact or fiction issue: "The bastards are making it up" (Wolfe, 1973, p. 11). The critics could not accept the argument that facts were social constructions, and all writing is narrative. It was as if the use of narrative was an option, when in fact, as Booth (1983) stated, "authors cannot choose whether to use rhetorical narrative strategies, including fictional accounts, the only choice is which ones will be used" (p. 116).

The critics held to the belief that a journalist should produce an accurate, balanced news story (Christians et al., 1993, p. 55). This story should be based on carefully researched facts, information gathered from credible sources (hopefully eyewitnesses), and the use of quotes spoken by real people (Agar, 1990, p. 80). The critics were unified on this point: "While wrong truths are always correctable, with facts, fictional facts are forever counterfeit" ("The Fiction of Truth," 1984, p. 13). Facts were facts and fictions were fictions, and the two could not be intermingled. The new writers were producing fabrifacts (Fishkin, 1985, p. 216), and fabrifacts cannot be disproven. These writers were sacrificing journalistic truth for dramatic effect (Agar, 1990, p. 78). Hence, the new writers were not producing objective news accounts or objective stories about what was really going on in society.

Second, the new writers had no agreed on method for validating their assertions.[17] Readers contended that it was not possible to determine if the writers had gotten the story right. Furthermore, their presence in the tale could well have disturbed and distorted the very scenes they were studying (Van Maanen, 1988, p. 135). Because they made up quotes, fabricated events, and quoted fictitious sources, the credibility of their texts was constantly in doubt (Agar, 1990, p. 80). The critics were most disturbed by the use of composite characters (Fishkin, 1985, p. 212). They felt that the new writers were being dishonest with the reader, who might believe they were reading about a real person (Hollowell, 1977, p. 30). Writers such as Sheehy (1973, p. 16) defended the use of this method, contending that it had a long and distinguished history in the *New Yorker* and that its use allowed them to "protect the privacy of perfectly decent people." The method also allowed the writer to "compress considerable amounts of documentary evidence from a variety of sources into a vivid and unified telling of the story" (Hollowell, 1977, p. 31).

Third, the writer's place in the new fiction was challenged. Some felt that too much of the writer was in the prose. Others felt too little was there (Van Maanen, 1988, p. 134), claiming that the writer's moral stance was hidden from view. These so-called neutral or objective texts were in fact neither neutral nor objective (Hollowell, 1977, p. 73). Still, some felt that the writer's place in society had gotten out of hand. These people had become celebrities, larger than the stories they were writing, making pretensions about doing something that was really not new at all (Hollowell, 1977, pp. 40-41, 49-50, 118).[18]

Fourth, these writers were doing "scoop ethnography. . . . Self-serving, pandering . . . tales [about] inconsequential topics" (Van Maanen, 1988, p. 135). When they wrote about important things, they did not connect their work to the scholarly literatures on the topic (Van Maanen, 1988, p. 135). This meant that the work had the feel of something new, when in fact the findings were not new at all (Van Maanen, 1988, p. 135). At the same time, much of their work was topical in nature and perhaps too close to the news of the day. This raised doubts about its durability (Hollowell, 1977, p. 148).

Fifth, these writers eroded the public's trust in the media and the government (Eason, 1986, p. 442). By making celebrities out of themselves, they became bad models for a new generation of journalists. Their use of literary techniques violated journalistic norms concerning objective storytelling (p. 439). They contributed to the disorder journalism was experiencing in the 1970s and 1980s as large numbers of women and minority group members entered the newsmaking labor force (p. 441).

This is the critical legacy Janet Cooke (1980) confronted when she presented a composite story titled "Jimmy's World."

The Janet Cooke and Related Stories

On April 16, 1981, the Pulitzer Prize Committee announced that it had withdrawn the 1981 Pulitzer Prize in feature writing from *Washington Post* reporter Janet Cooke (Maraniss, 1981, p. A1). Two days earlier, Cooke had been awarded this prize for her 1980 story "Jimmy's World." This was a 2256-word story about an 8-year-old African American heroin addict who lived in a drug-invested neighborhood in Washington, D.C. (Cooke, 1980). On the basis of 2 hours of taped interviews and 145 pages of handwritten notes, Cooke's story was accompanied by an artist's depiction of Jimmy being injected with a needle by his mother's boyfriend Ron, who was quoted as saying to Jimmy, "Pretty soon, man, you got to learn how to do this to yourself" (Cooke, 1980).

The story ran on the front page of the Sunday, September 28, 1980, edition of the *Washington Post*. Within hours, Washington, D.C. Mayor Marion Barry and Chief of Police Burtell Jefferson assigned (Maraniss, 1981)

> a task force of police and social workers to locate the 8-year-old cited in the story and to obtain medical treatment for him. When the child could not be located, Barry and Jefferson voiced deep skepticism about the validity of the story. Barry said he believed 'Jimmy' did not exist, or was a composite of several youngsters. (p. A25)

Other irregularities appeared the day after Cooke received the award. Officials from Vassar called Benjamin C. Bradlee, executive editor of the *Post*, and told him that Cooke had not graduated magna cum laude from Vassar; in fact, she had only attended the school as a freshman. Associated *Post* staffers in Ohio were told that Cooke had received a bachelor's and not a master's degree from the University of Toledo (Maraniss, 1981, p. A25). These reports lead to an investigation by the *Post*. Bradlee and Bob Woodward, assistant managing editor, told Cooke that they "had serious doubts about her story. . . . Bradlee told Cooke she had to prove Jimmy's existence as soon as possible" (p. A25).

Cooke's supervising editor, Milton Coleman, drove to the neighborhood where Cooke claimed Jimmy lived. She was unable to find his house. Post officials examined Cooke's files for the story, and there was no record of an original meeting with Jimmy and his family. After several hours of interrogation, Cooke confessed that "Jimmy did not exist" (p. A25).

A 26-year-old African American, Cooke claimed she had graduated magna cum laude from Vassar and held a master's degree from the University of Toledo. In forfeiting her prize, Cooke also admitted that her story and her autobiography were fabrications. Although she had previously stated that she had interviewed this boy, his mother, and his mother's boyfriend, she now confessed that she "had never met or interviewed any of these people and that she made up the story of Jimmy based on a composite of information about heroin addiction in Washington gleaned from various social workers and other sources" (Maraniss, 1981, p. A1). Cooke stated that "the article was a serious misrepresentation, which I deeply regret. I apologize to my newspaper, my profession, the Pulitzer board, and all seekers of truth" (Maraniss, 1981, p. A25).

Thus was exposed, in two swift days, the narrow dividing line between fact and fiction. The New Journalism (Eason, 1984; Hollowell, 1977; Wolfe & Johnson, 1973; Zavarzadeh, 1976) was put on the spot, and the legitimacy of the news media as a democratic forum was challenged (Eason, 1986, p. 431). In the wake of the scandal, journalists of course did not claim that the facts speak for themselves. The question became, instead, how did the story get published in the first place (Eason, 1986, p. 433).

If 1980 was a bad year for American journalism, 1981 was worse. *Washington Post* reporter Michael Daly published a story about a British army gunner in Belfast named Christopher Spell. It was soon revealed that Spell was a composite character and Daly was out of a job (Fishkin, 1985, p. 212). On December 20, 1981, the cover story in the "*New York Times Magazine* was a dramatic firsthand account of life inside Cambodia titled 'In the Land of the Khmer Rouge: An American Reporter Takes a Journey Into the Cambodian Jungle' " (Fishkin, 1985, p. 213; Jones, 1981). Reporters for the *Washington Post* "checked with Cambodian officials and concluded that Jones 'neither visited with Cambodian rebels . . . nor interviewed people quoted in the piece' " (Fishkin, 1985,

p. 213). Alexander Cockburn (as quoted in Fishkin, 1985, p. 213), writing for the *Village Voice*, "showed convincingly that Jones had invented material himself .. . [and had] plagiarized portions of his report from André Malraux's 1930 novel, *The Royal Way*."

Three of the nation's leading newspapers had been caught "passing off fabrications as fact" (Fishkin, 1985, p. 213). The *New Yorker*, with its eight-member fact-checking department, remained to be implicated in this situation (Fishkin, 1985, p. 213). The *New Yorker* had long held the reputation for being the most accurate publication in the world (Fishkin, 1985, p. 214). The magazine's editor, William Shawn, was fond of asserting that "at the *New Yorker*, not only accuracy but truthfulness is sacred. . . . I venture to say that the *New Yorker* is the most accurate publication not only in this country, but in the entire world" (as quoted in Fishkin, 1985, pp. 213-214; also quoted in Lipman, 1984, p. 1). On June 18, 1984, *Wall Street Journal* staff reporter Joanne Lipman published an article revealing that Alastair Reid, a prestigious *New Yorker* writer, had admitted to spending his entire career "creating composite tales and scenes, fabricating personae, rearranging events and creating conversations in a plethora of pieces presented as nonfiction" (Lipman, 1984, p. 1).

The story did not end. Ten years later, Janet Malcolm and the *New Yorker* would be charged with libel by Jeffrey N. Masson (Gross, 1993a, 1993b; Lincoln & Denzin, 1994, p. 576).[19] Malcolm and the *New Yorker* were accused by Masson of fabricating five quotations in her two-part 48,500-word *New Yorker* profile of him.

The Cooke, Daly, Reid, and Malcolm stories were widely read as indictments of the New Journalism (Christians et al., 1993, p. 118; Eason, 1986; Fishkin, 1985, pp. 212-215). How did they happen?

Janet Cooke and the *Washington Post*

It was a fast-moving sequence. Cooke gets the award on April 14, 1981. On April 16, the fabrication is exposed, and the *Post* issues an apology to its readers. On April 19, Bill Green, *Washington Post* ombudsman, presented an account of how the story was published (Green, 1981). It was a simple story: It was the failure of the editing system to work.

As Eason (1986, p. 442) observes, a complex system of accountability works in the process of news production. This process ensures that facts, fictions, and lies are kept separate. Reporters depend on sources who confirm the accuracy and truth of an event. Editors rely on reporters to discover reliable and valid sources. Reporters expect their editors to give them assignments that will lead to good sources and good stories. Editors expect that reporters using good sources will produce true news and valid stories. These stories are based on real people, not composite characters (Greenfield, 1981). Editors expect reporters to reveal their sources and to be able to verify that what they have learned in fact occurred. Editors will listen to tape-recorded interviews and check a reporter's field notes. In turn, executive and managing editors can ask weekly or other division editors to confirm the reports written by their staff reporters. A hierarchy of credibility is thus established. This means that reporters have to reveal their sources to at least one person in this chain of command. If this rule is waived, there is no way to verify the story, and it becomes an unchecked report. Newspapers may choose, as in the case of Watergate and "Deep Throat," to not reveal a reporter's sources to the general public (Michener, 1981, p. 79), but reporters are expected to reveal their sources to their editors. With this system of checks and balance in place, untrue stories are not supposed to get published.

The following is a summary of Green's account. Cooke was hired by the *Post* on January 3, 1980. Because they were impressed with her credentials, her presentation of self during the job interview, and with the stories she had written for the *Toledo Blade*, the *Post* only checked her references in a cursory fashion. She was soon assigned to Washington's drug-infested riot corridor (Green, 1981, p. A12). Her stories drew compliments from Ben Bradlee. In August of 1980, Cooke's supervising editor, Vivian Aplin-Brownlee, asked her to look into a new type of heroin being used on the streets of Washington. Cooke amassed "extensive notes and taped interviews with intriguing leads" (p. A13). When Aplin-Brownlee saw what Cooke had collected, she told her she had a story for the daily. Aplin-Brownlee would not see this emerging story again until it appeared in print. Cooke brought her materials to Milton Coleman, the city editor. He reported that "she talked about hundreds of people being hooked. And at one point she mentioned an 8-year-old addict. I stopped her and said, 'That's the story. Go after it. It's a front-page story' " (as quoted in Green, 1981, p. A13).

Cooke returned with a report that she had located the boy's mother. Coleman assured her that she could promise the mother anonymity. He did not ask for the mother's name or address. "He had promised Cooke confidentiality on her sources" (Green, 1981, p. A13). Coleman shared this emerging story with the *Post*'s managing editor, Howard Simmons, who also did not ask Cooke or Coleman to reveal any details on identity. Coleman reported that Cooke had told him that she had taken the boy's mother out to dinner, and that she had visited the mother's house. There were no further interviews with the boy or his family. Cooke reported to Coleman that Ron, the mother's lover, had threatened her with a knife: "If I see any police, Miss Lady . . . we will be around to see you (as quoted in Green, 1981, p. A13).

The original draft of the story contained exhausting detail about the mother's home and about Jimmy's dress and speech. The name Tyrone appeared on Cooke's first version of the story and Coleman assumed this was the boy's real name. Cooke also told Coleman the name of the elementary school "Tyrone" attended. Members of the *Post* staff assumed that Coleman knew who the child was, and other editors did not ask because they had guaranteed Cooke anonymity. Coleman helped Cooke redraft her story, and he checked details concerning the process of shooting up described in the story. Legal counsel made minor changes in the story.

Bob Woodward then called Cooke in and asked her about the story and was convinced of its truth. None of the *Post*'s senior editors checked the story. Coleman believed that "the extra eyes of the backup system would catch anything that I missed" (as quoted in Green, 1981, p. A14). On the evening of September 26, Coleman gave Cooke one last chance to pull her story and she declined. Confident that they had a true story, the *Post* ran the story in its Sunday edition. The rest is history.

Reactions from the Journalism Community

The responses of the American journalism community to the Cooke story reflected a nostalgia for a past when the practices of anonymous sources, unchecked reports, composite characters, scene setting, and fictionalized dialogue did not occur (Eason, 1986, p. 430). These were the practices associated with the New Journalism. As a complex interpretive community (Condit & Selzer, 1985; Glasser & Ettema, 1989; Reese, 1990; Zelizer, 1993, 1995, p. 79), with shared values and common understandings, American journalism responded as if with a single voice to the Cooke case. Reporters are supposed to tell the truth. Facts and fictions are not cultural categories produced by social and symbolic processes; they are real things, truthfully known (Eason, 1986, p. 431).

No one stepped forward to defend Cooke. The *Post*'s system of accountability had failed, and they too were at fault. They failed, in part, because the times had changed. Although the *Post* had gotten away with anonymous sources ("Deep Throat") in the Watergate case, they were betrayed by Cooke, who "was free to write whatever she wished" (Michener, 1981, p. 79). Objectivity and its loss were at stake. The nation "would perish" (p. 79) if readers could not trust their newspapers to tell the truth.

Journalism history was rewritten to explain the Cooke story. Cooke was placed outside the moral boundaries of the journalism community. As a deviant, she defined the rules that had been broken (Eason, 1986, p. 430). She was young, female, and African American. She had not served a long apprenticeship (Michener, 1981, p. 80). She worked for a newspaper that had achieved considerable notoriety in the Watergate scandal in which the investigative journalism practices of Woodward and Bernstein had brought down an American president. Cooke's work was connected to this history, and to the backdrop of the New Journalism, leading one member of the Pulitzer Prize (Judith Crist) committee to call her work not the New Journalism but the New Fiction (Tyler & Simmons, 1981).

Two decades of journalistic practice, the 1960s and the 1970s, the decades of the New Journalism and the new nonfiction, were taken to task. The problem turned on fact and fiction and reality. Greenfield (1981) is quite explicit, arguing against "the degraded condition of reporting in this country. . . . The increasingly slithery nature of the 'reality' much of that reporting seeks to convey" (p. A19). Greenfield goes on. The 1960s and 1970s bear witness to "a looser and looser and ever more self-indulgent and impressionistic conception of what is real and what is imagined" (p. A19).

For the journalistic community, the villain was the New Journalism and the related tradition of investigative reporting. These writing forms, with their "cloak of anonymous sources . . . [and] the use of composites had eroded public trust, and television docudramas further blurred the line between fact and fiction" (Eason, 1986, p. 439; see also Greenfield, 1981, p. A19). At issue was the composite character—a "dimly acceptable journalistic art form" (Greenfield, 1981, p. A19). Greenfield is adamant,

> There was a time when quotation marks were sacred, and their presence at either end of an utterance meant something specific. It meant that the recorded utterance had, *word for word*, been said by whomever it was attributed to, and for this the writer could vouch. (p. A19)

Judy Mann (1981) elaborated: "Our job is simply to tell people what is happening, to use the skills we have to obtain the truth" (p. B3).

John Hersey's (1980, p. 2) line, "None of this was made up," became the rallying call for the critics. Arguing from a reconstructed moment in time when facts were facts and fictions were fictions, Hersey contended that the new journalists had lost their faith in objectivity. At the same time, their investigative reporting strategies undermined governmental authority (Eason, 1986, p. 441). Cooke's story was now read through the narrative strategies of the New Journalism.[20] In their praise of subjectivity, the new journalists had turned reality into something that in the end becomes "fuzzy, vague, unrecognizable, and false (Hersey, 1980, p. 23; see also Glasser & Ettema, 1989, p. 6).

Two other issues were read into the Cooke story. The 1960s and 1970s opened up American society to the sound of new voices—stories about youth, women, gays and lesbians, African Americans, Asians, American Indians, and Latino(as) (Eason, 1986, p. 441). These voices were heard by the new journalists, and they represented a challenge to conventional journalism. Many presumed that stories about these groups could only be written by persons from these groups. Affirmative action hiring practices addressed this situation. These programs brought countless minority and female reporters into America's journalism community. Some argued that these reporters had not paid their dues and that they were hired because they filled affirmative action criteria, not because they were good reporters.

Cooke was part of this group: She was not just Janet Cooke, she was an attractive African American woman. Michener (1981) observed, "she was what is known as a twofer" (p. 80), and she "progressed so fast in her profession that she did not learn its great traditions" (p. 79).

Therefore, the argument comes full circle. The *Post* was culpable, taken in by this untrained African American female reporter. This reporter had learned her methods by reading the new journalists, who had contributed to the disorder the larger journalism community was now experiencing.

The answer to the crisis was clear: Return to that earlier time when the crises in representation and legitimation did not exist—the nostalgic past. The call to "None of this was made up," however, failed to address the underlying problematic situation. The 1960s and 1970s had ruptured and forever changed the media's relationship to its audience and to the federal government (Eason, 1986, p. 441). A white middle-class audience that believed what its government said could no longer be presumed.

The media, however, resisted change. It did not propose any significant changes in its production process—in the way stories were written, sources were used, or interviews were quoted. It just put greater pressure on its internal, complex system of accountability to ensure that accurate facts were being produced. Nor did the media propose any significant change in its relationship to the government or to its reading audience. In response to audience cultural fragmentation, "it put more emphasis on lifestyle sections" (Eason, 1986, p. 441). In response to the loss of trust in the government, the media continued their dependency on governmental sources for stories while asserting their own independence from these sources (p. 442).

Therefore, nothing changed, and Janet Cooke was banished from the community.[21] A victim of her own hubris, perhaps, but surely she made a moral judgment when she created her story—a call for help for persons like Jimmy. In this call, she was, as an investigative reporter, writing a human interest story, well within the moral boundaries of the larger community (see Cohen, 1981).[22] Her error was to be judged by the standards of another community, in which the lines between truth and fiction are never meant to be crossed. Her moral judgment was sound, her newsmaking judgment was not (see Glasser & Ettema, 1989, p. 15; see also Gans, 1980, p. 293).

The real Jimmy was never found. Reporters are still sent out to find and tell true stories. The information, spectator theory of journalism prevails (see Carey, 1989, pp. 76-86; also see the following discussion). Objectivity remains the goal, and although there may be (Glasser & Ettema, 1989)

> 'enduring values' upon which the claim to objectivity depends . . . such values are not consistent, and their application to the situation at hand is seldom clear. Appropriate objective standards are rarely self-evident, and the task of 'empirically determining' them is rarely simple. (p. 2)

Janet's story makes this clear. Furthermore, as Stuart Hall (1982) suggests, the very conditions that produce objectivity are themselves social productions.

Paraphrasing Glasser and Ettema (1989, p. 17), who paraphrase Hall (1982), the press actively fashions and simultaneously legitimates the very forms of objectivity it ostensibly conveys and uses when it evaluates news stories.[23] There can be no firm and solid division between newsmaking judgments (objectivity), the so-called facts of the real world, and moral judgments about these facts and their reporting—what is called the normative ought (Gans, 1980, p. 183; Glasser & Ettema, 1989, pp. 2, 15).

Janet Malcolm: The Journalist and the Psychoanalyst

During a 7-month period in 1982 and 1983, Janet Malcolm interviewed Jeffrey Masson, a psychoanalyst and former Sanskrit scholar, who had lost his job as secretary of the Freud Archives (Malcolm, 1984, p. 59). The tape-recorded interviews occurred in Berkeley, California, Manhattan, New York, and over the telephone. In 1983, Malcolm published a 48,500-word, two-part series in the *New Yorker* under the title "The Freud Archives." This series was then published as a book, with the same title, by Malcolm in 1984. The five quotes in question are contained in the 1983 *New Yorker* article. The profile was based on tape-recorded interviews with Masson. The federal jury ruled for Masson, concluding that Malcolm had fabricated the five quotations and that two of them met all of the criteria for libel as defined by the Supreme Court: They were made up or materially altered. Malcolm knew they were defamatory and acted with "reckless disregard" for their accuracy, and Masson had been damaged by them (Gross, 1993b, p. A1).

Four of the five quotes were not on tape, although Malcolm had typewritten notes that included three of them (Gross, 1993e).[24] Malcolm asserted that these quotations were real and not made up, and that Masson could not remember having said them. In the quotes in question, Malcolm put quotation marks around words she had rearranged through the compression of long interviews that occurred several months apart and in different places (Carmody, 1993). In one instance, the locale of the quoted material was changed by Malcolm's editor (also her husband) to simplify the narrative line (Carmody, 1993).

The following are the five quotations in question. The first quotation asserts that the members of the Freudian establishment considered Masson "to be like an intellectual gigolo." The second quote describes what he would do with Anna Freud's London Home; that is, "turn it into a place of sex, women and fun." In the third quote, Masson claims that after his 1984 book, members of the profession would consider him, after Freud, "the greatest analyst that ever lived." The fourth quote refers to a statement Masson made at a conference about the "sterility of psychoanalysis." The fifth quote, on the tapes but edited in print, has Masson saying that the director of the Freud Archives " 'had the wrong man' if he expected him to swallow his dismissal in silence" (Gross, 1993e).[25]

Masson's case turned on proving that Malcolm had maliciously and deliberately fabricated the five quotations, knowing that they were defamatory, while acting with reckless disregard for their accuracy (Gross, 1993b, p. A1). Malcolm's journalistic practices were at issue. Masson's attorney established that Malcolm combined or compressed "several conversations into one seamless monologue" (Gross, 1993d). He further contended that she rearranged events and created conversations that did not occur where she said they occurred. In one instance, Malcolm set a conversation in a Berkeley restaurant when it actually involved many remarks made in several telephone conversations and during a visit to her home.

It took eight jurors—seven women and one man—3 ½ days to reach a verdict: Quotes two and three were libelous. The jurors argued that Malcolm had been warned by the legal staff at the *New Yorker* about the "sex, women and fun" quote. They also believed that Malcolm altered the fourth quote to change its meaning. She had been given the opportunity to change it while working with her editor, and Masson had said that he wished he had not made that remark.

During the course of the trial, William Shawn, the legendary editor of the *New Yorker*, defended Malcolm's use of compression, which she used (Gross, 1993c)

> to turn months of interviews and impressions into a coherent narrative. . . . This is done frequently for literary reasons, it must never be done to distort or deceive anybody or done to the disadvantage of anybody. It is an acceptable technique with our kind of writers who are responsible people. (p. A10)

The jurors disagreed.[26]

Much is at issue in the Malcolm-Masson trial and related libel cases. Disgruntled subjects can now sue a writer, "on grounds that render irrelevant the truth or falsity of what was published (Malcolm, 1990, p. 7). A journalist's "demeanor and point of view . . . can become an issue to be resolved by jury trial, . . . Newspaper and magazine reporters . . . can . . . be sued for writing truthful but unflattering articles" (p. 7).[27]

Journalistic and ethnographic betrayal are always possibilities. The writer-subject relationship can be one of mutual exploitation. Subjects want their side of the story told. The writer wants a good story and may have few compunctions about representing the subject in an unflattering light, and some subjects make this easy to do.[28]

Accurately reproducing what a subject says is also problematic. The writer of nonfiction is under a contract to "the reader to limit him[her]self to events that actually occurred and to characters who have counterparts in real life, and he [she] may not embellish the truth about these events or these characters" (Malcolm, 1990, p. 153). All writing, however, requires narrative construction, fitting statements to contexts and persons, and making sense of what was said. "The literally true may actually be a kind of falsification of reality" (p. 154).

Tape-recorded, actual speech is filled with nuance, hesitation, and "bizarre syntax, hesitations, circumlocutions, contradictions" (Malcolm, 1990, p. 155). Transcribed speech, as discussed in Chapter 4, is embalmed speech—filled-out speech fitted to standard readable English, not "tape-recorderese" (p. 155). Reporters (and ethnographers) write dialogue in English (Malcolm, 1990):

> When a journalist undertakes to quote a subject he[she] has inter-viewed on a tape, he[she] owes it to the subject, no less than to the reader, to translate his[her] speech into prose. Only the most unchari-table (and inept) journalist will hold a subject to his[her] literal utter-ances and fail to perform the sort of editing and rewriting that, in life, our ear automatically and instantaneously performs. (p. 155)

Readerly prose, faithful to the content and meaning of a speaker's words, will not perfectly reproduce the actual, spoken text.

Tape-recorded speech has historically functioned as an aide to the writer's memory. Recent libel suits make it necessary for "journalists to have an electronic record of what a subject said" (Malcolm, 1990, p. 156). There is a danger here, however, because the journalist and ethnogra-pher may be turned into stenographers as lawsuits degenerate into what a subject did or did not say (p. 156). The idea of a reporter "inventing rather than reporting speech is . . . repugnant. . . . Fidelity to the subject's thought and to his [her] characteristic way of expressing him[her]self is the *sine qua non* of journalistic quotation" (p. 157). The task is obvious. Trustworthy quotation involves the translation of tape recorderese into English, maintaining, in every instance, fidelity to the subject's thoughts and intentions (p. 157).

As ethnographers move more deeply into experiments in narrative, steps must be taken to ensure that the words they put in subject's mouths were in fact spoken. In the case of composite characters, words that could have been spoken are rightfully employed. The compression of long stretches of narrative material into single monologues is appro-priate when fidelity to meaning and intention are maintained. The ethics of textual production argue for meticulous checking—the verifi-cation that particular statements were in fact made. Still, care must always be taken when contexts are changed, interviews compressed and edited, and events are reordered for dramatic purposes. The reader must always be informed about the author's narrative strategies of the author. There is no such thing as "a work of pure factuality, any more than there is one of pure fictitiousness" (Malcolm, 1990, p. 154). The degree of creative mediation that occurs in any text, including changes in what was said and what is reported, must be indicated. It is not that there is a single reality to which a text refers. To repeat the Wallace Stevens quote (as quoted in Updike, 1995, p. 21) at the opening of this chapter, "Reality is not what it is. It consists of the many realities which it can be made into."

What to Make of It All

The basic unit of analysis for the new writers was not the fact. They focused on the scene—the situation in which the event in question occurred or would happen (Wolfe, 1973, p. 50). As Zavarzadeh (1976, p. 219) stated, the nonfiction text "is written not *about* facts, but *in* facticities." These facticities are treated as extensions of real life in its multiple forms and in its many realities. These many versions of reality are then made visible and interpreted by the writer.

The new writers refused to locate reality in events per se. Rather, the real, in its multiple forms, was anchored in the experience of the text itself. This called for a new form of reading. They produced texts that challenged readers to read reflexively, to read between the lines, to erase the distinction between fact and fiction, and to reread experiences, altering prior understandings based on new information (Frus, 1994, p. xx). This new information was contained in the reflexive text that disrupted temporal sequence, rearranged events and their chronology, and constantly altered the past in light of new understandings (Frus, 1994, pp. 209-210). The reality of the text could not be verified in external experience or in concrete external facts (see Frus, 1994, p. xx). The facts were reconstituted in the telling and in the experience of reading.

The appeal of the New Journalism and the new writing was not that it offered "the certainty of the factual" (Frus, 1994, p. 233). The appeal was more complicated. The new journalists resisted the call to facts. They wrote, instead, in a way that questioned the "natural relationship between narratives and the 'reality' they appear to represent" (p. 233). They created reflexive texts requiring self-conscious readers. With their readers, these writers shared the view that the world outside was filled with "pseudoevents and precreated experiences" (p. 233). The new writing produced texts and textual experiences that closely corresponded to this view of the world (p. 233).

These works mirrored the reader's process of self-formation and self-understanding. They did this in their structured ambiguity and internal complexity. They did it in their hesitations and certain uncertainties and in the way they called attention to language and its use. They did it by challenging journalistic representations of truth, even as they challenged their own ability to represent reality. In these ways, these works created readers who shared the same uncertainties and who doubted the truths they were given by the media, the government, and by science. These works undid old dichotomies such as fact and fiction, journalism and science, and literature and ethnography. It is doubtful that we can go back to the age where such easy distinctions so automatically operated.

The critics, of course, would have none of this. Recall James W. Carey's (1989, pp. 76-86) analysis of the two views of newsmaking—the informational, spectator model and the storytelling, participative model. Traditional journalism (and ethnography) relies on a spectator, ocular, visual epistemology. This is a representational model. In it communication (and ethnography) is "a way of seeing things aright" (p. 77). Journalists secure accurate representations of reality, and these representations shape the formation of a correct, accurate, and well-informed public opinion (p. 81).

The storytelling framework rejects the visual model of communication. It emphasizes conversation, hearing, and listening as the chief participatory modes of knowing and learning about the world (Carey, 1989, p. 80). In this view, public opinion is formed through discussion, conversation, and storytelling. As Carey states,

> [The] purpose of news is not to represent and inform but to signal, tell a story, and activate inquiry. . . . We lack . . . the vital means through which this conversation can be carried on: Institutions of public life through which a public can be formed and can form an opinion. (p. 82)

To elaborate, we lack a communitarian journalism that treats communication and newsmaking as value-laden activities and as forms of social narrative rooted in the community, not in some atomized public (Christians et al., 1993, pp. xii, 113, 121).

The new writers attempted to create a new community of discourse in America—a community critical of what was happening in the cinematic society. They turned newsmaking and ethnography into storytelling. As performers, they brought good and bad news to the American public and attempted to open a conversation that would bring this country back to its senses. Seeing themselves as moral compasses, the new writers used narrative in new ways to tell new stories about themselves and their relationships to American society. They argued for a new way of telling things about society. They used their life stories, their autoethnographies, as "the dial of an instrument that records the effects of a particular stage of civilization upon a civilized individual (Spender, 1984, p. ix).

Their legacies are multiple and have yet to be built on.[29] Ethnography has not embraced, let alone learned from, the many narrative turns taken by these new writers. The preferred strategy, instead, has been to stand outside, as critics, or to take up the structural approach to narrative, learning how to dissect rather than how to write stories. This second variation on the narrative turn is the topic of the next chapter.

Notes

1. To repeat, the narrative turn sees culture as a performance and privileges the linguistic and textual basis of knowledge about society. That is, things are known through textual, narrative representations and performances (see Bochner & Waugh, 1995). All narratives are performative texts (see Frus, 1994, p. xiv). Following the modernist formulations of Polkinghorne (1988, pp. 13, 51, 111) and Miller (1990, pp. 66, 74-78), I define narrative as the performative process of making or telling a story. A story is the narration of a series of events in a sequence. A story and a narrative are thus nearly equivalent terms (Polkinghorne, 1988, p. 13). A story and a narrative contain certain basic structural elements, including plot, setting, characters, locale, and temporality. Stories begin with an initial situation. A sequence of events lead to the disturbance or reversal of this situation. The revelation of character and setting are made possible by this disturbance. A personification of characters (protagonists, antagonists, and witnesses) also occurs. The resolution of this predicament leads to stories in which there is a regression, progression, or no change in the main character's situation (Polkinghorne, 1988, p. 15). Postmodern, nonfiction writers, including Capote (1966), Mailer (1966, 1979, 1995), Thompson (1967, 1973), Wolfe (1969, 1973, 1987), and Didion (1968, 1979, 1992), challenge these conceptions of narrative (see Zavarzadeh, 1976, pp. 41, 84-88, 224-227).

2. A paradox must be immediately noted: What is experimental in one setting may be old hat in another. Some of the new journalists, for example, used the traditional methods of social realism (see Wolfe, 1973, pp. 31-32). What was radical was that journalists were using time-worn techniques invented by nineteenth-century novelists while challenging the notion of journalistic objectivity. Similarly, much experimental ethnography is experimental because it uses techniques not previously deployed in ethnographic writing. Few ethnographers have moved into nonfiction texts or into the kinds of postmodern writing discussed in Chapters 1 and 2 (e.g., mobile observers recording a moving world, etc.).

3. It is useful to immediately distinguish two branches, or versions, of journalism: the so-called objective, informational school that produces valid accounts of events and the so-called New Journalism (Sims, 1984, 1990; Wolfe, 1973), which emphasizes narrative and storytelling (Eason, 1981, p. 128). The first mode emphasizes the relation between the report and an event, whereas the second stresses the relation of the report to the reader (see Eason, 1981, p. 128). Informational journalism is evaluated on epistemological grounds, whereas narrative journalism is judged by aesthetic criteria, how well the story coheres, and so on.

4. The New Journalism has passed through four interrelated historical waves (Frus, 1994, pp. 134-135; Schudson, 1978, pp. 71-72, 75-81, 88-90, 121-122): the penny novel papers of the 1830s, the journalism of Pulitzer and Hearst in the 1890s and 1890s, culminating in the yellow journalism of the 1920s, and the movement labeled by Tom Wolfe as the New Journalism in the 1960s and early 1970s (Wolfe, 1973). The 1960 movement is alive and well in the recent works of Wolfe (1987), Mailer (1995), Didion (1992), Cramer (1992), and others.

5. If, as Doctorow (as cited in Fishkin, 1985, p. 207) asserts, there is no longer any such thing as a distinction between fiction and nonfiction, only narrative, then all narratives assemble their respective versions of fact, fiction, and truth. In this context (Denzin, 1989a, p. 23), a fact refers to events that are believed to have occurred. A facticity describes how facts were lived and experienced. A fiction is a narrative—a story that deals with real and imagined facts and facticities. Fictions are made up, fashioned out of real and imagined happenings (Clifford, 1986, p. 6). Truth references statements that are in agreement with facts and facticities as known and commonly understood within a community of knowers (Peirce, 1905). Ethnographic writings are narratives. Every work constructs its version of what is truthful and factual, what could have happened, what did happen, or will happen here. In contrast, Pauly (1990, p. 122), drawing on Heyne (1987), preserves the distinction between fictional and factual texts. Fictional texts make no claim to factual status or factual accuracy. Factual texts claim to be factual, and their facts can be checked and are subject to public debate. After making this distinction, Pauly (1990) then states, "all narratives are fictions" (p. 122). He conflates matters by invoking, but not naming, Peirce (1905), arguing that "to say a report is true is to affirm that it speaks the consensus of some actual community of interpreters. In turn, disagreements over truth signal appeals to different communities of interpretation, with their own standards of evidence, significance, and style" (Pauly, 1990, p. 122). Therefore, truth is a social construct, and narratives about the world are judged "according to their coherence and correspondence to to a world we recognize. . . . They do not correspond to the events themselves but to other narratives (Frus, 1994, p. xiv).

6. For example, serious American novelists (Faulkner, Hemingway, Fitzgerald, Gardner, Updike, Mason, Roth, Mason, Roth, Doctorow, Oates, Boyle, and Amis) write

fiction, whereas Mailer and Capote (in their nonfictional novels) are not doing great literature, and the new journalists—for example, Wolfe (1969), Talese (1972), Didion (1968), and Thompson (1973, 1967)—were dismissed for writing "zippy prose about inconsequential people" (Wolfe, 1973, p. 38; see also Frus, 1994, pp. 151-152; Pauly, 1990, p. 113).

7. A fourth form of representation, advertising, must be added to this list of postmodern discursive forms. Advertising texts have "become the site of representational politics" (Giroux, 1994, p. 4). These multimedia, performance texts constantly redefine the connections between public culture, everyday life, and "the politics of representation and the representation of politics" (Giroux, 1994, p. 5). Of course, these texts, as a form of collective, public fantasy, totally disregard the issues of fact and fiction, stressing instead the emotional power of the story that is told—the emotional identification of the viewer with the issues (and personalities) at hand. Thus, we have real people (Larry Bird and Michael Jordan) doing imaginary things (making baskets by bouncing basketballs over highways, tall buildings, and through narrow windows; the winner gets the Big Mac).

8. Thus, traditional journalism (in the information mode) invokes the norms of objectivity and impartiality and deploys a writing style that makes the narrator invisible while privileging the visual and honoring brevity (Frus, 1994, p. 58). In contrast, the New Journalism emphasizes the production of compelling stories that convince readers of the truth of a situation (Eason, 1984, p. 127). These works locate the narrator in the events reported on. There are important differences between those new journalists who work in the ethnographic realist mode and those who follow a cultural phenomenology (see Eason, 1984).

9. At least three approaches to storytelling can be taken: the modernist, totalizing novel or ethnographic text that imposes a narrative (and theoretical) framework on the events reported on (see Note 1); the postmodern, nonfiction novel that refuses to impose a modernist narrative framework on the events described; and the critical approach, which attempts to unravel the ideological foundations of the narrative itself (i.e., how it functions to bring order and meaning out of chaos). On this, Lentricchia (1990, p. 335) observes, "The storyteller's most powerful effect comes when he [she] convinces us that what is particular, integrated, and different in a cultural practice . . . is part of a cultural plot that makes coherent sense of all cultural practices as a totality; not a totality that is there, waiting for us to acknowledge its presence, but a totality fashioned when the storyteller convinces us to see it his [her] way."

10. Here, Whyte is referring to and answering criticisms of his work (see Whyte, 1992; "Special Issue," 1992).

11. Wolfe (1973, p. 38) disputes Capote, tracing the origins of the nonfiction novel to the works of Fielding, Dickens, Balzac, Sterne, and Smollett.

12. Hollowell (1977, p. 12) notes that African American writers (Malcolm X, Claude Brown, James Baldwin, and Elridge Cleaver) were also taking a lead in this discourse through the use of the autobiography, confessional, and personal essay.

13. This often led to the use of the technique called compression: "combining quotations spoken at different times and different places into a single monologue" (Gross, 1993e). Compression became a major issue in the Malcolm-Masson case.

14. When did the New Journalism and the writing of nonfiction texts start? Maybe it all started in 1957, the "year the Soviet Union's Sputnik shook America" (Zavarzadeh, 1976, p. 38). It might have started in 1963 when J. F. K. was murdered, or it might have started in 1968 when the political assassinations increased, ghettos went up in flames, students fought on American college campuses, an aging Hollywood idol became gover-

nor of California, and a new generation ran away from home in search of a new frontier. The novelistic drama of the Watergate hearings (1972-1974) further eroded the public's confidence in what a fact was (Zavarzadeh, 1976, p. 38). The center no longer held firm.

15. Working side by side with the nonfiction writers, the new journalists argued that they were reclaiming the territory long occupied by the realist novel (Wolfe, 1973, pp. xi, 40-41). According to Wolfe (pp. 40-41), mainstream fiction writers had given up realism. He called them the Neo-Fabulists (pp. 40-41), contending that they wrote about fictional characters as if they had no history, social class, ethnicity, or nationality. The traditional devices of realism, including dialogue, status detail, and point of view, were no longer used. These writers (Barthes, Borges, Gardner, and Marquez) wrote fables, fairy tales, and epic history, creating a void that the new journalists and the nonfiction writers attempted to fill.

16. Alternatively, following the distinctions in Chapter 2, the ethnographic realists wrote modernist texts, presuming a stable world recorded by a stable observer. The cultural phenomenologists presumed an unstable world recorded by a moving, mobile mind. They produced postmodernist texts.

17. This criticism persisted, even thought these writers inevitably referenced public documents and the interviews they conducted. Wolfe (1973, p. 52) called this saturation reporting.

18. In Hunter S. Thompson's (1979, p. 120) brand of the New Journalism, the gonzo journalist is a performer, a film director—the main character in the films he writes, directs, films, and produces. On this point, I thank Richard Bradley.

19. Actually the Malcolm-Masson case started nearly 10 years earlier in 1984, when it was dismissed by the original judge, dismissed again by an appellate court, and then ordered back to trial in 1991 by the Supreme Court, which limited the trial to five quotations (Gross, 1993a). A March 14, 1994, date was set for the retrial of the previous trial completed on June 2, 1993. The June 1993 trial found the *New Yorker* innocent of libel charges but held against Malcolm while disagreeing on the amount of damages to be paid Masson. In setting a new trial, the judge ruled that the amount of damages could not be separated from evidence on whether Masson had been libeled by Malcolm ("March 14 Retrial," 1993).

20. This reading rested on analogical reasoning because Cooke used a composite case; she was exemplifying the New Journalism. A version of the intentional fallacy (Chang, 1992; Wimsatt & Beardsley, 1954), using an author's intentions to interpret a text, was also operating. The fact that Cooke refused to discuss her story (Walsh, 1981) did not deter critics in their interpretation of her story as an instance of the New Journalism. Thus, the disconnected transgressions of the past were used to explain transgressions in the present. This is a version of what Richard Bradley (personal communication, August 10, 1995) calls proleptic history.

21. The association of daily and weekly newspapers in the Maryland-Delaware-District of Columbia Press Association gave Cooke the second-place award in the news story category for Jimmy's story. On April 23, 1981, they asked Cooke to return her award because the story was fabricated ("Press Group," 1981). On August 7, 1981, Cooke, the *Washington Post*, and several of its editors were sued for $8.8 million in damages for publishing Jimmy's story. The suit was brought by Washington, D.C. school board member R. Calvin Lockridge and his wife Mildred and a parent with children in the city school system who claimed that the story caused abuse, harassment, and public ridicule as well as forcing many people to take considerable time to find Jimmy. The same parties also asked for $6.5 million in damages for the District of Columbia, which "they said,

among other things, sustained a loss in its efforts to gain statehood as a result of the story" (" 'Jimmy' Story," 1981).

22. Consider the following: "Janet Cooke has made us aware of a problem. At least for a few weeks there was a lot of attention paid to the horror of juvenile addiction. Mayor Barry made a point of wanting to save 'the real Jimmy.' Well, children like 'Jimmy' are still out there" (Cohen, 1981, p. A12).

23. Ironically, Cooke's story and biography remained "true" until she won the Pulitzer Prize and the authorities from Vassar and the University of Toledo started the process that lead to the discovery of the discrepancies in her personal history and then in "Jimmy's" story.

24. At the time of the trials, the notes to document Malcolm's assertions were missing. On the night of August 11, 1995, the missing notes were found by Malcolm's granddaughter (Stout, 1995, p. B1; see also Lewis, 1995).

25. Masson's legal complaint against Malcolm was amended and revised four times. Masson removed complaints that described his sexual promiscuity (having slept with over 1,000 women), his desire to single-handedly bring down psychoanalysis, and his ability to speak fluent German after 6 months in Munich. These statements were documented on Malcolm's tapes (Gross, 1993e).

26. The case went back to trial in November 1994 when a jury in San Francisco "essentially ruled in favor of Ms. Malcolm. It found that while two of the five disputed quotations . . . were false and defamatory, none were written with the recklessness that constitutes libel" (Stout, 1995, p. B1).

27. These observations on journalistic betrayal were written by Daniel Kornstein (and quoted by Malcolm). Kornstein defended Joe McGinniss, the author of *Fatal Vision*, a nonfiction novel about convicted triple murderer Jeffrey MacDonald. MacDonald had sued McGinniss for libel. Malcolm's (1990) book, *The Journalist and the Murderer*, is the story of this trial. Malcolm's book was read by critics as her response to her trial with Masson, and in an Afterword, she takes up the Masson suit, which had not yet come to trial (see also Malcom, 1992).

28. Malcolm also speaks of her sense of betrayal when members of the journalism community accused her (before the case ever went to trial) of fabricating quotations and manufacturing dialogue. She states, "I will no doubt always be tainted—a kind of fallen woman of journalism" (Malcolm, 1990, p. 152).

29. This legacy will be elaborated in Chapter 9 when I discuss public journalism (Charity, 1995).

6

The Private Eye

Ethnography is . . . a superordinate discourse to which all other discourses are relativized and in which they have their meaning and justification.
— Tyler (1986, p. 122)

Crime fiction's intrinsic interest in society—in the law and in the violation of the law—inevitably involves an exploration of the experience of modernity, of what it means to be caught up in this maelstrom of perpetual disintegration and renewal, of struggle and contradiction, of ambiguity and anguish.
— Thompson (1993, p. 8)

Photography made it possible for the first time to preserve permanent and unmistakable traces of the human being. The detective story came into being when this most decisive of all conquests of a person's incognito had been accomplished. Since then the end of efforts to catch a man in his speech and action has not been in sight.
— Benjamin (1973, p. 48)

My topic is crime fiction, detective stories, the Private Eye.[1] In this chapter, I extend my analysis of the new journalists by examining another form of storytelling, the writing of the "Private Eye"—mystery, crime, and detective fiction (see Black, 1991; Bloch, 1988; Cawelti, 1976; Chandler, 1972; Fiedler, 1982, pp. 498-500; Glover & Kaplan, 1992;

Haycraft, 1972; Holquist, 1983; Jameson, 1992, pp. 33-39, 45-47; Knight, 1980; Krieger, 1991, p. 60; Porter, 1981; Symons, 1985).[2] I compare the private eye to the new journalist, and the new ethnographer, arguing that the postmodern detective pushes the boundaries of the new ethnography in new and important ways, in ways that call for a redoing of ethnographic writing.[3] I disagree with Tyler. Postmodern detective writing, not ethnography, has become the superordinate discourse to which all other discourses should now be compared.

The detectives, like the journalists, teach readers how to confront and manage the unpresentable features of the postmodern world, including violent, horrible, messy crimes, incest, child and spousal abuse, murders, rapes, rotting corpses, decapitated, butchered bodies, blood everywhere, and the stench of death. They also present the tools of death: knives, axes, guns, and poison. Crime fiction domesticates capitalism's murderous violence. Dead bodies produced in domestic and imperial wars are brought home—murder in the bedroom and the kitchen, not the battlefield. The facts of crime fiction, murder, are not new. The crime writers merely tame death and violence and make it presentable; like good Victorians they often (but not always) keep the gore offstage—in the past.[4]

Thompson (1993, p. 8) is correct. In crime writing, all the contents and discontents of modernism and postmodernism are played out. At the same time, this writing form gently and persistently creates readers who now demand a more active place in the stories they are given about society and its dealings. The objective, realist text no longer works for this reader, who asks for open-ended stories about the postmodern and its discontents.

As Glover and Kaplan (1992, pp. 215-216) observe, contemporary detective writers confront, struggle with, and attempt to bring meaning to these discontents, which are multiple and include a rewriting of the politics of 1960s to fit a cultural conservatism of the 1990s; the restless, relentless intrusion of sexual politics into the American landscape, with a corresponding challenge to mythic, masculine heterosexuality and a concern "for a less macho, less misogynist homosociality . . . but a [persistent] horror of both male and female homosexuality" (Glover & Kaplan, 1992, p. 225); the entry of African American (Mosley, Green, and Haywood), Latina(o) (Ramos, 1993, 1994), Native American (Hager and Page; see Breen, 1994), feminist (Grafton, Muller, Van Giesen, and

Stabenow), and gay and lesbian (Hansen and Scottoline) crime writers into this political arena;[5] a reformed masculinity that shores up law and order (Glover & Kaplan, 1992, p. 222); a democratizing of public space, in which proactive women are no longer out of place nor only sexual objects or femme fatales; and an increased respect for the domestic popular as the site at which the New Right has attempted to exercise its hegemony (Glover & Kaplan, 1992, pp. 216, 222).

These are the topics that define the contradictory, ambiguous, and violent features of the postmodern moment. Crime writing (and the New Journalism), more than ethnography, have taken up these problems as their domain.

The postmodern detective, unlike his or her modernist counterpart, is no longer an objective observer of the world. This figure stirs up the world and is changed as a result of that project. In bearing witness to the unpresentable, this figure is morally tainted, jaded, and at times destroyed by what has been seen. Most critically, the postmodern detective stands exposed in the stories that are told: His or her personal, private life is central to the mystery, which becomes a version of an autoethnography. Like the new journalists (Mailer and Didion), crime writers question the relationship between facts and truths, telling at the same time moral stories about society, including speculations about "justice and injustice, good and evil" (Paul, 1992, p. 450) and the problems of human nature.[6] Producing texts that may play tricks on the reader, crime writers tell stories that require self-reflexive readers—readers who will not be seduced by a text's multiple verisimilitudes (the apparently guilty party is innocent, the apparently innocent party is the villain, etc.).

In challenging the traditional distinctions between fact and fiction, the new detectives, like the new journalists, disrupt the natural relationship between narrative, reality, facts, and truth. Pushing always to reveal the multiple truths that lurked behind the so-called facts that defined any situation, these writers locate reality not in facts or events but in the experience of the text. The truth of an experience, as presented by the writer, was thereby created by the reader who was drawn into the structures of verisimilitude that defined the text and story in question.

The crime writer creates a text in which all doubt is cast on the "possibility of distinguishing the prior from the later, the 'original' from copy or repetition, and before from after" (Frus, 1994, p. 213). In this writing form, the present is always being reconstituted, given new meanings each time it is confronted with newly formed interpretations: There is no primal present, no primal past, and nothing is absolute (Derrida, 1967/1978, p. 212; see also Frus, 1994, p. 213).

Postmodern detective writing extends the project of the new journalists. This writer also produces news about society while always doubting the authority of those who write what passes as truth and knowledge in the culture. In troubling traditional notions of truth, the new journalists inevitably worked within a self-contained four-sided system that also defines traditional fictional and nonfictional crime narrative (Frus, 1994, p. xx). Starting always with an event, a happening, a crime, an epiphanic event in the life of someone, they then identified a criminal or villain, a victim, and a sleuth (law enforcement officer or private eye). The new journalists added a new element to this traditional equation. They became stand-in sleuths—for example, Capote telling the murder of the Clutter family, Mailer taking on the Kennedy assassination, and Malcolm writing about the journalist and the murderer.

In the hands of Mailer, Malcolm, and Wolfe, the traditional villain-victim-sleuth model of detection was radically altered because a conspiratorial mode of inquiry was adopted. In this mode, still employed by the crime writer, the villain was no longer an isolated individual, but a larger collectivity—the media, the military, or the government. The victim was often the public-at-large seen through the suffering of a particular person (see Jameson, 1992, pp. 33-39). The journalist would work hand in hand with the detective or prosecutor, who explains "the crime by reconstituting how it 'must have happened' " (Frus, 1994, p. 196). In turn, the journalist would rereport the story, "imitating or supplementing the detective's story by recapitulating the solution in what becomes the privileged" (Frus, 1994, p. 196) or contested telling. A new way of telling stories about society was produced (journalist as sleuth), and these new storytellers met with considerable resistance, as discussed in Chapter 5.[7]

Unlike the journalist, who seeks out news and enters into an often dubious ethical relationship with those written about, the detective seldom initiates inquiry. The detective is hired to solve a problem and in so doing enacts an ethics of practice that privileges the client relationship. This ethical code, however, translates into a personal moral code that may lead the detective to work against the so-called best interests of the client.

As a form of realistic fiction, traditional, modernist crime fiction uses many of the literary techniques followed by the new journalists: the scenic method, the use of realistic dialogue, a blurring of writing genres, a treatment of facts as social constructions, the use of multiple points of view, a focus on social manners, and the presentation of a moral theory of society and human nature.

To repeat, I dispute Tyler's (1986, p. 122) claims for ethnography. Among the virtues Tyler appropriates for postmodern ethnography are its use of fragmented dialogical discourse, its ability to defamiliarize the familiar, the use of allegory, the rejection of the objective observer, and its tendency to take the reader into strange lands. These claims in hand, Tyler (p. 136) then observes, "No, there is no instance of a post-modern ethnography."

Tyler's (1986) inability to point, except obliquely, to the work of a few (e.g., Tedlock, 1983) supports my argument. The New Journalism and detective, crime, mystery, and suspense fiction have become the dominant discourses of the postmodern. These works, in their postmodern versions (see below), have taken on the features Tyler wants to give to postmodern ethnography. In the politics of the popular, and in the discourses of daily life, crime writers, not ethnographers, have seized the day. Ethnographers have much to learn from these writers. I describe, then, the lessons to be learned from the private eye.

My analysis will primarily focus on two contemporary crime fiction writers: James Lee Burke (1987, 1988, 1989, 1990, 1992a, 1992b, 1993, 1994, 1995) and John Straley (1992, 1993, personal communications, November 3, 11, 29, 1994, January 25, 1995, November 2, 1995; 1996).[8] (My discussion will also be informed by the work of several other contemporary crime writers,[9] including Walter Mosley, Manuel Ramos, Pago Ignacio Taibo II, Joseph Hansen, Lawrence Block, Tony Hillerman, and such diverse "Sisters in Crime"[10] as Lisa Scottoline, Sara Paretsky, and Sue Grafton.)

First, however, I must briefly trace the history of crime fiction. This history moves from nineteenth-century mass media stories about murder and crime to the creation of the fictional private detective who solves crime puzzles and to moral and metaphysical stories about crime and the meanings of life in an increasingly fragmented and disjointed postmodern world. This history corresponds to the history of ethnography outlined in Chapter 1, including the major moments in capitalism (market, monopoly, and multinational), the three dominant aesthetic formations in the twentieth century (realism, modernism, and post-modernism), and the five moments in ethnography (traditional, modernist, blurred genre, crisis of representation, and the present).

From Crime to News to Moral Fiction

In one version of the origin story, the detective story emerges in the mid-nineteenth century with the appearance of the modern police force in the democratic societies (Bloch, 1988, pp. 246-247; Haycraft, 1972, p. 7; Thompson, 1993, pp. 3-5). This apparatus necessitated the collection of evidence that could be brought to bear in criminal trials. Thus were created professional and amateur private criminal investigators who collected such materials. The science of criminalistics appears by mid-century, and the agents of the state were soon using photography as a method of recording crimes and keeping track of criminals and their associates.

With the modern police force and the science of criminalistics came the modern social sciences (sociology, anthropology, and psychology), and with psychology came Freud's psychoanalytic movement. The psychoanalytic case study would be presented as a mystery (Porter, 1981, pp. 243-244), the discovery and unraveling of buried psychic traces bearing on the meaning of life (eros, sexuality) and death (thantos, violence). These meanings were made visible through the eyes and words of the psychoanalytic voyeur who could interpret seemingly insignificant (and at times problematic) surface details littering the patient's life—the belief that everything means something.

The mass circulation newspaper, the pulp magazine, pulp fiction, and media stories about serial murders were popularized during this same time period (Symons, 1985, pp. 43-44). The modern novel enters this space—for example, Dickens's serialized stories about the horrible urban conditions that produced crime (Cawelti, 1976, p. 58). By the end of the century, there would be the institutionalization of the cine-matic apparatus and the creation of cinema's voyeur (Denzin, 1995a, pp. 4-25). This voyeur would soon be a private investigator using the science of criminalistics to capture urban criminals. There was a large, middle-class mass market ready to read (and see) stories about murder and murderers.

Therefore, as indicated previously, the crime writers domesticated violence. Drawing on the facts of daily life, as reported in the media, readers were taught to read and appreciate violent stories about unhappy people who murdered one another. Readers were taught the methods of crime detection, including logic, forensic science, participant observation, document analysis, interviewing, and introspection. They learned how to distinguish true from false clues. These hard facts were then fitted to a mystery in which the detective solved the crime in question.

In these moves, the nineteenth-century crime writers helped solidify the realistic novel as a distinct genre. The crime writers gave the realist novel concrete subjects (dead bodies, victims, and murderers) and concrete methods for separating facts from fictions and lies from the truth. In so doing, they helped the realist novel solve two problems (Clough, 1992, p. 20; McKeon, 1987, p. 22). The first problem was empirical—namely, how to authorize the truth of a representation when measured against the demands of empiricism. The second question turned on the construction of a realistic, self-made, autonomous subject whose experiences could be seen as occurring in the real world of real experience. The realist novel attempted to solve these questions by presenting stories that were narrated by unified subjects (and omniscient authors). These persons reported on their own (and other's) experiences, continually making distinctions between facts and fiction. Of course, this was the precise project of the mystery story.

The Classic, Traditional Model

According to another version of the origin story (Cawelti, 1976, p. 80), in the beginning was Poe (1966), who in three detective stories published between the years 1841 and 1845 (Haycraft, 1972, pp. 13-14) created the formula for the classic detective story.[11] In *The Murders in the Rue Morgue, The Mystery of Marie Roget,* and *The Purloined Letter,* Poe

(1966) defined four essential features (situation, patterns of action, characters, and setting) of this new fiction that carried important links to the Gothic novel. The crime novel should begin with a crime that has already occurred (Block, 1988, p. 255; Jameson, 1983, p. 147), with the mystery centering on the identity, motive, and means of action of the criminal.[12] The crime presented, the story must then evolve through six main phases: an introduction of the detective, a further description of the crime and its clues, the investigation itself, an announcement of its solution, an explanation of why the crime occurred, and a denouement (Cawelti, 1976, pp. 81-82). Four main characters must be developed: the victim, the criminal, the detective, and those threatened by the crime (Cawelti, 1976, p. 91). Finally, the story (and crime) must be located in a setting marked off from ordinary civil society—for example, a locked room or an isolated country house.

Thus, classic British (and American) crime fiction unfolded. Confined to these essential structures, male (Bentley, Carr, Doyle, Innes, Collins, and Chesterton) and female (Christie, Wells, Sayers, Tey, and Rinehart) writers could easily fit this formula to the stories they told.

These stories presented a brilliant detective who was eccentric, aloof, and detached from society, given to keen intelligence, adept at logic, but gifted with a poetic or intuitive imagination that allowed entry into the minds of victims and criminals (Cawelti, 1976, p. 148). He or she was able to locate the guilty party when the police failed, although the police often assisted this person in the quest for truth. In this quest, the detective's life was seldom threatened, and only infrequently was the detective personally involved with the victim, the victim's family, or with the criminal. In a typical telling, a parade of suspects would be brought forth and interrogated. These suspects would be eliminated, one by one, as the detective, in a spectacle of discovery, isolated and unmasked the guilty party.

These were crimes of passion, some sexual, most violent, usually against family members. The classic detective story was a tale about the middle and upper classes and their problems.[13] These stories aestheticized crime; they turned acts of passion into intellectual puzzles that could be solved by a rational mind (Cawelti, 1976, pp. 99, 107). At the same time, they contained violence within the family, inevitably offering a rational explanation for the violent conduct of a particular family member (p. 105).

As such, their novels differed from the realistic, social problems-based melodramas of Dicken's and other nineteenth-century writers who exposed the hypocrisy and guilt of a callous middle-class society (see Cawelti, 1976, pp. 58, 104-105). The crime writers validated the existing social order and validated the belief that crimes were a matter of individual motivation (p. 105). In the end, order was always restored, society was back at peace with itself, and the detective retreated to his or her chambers to contemplate poetry, art, classical music, gourmet cooking, orchids, or a good pipe. Like good traditional and modernist ethnographers, these writers told objective tales about society and its moral problems.

The Hard-Boiled Model

This model held until the early 1920s when the American hard-boiled detective story emerged on the scene.[14] In successive decades, Hammett (1930s), Chandler (1940s), and Macdonald (1950s-1970s) redefined the genre, and their legacies linger to the present day in the soft-boiled story.[15] Working with Poe's basic structures, this group of writers personalized the detective, making him part of society and a coparticipant in the crimes investigated.[16] This man of the world had a personal moral code, and he lived alone, on the fringes of the social, in seedy offices in disreputable regions of the city. He had ties to the underworld, and he was friends with ex-cops, prostitutes, pimps, burned-out journalists, and sometimes had a friend on the police force (Cawelti, 1976, pp. 152-153). He also knew people of great wealth. He was one with this society that he stood alienated from. His quest was always for personal justice. He was detective, judge, and executioner. He brought justice to those who had been victimized by a corrupt society in which respectability and power masked evil and corruption.

No crime was ever simple; it involved complex webs of interconnected deceptions, misrepresentations, and betrayals, often more than one murder, and frequently the detective had a personal relationship with the criminal who was a woman—a femme fatale. The hard-boiled detective would become a victim of violence, be tempted by bribes, be hired by the villain, and even face the loss of his license. This antihero was tough, sentimental, a cynic, and used to brutality. He understood that evil was everywhere, caused by the structures of wealth capitalism permitted, and amplified by Oedipal relationships buried deep in the repressed pasts of corrupt and powerful families (Cawelti 1976, p. 150; Macdonald, 1970, p. x).

In critiquing capitalist society (Cawelti, 1976, p. 173), the hard-boiled writers redefined the genre.[17] They turned a form that produced intellectual puzzles into a forum for social criticism. They moved their writer directly into the social world and eschewed simple intellectual, rational solutions to complex social and personal problems.

The classic writers maintained a wall—a division between civil society and private, domestic life. The hard-boiled detectives tore this wall down, erasing the boundaries between the personal and the political and the social and the civil. Civil society was a battlefield, a war zone, and a fraudulent place where violent acts occurred on a regular basis. Their antihero could make things right. These writers set the stage for the crisis of representation that would occur in the genre when the next generation of writers began to tell somewhat different stories about crimes and their victims.

The Soft-Boiled Model:
The Death of Modernism

It remained for others to modify this model, which held steady through the 1960s when a new group of writers, not unlike the new journalists, entered the field.[18] Increasing numbers of ethnic, feminist, and gay and lesbian writers began to rework the hard-boiled model. They brought their own cultural, gender, sexual, and ethnic standpoints to bear on the crime problem in America, frequently pointing, as did Macdonald, to the family (incest, rape, and sexual violence) as the source and site of the problem. They softened and blurred the model. They gave the detective a family or a long-term relationship. Women were no longer femme fatales, and gay men could be masculine and solve crimes and have their own code of honor. Macho, insensitive, sexually aggressive, handsome, and violent men were now the enemy.

These writers began to articulate a politics of culture and domestic life that went beyond the hard-boiled critique that focused on capitalists on the one side and wealthy families on the other. They reopened the domestic sphere as the place where cultural, not just economic, politics were played out. Here, they returned to the classic British model. By openly engaging sexuality and desire, however, they uncovered and exposed the repressed sexual code that governed the Victorian mystery. Less inclined to pursue their own code of honor (but not above doing so when necessary), these writers realigned the genre with the state and the police, often working hand in hand with these agents of social control.

The Postmodern Turn

Finally, the postmodern turn, and not just the metaphysical "detective" stories of Robbe-Grillet, Borges, Nabokov, Pynchon, Reed, Marquez, and Dillo are discussed (Cawelti, 1976, p. 137; Holquist, 1983, pp. 165, 172-174; Thompson, 1993, p. 168). The metaphysical detectives produced stories that inverted Poe's classic model—the syllogistic model that inevitably restores, through action and ratiocination, order to a disorderly world. Cawelti (1976, p. 137) calls these works anti- or inverted detective stories. In them, the reader confronts hesitating investigators, facing absurd situations, plots that consist of no plot, mysteries not about death but about life's absence of meaning, worlds without meaning, chaos, and the inability of any kind of narrative or psychological model to bring meaning to a violent world (Holquist, 1983, p. 173).

These novelists opened the door that the new postmodern, post-hard-boiled writers like Burke and Straley step through. The post-hard-boiled writers have their feet in three worlds at the same time: Hammett, Chandler's (and Hemingway's) hard-boiled, macho tradition; the soft, domestic, damaged variations on this tradition; and the metaphysical insights of Borges and Robbe-Grillet. They are cynical but doubtful, and no overarching moral code works any longer.

Their works exhibit but go beyond those features Tyler wants to bring to the postmodern ethnography (fragmented dialogical discourse, defamiliarizing the familiar, using allegory, the rejection of the objective observer, and taking the reader into strange lands). These qualities, however, produce, at best, a ludic postmodernism (Kincheloe & McLaren, 1994, p. 143): Playful texts that risk reinscribing the status quo while reducing ethnography to the invention of new forms of textuality. The post-hard-boiled detectives seek a materialist, resistance postmodernism. Their utopian and dystopian texts intervene in the world, producing material changes in the lives of people.

At the same time, these writers attempt a form of discourse that captures a mobile, unstable consciousness recording its relationship to an ever-changing external world. This complex world, with its multiple perspectives, is then connected to a constantly changing external world, in which nothing is firm or certain. Consequently, there can be no single truth; the only truth is that of self-discovery—the moral rebirth of the detective.

Straley and Burke embody these tendencies. They struggle to bring ethnography (and detective fiction) back to a moral and ethical center that locates the "other" in us. Their texts are not records of experience, but rather they become the means for the reader's moral experience. In these works, the detective journeys through the familiar and the unfamiliar to find the truth about himself. He is the agent of this discovery, the means to truth. He works within and against the laws, not of science, but of society and its moral order. Science and politics have corrupted the social and destroyed nature. They have violated the first law of nature: The more humans attempt to control anything, the more uncontrollable it becomes.

James Lee Burke

His name is Dave Robicheaux. He is a detective for the New Iberia Parish Sheriff Department, a small town located east of New Orleans and southeast of Baton Rouge near the Atchafalaya Basin and the Gulf of Mexico. Now the subject of eight highly praised, best-selling novels (see Carter, 1992), Burke's Robicheaux is a contemporary version of Chandler's hard-boiled detective. He is damaged, however, one of the walking wounded, given to bouts of violence and troubled by dreams and nightmares that seem to return to Vietnam and its aftermath in American culture. He fights to stay sober. His stories are told in the first person, constantly merging, through visual flashbacks, the past with the present. Best read cinematically, or televisually, as a collage of interconnected scenes and complex story lines, with constant close-ups of Dave, the series moves back and forth between Western Montana (Missoula) and Southern Louisiana (New Orleans and New Iberia).[19]

Dave confronts people who have names like Bobby Earl, Bama, Tante Lemon, Lester Benoit, Patsy Dap, Sonny Boy Marsallus, and Glo ("You treat me right, I light up. I light up your whole life" [Burke, 1995, p. 101]). His close friends call him "Streak" because of the white spot that marks his otherwise black hair. He loves the French Quarter and is close friends with working-class Cajuns, blacks, pimps, hookers, ex-cops, the rich, and the powerful. He deals with violence on a daily basis: "A prostitute icepicked by a psychotic john. . . . Two homosexual men burned alive" (Burke, 1987, p. 11) or a social worker bludgeoned to death with a claw hammer (Burke, 1995, p. 18).

A Vietnam veteran, he is nearing 50 and tries to run or work out everyday. A recovering alcoholic, he has an Alcoholics Anonymous (AA) sponsor (Tee Neg) and goes to AA meetings (Burke, 1992a, p. 218). He has been married three times. His first wife divorced him, and his second wife, Annie, was murdered. His present wife, Bootsie, has lupus. They have an adopted daughter from Salvador named Alafair who is now almost 14 years old (Burke, 1995, p. 23). Alafair has a horse named Tex and a pet three-legged coon named Tripod who wreaks havoc in Dave's boat and bait shop.

Located on the bayou, a few miles outside New Iberia, the bait shop is managed by Batist, an ageless, illiterate African American man "as black and solid as boilerplate" (Burke, 1995, p. 42). A hundred yards back from the bayou sits his house, which was built by his father who spoke Cajun French and died in an oil derrick fire when Dave was a teenager. Dave's best friend is Cletus Purcel, a private investigator and an ex-policeman—a large, tough man who always wears a powder blue porkpie hat and tropical print shirts. He is a heavy drinker, "His green eyes [were] lighted with an alcoholic shine" (Burke, 1994, p. 12), and his face bears a scar "as thick as a bicycle patch, perforated with stitch holes, where he had been bashed with a pipe when he was a kid in the Irish Channel" (Burke, 1994. p. 12).

Robicheaux is given to lyrical descriptions of his world (Burke, 1988):

I was just off the Southwest Pass, between Pecan and March islands, with the green, whitecapping water of the Gulf Stream to the south, and the long, flat expanse of the Louisiana coastline behind me. . . . Dead cypress strung with wisps of moss, and a maze of canals and bayous that are choked with Japanese water lilies whose purple flowers audibly pop in the morning. . . . It was May and the the breeze was warm and smelled of salt spray. (p. 1)

Dave is bothered by dreams. "He waited for me in my dreams . . . a metamorphic figure who changed his appearance every night (Burke, 1990, p. 20). Also (Burke, 1993),

My dreams take me many places: Sometimes back to a windswept firebase on the top of an orange hill gouged with shell holes; a soft, mist-streaked morning with ducks rising against a pink sun while my father and I crouched in the blind. . . . But tonight I was back in the summer of my freshman year in college, July of 1957." (p. 3)

Robicheaux has a theory of human nature: It divides the world into the following categories. First are the walking wounded, "the ones to whom a psychological injury was done that they will never be able to define" (Burke, 1992a, p. 280). These people, "who cause psychiatrists and priests to sigh helplessly" (Burke, 1992a, p. 280), live in a world inhabited by evil people. There are two types of evil persons: the morally insane and the politically evil—the "dark players . . . the oil and chemical companies . . . the developers . . . the Mafia" (Burke, 1992a, p. 30) and the "elected political officials" (Burke, 1992b, p. 45). Society takes two approaches to such persons. The morally insane, the sociopaths, psychopaths, mainline recidivists (Burke, 1992a, p. 57), maniacal killers, sex criminals, sadists (Burke, 1992b, p. 45), and other atavistic members of the pool (Burke, 1992a, p. 60) are locked up or otherwise provide employment for social workers, jailers, truant officers, psychologists, and public defenders (Burke, 1992a, p. 76).[20] In contrast, the bigots, Klansmen, Aryan Brotherhood, anti-Semites, and the politically evil are "out there by consent" (Burke, 1992a, p. 304).

In making bargains with the politically corrupt, we get, Robicheaux contends (Burke, 1992b, p. 47), the kind of society we deserve. In the end, however, evil persons will fall. This will happen because of the efforts of good people who become engaged, and make themselves visible, and because of the arrogance of power, which always corrupts (pp. 44, 49).

Evil can, however, strike out at anyone: Seemingly randomly, an ordinary person suddenly finds that "they have been arbitrarily selected as a victim of an individual or a group about whom they have no knowledge and against whom they've committed no personal offense" (Burke, 1995, p. 73). In these moments, like Chandler's detective, Dave steps forward and "down these mean streets a man must go who is not himself mean, who is neither tarnished, nor afraid. . . . The detective . . . must be such a man. He is the hero; he is everything" (Chandler, 1972, p. 20). Dave is tarnished, but he is a hero and he is not afraid. He is a good person, and when he steps forward to help the helpless the problems always seem to come home to threaten his family.

The series is self-reflexive, turning back on itself, elaborating and developing characters as they age (Alafair, Cletus, Bootsie, and Dave), and connecting their past histories to their current situations. In each work, Robicheaux struggles to find a place for himself in a world that is increasingly out of control. At the same time, the series writes itself alongside contemporary American history. It constantly critiques the violence that has accompanied the cultural conservatism of the past two decades, seeking always to find a place for a new straight, gay, lesbian, or bisexual man or woman who might enjoy some dignity, intimacy, and personal happiness in this violent, unstable world.

His America is the new but the old South, where the legacies of a violent racial history (the Civil War) are folded into old southern myths about a gentile aristocracy. These myths settle over local communities, such as New Iberia, where poor blacks, Cajuns, and middle-class whites interact in a beautiful, tranquil, bayou pastorale setting governed by complex rules of racial etiquette that maintain an ancient color line.

Violence cannot be kept out of this world, and the violence that Burke continually returns to has its roots in an America that has lost its innocence. The following are his topics, which are told through Dave's attempts to maintain some sense of order, justice, and community in New Iberia (Burke, 1992b): Neocolonialism, Vietnam, prisoners of war, Watergate, the Iran-Contra story, the international drug economy (from the Golden Triangle to Latin America), the war on drugs, the Middle East, mercenary armies, an unworkable prison, welfare, and educational system, the CIA, FBI, DEA, Desert Storm, a new generation given to random violence, organized crime, the racist, conservative political legacies of Reagan and Bush and now Gingrich.

Into Dave's life enter figures with connections to each of these story lines: Nicaraguan, Columbian, and local drug dealers (Burke, 1987, 1988, 1995); corruption and violence in the oil industry (Burke, 1989); Vietnam War heroes who are drug dealers (Burke, 1990); the CIA, the mob, and Klansmen (Burke, 1992a); a serial murderer and the New Orleans mob (Burke, 1993); Neo-Nazis (Burke, 1994); and violence toward black sharecroppers (Burke, 1995). The stories typically involve Dave (and Cletus) in a triangular conflict, pitting the two of them against local mobsters and hired assassins who are attempting to destroy either one of the world's walking wounded or a member of the underclass, often local Cajuns or blacks.

A Stained White Radiance[21] (Burke, 1992a) is characteristic of the series. The plot is typically complex. Bootsie's lupus is out of control and she is suffering from steroid psychosis. Someone is out to do harm to the three siblings in the Sonnier family: Drew, the attractive older sister, twice married, and founder of the local Amnesty International chapter: Lyle, a Vietnam veteran (with whom Dave served), now a televangelist; and Weldon, the wealthy brother who is an oilman. Weldon, who also served in Vietnam and flew for Air America, a front for the CIA, is married to Bama. Bama is addicted to drugs. Her brother is Bobby Earl, a politician with connections to the Klan, the American Nazi movement, and to Joey Gouza, a New Orleans mob figure, and drug dealer with ties to Jack Gates, a gun runner. The father, Verise Sonnier, long thought dead, has reappeared with a new name—Vic Benson.

The story begins with Dave's history of the Sonnier family (Burke, 1992a):

> The background of the Sonnier children was one that you instinctively knew you didn't want to know more about. . . . As a child I saw the cigarette burns on the arms and legs of the Sonnier children. . . . I came to believe that [they] grew up in a furnace rather than a home. (pp. 1-2)

A shot is fired at Weldon's house and Dave is called to investigate. In short order, a new policeman on the force is killed at Weldon's home; Dave is attacked by two lowlifes, Eddy Raintree and Jewel Fluck; Bootsie and Alafair are threatened by phone calls; Bootsie gets better with new drugs; Cletus picks fights with Joey and Bobby Earl; Dave has nightmares about Vietnam; Drew drives a nail through her hand, charging Joey with the crime; Lyle tells Dave how he and Drew and Weldon killed their father's mistress, Mattie, after their mother died; and their father was presumed killed in an oil rig fire. Dave suspects that Joey Gouza controls Bobby Earl and is out to harm the Sonnier family as a way of controlling Bobby. Weldon plays a tape, revealing how he double-crossed Joey and Jack Gates on a drug run to Columbia. Bobby is jailed and the violence toward the family continues. The story climaxes at a political rally for Bobby Earl, after a family reunion at Lyle's when the three children confront their long-lost father. Vic (Verise) attempts to murder Bobby Earl, mistaking him for Weldon. Dave and Batiste capture Vic and save Weldon. In the denouement, Dave, Bootsie, and Alafair take their family vacation to Key West. Joey Gouza is still in prison. Bobby Earl went on to greater political power, Vic is in jail, and Dave saves Alafair from a nurse shark as they snorkel off a coral reef.

Dave summarizes the mystery (Burke, 1992a):

I had been determined to prove that Bobby Earl was fronting points for Joey Gouza, or that he was connected with arms and drug trafficking in the tropics. I was guilty of the age-old presumption that the origins of social evil can be traced to villainous individuals. . . . Bobby Earl is out there by consent. (p. 304)

This is a postmodern telling of a quasi-police procedural because Dave, after all, is a policeman. The story unfolds in criss-crossing, overlapping "Fellini-esque" episodes that illuminate each of the key characters. ("The animals in the circus car crashed wildly about in their wire cages. I touched Eddy Raintree lightly on the shoulder, and it rotated downward with gravity on the severed tendons in his neck. One of the gandy walkers vomited" [Burke, 1992a, p, 155]). Victims (Sonniers, Bootsie, and Alafair), crimes, and suspects (Joey, Bobbie Earl, and Vic) multiply as individuals bring different stories to Dave. Each story confounds the investigation, pointing Dave away from Vic and toward Joey. In fact, however, the stories are intertwined. Weldon has an incriminating tape Joey wants, and hence Joey authorizes the attacks on

Weldon and his family. Vic has returned and seeks vengeance against his three children. Weldon dared to do what Vic would not do; that is, drill for oil on the family property. Weldon and his siblings killed Vic's mistress.

Hence, the violence comes from two sources: the personal and the political. Each set of crimes has its own structure of rationality, but different clues point in different directions. In following one set of clues, those pointing to Joey, Dave is led away from the other clues that point to Vic. The family assists in this, covering up both Vic's reemergence in their lives and lying about their involvement with Joey and his connections to Bobby Earl. At the same time, Dave is trapped in his situation with Bootsie, who is suffering from her psychotic reactions to her disease. Nothing is exactly as it appears. What is apparently true turns out to be false, what is false turns out to be true, and there are certain truths that Dave cannot use because they would harm good people (Burke, 1992a, p. 262), including reporting the fact that Drew drove the nail through her own hand.

Thus, the detective is in the center of three overlapping story lines: his life with Bootsie and Alafair, the Sonnier family's attempt at salvation redemption, and the story of Bobby Earl and his involvement with organized crime. The detective finds that no account of reality is stable. Drew, Lyle, and Weldon keep changing the information they give him. Bobby Earl and Joey Gouza do the same, and even Vic denies knowing his own children. Multiple verisimilitudes and multiple truths are operating: Bobby Earl is loved by his blue-collar, redneck constituency, but he is evil and corrupt; Bootsie is the best person Dave has ever encountered but she may die or go crazy.

What is the truth? Which is the correct verisimilitude? Evil people do evil things but not necessarily the evil things you think they do. Good people do bad things: Does this make them bad? Bad people do good things, and so on.

The detective confronts this underlying truth. He lives in a constantly changing unstable world. He can never make his perceptions and beliefs veridical with this world. To attempt to do so is to risk insanity.

Robicheaux's AA sponsor, Tee Neg, summarizes the situation Dave confronts, noting that he cannot accept the fact that the new South is not like the old South, when (Burke, 1992a) you and me and yo' daddy went all day and everywhere and never spoke one word of English. You walk away when you hear white people talking bad about them Negro . . . but you keep pretend it's like it used to be. Get mad about what you can't change and maybe you'll do it just like Tee Neg done [get drunk]. . . . It ain't never gonna be the same. That world we grew up in, it's gone. (pp. 219-220)

More is involved—Bootsie's illness (Burke, 1992a):

I realized the error of my thinking. . . . The problem wasn't her disease. It was in mine. I wanted a lock on the future. I wanted our marriage to be about the governance of morality and chance. . . . I hadn't bothered to be grateful for the things I had. (p. 186)

Two messages, two vital truths; one connected to the past, and the other to the present. Robicheaux cannot change the new South; pure nostalgia draws him back to a racial order that will never be again. His idealized world has changed and he cannot bring it back. Second, he already has everything he needs. He cannot control the future, but he has Bootsie today, and for this he must be grateful. He can neither live in the past nor attempt to control the future. This is AA philosophy, another version of the "Serenity Prayer," which asks the person to accept what cannot be changed while having the courage to change what can be changed and the wisdom to know the difference.

This is what the Burke series is all about—allegories about a world out of control. Robicheaux confronting, over and over again, challenges to his beliefs in a mystical, pure South, tests of his willingness to accede to a past that is gone, and challenges to his integrity, which ask him to rise up and fight for what he believes in. In these actions, Dave Robicheaux rewrites Philip Marlowe's project. Gone is the lonely detective who has neither friends nor family. Gone is the mythic figure who stands strong and tall against a world of evil. Dave never undoes evil, and only occasionally is complete justice ever achieved. Justice works locally: the Sonnier family back together again and Dave at home with Bootsie and Alafair. Gone is a moral code that makes the detective judge and executioner. Burke's detective loses control and acts violently and is brought up short by the law (his constant suspensions). Against all this, however, hovers this moral code taken from AA, one of the last homes for the damaged, postmodern, macho detective. Without his sanity and his sobriety, all else would fall away.

In this, Burke's hero is turned into an ordinary figure, a member of the walking wounded, a fallen figure who learns over and again a single lesson—the world has changed and the changes cannot be undone. Cecil Wayne Younger, John Straley's private detective, knows this too, but his lessons go beyond this point: They involve deep interrogations about what passes for truth in today's postmodern world, including the truths of myth and folklore. Straley's autoethnographies, like Burke's, constantly expose the investigators frailties and self-weaknesses, making the investigator's moral journey a central part of the mystery at hand.[22]

John Straley

He is a damaged man, maybe an alcoholic, the ne'er-do-well son of a recently deceased famous Alaskan Judge.[23] His world is situated in Sitka, Alaska, a small coastal town of 8,000 people located about 70 miles by air from Juneau. Younger lives with, and is the unofficial guardian of, an autistic man named Toddy. He and Toddy are both 36 years old. Cecil runs a private "investigator's service in a town with no business" (Straley, 1993, p. 6).

Cecil plays at being Sam Spade in Sitka (Straley, 1992, p. 50)—a subartic gumshoe (Straley, 1992, p. 34), sometimes called one of the Hardy Boys (Straley, 1993, p. 9)—and ironically compares himself to Chandler's Marlowe, noting though, that "mysterious blondes never go to Sitka when they want to hire a detective to find a rare coin stolen from their father's mansion" (Straley, 1992, p. 32).[24] He takes rape, assault, and murder cases but no divorce or insurance work (Straley, 1992, pp. 32-33), unless he is completely broke. He has a bad reputation and has few friends, but he is not like one of those private detectives on TV because he is never in control of anything (Straley, 1992, p. 179). Younger has no drivers license, preferring cabs or walking, and he does not carry a gun. He abhors violence.

His sister is a lawyer who teaches at Yale. Cecil studied music and art history at Reed college but was thrown out. He got into drugs, went to Africa and Asia where he studied religion and music, and traveled the South singing in choirs. His father got him a job as an investigator with the Public Defender Agency in Juneau hoping to shame him into going to law school (Straley, 1992, p. 50). He got into trouble with cocaine and a "small matter of suborning perjury . . . and did a little time" (p. 50). He stayed sober until his father died. He then "played the drunken aesthete" (p. 51) until his girlfriend, Hannah Elder, a recovering alcoholic social worker, threw him out. "She wanted more than ego, irony and alcohol" (p. 33).

He likes jazz and the blues (Billie Holiday and Miles Davis), reads Roethke and Wendell Berry, and watches the old *Thin Man* movies. He does not like AA (Straley, 1992, p. 165) and is continually on and off the wagon ("I hate being on the wagon. It's like getting my life back but losing one of my senses" [Straley, 1993, p. 13]). He likes being drunk because only drunks understand that "reality is basically an ironic joke that no one gets" (Straley, 1993, p. 17).

A defense investigator, people hire him to imagine their innocence (Straley, 1993, p. 3), to find that version of the truth that is most acceptable (Straley, 1992, p. 9), the version that makes the most sense (Straley, 1992, p. 225). Unlike the police, who collect facts and the oral history of a crime (Straley, 1992, p. 5), Cecil gathers folklore, and in the end he is a storyteller with no authority, "no badge, and no flashing blue lights" (Straley, 1993, p. 3). The police base their reports on the facts, but these reports do not always make sense, and they do not make things right. Cecil gives his clients stories that make sense (Straley, 1992, p. 225). The stories he collects and tells are the old stories: Myths that "don't have anything to do with the facts; they're the box that all the facts came in" (Straley, 1992, p. 225). An investigator of oral culture and a collector of folklore, he looks for different versions of the same story, understanding that fiction is a way to get at the truth (J. Straley, personal communication, November 3, 1994) and that life stories are constantly being revised to fit the situation people find themselves in (Straley, 1992, p. 120). Cecil seeks the truth of life fictions and not that version of truth that is based on the so-called hard facts of a criminal case.

Straley's territory is Alaska and what is happening to this state in the last years of the twentieth century, but he asks, where is the "Real Alaska?" (Straley, 1992, p. 106). To some Straley writes,

> Southeastern Alaska is a suburb of San Francisco, inhabited by drug-addled phoneys and bureaucrats, with a few loggers and fisherman holding against the odds. The phoneys and the bureaucrats have an image of the modern white resident of the north as a 400-pound Oklahoma building contractor with a 50-pound gold nugget watch-band and an antebellum attitude toward the darker races. (p. 106)

Alaska is a postmodern site. In a downtown bar in Anchorage, for example (Straley, 1992),

> You can find a deranged redneck watching a Rams game on the wide-screen TV alongside an arts administrator who is working on a production of *Waiting for Godot* to tour the arctic villages. Both of them will walk around the Eskimo man bundled up asleep on the sidewalk, but the arts administrator will feel an ironic sense of history. (pp. 106-107)

Anchorage embodies the real Alaska: "Gold, wars, earthquakes, oil, environmental disasters, everything was good for Anchorage. Except peace and stability" (Straley, 1993, p. 154).

Straley's stories are set in this conflicting social and moral order, the last frontier, where Native Alaskans find their lives defined and shaped by this neocolonial nightmare, the Disneyland of the north. Cecil's sensibilities align him with the underdog—drunks, alcoholics, hunters, native Tlingit and Yupiks, crazies, and iconoclasts. He is against those who would take control of the Alaskan earth and destroy it in the name of progress (Straley, 1993, p. 157). Straley seeks a sacred relationship to the earth, nature, natural beauty, the rhythm of the seasons, the symbolic meanings of bears, ravens, whales, the wind, and the rain, and fears that human beings are destroying themselves and this world. This is a radical environmentalism (J. Straley, personal communication, November 11, 1994), of sorts, which locates the enemy in the machineries and cultural logics of transnational, corporate capitalism and patriarchy.[25]

Cecil wages a battle against these cultural logics. He understands that the rapes, murders, alcoholism, and family violence that he encounters can be directly and indirectly traced back to these cultural formations. The laws of the state protect the rich (Straley, 1993, p. 157). The people Cecil works for find their lives and their fates twisted to suit the privileged class, which is hip deep in the environmental destruction of Alaska. (Cecil's nemesis, and old family friend, George Doggy, embodies this contradiction—a man who works for the state but always seeks justice.)

Like Dave Robicheaux, Cecil has a theory of human nature, but his is perhaps more existential than Burke's. Here, Straley is like Tony Hillerman's Joe Leaphorn (see Breen, 1994, p. 50): A skeptic about God, he believes that there are always multiple stories about and multiple causes for everything. Underneath, the universe is rational and orderly, although stories and causes are not necessarily the same. Like Hillerman's Jim Chee,[26] however, Cecil is drawn to the truth of the old ways and experiences conflict when the two belief systems collide. Humans are responsible for their own actions, existence defines essence. Humans do evil when they retreat from, or fail to embrace, this natural, ethical order. Trouble comes into the world when these two moral orders, nature and the social, come into conflict: when humans attempt to impose their will on the natural, moral order. Evil, violent actions are caused by self-weakness, self-doubt, the actions of others, greed, and such cultural diseases as alcoholism and family violence.

Unlike Hillerman, who writes about native people, Straley writes (mainly) about crazy or damaged white people.[27] Still, he finds in native myth and folklore a sacred, ritualistic cultural logic that honors a natural, orderly, but violent social world. This order is given, at a deep level, in the old myths and in native folklore. In a site like Alaska, there is an ongoing tension between folklore, the truth of the old stories, and the orderly, rational, white male mind. Still, these old quasi-religious stories contain the seeds of a magical realism; at one level their teachings are true. Humans make their way through this world by respecting nature and following the old myths.

Cecil respects and follows these myths. He also embraces the lore and ethics of the hunter, seeing in the hunter's mind something that is both personal and meditative (J. Straley, personal communication, November 29, 1994). The hunter (investigator) respects his prey (suspects) and becomes one with the prey, always honoring the dead and praising their spirit (J. Straley, personal communication, November 29, 1994). Here, there is a merger of the ancient stories of the north with the projects of hunting and being a private investigator (J. Straley, personal communication, November 29, 1994). These tales ask the hunter to always be respectful of the prey, the enemy, to see in the hunt, the investigation, an ancient struggle between truth, power, and justice (Straley, 1992, pp. 55-58; 1993, pp. 199-204).

The rules are changing for the new investigator (PI)—he is not like Marlowe, the hunter of old. The new PI is trying to find new rules that apply in this changing world (J. Straley, personal communication, January 25, 1995). As a result, the PI's self is constantly being changed; the old rules no longer apply. This PI asks the world to reveal itself through its stories. Every story contains a kernel of truth, and Cecil seeks the multiple truths and verisimilitudes that reside in these stories. His is the "eye/i" of the culturally sensitive ethnographer, not the all-seeing "I" of Marlowe whose eyes render the world immediately visible and understandable.

In Cecil's world, nature becomes a stand-in for the self. John Straley (personal communication, January 25, 1995) inverts Aristotle's theory of narrative that reduces stories to three forms: human-human, human-nature, and human-self. In Straley's tales, self is folded back into nature. The struggles between humans are always mediated by a natural, ethical order that attempts to restore balance to the world. He approaches this world with a cautious, intelligent optimism grounded in a faith in common sense and the fictional truths of those old stories of the north that are always within range of being heard, if one but listens (J. Straley, personal communication, November 3, 1994).

The Woman Who Married a Bear (Straley, 1992) is a neo- or postcolonial racial and ethnic Oedipal tale, a parable about what happens to native Indians when they marry whites. The novel takes place in 1984, 2 years after the murder of Louis Victor. It is a murder mystery based, in part, on a tale related to Straley by a Tlingit woman who told him about "a woman who married a bear and had children by him" (Straley, 1992, p. i).[28] In the end of the story, the children kill their father and eat him, leaving his body on a rock.

Louis Victor's mother, Mrs. Victor, an old Tlinget woman in a nursing home, hires Cecil to find the true story about her son's death: "My son has been murdered and I want to know the whole truth. . . . I know how it happened. . . . I want to know why" (Straley, 1992, pp. 9-10). "There was trouble in my son's family. . . . He would visit me. . . .

He always wanted to hear those Indian stories. I would tell him the same stories my father and uncles told me" (p. 11).

The circumstances of the case are the following. Louis was a big game guide, an "Alaskan stereotype—strong, proud, Tlinget man, good with a gun, good finding the game" (Straley, 1992, p. 86). He was murdered on October 3, 1982, near his hunting cabin at Prophet Cove on Admirality Island. Louis left two teenage children named Lance and Norma and a wife Emma, originally from San Francisco, whose two strong brothers objected to her marriage to Louis. Louis had a Yupik girlfriend named Rachel, and Emma had a sexual relationship with Walt Robbins, who was Louis's partner. Walt had an 18-year-old daughter, De De, who was infatuated with Lance but was pregnant by a Filipino boyfriend named Rudolfo Anastanso. On October 15, Alvin Hawkes was sentenced to 40 years in prison for the murder of Louis Victor. Hawkes, who worked for Victor, claimed that a transmitter implanted in his inner ear gave him instructions to murder Louis, who was about to be killed by the great power (Straley, 1992, p. 26). On the eve of the trial, De De Robbins, the only other witness to Louis's murder, committed suicide.

In May 1992, Louis hired Alvin Hawkes as a deckhand on his charter boat. On October 2, Hawkes was preparing a remote cabin on Admirality Island for a group of hunters. On October 3, Hawkes radioed Victor indicating he was having trouble. Victor, Lance, and Norma took their boat, the Oso, from Juneau to the island. Walt Robbins and De De traveled with them in Walt's boat. Walt saw Louis go ashore with his rifle and talk with Hawkes. The next morning, Hawkes claimed that Louis had gone crazy and tried to kill him. Hawkes was covered with blood. Lance said he saw Hawkes throw a rifle in the bay early that morning. Louis' body was found about a half mile from the cabin. It had been partially consumed by a brown bear. The head was propped on a rock (Straley, 1992, p. 25). The autopsy report indicated that Louis had been killed by a gunshot wound to the head. De De was a witness to the fight between Hawkes and Louis, but she said it looked more like "horseplay than a real fight" (p. 27). She and her father left the next morning before the report of the murder. De De's death, on the eve of the trial (she was found floating next to the docks in Bellingham, Washington), was reported as a suicide when her diaries revealed that she was pregnant.

These are the facts: a drunken detective, two deaths, a convicted man in prison who hears voices, and a mother who wants another story of how and why her son was killed. Pointing to two boxes of files and trial transcripts, Mrs. Victor states, "Shouldn't I feel I know the whole truth after I read two boxes of papers? I don't. . . . This is not the story of how my son died" (Straley, 1992, pp. 11-12).

A classic mystery, the death has already happened, but as the first mystery unfolds (i.e., who killed Louis Victor), other mysteries begin to appear. Shortly after Cecil takes the case, Toddy is shot. Who shot Toddy? Was Cecil the intended victim? Did De De really commit suicide or was she killed by Lance, as Walt Robbins seems to think? In the course of investigating the trial, Cecil discovers a closed file that contains information about the possible sexual abuse of Norma by Louis. Did Louis sexually abuse his daughter and beat up his wife? Walt Robbins reveals that Emma's brothers had an ugly, racist fight with Louis over his Yupik girlfriend, and that Louis soon broke his promise to not see Rachel again.

Cecil collects stories about the case, checking telephone and flight records, reading files, interviewing every witness, and putting himself in "position for information to come to me" (Straley, 1992, p. 83). His investigation involves a series of airplane journeys from Sitka to Juneau, Stellar, Anchorage, and back again to Sitka. Each flight yields a new story, each story is a different version of Louis Victor and why and how he was killed. Although the state's version is discredited by Cecil (Hawkes hears voices), it is accepted by Emma (Straley, 1992):

> My husband is dead, and the man who killed him is in prison. . . . Our family has been destroyed. . . . The family is the only thing worth dying for. . . . If its worth dying for, its worth killing for. . . . Kill Alvin Hawkes. But don't defile our family. (pp. 102-103)

Lance and Norma (Straley, 1992, pp. 143-44) slightly alter the facts of the case, indicating that they saw lights in the cabin the night of the murder. Cecil challenges them (Straley, 1992):

> So, now you're saying that you were on deck that night. . . . I can't help worrying about two people [Alvin and De De] who could place you

on deck. . . . But I suppose you don't have to worry. They'll both be gone for a long time. (p. 144)

Walt Robbins doubts that his daughter committed suicide and suspects Louis's children are involved (p. 154). Edward, Cecil's Yupik friend from high school, keeps telling Cecil to learn the story about the "human being who marries a bear" (p. 169) and tells him Emma's brothers, big shots in the San Francisco police department, threatened to kill Louis. Sy Brown, Hawkes' attorney, accepts the facts of the case, noting only that Louis had been placed on a year's probation and sent to an alcohol program after he was accused of beating his wife: "he led a good life, with one minor transgression, and he made serious amends for that. . . . He quit drinking" (pp. 86-87).

Robbins agrees to take Cecil to Louis' cabin if Cecil can get to Juneau. A drunken flight later, waking up on the floor of a Juneau hotel room, Cecil is confronted by Louis' mother, who tells him the story of the woman who married a bear (Straley, 1992, pp. 182-185).

The following is the story she tells him. "A long time ago there was this girl. . . . This girl married a brown bear" (Straley, 1992, p. 183). The woman moves away from her family and her two brothers. She and the bear have two babies, which are half-bear and half-human (p. 183). The babies are good hunters and are curious about their uncles. One day, the uncles see the two bear-human babies. The babies run and tell their mother. Their bear father says they have to move away. The mother cries and said she did not want to move. The bear father tells her if she will not leave, he will return to his bear wife because it is not safe for him. The bear father goes hunting. The mother tells her children that they must kill their father and leave his skin on the rocks so the uncles would find him and know the bear was not hunting near the village. The children kill their father and eat him and then "lay his skin out on the rocks for their uncles" (p. 184).

Walt and Cecil journey to the island. Cecil is confronted by a huge bear (shades of Faulkner) who runs over him: "She stood with apparent grace and power like Michelangelo's *David*" (Straley, 1992, p. 207). He hears voices and sees Emma's float plane in the harbor. In the cabin, Lance has a gun on Walt while Norma and Emma watch. Cecil secretly tape records the conversation that ensues—a spectacle of discovery.

Norma reports that Lance killed De De, fearing she would contradict their story about not being on deck that night (Straley, 1992, p. 211). Walt pleads with Emma, "Why? Why any of it?" (p. 213). Emma retorts, "He humiliated me. He humiliated his children. Then he wanted a divorce. . . . These are my children. It's true they are half his" (pp. 213-214). Norma confesses (Straley, 1992):

> Why did I shoot him. . . . I hated his being Indian. . . . I hated the way his hands felt when he had been drinking. . . . I hated it . . . but . . . I loved picking berries with him. . . . I loved Papa. I never planned to shoot him. (pp. 214-216)

Emma then confesses to mistakenly shooting Todd when she intended to shoot Cecil. She then murders Walt. Emma and Lance attempt to escape in the plane. Lance shots Cecil as Cecil fires a bullet into the plane, which crashes in the bay as Norma tries to run away.

Cecil has it all on tape. Emma has committed her story to tape as well, telling the police that Cecil killed Walt, that Walt killed Louis, and that Cecil threatened to kill Walt unless he paid him to keep quiet about his murdering Louis (Straley, 1992, p. 225). Mrs. Victor wants a good attorney for her grandchildren, and she accepts Cecil's story because it makes sense. Cecil summarizes the story (Straley, 1992):

> We didn't mention the woman who had married a bear and I didn't ask her if it was a true story. I didn't even ask her if she had just told it that way to ease me along the path of her own suspicions. (p. 225)

Five mysteries folded into one. Did a woman marry a bear? Yes, if you understand a bear to be an Indian. De De was murdered—it was not a suicide. Emma shot Toddy. Hawkes did not kill Louis. Louis loved an Indian woman, and he did sexually abuse his daughter.[29] Norma and her mother never forgave him. He was an Indian and he fell in love with another woman and wanted a divorce. A scorned femme fatale, Emma Victor kills to save her family's reputation. Three murders with three different murderers. Cecil, the subartic sleuth, has discovered the truth of those old stories, those old myths: Indians get in trouble when they marry white people.

Thus, there is a factual basis to the old tales that are fictions—myths fitted to concrete life situations. Mrs. Victor's story about the woman who married a bear was true—a true fiction. Here, Straley joins Patricia Hill Collins's (1991, p. 210), who argues for the central importance of those meaningful lived experiences that have been inscribed in a powerful cultural text. Collin's blues, Straley's tale, and Mrs. Victor's story are all symbolic representations of deep cultural truths, and great wisdom resides therein.

Straley delays the telling of this story, allowing Cecil to collect the other stories about the murder, understanding that these stories only contain partial, self-serving versions of what happened. Cecil must first journey through and interpret these other versions of what happened. Only after these other stories have been exhausted does Cecil receive the full version of the story about the woman who married a bear. The hearing of the story, then, is a journey into the heart of Native Alaskan culture. This journey includes Cecil's drunken trips back and forth across the Alaskan landscape. (This drunkenness parallels the alcoholism that inflicts the Native Alaskan.) These drunken trips place Cecil above and outside the very world he needs to penetrate. It is no accident that he awakens from a drunk to witness Mrs. Victor and her nephews dressing a deer in a Juneau hotel room. Here, in this room, Native culture secures its place in the "real" Alaska: a dead dear dressed out in a white man's bathtub.

In the end, Cecil is back where he started. As in the book's opening sequence (Straley, 1992, p. 4), a raven with a red thread wrapped around his foot circles overhead: "Raven, the trickster: the missing piece of darkness" (p. 4). Cecil pays someone to let him sleep the night in the locked cathedral (p. 225). The shamus has come home, discovering in this journey that the stories he is told only temporarily keep him from insanity (p. 147), from completely unraveling and falling apart, and maybe then understanding, if only momentarily, that "There is nowhere to stand but in absence" (p. 4).

This is what *The Woman Who Married a Bear* (Straley, 1992) is all about—stories that fill the absences. If murder "is about the death of memory" (Straley, 1992, p. 198), the ultimate absence, then these stories always unravel, forcing us to confront and to come back to the last missing piece of darkness; no big sleep here, just a simple question—Who am I?

Denouement

It is a truism, as the post-Oedipal feminist theorists remind us (Clough, 1994; de Lauretis, 1984, p. 118; see also Lottman, 1979), that there are only two basic plots in fiction: "one, somebody takes a trip; two, a stranger comes to town" (Smith, 1995, p. 7). In practice, this observation translates into a gender: Men take trips and woman stay home.[30] This mythical model thus creates two positions of possible sexual difference: "male-hero-human; and female . . . non-man" (de Lauretis, 1984, p. 121)—woman as space, void, as nonhuman.

The previous truism spreads to ethnography and to detective fiction. The ethnographer—always a stranger, usually a male—takes a trip and comes into somebody's town. The detective always travels, moving from some home base, to the crime scene, venturing then into the places and sites where victims and suspects reside, and then home again, wherever home happens to be. The criminal scene is always familial—a symbolic site of sexual violence, crimes of incest, rape, physical violence, and murder. The murders that occur are ritual sacrifices, acts that symbolically serve to re-establish the moral order, which is based on sexual difference and sexual desire (de lauretis, 1984, p. 119).

The stories discussed in this chapter are thus two postmodern Oedipal stories. Thus, Vic Benson (Verise Sonnier), like a nearly blind Oedipus wandering the earth, desires to destroy the children who murdered his mistress. Vic travels home to haunt and destroy his damaged family. He wishes to punish them for his crimes including the death of their mother, which he caused (Burke, 1992a, p. 86). Dave Robicheaux restores order to this Oedipal struggle as he seeks to find his own place with Bootsie and Alafair.

Possible incest and surely sexual abuse exist in the Victor family. Emma will do anything to save her family, even if her children are half bear. Emma Victor symbolically murders Louis (by sanctioning Norma's actions) because Louis betrayed his sexual contract with her. More deeply, however, Louis turned Emma into a nonhuman because the woman who marries a bear is now only half human. Forced to leave her home because of her marriage to Louis, she can only return home if she kills the bear, Louis, the nonhuman. This is an Oedipal tale with a vengeance (de Lauretis, 1984, p. 157). The scorned woman saves her family through this violent act and symbolically reclaims her status as woman and mother. In the process of claiming justice, however, she becomes femme fatale, and in the end she and her daughter are the objects of Cecil's investigative gaze.

Cecil is trapped in this ambiguous world of sexual desire and power. The sexual story he uncovers, which establishes the truth of Mrs. Victor's fable, is a story of possible incest and the violation of the incest taboo. This, however, is an incest tale with a twist. In marrying Louis, Emma exchanged her white femininity for the raw sexual desire she experienced with Louis, the bear. She became less than human, but more of a woman, as a result of this exchange. Louis betrays her twice over—he has an affair with an Indian woman, and he attempts to seduce his daughter. She had no choice but to kill him. They both become victims of a violent racial and ethnic stratification system that dishonors Native culture and cultural differences.

Cecil's ambiguous relationship to himself, in part a product of his constant battle with alcohol, allows him to believe that everything he knows is "a transitory illusion" (Straley, 1993, p. 183). This makes his future "a fictional dream and [his] past a remembered one" (p. 183). Underneath these illusions, however, hover the constant presence of his dead father—the famous ex-judge, the man of pure rationality—and his mother—"the first person to tell me the earth was round. She said it had been discovered by women waiting for their husbands to return from the sea" (p. 125). His mother, who refuses to dispose of his dead father's clothing, loves stories about romance, longing, and death (p. 126). Cecil is trapped in between these stories of love, romance, and death. He is unwilling to live the controlled life Hannah offers (p. 217).

In such a life he would have to be the permanent hero, or at least forego his penchant for stirring up the world and collecting stories, and he would have to be sober. His affinity for alcohol allows him to escape and deny the Oedipal solution (and trap) his father, mother, and Hannah make available to him. Like Rigby Reardon, the Steve Martin hero of *Dead Men Don't Wear Plaid* (1982), Cecil constantly spoofs the hard-boiled detective genre. His recurring camp-like impersonations of the tough-guy PI identity allow him to never be fully in nor never fully outside the Oedipal triangle. He is most comfortable with his nonthreatening, homosocial relationship with Toddy.

Cecil represents two versions of the same thing—traveling ethnographies and voyeurs on the road: the Oedipal story writ large (and small); the wandering stranger seeking buried truths about him- or herself and the past. Thus returning always to Oedipus's dilemma—Who am I, who is my mother, who is my father—sexual intrigue, homosocial, and heterosexual tales about the family and its inability to ever completely and successfully repress the deep, dark secrets about itself.

Burke and Straley, however, are not content to leave their stories at this level, and here they speak most directly to a critical, resistance, postmodern ethnographic project. Like the new journalists, both writers situate their projects in this postmodern moment and its discontents, the personal troubles and public issues (Mills, 1959) that breed a self-poisoning form of self-hatred and existential anxiety that merges with feelings of dread, envy, anger, false pride, and fear. These are the very emotions that feed on the conditions that produce the violence toward self and other that their detectives investigate. These emotions are lodged in a recalcitrant transnational cultural order that peevishly asserts that because the local is always global it is politically correct to think locally and act globally. The global, however, defines and controls the local; there is no escaping the box we are in. What is best for Exxon in Alaska, or Africa, or south Louisiana is best for me when I fill my 11-year-old Toyota with gas in Champaign, Illinois. We confront the cultural logics and corporate machinery of late capitalism. This logic and its machinery place us in the middle of a race, class, and gender war. This faceless, irrational, bureaucratic conglomerate, which traverses local, state, and national boundaries with electronic ease, will destroy anything that threatens to impede its progress.

Burke and Straley long for a time when such was not the case. Their's is not the romantic nostalgia born of pure innocence, however, because the past cannot be returned to. Their utopias are purely imaginary—Dave and Bootsie and Alafair under the pecan tree or Cecil and Hannan in an island sauna, sheltered from the violent storm. No real utopias here, except in those lonely places in nature where man has yet to tread. These too are imaginary, however, because the violence of capitalism is present everywhere; oil on the waters, dead birds on the shoreline, and fish that now spawn at the wrong time because their biological clocks have been altered by chemical spills.

Therefore, these are always traveling stories: Someone takes a trip and a stranger comes to town. Today, however, as Burke and Straley understand, you do not have to leave town. The world and its troubles come to you, so there is now only one story: the story about constant displacements—how do I make sense of myself in this world that will not go away? Nothing is unpresentable or unfamiliar, and it is no longer possible to separate the prior from the later, the original from the copy. These traveling tales, then, seek a shifting moral center in the midst of this sea of change, but this moral center no longer holds, as Cecil shows us.

The postmodern detective story is about the death of the last frontier and what we do about this death: There is no there to go to anymore. We are left, then, with tiny moral tales. These tales work outward from the local to the global, entangling the global in the local dealings that produce the violence that surrounds us everywhere. Oedipus does battle with capitalism. Paraphrasing de Lauretis (1984, p. 184), who quotes MacKinnon (1982, p. 515), local violence is to the detective story "what sexuality is to feminism [and] what work is to Marxism: that which is most one's own, yet most taken away." Local violence is always personal and political, moral and social, and always about that which is "most defining of the [gendered] self and [that which is] most exploited or controlled" (de Lauretis, 1984, p. 184).

Local violence, murder, Straley reminds us, is about memory and its loss, its destruction, and the attempt to erase the past and control the future. It is about violence and the loss of self. Here, inside time, the postmodern detective writers attempt to restore this lost memory, showing that it can never be erased because its traces always leave a stained white radiance.

Notes

1. I follow Thompson (1993, p. 3) in my definition of this genre, which conflates mystery, spy, crime, and detective fiction: " 'crime fiction' is used to denote all the genres and subgenres that concern themselves with violation of the law, whether or not this violation actually took place, and whether or not this violation is sanctioned by the novelist." This violation, or crime, is an important catalyst for action in the story (Zeman & Zeman, 1992, p. 436). To this definition I add Haycraft's (1972, p. x; see also Porter, 1981,

p. 5) proviso that such fiction must "be mainly occupied with detection and must contain a proper detective (whether amateur or professional)." I will, however, resist (as does Thompson) any firm genre-driven reading of this form (see Todorov, 1977, p. 51; Denzin, 1995a, p. 111, on whodunits, thrillers, and suspense and adventure spy variations within the genre). Subgenres include the soft- (Block, Parker, Leonard, Schopen, Straley, Burns, Constantine, and Parker) and hard-boiled (Chandler, Hammett, Macdonald, and Ellroy) private eye, true crime, the police procedural (McBain, Harvey, and Hillerman), thrillers (Wood) and suspense (Brett), whodunit, conspiratorial, spy (Le Carre), historical (Meyers), regional, cozy (Curzon), domestic, formal English model and its variations (Doyle, Chesterton, and Christie), closed door, comic, and supernatural. Across these types are then inserted writers who privilege race, ethnicity, religion, gender, sexuality, self-weakness (mental illness, drug addiction, and alcoholism), and politics, giving rise, for example, to the soft-boiled, gay, militant feminist private eye or the soft-boiled private eye who is a male recovering alcoholic (Block), the gay black PI (see Pronzini & Greenberg, 1985a, 1985b), and so on.

2. The private eye is like the investigative journalist (Glasser & Ettema, 1989), using the tools of the voyeuristic, investigative trade to expose evil and wrongdoing in the social order (see Schopen, 1989, 1990).

3. Some argue that the "detective-mystery-espionage-thriller genre . . . is virtually the only *serious* fiction being written today" (Cline, 1989, pp. 317, 320). Chappell (1993, p. 17), for example, contends that Warren's *All the King's Men* (1946), is a novel that crosses the boundaries between so-called serious and detective fiction. Of course, Edmund Wilson's (1946) indictment of classical mystery fiction is often correct: "the explanation of the mystery, when it comes, is neither interesting nor plausible enough. It fails to justify the excitement produced by the picturesque and sinister happenings, and I cannot help feeling cheated" (Wilson as quoted in Wolcott, 1995, p. 101; see also Porter, 1981, p. 2). The same criticism could be brought to much of what passes as contemporary ethnography (Richardson, 1994a, p. 517).

4. Among the recurring arguments (see Cawelti, 1976, pp. 98-105; Porter, 1981, pp. 255-256; Thompson, 1993, p. 8) for the genre's popularity are the following: the psychoanalytic (it re-creates the primal sexual scene); the democratic, anticrime (it embodies the democratic respect for law and order); the Christian (it absolves us of guilt by punishing the murderer for crimes we would like to commit); the intellectual (it allows the reader to solve a complex puzzle); the postmodern (it brings order to the disordered postmodern world); and the critical school (it reproduces the myth and importance of the individual hero in a violent, corrupt world).

5. It is impossible to give a definitive list of writers under each of these categories (see Pronzini & Greenberg, 1985b, for a representative summary through the mid-1980s). *Ellery Queen's Mystery Magazine*, *The Armchair Detective*, and *The Drood Review* regularly publish and report on the new (and classic) fiction in this genre, including the annual awards that are given *(The Ellery Queen, Edgar Allan Poe, and Shamus Awards)*.

6. There is a long literary and film tradition that turns journalists into detectives, including *Citizen Kane* (1941), *All the King's Men* (1949), *The Parallax View* (1974), *All the President's Men* (1975), and recently *I Love Trouble* (1994) (see Denzin, 1995a, pp. 23-24). A variation is given in the reporter who works with the detective (Cawelti, 1976, p. 152)—for example, *The Dead Pool* (1988) and *The Mean Season* (1985).

7. In film form (*The Parallax View, The Conversation, JFK*, and *The Manchurian Candidate*), the collectivity also functions as a detective, attempting to destroy the solitary, often psychotic detective (Denzin, 1995a, p. 165).

8. Both writers have won major awards: Burke, the *Edgar*, and Straley, the *Shamus*. Burke's eight Dave Robicheaux's mysteries have appeared on the *New York Times* best seller list for fiction. Straley has been compared to Tony Hillerman.

9. These writers move most fully across the themes discussed previously—namely, those connected to the discontents identified by Glover and Kaplan (1992).

10. An organization of female mystery writers and readers, with more than 2,200 members in 11 foreign countries. Sisters in Crime is responsive to the fact that although in 1987 over 37% of the published, hardcover mysteries were written by women, less than 17% of the mysteries reviewed (in the *New York Times*) were written by women (Hart as cited in Silet, 1993, p. 49).

11. Other origin tales trace the mystery story back to Oedipus, also noting that murder and its detection were favorite themes for "Greek, and Roman dramatists, and for Shakespeare and other Renaissance tragedians" (Cawelti, 1976, p. 52).

12. According to Haycraft (1972, pp. 10, 12; see also Holquist, 1983, p. 157), Poe also gave the genre the following conventions: use of the least likely person theme, the scattering of false clues by the real criminal, the extortion of a confession by the use of psychological means, the eccentric detective, the stupid foil, the well-intentioned but floundering member of the police force, the locked-room convention, deduction by means of "putting oneself in another's position" (Haycraft, 1972, p. 12), concealment by the means of the ultraobvious, the staged ruse, and the condescending and expansive explanation when the crime has been solved.

13. The oedipal overtones are very strong, nearly universal. It appears that a *sine qua non* of the genre is the unhappy family (or pseudo-family) facing a crisis using a planned or unplanned violent act as a means of addressing the crisis.

14. Penzler (1995, p. 404) argues that Carrol John Daly wrote the "first story about a 'hardboiled dick' . . . The private eye story was essentially his creation. . . . It took Hammett to bring art to the hardboiled novel."

15. Of course, their major works (*Maltese Falcon, The Big Sleep,* and *Harper*) were turned into movies, with Humphrey Bogart playing Hammett and Chandler's Sam Spade and Philip Marlowe and Paul Newman playing Macdonald's Lew Archer.

16. Porter (1981, pp. 176-178) argues that the popularity of the American private eye in the late 1920s (just before the great depression) corresponds to "a major crisis of American individualism as the political philosophy of industrial capitalism."

17. Recall Hammett's analysis of capitalist corruption in *Red Harvest* (see Cawelti, 1976, p. 173; see also Hammett, 1980).

18. According to Porter (1981, p. 183), the hard-boiled tradition had no place for women; the culture had "generated no precedent for a tough-talking, worldly-wise woman, capable of defending herself in the roughest company, who also possessed the indispensable heroic qualities of physical attractiveness and virtue. A woman in the private eye's role would have been conceivable only as fallen or comic." Sisters in Crime brought this picture down.

19. The series has been optioned by Alex Baldwin's film company, with Baldwin playing Dave (Carter, 1992, p. 47).

20. Some of the morally insane become members of paramilitary organizations, and the majority of them are "self-deluded, uneducated, fearful of women. . . . Some of them have been kicked out of the service on bad conduct and dishonorable discharges" (Burke, 1995, p. 49).

21. From Shelley, "Something stains the white radiance of eternity" (Burke, 1992b, p. 45).

22. In "real" life, John Straley (personal communication, November 3, 1994) works as a private investigator.

23. Like Jack Burden in Warren's (1946) *All the King's Men*, Cecil is also descended from one of the state's most aristocratic and politically influential families (regarding Warren's novel, see Chappell, 1993).

24. An obvious reference to Raymond Chandler and the two film noirs *Time to Kill* (1942) and *Brasher Doubloon* (1947), which were based on the same Chandler story.

25. These themes are more thoroughly explored by Straley (1993). The fourth, yet to be published, novel in the series explores class and labor issues (J. Straley, personal communication, November 3, 1994).

26. Chee is both a policeman and a practicing shaman (Breen, 1994, p. 26).

27. John Straley (personal communications, November 3, 11, 29, 1994) rejects the label that calls him the Tony Hillerman of the north, although he points to Hillerman's influence (landscape) as well as to the influences of Hammett and Mosley (atmosphere), Sue Grafton (character), Richard K. Nelson's (1983, 1989) native ethnographies, and the nature poets and fiction writers (Lopez, Dillard, and Rogers).

28. Straley (1992, p. i; see also Snyder, 1990, pp. 155-175) notes that this story takes several version, which have been collected by folklorists. In one version, a man marries a bear, and in the other, a woman marries a bear.

29. On this point, John Straley (personal communication, November 2, 1995) states, "For the record, I never resolved in my own mind whether Victor Louis sexually abused his daughter. To me that is an unknown element in the story."

30. Sisters in Crime trouble this equation.

Ethnographic Poetics and Narratives of the Self

Bury stars in deep ground
With words like rushing water
Follow the yellow coil in the cat's eye
To an empty room
And listen

          —Diamond (1985a, p. 264)

Poetry?
   as ethnography?
ethnography?
   as poetry?

          —Diamond (1985b, p. 13)

Another version of the narrative turn includes ethnographic poetics[1] (Marcus & Fischer, 1986, pp. 73-74) and narratives of the self,[2] the self-referential literary productions of ethnographers (Benson, 1993)—performance texts turned inward waiting to be staged: poems (Brady, 1991a; Prattis, 1985a; Richardson, 1994b; Timmermans, 1994), dramas (Grindal & Shephard, 1993; Paget, 1993), fictional novels (Stewart, 1989), autoethnographies (Ellis, 1996; Kohn, 1994; Pfohl, 1992; Shelton, 1994, 1995a, 1995b; Travisano, 1994; Wolfe, 1992),[3] autobiographies

(Geertz, 1988, 1995), memoirs (Gottlieb & Graham, 1993), reflexive fiction (Ashmore, 1989, p. 51), narrative collages (Pfohl, 1992), parallel texts (Ashmore, 1989, p. 66), remembrances from the field (Ellis, 1995b), diaries, stories about writing stories (Richardson, 1995), documentary film (Harper, 1994), the use of fictive devices to write ethnography (Krieger, 1983, 1991; Mitchell & Charmaz, 1995), experimental versions of the New Journalism (Rinehart, 1994), "indigenous oral narratives as literary forms" (Marcus & Fischer, 1986, p. 73), and a field of messy texts (Clough, 1995; Fontana, 1992; Marcus, 1994).

Here, I examine a sampling of these experimental works, treating them as pivotal writing forms to be engaged and discussed in ethnography's sixth moment. I will read these works against Trinh's model of the text, a model that challenges the realist ethnographic project and those experimental variations that remain connected to such terms as lived experience, authenticity, verisimilitude, and truth.[4] I will offer a set of interpretive criteria for reading and writing these textual forms.

A two-sided thesis organizes my interpretation of these literary writing forms. First, experimental writing must be well-crafted, engaging writing capable of being respected by critics of literature as well as by social scientists (see below). Second, the self-referential literary productions of ethnographers must do more than put the self of the writer on the line or tell realist, emotional stories about self-renewal, crisis, and catharsis. It is not enough to write moving tales of the self that emotionally move the reader. Self stories should answer, at one level, to the criterion of cultural criticism, to Brecht's concept of Epic, or Dialectical Theatre, and Sartre's engaged literature. Such works should be a stimulus for social criticism and social action—a joining of the personal, the biographical, with the political, the social. That is, the tale being told should reflect back on, be entangled in, and critique this current historical moment and its discontents (Clough, 1994, p. 170; Ellis, 1995c, pp. 164-166; Richardson, 1995, p. 194).

I begin with a brief aside on reading the new writing then discuss the history of these textual experiments in anthropology and sociology, offering exemplars from each field. I turn next to the assumptions that organize this textual form, moving back and forth between poetics and self-narratives. This will necessitate an analysis of the criticisms of the form, as well as a discussion of reflexivity, because as

Marcus (1994) observes, the messy textual experimentations that define ethnography's contemporary moment are all shaped by the "crucial turn . . . taken toward self-critical reflexivity in ethnographic writing" (p. 568). Much of what passes as new, however, may, under another framework, be old hat.

Reading the New Writing

Perhaps we can thank Richard Rorty for all or some of this. In promoting the turn to narrative in the human disciplines, Rorty (1989, p. 60) has argued that our liberal society needs social texts that promote compassion, texts that persuade and show us how to feel the sufferings of others. For Rorty (after Dewey), the poets (and novelists) have always been the moral prophets of humanity (p. 69). The task of producing compassionate understanding thus falls to (Rorty, 1989)

> Ethnography, the journalist's report, the comic book, and the docudrama, and, especially the novel. . . . The novel, the movie and the TV program have, gradually, but steadily, replaced the sermon and the treatise as the principles of moral change and progress. (p. xvi)[5]

Speaking for ethnography, poems, stories, and novels (fiction and nonfiction) become experimental ways of implementing Rorty's (1989) project; the fiction and nonfiction social science text of the exegetical, testimonial, and notional varieties can produce social good. Therefore, the narrative turn opened wider a space that was already occupied by a few adventuresome anthropologists who had taken to writing poems and fiction—sometimes for their peers and sometimes using pseudonyms (see History below).[6]

Like the new journalists, the new social science writers divide into two groups—the ethnographic realists and the cultural phenomenologists. The realists see stories in society, waiting to be written, and the phenomenologists write from the inside out, their own stories become cultural texts. Both groups situate themselves in the stories told so the new writing always carries traces of autoethnography, the personal memoir, and the confessional.

These were (and are) realist, modernist tales, tales about personal loss, recovery, and the self writing its way out of a painful past, sharing experience so others can also move forward: ethnographic therapy (Prattis, 1985b, p. 275), social science helping others, and moral texts. This is Tom Wolfe's New Journalism using nineteenth-century social realism as a vehicle for doing narrative at the end of the twentieth century.

In the end (and the beginning), the new social science poets and storytellers become modernist observers telling realist tales, deploying a parallax view, and recording a constantly changing internal and external world. Seldom are the modernist narrative strategies subverted because the new texts seem to always presume a fixed or semifixed standpoint for the ethnogaphic gaze. Thus, an affinity for lived experience and its reconstruction is maintained. These works become vehicles for the reproduction of a series of humanistic sensibilities that valorize the feeling, knowing, self-reflective individual. The texts are often records of or reflections on experience. This makes it more difficult for the text to become a means for the reader's own moral experience.

The new social science writers are not like the metaphysical, postmodern mystery writers who write about hesitating investigators confronting absurd situations in which all narrative forms somehow fail. Too often, there is a ludic strain in this work—inventive texts that do not go far enough in challenging the status quo. At times, these writers risk reducing ethnography to the invention of new forms of textuality. The post-hard-boiled detectives are a model here because some of them at least attempt utopian and dystopian texts that intervene in the world.

Here, the new language poets are instructive (Ross, 1988, p. 370). The new language poets move beyond the haiku, prose, rhymed quatrains, and free verse poetry of the modernist, objectivist, populist, new criticism, and Beat traditions. They attempt to create a Marxist, critical poetic form that examines and exposes *"our patterns of consumption at the commodity level of meaning"* (p. 373). This poetry focuses on the sentence as that unit of language that carries the commodity level of meaning (p. 373). The writer works at the level of the sentence rather than at the " 'imaginary' level" (p. 375). The new sentence, as it is called, defamiliarizes language, decontextualizes the present tense, and uses cinematic devices like jump cuts and multiple points of view (p. 375).

The following is an example from Jean Day's "Ticonderoga" (as quoted by Ross, 1988):

> We came to the landing place with buck knives and whale grease for the job. The garbage had yet to be put out. Barges up and down the river intersected long treeless vistas of acquisition. Sugar in the pan was pornography in the minds of men. That intimacy saved for green grass. Your flow. A product said, "Hit me with a club." . . . I thought I wanted to intend and determine. (p. 374)

There is no single story told here, only a series of sentences, each to be taken on its own. Each sentence, embedded in what comes before and after, questions the very act of writing and creating images. The notion of a poem that tells a story is undone. The issue is how language creates experience. The use of the new sentence allows the writer to deconstruct the very ways in which a commodity economy linguistically presents itself to its members (knives, garbage, barges, pornography, and intimacy). Only a few of the new (and old) poets in ethnography work from this tradition.

History

The move to poetry and first-person texts is not recent. Its history extends back to the founding figures of ethnography, from Fraser to Malinowski, Evans-Pritchard, and Benedict (see Clifford, 1988, pp. 46-48), forward to the contemporary moment (Clifford, 1986, pp. 13-17): Rosaldo (1989), Anzaldua (1987), hooks (1990), Ellis (1995a), Richardson (1995), Wolfe (1992), Benson (1993), and Brady (1991a). This history is complex and travels in several directions at the same time, constantly criss-crossing ethnography's fourth and fifth moments (see Atkinson, 1992, pp. 37-50).[7]

Anthropology

In anthropology, this history appears to include the following: re-readings, in the 1970s and 1980s, of classical works from ethnography's traditional period (Malinowski's diaries); the appearance, in the 1970s, of a series of texts reflecting on the fieldwork experience (Marcus & Fischer, 1986, p. 34); the crisis of representation occurring in ethnography's fourth moment, with connections to feminism and poststructuralism; a subterranean literary tradition, extending from the 1930s through the 1980s, associated with the poetic and literary writings of Sapir, Benedict, Edith Turner, Laura Bohannan, Marjorie Wolfe, Marjorie Shostak, Elisabeth Fernea, and others (Bruner, 1993, p. 5); the self-conscious emergence, in the 1960s, of a generation of anthropological poets, including Stanley Diamond, Dennis Tedlock, Dell Hymes, Gary Snyder, and Paul Friedrich (Brady, 1991b, p. x; Bruner, 1993, p. 4; Prattis, 1985a); the emergence, within the same time period, of the field of ethnopoetics (Brady, 1991b, p. x); the exploration, after *Writing Culture* (Clifford & Marcus, 1986), of new representational forms (see Dorst, 1989); an increasing interest in the 1980s by cultural anthropology in poetics that led to the formation of poetry reading sessions at annual meetings, as well as the creation of a new journal, *Anthropology and Humanism Quarterly*, which was committed to publishing experimental works by anthropologists (Brady, 1991b, pp. x-xi).

Anthropological Poetics

This history culminates in the present, where it is now commonplace for cultural anthropologists to be conversant in the experimental narrative tradition and to be receptive (at one level at least) to poetry, first-person narratives, short stories, and ethnographic dramas (Benson, 1993; Rose, 1991).

Consider Friedrich's (1985, p. 102) poem, "Industrial Accident Mexico":

> . . . *pouring insecticide over the arching rootlets*
> *of young fruit trees in Colima,*
> *sweating from the exertion,*
> *on his knees leaning too low,*
> *breathing in too deeply—*
> *he can hardly suspect*
> *that that poison*
> *will filter down to the tender rootlets of his brain.*
> *Nor does the owner of the plantation,*

nor his mistress beside him in the afternoon sun,
watching, and admiring the Indian's biceps,
foresee the young wife
beside the living corpse—its twitching—
later—back in the village.

Sociology

Sociology's history is shorter—slightly longer than a decade. It can be written in terms of the works of but a handful of writers, including John Johnson (1976), Irving Zola (1982), Susan Krieger (1983, 1991, 1992), John Van Maanen (1988), Arthur Frank (1991), Patricia T. Clough (1992, 1994), Stephen Pfohl (1992), Edward Rose (1995), Laurel Richardson (1994a), and Carolyn Ellis (1995a). As these names suggest, sociology's history with experimental narratives attempts to address three problematics: the reflexive fieldwork text, the personal illness and autobiographical narrative, and the crisis of representation in ethnography's fourth moment.

John Johnson's (1976) highly reflexive *Doing Field Research* introduced the personal voice into the classic fieldwork text, a voice that would be further categorized and elaborated in Van Maanen's (1988) *Tales of the Field*. Van Maanen's book moved across realist, confessional, and impressionistic texts. Citing representative works within each genre, this work opened the door for more serious considerations of sociology's literary turn. Susan Krieger's (1983) highly experimental and controversial *Mirror Dance* (Clough, 1994, pp. 160-162; Krieger, 1992; Stevens, 1992) engaged feminist, queer, and standpoint theories, and in its refusal to be a traditional ethnography opened the way for new explorations in the personal essay as the site for the expression of the subjective self (Krieger, 1991). Edward Rose's (1995) ethno inquiries call for a poetic ethnographic discourse that returns sociology to the study of the everyday world, to native language, and to the poetic meanings of ordinary words. Stephen Pfohl (1992) unhinges this world from within using collages, personal confessions, poetry, and militant art forms to bring the insanity of the postmodern world alive (Shelton, 1994, 1995a, 1995b).

Clough (1992) brought a feminist, materialist, and psychoanalytic poststructuralism into the interpretive, ethnographic, and symbolic interactionist traditions, rereading Blumer, Goffman, and Becker. Clough (1994) then moved to a deeper, critical reading of feminist theory, exposing the boundaries of the psychoanalytic, materialist, queer, and standpoint epistemologies. By the early 1990s, Laurel Richardson (1991, 1992, 1993, 1994a, 1994b, 1995, in press; Richardson & Lockridge, 1991) was presenting ethnographic dramas and performance texts at annual meetings of the Society for the Study of Symbolic Interaction. She was also writing poetry and arguing for the poetic representation of interview materials. During the same time period, Carolyn Ellis (1993, 1994, 1995a, 1995b, 1995c, 1996; see also Shelton, 1995a), drawing on the personal illness narrative tradition fashioned by Zola (1982) and Frank (1991), forged an emotional sociology out of personal narratives surrounding the death of loved ones in her life. Clough wrote theory, Richardson wrote poems, and Ellis wrote short stories as well as a long semiautobiographical work.

Sociological Poetics and Self-Narratives

Consider the following poems from Laurel Richardson's (1994b) set of nine poems titled "Marriage and the Family":

Marriage

I used
to think it was
cute to have a lit-
tle shadow go in and out
with me

                                        —Richardson (p. 3)

Being Single Is

drying a wishbone
by the kitchen window
'til the bone is chipped

to bits by trinkets
placed beside it,
or it rots, because

there is no one
to take one end
you the other

pulling, wishing
each against each
until the bone
breaks

—Richardson (p. 5)

Now death is discussed. Carolyn Ellis's (1995a) *Final Negotiations* is a moving story of love, loss, and chronic illness. This autoethnography ends with the death of Gene Weinstein, Ellis's partner of 9 years. The death occurs in a hospital room. Ellis is at Gene's side (Ellis, 1995a):

> Friday, February 8, 1985. . . . Shutting the door, I stand next to him. "Let go, baby. It's time. The journey will be OK. You're going to feel much better now. You've fought a valiant fight." . . . Suddenly, I rush to the phone and call Beth at her friends' house . . . When I return to his side, his eyes are open. They don't blink. I feel close as I hold his hand, now almost lifeless, and I continue encouraging him . . . He looks like an old man. His pulse is faint, but I can still hear and feel life . . . His breathing stops again . . . It doesn't return. I watch for a while. I hold the hand that is now lifeless. (p. 295)

Three unconventional texts: Friedrich and Richardson's poems about work, death, marriage, and the family and Ellis's description of the dying moments in her partner's life. Thus, these two disciplinary histories from anthropology and sociology converge on the site of the body, lived experience, and culture. These representative texts open the spaces in ethnography's sixth moment for a renewed commitment to the exploration of new narrative forms of representation—what Marcus (1994, p. 567) calls the messy text (see below).

Interpretive Assumptions

The following assumptions structure the poetic, narrative text. First, these experimental works ostensibly push and extend the bounda-

ries of the traditional, ethnographic model of textuality, perhaps answering Tyler's (1986, p. 122) call for a postmodern ethnography. They
blur and shade into performance texts (Chapter 4) and draw upon and
use many of the literary devices used by the new journalists (Chapter
5), including the erasure of the usual distinctions between fact and
fiction (Krieger, 1983, pp. 185, 189; 1991, p. 33; Ellis, 1995a, pp. 312-318),
the use of scene setting, dialogue, multiple points of view, composite
characters and scenes, and an emphasis on showing, not telling (Ellis,
1995a, p. 312), and experiments with flashbacks, foreshadowing, interior monologues, and parallel plots. With the new journalists, the basic
unit of analysis is not the fact but the scene, the situation in which an
event occurs. Stories and poems are written in facts, not about facts.

Richardson's nine poems on marriage and the family, for example,
always begin with family scenes and then take up the topics of legacy,
marriage, doctors, custody, being single, and being surrounded by men.
These poems present scenic experience without being explicitly ethnographic: They show, not tell. In so doing, they answer yes to Diamond's
(1985b, p. 13) questions: Poetry? as ethnography? ethnography? as
poetry? Friedrich poetically plunges the reader into the public under-
side of industrial Mexico. A young Indian pouring insecticide on the
roots of a fruit tree will soon die from this poison. The plantation owner
and his mistress only see a muscular young male Indian in the afternoon sun.

Also, as if she were extending Diamond, Ellis shows that yes, the
personal narrative can also be ethnography. She brings the reader into
the hospital room on the day Gene dies. We see her alone with him,
talking with him, holding his hand, we feel her rush of emotion, the
impending doom: She knows he is dying, if not now already dead. Ellis
uses self-dialogue, scene setting, and her conversation with a silent
Gene to tell the reader what is going on in the moment of death. These
materials provide evidence that the events she is describing are authentic and not figments of her imagination.

Second, the modernist goal of representing lived experience is
emphasized; the writer moves outward from a personal, epiphanic
moment to a narrative description of that experience (Ellis, 1995a, p. 30;
Richardson, 1994b, p. 9). Richardson highlights epiphanic moments in
a marriage, birth, death, divorce, and being single. Friedrich marks

death in the worksite, and Ellis does the same, only in the hospital room. With regard to poetry, Richardson (1994b) states,

> If a goal of ethnography is to retell 'lived experience,' to make another world accessible to the reader, then, I submit, the lyric poem, and particularly a sequence of lyric poems with an implied narrative, come closer to achieving that goal than do other forms of ethnographic writing. (pp. 8-9)

This, however, is no simple retelling of lived experience. The poetic form, as used by Richardson and Diamond (Rose, 1991, p. 231), juxtaposes voice (the implied and real narrator), temporality, point of view, and character. Richardson's (1994b) poem, "Marriage," begins with "I," the real narrator, the writerly self, but this is an "I" that is in the past ("I used to think"). This "I" is now writing in the present as the implied narrator of the remembrance, writing about a little shadow that no longer goes in and out with her. Is this the shadow of a former self, no longer seen, or is this shadow still present and no longer regarded as cute?

Who is doing the looking at the wishbone by the kitchen window sill? Richardson (1994b) shifts point of view within the poem. The author is absent but implied in the poem's title, "Being Single Is." Being single is then defined by the wishbone, being chipped to bits, rotting, and breaking. Being single, however, is also about being alone, having no one to take the other end of the bone, and no one to wish with.

Third, the experimental text privileges emotion and emotionality, arguing that a main goal is to evoke emotional responses for the reader, thereby producing verisimilitude and a shared experience. Ellis (1995a, pp. 315-316, 318) is quite clear on this, stating that evocation of emotion was a primary goal of her text: "I felt that [the] evocative composite would be powerful enough that readers would put themselves into the experience" (p. 315). This emotional response becomes a measure of the texts validity—for example, encountering, through Ellis's eyes and hands, Gene's lifeless hand. Ellis states, "In evocative storytelling, the story's 'validity' can be judged by whether it evokes in you, the reader, a feeling that the experience described is authentic, that is believable and possible" (p. 318).

Richardson (1994b, p. 9) underscores this position as it applies to poetry: "A lyric poem 'shows' another person how it is to feel something." Friedrich sees (and feels) industrial murder on a hillside in Mexico, allowing us to see (as he undoubtedly did) the young Indian, on his knees, breathing too deeply the fumes from the poison. Suddenly, point of view shifts and we see from the standpoint of the the landlord and his mistress who are enjoying the majesty of the vista. Then we see death in the eyes of the young worker's wife who will soon be a widow.

Fourth, this felt text uses evoked emotion as the method for establishing its claims to authority. Narrative truth or the truth of fiction is emphasized—writing a good story or a good poem that persuades and moves the reader (Ellis, 1995a, pp. 316-317; Richardson, 1994b, p. 9). We do not doubt the certainty of Friedrich's vision or the depth of Ellis's sorrow. Narrative truth plunges the reader into a believable emotional world in which past, present, and future merge into a single but complex interpretive experience.

The reader submits to the text's causal version of how and why something happened. We know this Indian worker will die from chemical poisoning. We neither doubt nor question the truthfulness of Ellis's description of Gene's death. Richardson paints a powerful image of the painful sorrow and loneliness felt by a single woman.

Four narrative strategies—empirical omniscience, synchronic narration, personal testimony, and the notational recording of lived experience—combine to secure this effect.[8] The narrative point of view in the Friedrich, Richardson, and Ellis texts is that of an author who knows everything about the events in question. This is empirical omniscience. It allows each writer to also use synchronic narration, stopping the flow of time and presenting multiple interpretations simultaneously. Thus, Ellis tells us the time of Gene's death, and then freezes time, showing first hers, then the nurses', and then the social worker's reactions to this situation. Each writer, as omniscient observer, uses their own body and self as a site of personal testimony registering, in this way, the emotions they want the reader to feel. These feelings are connected to the carefully constructed notional text that re-creates the lived experience being transmitted to the reader.

Fifth, to achieve these emotional effects that produce narrative truth, language is used in a special way—in a way that compliments these four narrative strategies. Lyric poetry, for example, consciously manipulates "sound patterns, rhythms, imagery and page layout to evoke emotion" (Richardson, 1994b, p. 9). Emotions are made concrete, tied to specific images (shadows or wishbones in window sills), feelings, and moods, evoking, in this way, epiphanies in people's lives (p. 9).

Ellis (1995a, p. 314) extends this strategy to the personal narrative, suggesting that conversation, dialogue, and scenes help "to capture emotions." Prattis (1985b, p. 274) elaborates, noting that poets, in their rhythmic use of language, evoke senses of motion, ambience, taste, smell, color, local landscape, and voice. They make the strange familiar and bring the reader directly into a field of experience that moves outward from the writer's feelings (Prattis, 1985b, p. 280). The figurative language of the poetic text is a language of self and other, and a language that reveals the mundane, the banal, and the sublime in daily life. The poetic text creates a sense of awe, reverence, astonishment, and respect for the experiences described.

Sixth, and perhaps more critically, this use of language breaks down the hierarchical barrier between writer and reader, creating a context in which equals mutually engage a shared experience (Ellis, 1995a, p. 329; Richardson, 1994b, p. 11; Rose, 1991, p. 232). Rose (1991, p. 231) discusses how this works in Stanley Diamond's poetry. The following is an except from a Diamond poem (as quoted in Rose, 1991):

> *What do you know of the bear*
> *His body, my spirit. (p. 230)*

This poem begins with an implied narrator, Diamond in the persona of a shaman (Rose, 1991, p. 223), and then moves to the character of the bear, in which the bear's body "is juxtaposed immediately with *my spirit*, and the two become one—the Other united with the self in a simultaneous perspective" (Rose, 1991, p. 231). Diamond takes on the voice of the cultural other; we are placed at a site at which we confront the bear. The reader, aware of Diamond's presence ("What do you know of the bear"), also confronts the implied author (the shaman and the bear) who stands in front of Diamond.

Diamond, like Richardson and Friedrich, appears as a "brooding presence, a universal observer" (Rose, 1991, p. 231) who has had certain human experiences and who has penetrated to the essence of those experiences. An objective rendering of the experience is not given, nor is the position one "of alienation; it is one of embrace. The observer moves toward the observed, and draws, in turn, the observed closer to the observer, suspending both in a new space, somewhere not wholly here and not wholly there" (p. 231). In this new space, the reader is invited to explore the insights, feelings, and emotions experienced by the writer. The writer is not the scribe producing an objective tale.

This self-reflective use of language violates old norms of observer objectivity and promotes new forms of subjective understanding. The inner experience of the writer is made public, making the self both the object and the subject of inquiry (Richardson, 1994b, p. 11). This strategy makes the strange familiar and brings the reader directly into a field of experience that moves outward from the writer's feelings. A new dialectics of experience is achieved (Prattis, 1985b, p. 267). We confront the bear in Diamond's poem: Is he us? Poetry, and the personal narrative, become tools for reflexive knowledge, allowing the writer to see the "other" as an extension of the writing-observing self (Prattis, 1985b, p. 268). Lyric poems thereby reduce the distance between the " 'I' and the 'other' and between the 'writing-I' and the 'experiencing-I' of the writer" (Richardson, 1994b, p. 11). Self stories are then produced. Anthropologists such as David Price (1985) challenge the story that is told:

Preface to My Thesis

Welcome to a very outre *film*
by a very avant garde *director,*
It purports to be a story
of some Indians in South America
Which I made with my own little camera.
The astute observer will note, however,
that it is really the story of me,
filmed through a strange lens
whose optical principles
no one understands. (p. 220)

Seventh, there is, in this self-reflexive use of language, a search by poets and anthropologists like Stanley Diamond for the sublime, a sense of ironic awe found in the horrible and in the pain of the world (Rose, 1991, p. 227).

Sunday in Biafra

The buzzard's radium eye is mild—
he scans the silhouette of bone
within the wasted child

He is lean
the shadow of a swan
lean
as the animal he feeds upon

He mates
He dreams he mates
in crossed shadows
under the gorged moon.

—Diamond
(as quoted in Rose, 1985c, p. 32)

Starving children in Biafra on a Sunday afternoon—the strange, the horrible, and the disturbing sublime. A lyrical moment of death, the banal transformed into tragedy without emotion or sentimentality (Rose, 1991, p. 227).

Diamond (as quoted in Rose, 1991, p. 227) describes his pursuit of the sublime:

The sublime is the poetry that interests me the most, and by that I would mean, the way in which the pain and the fatality of existence can be the context for the most marvelous symbolic constructions of the human spirit. The constructions, let us say language, explode the context in ways that are mysterious. The symbol becomes substantial. . . . The context from which it is hatched crumbles. Now that is the achievement. (p. 227)

The buzzard feeding on dead children, dreaming, and mating.

Eighth, by "stimulating [the] conscious awareness of repressed materials within the anthropologist's own unconscious" (Prattis, 1985b, p. 275), the poetic form produces a therapeutic experience for the reader and the writer. This is a form of narrative self-completion and self-revelation that is perhaps not otherwise achievable. Some reject self-understanding as the "only goal worth pursuing" (Ellis, 1995a, p. 327), but use the method of emotional recall to retrieve the emotional content of previous experiences (Ellis, 1995a, p. 310).

Doubts may persist, however, because this therapeutic and evocative text may only produce the illusion of knowing.

Come Seem With Me

Grant me the mask
Take for granted the mirror.
And we can pretend
To the act of recognition.
We can perform
The act of knowing.

—Duff (1985, p. 161)

Thus, the poetic and narrative text make public what sociologists and anthropologists have long kept hidden: The private feelings, doubts, and dilemmas that confront the field-worker in the field setting. These doubts and dilemmas reveal that the field "lies to a great extent within us" (Prattis, 1985b, p. 277), thereby raising the question, "just what are [we] doing in other people's cultures?" (p. 277).

The question is more than rhetorical; its answer lies within our own experiences and within that institutional apparatus that directs ethnographers to travel to strange places so they can return home with a story to be told: "One tribe, one ethnographer" (Van Maanen, 1995b, p. 16), each ethnographer producing an account that is "the close study of a culture as lived by a particular people, in particular places, doing particular things at particular times" (p. 23).

Fred Westerman (1985, p. 237), a member of the Dakota nation, questions the logic of this journey and its product. The following poem by Westerman mocks this project, and it warns of our presence in the cultures of others:

Here Come The Anthros

And the anthros still keep coming
like death and taxes to our land
To study their feathered freaks
with funded money in their hand.
Like a Sunday at the zoo
the camera could go in
taking notes and tape recordings
of all the animals at play

Here come the anthros
Better Hide your past away
Here come the anthros
on another holiday. (p. 237)

Ninth, in emphasizing the personal, a new kind of theorizing occurs: Works are filled with biographical and not disciplinary citations (Shelton, 1995a, p. 84). A minimal, almost atheoretical, sociology or anthropology is created, and personal experience is not mediated by complex theoretical terms. Experience is meant to speak for itself (p. 84). A text becomes a place where the writer carries in a dialogue with significant others. Oedipus may not be reinvented (p. 84), but the familial soaks through the text that may run dangerously close to the melodramatic (pp. 84-85).

In summary, the experimental text simultaneously breaks from and continues the ethnographic tradition of representing the experiences of others. These new textual forms question the "certainty and authority of the [traditional] scholarly text" (Atkinson, 1992, p. 38). They reject the search for absolute truth and pursue a form of narrative truth that is suspicious of totalizing theory, breaking down, in the process, the moral and intellectual distance between reader and writer (p. 38).

In these ways, poetic and narrative texts humanize the ethnographic disciplines (Ellis, 1995a, p. 336; Prattis, 1985b, p. 277). These texts are organized under a postmodern aesthetic assumption concerning the sublime to make what was previously unpresentable part of the presentation itself (see Lyotard, 1979/1984, p. 81). Here, there is a different use of the sublime (see Rose, 1991, p. 227). Modernist ethnographers (and poets) stood outside their texts so as to produce a sense of awe or reverence or respect for what is being written about. The writer was missing from the text. The postmodern writer also seeks the sublime, but it is a new sublime—a nostalgic sublime that transgresses Diamond's poetry of pain. The new scribe seeks a sense of respect and awe for the lost writer who experiences what is being written about. What was previously unpresentable (the writer's experiences) is now what is presented. Paradoxically, that which is most sought after remains the most illusive.

In this gesture, these works have obvious parallels with mystery fiction, which also presents the unpresentable back to the culture. The experimental writers are seeking new moral truths about the investigative, reflexive ethnographic self. At the same time, many of these writers are attempting to write cultural criticism, as they fashion new understandings of the gendered, writing self trapped in the twilight years of this century. In this respect, they enact another version of the standpoint epistemologies discussed in Chapter 3.

Criticisms

The poetic, narrative text has been criticized on several grounds: Grounds that are directly connected to the defining features of the genre—namely, the emphasis on the personal, reflective text and the absence of a public method that would allow critics to assess the so-called validity of the author's assertions (Charmaz, 1995; Dawson & Prus, 1993, 1995; Farberman, 1991, 1992; Kleinman, 1993; Kunda, 1993; Lofland, 1993; Nader, 1993; Sanders, 1995; Snow & Morrill, 1993, 1995b).

These are basically the same criticisms that were brought to the New Journalism (Agar, 1990; Farberman, 1991, p. 476; Van Maanen, 1988, pp. 134-136, 1995b, pp. 13-23);[9] that is, the charges surrounding the fact-fiction problem and the attempts at being too literary (Snow & Morrill, 1995b, p. 361; Wolfe, 1992, p. 139); narcissism and self-indulgence (Nader, 1993); self-reflexivity (Atkinson, 1992, p. 50; Kleinman, 1993; Marcus, 1994, p. 569); the privileging of discourse over representation, description, and analysis (Charmaz, 1995, p. 49; Snow & Morrill, 1995a, p. 347); the absence of guidelines for doing nuts and bolts research (Kleinman, 1993; Snow & Morrill, 1995a, p. 348), including showing how the voice of the other should be presented in the new text (Snow & Morrill, 1995a, p. 347); being too theoretically reticent (Atkinson, 1992, p. 44) or giving up key sociological terms (Farberman, 1991, p. 474); and promoting a form of textuality that carries a "faintly nativist aroma. . . . [A] sort of tribal rage . . . [that] culminate[s] in orgies of nihilist ecstasy" (Farberman 1991, p. 476; see also Clough, 1992).

Others (Schmitt, 1993, p 140; Shelton, 1995a, pp. 85-86) suggest that the emotional, narrative text only creates the illusions of intimacy and verisimilitude. In its evocative mode (Tyler, 1986, p. 130), this form of writing "rather than 'representing' . . . frees ethnography from mimesis." There is a danger, however, because the text may become wholly self-referential, thereby losing its connections to the world it wishes to criticize (Atkinson, 1992, p. 50). The effect is a "hallucination of emotional intimacy" (Shelton, 1995a, p. 86), which does not disclose or critique how the "emotional is invisibly constituted by institutional structures" (Shelton, 1995a, p. 86). Still, some (Clough, 1994, p. 133) suggest that the new writers presume an essential, unified subject who can write about similarly situated others, never questioning the complex fault lines that constitute the site called lived experience.

As discussed previously, Marcus (1994, p. 568) suggests that these new textual forms involve experimentations with self-reflexivity. Read thusly, the previous criticisms may be directly and indirectly subsumed under what can be termed the reflexive critique. That is, the new writing forms reflexively challenge old ways of writing. The reflexive critiques of these texts are launched from this center point.

Reflexive Critique

The poetic or narrative text is reflexive, not only in its use of language but also in how it positions the writer in the text and uses the writer's experiences as both the topic of inquiry and a resource for uncovering problematic experience. It is impossible not to be reflexive because essential reflexivity is a part of language—an integral feature of all discourse (Marcus, 1994, p. 568; see also Ashmore, 1989; Ashmore, Myers, & Potter, 1995; Boyers, 1995).

Modifying and extending Marcus (1994, pp. 568-573), it is possible to identify six styles of reflexivity in the new ethnographic writing: subjectivist, methodological, intertextual, feminist or standpoint, queer, and feminist materialist (Clough, 1994, p. 168). These six styles encompass and extend the criticisms discussed previously. They also intermingle and are often present in a single work; they are marked, however, by distinct differences.

Subjectivist Reflexivity

In practice, subjectivist reflexivity "is associated with self-critique and personal quest, playing on the subjective, the experiential, and the idea of empathy" (Marcus, 1994, p. 569). This form of subjectivity has been met with the most criticism, leading to the charges of solipsism and narcissism noted previously and the complaint that this form of writing dead-ends in the self-indulgences of the writer (Marcus, 1994, p. 569; Wolfe, 1992, pp. 59, 137-139).

Bruner (1993, p. 2) has addressed these charges, noting that the emphasis on the poetic, subjective self raises the question of how much of that self is to be presented in a given ethnographic text. This too is often presented in terms of a false dichotomy, "the extent to which the personal self should have a place in the scientific, scholarly text" (Bruner, 1993, p. 2). This division between the personal and the scientific self falsely presumes that it is possible to write a text that does not bear the traces of its author (Lincoln & Denzin, 1994, p. 578). Of course, this is an impossibility because all texts are personal.

A balance is required; "No one is advocating ethnographic self-indulgence" (Bruner, 1993, p. 6). The goal is to return the author to the text openly in a way that does not "squeeze out the object of study" (p. 6). There are many ways to achieve this balance, including those noted previously (fictional narratives of the self, dramatic readings, poetic texts, short stories, and plays). Bruner wrote that the writer must always guard against "putting the personal self so deeply back into the text that it completely dominates, so that the work becomes narcissistic and egotistical" (p. 6).

On the positive side, this form of reflexivity, when it transcends the confessional text, has served to unmask the "epistemological and ethical grounds of anthropological knowledge" (Marcus, 1994, p. 569). It has undercut the belief in ethnography as a method that produces objective knowledge about the world. In so doing, it has created the spaces for the openly collaborative and multivoiced text (Gottlieb & Graham, 1993; Stoller & Olkes, 1987). It has also, however, led to the production of works that privilege and reinforce the point of view and "voice of the lone, introspective field-worker without challenging the paradigm of ethnographic research at all" (Marcus, 1994, p. 569).

Methodological Reflexivity

Methodological reflexivity represents an attempt to sustain methodological objectivity by using the researcher's objective position as a tool for producing a reflexive text that privileges theoretical discourse or the virtues of the standard realist, ethnographic text (Charmaz, 1995; Dawson & Prus, 1993, 1995; Schmitt, 1993). Critics of the new writing have invoked methodological reflexivity as a form of criticism contending, paradoxically, that the new writers are not reflexive enough.

Methodological reflexivity is used to address and highlight the so-called solipsistic problems of subjectivist reflexivity (Dawson & Prus, 1993, 1995). This form of reflexivity, which is also evidenced in critical ethnography (Carspecken & Appel, 1992) and in certain versions of cultural studies (Radway, 1988), emphasizes theoretical discourse and empiricist inquiry. Methodological reflexivity reflects a commitment to objective inquiry and to a belief that there is a world of intersubjectively constituted facts out there ready to be discovered by the ethnographer (Dawson & Prus, 1995, p. 114). This, however, is a negotiated, constantly changing world (Schmitt, 1993, p. 126)—a secondhand world that is mediated by cultural understandings. Nothing is ever just revealed. We only know this world through our representations of it.

In practice, methodological reflexivity often leads to texts that combine poetic and first-person narrative accounts with standard, ethnographic arguments (Wolfe, 1992). In this model, ethnography "retains its identity as a method . . . [asserting that] reflexivity is valuable only in methodological terms as a research tool" (Marcus, 1994, p. 569). Thus, Wolfe's (1992) *A Thrice Told Tale*, which consists of a short story, field notes, and an *American Ethnologist* article, functions to privilege methodological reflexivity—a reflexivity, Wolfe contends, that is already endemic to feminist studies (p. 132). She compares her short story, *Hot Spell* to her *American Ethnologist* article and reads the story as a confessional tale (Van Maanen, 1988). She argues that her realist ethnography does a much better job of objectively describing the events contained in her story. "Fiction . . . is no substitute for a well-written ethnographic account" (Wolfe, 1992, p. 59).

Intertextual Reflexivity

This form of reflexivity locates any work within a larger field of discourse while drawing on, elaborating, and commenting on that discourse. The new writing is often criticized because of its location within a larger textual field—the literatures of poststructuralism and

postmodernism (Charmaz, 1995; Dawson & Prus, 1993, 1995; Farberman, 1991, 1992; Sanders, 1995). The criticisms that are brought to this
larger field of discourse are then generalized to the new writing.

This is a misguided reading of intertextual reflexivity. Experimental
ethnography uses the previously written as a backdrop for experimental commentary. For example, Stanley Diamond's poems on Eskimos
(Rose, 1991, p. 225) and Edith Turner's (1993) story about the time
"Jimmie Nashanik Was Lost on the Tundra" recover a repressed term in
anthropology—namely, the native's perspective. In a series of narrative
reversals, including the use of native dialogue, imagery, and dialect,
these two texts bring the Eskimo perspective alive. These narrative
reversals expose the ways in which this voice has been previously
written over by those white, male anthropologists who have presumed
to speak for the Eskimo (Rose, 1990, p. 47). These narrative experiments
are critiques of existing culture writing. The Diamond and Turner works
exist in an intertextual field, which is increasingly filled by native
writers and an indigenous literature that no longer requires translation
by the white, male anthropologist.[10]

Standpoint Reflexivity

Many of the standard criticisms of the new writing argue from the
standpoint of the objective observer who is committed to writing some
version of a realist tale. These critics charge the new writers, who they
call the ethnographs, with producing political texts and with losing
sight of the goals of science (Farberman, 1991, p. 475).

All texts, however, are shaped by the writer's standpoint, by one's
location within culture, history, and by the structures of race, class,
gender, sexuality, age, family, and nation. Standpoint reflexivity, long
associated with the feminist perspective (Wolfe, 1992, p. 132), questions
this positioning, recognizing the "situatedness and partiality of all
claims to knowledge" (Marcus, 1994, p. 571). This leads to the production of messy, experimental texts (see below). These texts are always
open ended and incomplete. They invite critique and critical response
from others[11] who embody different standpoints (Marcus, 1994, p. 572).
Thus, an ethics of practice based on a politics of antiessentialism is
encouraged. Each writer produces a partially situated text that opens

up a previously repressed, ignored, or overinterpreted corner of cultural life.

As Trinh (1989, pp. 29, 35; 1991, p. 124) has observed, however, the experimental texts associated with feminist standpoint reflexivity have often been dismissed by male, postmodern writers (Caplan, 1988/1989, p. 16; Mascia-Lees, Sharpe, & Cohen, 1993, p. 230; Wolfe, 1992, p. 50). Feminists who have experimented with new writing forms have been accused of not theorizing new textual forms (Clifford, 1986, pp. 20-21), of not having contributed "much to the theoretical analyses of ethnographies (Clifford, 1986, p. 20), of not being conversant with "rhetorical and textual theory" (Clifford, 1986, p. 20), of engaging in a "sterile form of identity politics" (Marcus, 1994, p. 572), of producing confessional texts, or of writing just like men. Women writers are caught between Trinh's (1991, p. 124) Quiller-Couch and Lady Painter syndromes.

Caplan (1988/1989) summarizes this dilemma: "When women were using the experimental approach to ethnographic writing, much of it was dismissed as 'self-indulgence'; now that it is being done by men, it is called experimental" (p. 16; also quoted in Wolfe, 1992, p. 50). Wolfe (1992) elaborates: "In other words, men explore new paradigms; women mess around on the fringes of knowledge/art/literature/whatever" (p. 50; see also Boyers, 1995).

Queer Reflexivity

The first four forms of reflexivity emphasize lived experience, an epistemology of experience based on the standpoint of the self-reflexive individual in the world (Clough, 1994, p. 145). A generic model of the the person as a unified, gendered subject with agency and self-identity organizes this framework (p. 149). The reflexive, personal narrative or autobiographical text becomes a site for the expression of this agency— a place where lived experience is articulated and given expression, often in great emotional detail.

Queer theory challenges this model on three grounds. First, this commitment to the representation of lived experience ignores the problem confronted, but never resolved, by the standpoint theorists— namely, the fact that experience is always mediated by language, ideology, and desire (Clough, 1994, p. 74). The world cannot be known directly through experience, nor can any text directly represent raw experience (Clough, 1994, p. 73). There is thus a tendency to confuse the problems of capturing lived experience with its representation (Ganguly, 1992, pp. 62-63). The emotionally evocative text re-creates a world that the writer imagines and feels.

Second, the concept of an autonomous, gendered self with agency is regarded as a fiction. This fiction is created by an epistemology of the closet that presumes a normative heterosexuality for all gendered subjects. This sexual subject is produced by a cultural matrix that values only certain, accepted gendered and sexual identities—the normal heterosexual (Butler, 1990, p. 17). Accordingly, for queer theory, the concept of reflexive agency is located not in an unified subject-author but rather in subversive bodily acts, the body being the site at which agency is realized (Clough, 1994, p. 155).

Third, by deconstructing the notion of a unified subject with agency, queer theory questions the "autobiographical framing" (Clough, 1994, p. 155) that structures the poetic and personal narrative. These narratives are called into doubt because they too frequently enact the very epistemology of the closet that queer theory wishes to reject. Given this stance, the struggle is to find a narrative voice that writes against an epistemology that favors lived experience as the site for reflexivity and self-hood (p. 157). Thus, subjective reflexivity is regarded as a trap that too easily reproduces normative conceptions of self, agency, gender, desire, and sexuality.

Many versions of queer theory refuse to take up unconscious authorial desire as a topic and site of writing (Clough, 1994, p. 157). As a consequence, much writing in this tradition remains embedded in "the hegemonic discourse of heterosexist, white, propertied masculinity with which desire is entangled" (p. 157). The following form of reflexivity engages this project.

Feminist, Materialist Reflexivity

Clough's (1994) feminist, materialist analysis of reflexive textuality also breaks with the personal narrative and autobiographical model of the standpoint epistemologies. It problematicizes the concept of a subject that can know itself outside unconscious desire. At the same time, it calls for a relentless critique of that form of writing (and narrative desire) that presumes a unified identity capable of writing about the lives of others (Clough, 1992, p. 5) without writing about itself.

Clough (1994, p. 137) expands this critique by drawing on postcolonial criticism that, in the hands of Trinh, insists on collapsing the distinctions between "the social and the literary . . . fantasy and reality, fiction and history . . . literary criticism and social science" (p. 138). Following Trinh, Clough argues that the literary text too often becomes a place where a sanctioned ethnographic voyeurism occurs—a textual voyeurism that erases "gender, racial, class, ethnic, sexual and national differences" (p. 137). In the process, the distinctions between literary texts, literary criticism, and social science research are forever blurred.

To summarize, these six forms of reflexivity cannot be pulled apart; every text exhibits features of each.[12] Still, objective reflexivity is an illusion, inevitably undercut by the writer's particular situated standpoint. This standpoint yields a set of personal understandings that always locate any text in an field of previous writings and interpretations. Queer and feminist and materialist reflexivities undermine standpoint reflexivity at that precise point at which a knowing authors sits down to write a life story.

Reflexivity, however, is not an option. The trick is to balance the subjective with the inscriptive and to continue to produce texts that bring news from one world to another, understanding that at some level a reflexive poetic informs all that we write.

Read through the reflexive lens, the standard criticisms of the personal text (as discussed previously) dissolve into a politics of reading. The new forms of textuality are rejected because they undermine from within the hegemony of the standard social science text. Critics ask the new work to do things it is not organized to do. The new writing is not intended to be descriptive ethnography, nor is it a form of grounded theory wherein one can find a plethora of theoretical terms that are used to map the empirical world. The new writing does not take up conventional approaches to validity; instead, it values terms, such as narrative truth, and the emotional power of the text. The standard criticisms do not engage the logic of the form itself. The conventional critics write, then, around the edges of the new writing, never confronting or working through the epistemological critiques that organize the project. In contrast, the queer and feminist materialist critics cut to the core of the new writing. These theorists expose the major points of contention that turn on lived experience and the personal, emotional text.

Reflexive, Messy Text

Recall Trinh's criticisms (discussed previously) of the aesthetic strategies employed in the documentary film. These criticisms apply to much of the new writing because here too a documentary style is often used. This style creates the illusion of giving the reader direct access to reality. This style embodies a relentless pursuit of naturalism, which presumes a connection between lived experience and the written word. This style seeks its own version of authenticity by invoking the spoken speech of real, ordinary people in real situations. Lived time is described, and there are close-ups of real people doing things together (Shelton, 1995a, p. 86). Often, the writer is outside the situation being described, hidden—an unobtrusive camera—reporting, even on self-activities. Objective truth is captured and dramatized in the words of the text that uses the talk, testimony, and personal feelings of plain folk. These narrative strategies are intended to convince the reader that they should have confidence in the truth of the written word.

This naturalized, emotionally responsive documentary style thus inserts itself in the ethnographic apparatus, becoming part of the larger cinematic move in American culture—the move to capture the real and to give the real the aura of authenticity and immediacy. Therefore, in some hands the new writing forms reproduce the very representational technologies these authors wish to transcend. Hence Trinh's criticisms.

These criticisms open the door for the reflexive, messy text (Marcus, 1994, p. 567): texts that are aware of their own narrative apparatuses, that are sensitive to how reality is socially constructed, and that understanding that writing is a way of "framing" reality. Messy texts are many sited, intertextual, always open ended, and resistant to theoretical holism, but always committed to cultural criticism (p. 567).

The new reflexive writing becomes, then, a way of "framing reality" (Trinh, 1991, p. 188). Self reflexivity, however, does not translate into personal style or into a preoccupation with method. Such writing refuses to impose meaning on the reader; the text becomes a place where multiple interpretive experiences occur. A responsible, reflexive text (p. 188) announces its politics and ceaselessly interrogates the realities it invokes while folding the teller's story into the multivoiced history that is written. Such texts make readers work while resisting the temptation to think in terms of simplistic dichotomies; difference, not conflict, is foregrounded.

Ethnopoetics and narratives of the self are messy texts: They always return to the writerly self—a self that spills over into the world being inscribed. This is a writerly self with a particular hubris that is neither insolent nor arrogant. The poetic self is simply willing to put itself on the line and to take risks. These risks are predicated on a simple proposition: This writer's personal experiences are worth sharing with others. Messy texts make the writer a part of the writing project. These texts, however, are not just subjective accounts of experience; they attempt to reflexively map the multiple discourses that occur in a given social space. Hence, they are always multivoiced. No interpretation is privileged. These texts reject the principles of the realist ethnographic narrative that makes claims to both textual autonomy and epistemological validity (Bruner, 1993, p. 1; Clough, 1992, p. 4; Lee & Ackerman, 1994, p. 350).

Like Ronai's (1995) layered account and Burke's and Straley's postmodern mysteries, messy texts move back and forth between description, interpretation, and voice. These texts erase the dividing line between observer and observed. In them, the writer is transformed into a scribe who writes for rather than about the individuals being studied (see Lee & Ackerman, 1994, p. 349). Still, these texts make the writer's experiences central to the topic at hand. The messy text produces local, situated knowledge about the practices of a given group and its culture. There is always a stress on the historical contingencies and social processes that shape and play on the situations and persons under study. The messy text re-creates a social world as a site at which identities and local cultures are negotiated and given meaning.

The reflexive, epiphanic, messy text redefines the ethnographic project. The writer-as-scribe for the other also becomes a cultural critic: a person who voices interpretations about the events recorded and observed. At the same time, as the scribe of a messy text the writer shapes the poetic narrative representations that are brought to the people studied. These works are a testing ground on "which qualitative social science is being remade in the absence of authoritative models, paradigms, or methods" (Marcus, 1994, p. 573).

There are multiple risks here. As Hymes (1985) argues, in discussing the anthropological poet such writers must answer to the standards of two crafts—poetry and ethnography. One may succeed at one, writing good poetry, and fail at the other, not producing a text that conforms to the new ethnographic criteria. One may also write bad poetry or bad ethnographic fiction and produce a good ethnography, and so on. Unfortunately, Hymes's discussion creates the illusion of a false dichotomy—poetry versus ethnography. Good ethnography always uses language poetically, and good poetry always brings a situation alive in the mind of the reader. These dangers, however, have always been present, from the moment anthropologists introduced photography into their work (e.g., Bateson & Mead, 1942; Mead & Bateson, 1978) to the latest attempts by sociologists and anthropologists to write poetry.

There is also a third risk, a third craft to be mastered—the craft of cultural criticism. A critical text must avoid banality (Morris, 1990, p. 23) or the repetition of politically correct arguments about the current state of affairs in the world based on the study at hand. The craft of cultural criticism allows the writer (and reader) to move from the local, the particular, the personal, and the biographical to the political, the general, and the global. The writer exposes those institutional and cultural apparatuses that insert themselves in between the personal and the political and the individual and the social.

More deeply, the biographical, poetic impulse must produce bodies of critical, interpretive work that reflexively build on one another. It is not enough to produce isolated critiques. If the biographical is to be taken seriously, then each writer has an obligation to create a body of work that embodies a particular ontological, epistemological, and political vision of how things can be made better. Serious novelists, the new journalists, and mystery writers have long understood this. Writers, such as Burke and Straley, struggle to write political texts that are messy, poetic, ethnographic, and utopian.

The multiple risks include narcissistic texts, texts preoccupied with their own reflexivity, good and bad poetry, politically correct attitudes, too much concern for language, and utopian impulses predicated on the belief that the recovery of the previously repressed self can produce liberation and freedom. Combined, these risks can produce a neglect of ethnography's central purpose: to produce meaningful, critical discourse about the many worlds we all inhabit (Geertz, 1988, p. 147).

As the distinctions between the new writing and conventional social science research are troubled, however, a major problem remains. The traditional reflexive social science impulse is to turn everyone into the object of an analytic gaze (Clough, 1994, p. 162). Ethnography's literary impulse simply turns that gaze inward, leading to the production of "self-revealing autobiographical accounts" (p. 162). An impasse is confronted. There is a pressing need to invent a reflexive form of writing that turns ethnography and experimental literary texts back "onto each other" (p. 162) so that the liabilities of each form are somehow transcended. This is the aim of the messy text.

Whether one writes poetry, short stories, produces photographic essays, an ethnographic film, or writes popular songs, the goal in bringing news from one world to another, as Raymond Carver (1989a, p. 24) observes, is to neither shock nor brutalize the reader. Experimentation is not an excuse or a "license to be careless, silly or imitative" (p. 24). How the news of the new text is read is the topic of the next chapter.

Notes

1. I take this phrase from Marcus and Fisher (1986, p. 73), but distinguish *ethnopoetics*, "the emics of native poetries that are midwifed by western poets" (Rose, 1991, p. 220), from *native poetry*, the poetry of traditional, native poets, and *ethnographic poetics*, the poetic productions of ethnographers. Within this last category, following Rose (1991, p. 221), I distinguish between personal poetry, which is unshaped by the anthropological experience, and those poetic productions that meditate on this experience and rearticulate it within the poetic frame.

2. I take this phrase from Richardson (1994a, p. 521), referring to self stories or narratives (plays or fiction) that connect the personal experiences of the writer to the ethnographic project at hand. Self-narratives, which draw on the autobiographical genre (Krupat, 1994), are typically self stories about the field experience, writing stories (Richardson, 1995), or personal loss narratives (Ellis, 1996; Frank, 1995), including the loss of innocence, health, or a loved one.

3. *Autoethnography*: Traditionally, "the cultural study of one's own people" (Van Maanen, 1988, p. 106; see also Hayano, 1979, 1982), but more recently a turning of the ethnographic gaze inward on the self (auto), while maintaining the outward gaze of ethnography, looking at the larger context wherein self experiences occur (see Ellis, 1996).

4. As if in response to the standpoint theorists (Chapter 5) who failed to show how lived experience could be represented in a text, these experimental writers repeatedly attempt to bring the experience of the other (and the writer) into the texts that they write. They bypass the representational problem by invoking an epistemology of emotion, moving the reader to feel the feelings of the other.

5. I have elsewhere (Denzin, 1992a, pp. 129-130) criticized Rorty's views in terms of his private-public distinction, his view of "good" literature, his political aesthetic that dissolves into a passive pragmatism, and his uncritical view of the media.

6. Of course, this space was already opened by the writing moves connected to the standpoint epistemologies (Collins, 1991), the "new" sociologists of science (Mulkay, 1985), as well as the ethnopoetic (Tedlock, 1983) and performance text (Turner, 1986b) and the textual experiments of the New Journalism.

7. Here, I chart the history in anthropology and sociology; other disciplines will have slightly different histories.

8. Of course, these are common strategies used by nonfiction novelists.

9. Thus, Ellis (1995a, pp. 322-323) summarizes the criticisms of her work: "This is only her experience;" "Not sociology;" "Too raw;" "Too much of the author;" "A methodological nightmare;" "Not enough theory;" "Not objective;" and "Too involved."

10. Krupat (1994, p. 3) notes that the "auto" part of autobiography is alien to Native American understanding. The "graph" (alphabetic writing) part of autobiography was also alien: "Tribal people were oral people who represented personal experience performatively and dramatically to an audience" (Krupat, 1994, p. 3) and not in written form, as in a Western autobiography (see also Tedlock, 1983, pp. 247-248).

11. To repeat, the Quiller-Couch syndrome refers to masculine and feminine types of writing. The Lady Painter syndrome "refers to a statement by a male painter, who . . . postulates, 'When she's good, we call her a painter; when she's bad, we call her a lady painter' " (Trinh, 1989, p. 27).

12. A seventh form of textual reflexivity can be identified: the one connected to ethnomethodology and the new science studies (see Ashmore, 1989; Ashmore et al., 1995; Boyers, 1995; see also Mulkay, 1985).

PART 3

Whose Truth?

CHAPTER

8

Reading Narrative

What we 'look for' is un/fortunately what we shall find. . . . It is perhaps difficult for an analytical or analytically trained mind to admit that recording, gathering, sorting, deciphering, analyzing and synthesizing, dissecting and articulating are already 'imposing our [a] structure,' a structural activity. . . . Rare are those who realize that what they come up with is not 'structure of their narratives' but a reconstruction of the story.
—Trinh (1989, pp. 141-42)

I get the feeling that somewhere in some English publisher's vault there is a master disk from which thousands of versions of the same article about pleasure, resistance and the politics of consumption are being run off under different names with minor variations.
—Morris (1990, p. 21)

Every reading modifies its object.
—de Certeau (1984, p. 169)

As discussed in Chapter 5, the narrative turn in the social sciences presumes that social texts, including recorded or visual texts, interviews, fieldwork notes, transcribed conversations, speeches, film, music, advertisements, personal, electronic, and archival documents, can be rigorously and scientifically analyzed through the methods of narrative analysis (for reviews, see Feldman, 1995; Goodson, 1995; Hatch & Wisniewski, 1995; Polkinghorne, 1995; Psathas, 1995). In this way, the move to narrative is legitimized. With the proper structural tools, readers-as-analysts could produce reliable, valid, and consensual readings of social texts. Texts and stories are turned into analyzable documents about which certain scientific truths can be said.

This move to legitimize narrative through the use of analytic methods travels in three directions at the same time. First, the analytic approach to narrative serves to discipline a particular form of reading and writing—that form that treats the text as a mirror of reality (Clough, 1992, p. 133; Schneider, 1991). A disciplined reading unravels the structural logic that organizes any given text. This analysis frees the scholar to use the text as data for hypothesis testing or theory construction. The project of science is preserved.

This move, however, is countered by the poststructural critique of science, realism, and the realist text (Clough, 1992, p. 132; Hall, 1985). Poststructural critics argue that the purely analytic approach to narrative suppresses the underlying narrative logic of the text. This logic, as discussed in Chapters 6 and 7, articulates codes of sexual and cultural difference. Thus retellings of the Oedipal struggle are produced wherein the narrator or ethnographer's identity is transformed into an emotional story of self-discovery or self-healing (Clough, 1992, p. 135).

A text is not a mirror of reality; rather, a text is embedded in the narrative logics of science, sexuality, desire, and capitalism. These logics valorize, as discussed in Chapter 7, conceptions of a unified subject who can directly write about lived experiences in the everyday world. Poststructural readings aim to undo this logic, showing how it reinforces particular versions of sexuality, gender, power, knowledge, and science. This form of narrativity is meant to redirect ethnography "toward constructing itself as social criticism, rather than as social science" (Clough, 1992, p. 134).

In challenging the realist view of the text, poststructuralists argue that narrative is no longer embedded within the dominant traditions of naturalism. The hyperrealistic narrative has become the prevailing form of narrativity (Reevell, 1995, p. 703). The hyperrealist text is radically intertextual, anchoring itself in multiple media discourses at the same time (MTV, news, soaps, melodrama, etc.). This text refers back to itself, often mocking the real world and its conventional representations. This form of textuality contests the "naturalized moral order of 'real life' " (p. 703) as given in the traditional realist, narrative text.

As the poststructural critique gains force, it is confronted by critics who have leveled two charges against this particular version of the narrative turn. On the one hand, critics have mocked and ridiculed the new narrative theories of textuality, bringing negative views of postmodernism and poststructuralism to bear on these reading strategies (see Farberman, 1991, 1992; Geertz, 1988, p. 131; Prus, 1996, p. 222; Sanders, 1995, pp. 90-94; Snow & Morrill, 1995a, p. 347; Wolfe, 1992, p. 137). On the other hand, many question the texts that are analyzed, contending that they are either not worthy of analysis, because they belong to the realm of the popular, or that sociologists and anthropologists should not be reading them in the first place (Geertz, 1988, p. 135; Sanders, 1995, p. 94).

These are more than misguided criticisms. They are political critiques that aim to preserve a certain province for ethnography and ethnographic reading and writing. Ethnography is about valid and accurate descriptions of the social world (Van Maanen, 1995b, p. 23). Ethnography is not social criticism, and it is not about narratives that inscribe sexual identity or put the author's identity in the forefront of the story being told (Agar, 1990). For these critics, the old dictum, one tribe, one ethnographer, still holds, and to this is added the rule, the old ways of doing things still work: Do not experiment, do not criticize.

In this chapter, I examine these approaches to narrative, thereby making more explicit the reading strategies I have used throughout this study. I will isolate a generic, narrative model of textual analysis, giving special attention to standpoint,[1] resistant (Stabile, 1995), and content-based models. I will contrast these closed narratological frameworks to open, or performance-based, systems that reflexively embed the reader (and analyst) in a text's multiple material and historical realities.

Two Approaches to Narrative

These two reading styles overlap with the two approaches to narrative outlined by Polkinghorne (1995, p. 12)—what he terms the analysis of narrative and narrative analysis. The analysis of narrative involves the collection of stories, or narratives. These stories are then subjected to a paradigmatic analysis using concepts derived either from preexisting theory—for example, psychoanalysis—or inductively from the empirical materials themselves. In contrast, narrative analysis involves the collection of "events and happenings" (Polkinghorne, 1995, p. 12), which are then synthesized "by means of a plot into a story or stories (e.g., a history, case study or biographic episode). Thus, analysis of narrative moves from stories to common elements, and narrative analysis moves from elements to stories" (Polkinghorne, 1995, p. 12; see also Denzin, 1989b, p. 39). Modifying Polkinghorne, I will call these the analytic and storied approaches to narrative and contrast them to the storytelling model of Trinh (1989), a model that values "Grandma's story" and its telling (Trinh, 1989, p. 150).[2] I seek a return to Grandma's story and its telling.

The double crisis of representation and legitimation outlined in Chapter 1 frames my discussion. The crisis of representation, to repeat, addresses the problem of how to represent, and interpret, with some degree of certainty the multiple meanings that circulate in an ethnographic text. The crisis of legitimation asks how a reader can authorize any given reading. It asks, How do we judge an interpretation, when all external, or foundational criteria have been challenged? The critics of the narrative turn dispute this crisis, claiming that the new practioners are creating a crisis by their actions. Without this narrative turn, there would be no crisis of representation or of legitimation. I begin with problems of definition and interpretation.

Interpretive Assumptions:
The Reader in the Text

The following assumptions organize my argument. First, every text is a multiplicity of other texts existing within "a network of intertextual relations" (Frow & Morris, 1993, p. xix; see also Morris, 1988, p. 244). A text is always entangled in other texts. Two forms of the text must be immediately distinguished. Both forms are interpretive structures, and both forms involve processes of reading and writing. The first form is the text produced by the writer: a story, poem, realist ethnographic report, a film, a piece of music, an advertisement, a piece of New Journalism, or a performance work. This text is a complex interpretive document involving the writer's attempts to articulate some set of understandings about a particular situation, cultural form, or social process. I call this the original text; it becomes the site for new interpretive work. The second form, also a critical, interpretive text, now inserts itself inside the original document, offering new interpretations and readings of what has been presented.

Thus, when Meaghan Morris (1993) "reads" Henry Parkes Motel, a specific motel in Tenterfield, Australia, she reads the legend behind the motel, the inscriptions inscribed in the front wall of the inn, the myths surrounding Henry Parkes, and the stories Australians have come to tell about this historical figure. Meaning is never constructed on "a single level of inscription" (Frow & Morris, 1993, p. xix). A text always involves practices, institutional structures, and the complex forms of agency they entail, "[including] particular flows of power and knowledge, as well as a particular semantic organization. . . . There can be no privileged or 'correct' form of reading" (p. xix). This means that readers must always embed their interpretations in the larger intertextual arenas that surround, define, and shape the text in question.

Indeed, all texts have multiple authors and readers, or audiences. Webster (1982, pp. 106-108) elaborates, suggesting that every text has at least four audiences: the intended, the actual, the ideal, and the fictional. Thus, the intended audience of this chapter is you, the reader, and the ideal audience is one who has followed my arguments to this point. The actual audience may not be the one I intend. Were I to shift to a fictional voice, producing a dialogue between several voices, yet another audience, the fictional would be created. In so doing, I would then create another version of myself as author—in this case, a fictional writer. This fictional version of myself would interact with the intended, actual, and ideal versions of myself as the author of this text. This version of who I am is now embedded in the many voices of others. Who is writing and reading this text? In short, texts, as Bakhtin (1986) notes, are never monolithic productions. Multiple levels and layers of meaning always exist, and this multiplicity can seldom be captured within the confines of a single, structural, narrative scheme.

Second, as discussed previously, every text embodies a narrative logic concerning discursive authority, sexual difference, power, and knowledge (Clough, 1992, p. 5). This logic is repressed and displaced in the story the text tells; it must be exposed and analyzed.

Third, in presenting their particular version of reality, ethnographers privilege the visual, writing in a way that allows the reader to see and feel the world being described. Four visual regimes are central to this aspect of the ethnographic writing project: the Cartesian, Baconian, Baroque, and hysterical (Denzin, 1995a, p. 41; Jay, 1988, pp. 3-4, 18-20). The Cartesian regime presents the insights of a solitary, objective voyeur. The Baconian vision is fragmentary and descriptive. The Baroque eye stresses a surplus of images and a complex form of textuality. The hysterical eye focuses on that which cannot be captured objectively. These four visual regimes are differentially present in any given work; their presence must be identified and analyzed.

Fourth, the goal of any reading practice is not to reproduce a so-called standard version of the knowing subject of cultural studies or of contemporary ethnography (Morris, 1990, p. 23). A four-step model structures this form of reading (and writing). First, the investigator tacitly (or explicitly) endorses the enabling theses of contemporary ethnographic (and cultural studies) theory (pp. 21-22): Everyday people are not cultural dopes but active constructors of meaning; everyday patterns of action cannot be reduced to the mirrors of cultural or economic production; and everyday life is about dreams, hopes, fears, and desire and consists of a "multiplicity of fragmented and contradictory discourses" (p. 22).

Second, the analyst obtains a record of the subject's words and experiences. These words are either located in the text being analyzed or reproduced by the writer in an ethnographic text. Third, although a part of the everyday world, the subject's experiences must be translated into theoretical terms. This is the case because, at one level, the subject is still a cultural dope. He or she does not understand the historical forces that shape everyday biographical life. Only the analyst understands these forces. Fourth, the scholar then comments on the subject's experiences from within this theoretical model. Such readings use the voices of informants and the texts of popular culture to show how people resist cultural domination while producing their own versions of a complex and contradictory resistance culture (Morris, 1990, p. 25). Alternatively, these readings show persons to be the victims of this culture. Analysts can also use interpretations as a way to build complex, dense, or grounded theory or to fashion cultural criticism.

These politically correct writings and readings often exclude the writer's (and reader's) place in the text or the larger society. Nor do these works establish the writer's place outside the world studied; that is, in the institutions of higher learning (Morris, 1990, p. 31). This too often leads to the production of self-serving, tautological texts that become vehicles for the display of the writer's critical skills and populist affinities (p. 31).

This model foregrounds resistance, arguing that media texts, subversively read, contain the seeds of resistance to the larger, hegemonic cultural system. This stance implies an underlying logic of cause and effect, and a logic of political progression (Stabile, 1995, p. 406). Shifts "in ideology appear as fissures or cracks in hegemony. . . . Resistance is the necessary reaction to hegemonic attempts at containment, power is maintained, and then contested, and contradictions appear that cannot be suppressed" (Stabile, 1995, p. 406). Such readings, however, often fail to reflexively take account of the historical and material conditions that surround the field of discourse being analyzed (Stabile, 1995, p. 406). This results in those banal readings of the popular that Morris (1990) finds so distasteful.

Fifth, reading as an interpretive activity must be recovered, rescued from those analytic and storied frameworks (narratology, positivism, and postpositivism) that seek to anchor a reading in a fixed text, using a closed interpretive framework. Reading has no fixed place: "Barthes reads Proust in Stendahl's text; the television viewer reads the passing away of his [her] childhood in the news reports" (de Certeau, 1984, p. 174). Although the act of reading cannot be separated from the readable text, "the text only has meaning through its readers; it changes along with them" (de Certeau, 1984, p. 170). To read ethnographically is to travel (Morris, 1990, p. 30), to dream, and to be elsewhere (de Certeau, 1984, p. 173). The ethnographic reader "produces gardens that miniaturize and collate the world. . . . [The reader] is thus a novelist" (de Certeau, 1984, p. 173). This is not the reader of contemporary narratology—the reader anchored in a specific text.

There are two standard versions of this reader—positivist and postpositivist. The positivist reader displays curious alignments with structuralism and applies a set of external criteria (validity, reliability, and objectivity) to the interpretive process. Fixed-text reading strategies, from rhetorical to dramaturgical, semiotic, content, interaction, and conversation-based models, are illustrative of this position (Feldman, 1995; Psathas, 1995; Silverman, 1993, pp. 59-143; see below). (This is Polkinghorne's, 1995, analytic approach to narrative.) Post-positivism, the second standard interpretive position, attempts to formulate criteria unique to narrative inquiry, including whether or not a particular interpretation permits the formulation of grounded theory or generates findings that are trustworthy, persuasive, plausible, coherent, credible, generalizable, and internally reflexive (Reissman, 1993, pp. 64-70).

These two versions of the reader are supplemented, in the cultural studies literature (see Grossberg, 1992, p. 20-21), by three additional positions: the resistance, realist-functional, and processual-conjunctural models. Together, these models articulate different causal approaches to the text and its meanings in the worlds of everyday life. The resistance model connects particular social practices (torn jeans or looting after riots) to the subversion of the hegemonic cultural order. The realist-functional model presumes a necessary causal link between a text (sexist photographs) and social practices (sexism). The conjunctural model is radically contextual, materialist, antiessentialist, and antireductionist (p. 21). It locates a text and its meanings in a set of cultural practices, which are in "complex relations with other practices which determine, enable and constrain the possibilities and effects" (p. 21) of any practice (text) on any other practice of text. These five reading models must be carefully navigated as conjunctural readings are developed.

Sixth, in confronting a text the reader creates a world of experience. Like a bricoleur, the reader takes the materials at hand and creates an experience that may bear little relationship to the so-called objective text at hand (de Certeau, 1984, p. 174). The reader-as-bricoleur refuses to confine interpretation to a predetermined conceptual scheme. This reader, however, is knowledgeable about the many schemes now available for critical interpretation, including recent versions of television criticism (Allen, 1992; Hay, 1992) and what I term the standpoint theories—those theories that privilege sexuality, gender, class, race, age, nationality, and ideology.

Seventh, this reader understands that all readings are done for a purpose: to read politically and poetically, and to fashion interpretive, ethnographic, and performance texts that have the capacity to "articulate loss, despair, disillusion, anger" (Morris, 1990, p. 31), and, I would add, joy and love. The desire is not to put words or interpretations in people's mouths but to create the spaces so their voices can be heard, to write (and read) with them, for them, and not about them. Such readings are more than cathartic productions: They are instigations to action.

Eighth, it is necessary to analyze how any given text constructs and then negotiates the meanings brought to authors, readers, and speakers, thereby giving authority to a particular reading or interpretation (Frow & Morris, 1993, p. xxiii). Following Hall (1980), Morris (1990, p. 23), and Fiske (1992, pp. 292-293; White, 1992, p. 191), three levels, or forms, of meaning (and reading) can be distinguished: the dominant (realist), the negotiated (preferred), and the oppositional (subversive).

Every text situates a reader in a dominant discourse or ideology. Recall the discussion in Chapter 5 of Bill Green's (1981) account of how Janet Cooke (1980) came to write her story, "Jimmy's World." Green gave a realist accounting of the sequence of events that lead to Cooke's story being published. He situated his story in the dominant discourse concerning how newspapers oversee the writing of news stories. Green created a preferred reading of his story. This reading can be contrasted to the negotiated reading brought to the story by particular readers who accepted the dominant ideology but fitted it to their situation. Thus, James Michner (1981, p. 80) modified Green's reading to explain how Cooke was given a privileged position by her supervisors at the *Post*. In contrast, Judith Crist (Tyler & Simons, 1981) rejected Green's account completely and offered an oppositional reading, bringing the label of the "New Fiction" to Cooke's work.

Every reading challenges or destablizes a text, questioning its representations of reality. Hall's model of reading suggests that any text can be read (and written) at three levels (realist, preferred, and subversive), each level opening up another version of the story being told. The goal is to exhaust, within a given reading, the meanings located at each of these levels.

Ninth, readings are done against "the sting of memory" (Ulmer, 1989, p. 209). That is, the reader seeks texts that invoke the punctum or sting of memory, personally significant epiphanic moments represented in a particular work (Ulmer, 1989, p. 209). The meanings brought to this moment are then unraveled, read in terms of Hall's three forms of interpretation. Morris (1993), for example, reads Baudrillard's theory of television as fatal seduction against her family's experiences with American television and the *I Love Lucy Show*, recalling those moments when her father and mother yelled back and forth at each other over the level of volume on the television set.

My tenth assumption concerns an ethics of reading. A dialogical ethical model of reading must avoid the four morally problematic performance stances identified in Chapter 4. These four stances (The Custodian's Rip-Off, The Enthusiast's Infatuation, The Curator's Exhibitionism, and The Skeptic's Cop-Out; [Conquergood, 1985a, p. 4; see also Hill, 1995]),[3] may be fitted to the reading process. Custodial readers look for good texts to read and, like the enthusiast, fail to become deeply involved in the cultural settings that surround the text in question. These two stances trivialize the other and the text in question. The skeptic, or cynic, in contrast, values cultural differences and takes the position, to repeat Conquergood's example (1985a, p. 8), that "only blacks can understand and perform black literature." To paraphrase Conquergood (1985a, p. 8), this position refuses to face up to the ethical tensions and moral ambiguities involved in the interpretation of culturally sensitive materials. The curator is a reader who sensationalizes cultural differences, exploiting texts that present the culturally troubling other (Conquergood, 1985a, p. 7).

These four stances privilege dominant or preferred readings and reproduce cultural stereotypes. They shut down dialogue, failing to make the conversation between text, reader, and audience ongoing and open ended (Conquergood, 1985a, p. 9).

Finally, a two-edged problematic must be confronted. The reader and writer of the ethnographic, or cultural, text are coproducers of the very text that is being written and read. The reader creates the object of analysis. This object, the ethnographic or cultural text, however, is about the other. The second problem is clear. How do writers (and readers) speak of the other while being implicated in the very representations (and interpretations) that bring the other into existence? I will offer a model of narrative that addresses these two problems. First, however, the generic model of narrative analysis is discussed.

Generic Model of Narrative Analysis

The generic model of narrative analysis unfolds through five inter-related steps, culminating in a formal analysis that is driven by a theory of textuality and meaning.[4] The investigator begins first by selecting the type of text to be analyzed, often distinguishing between transcripts of what people say (transcribed interviews) and existing documents, a photograph, a scene in a film, a piece of popular music, or a body of ethnographic work (see Frey, Botan, Friedman, & Kreps, 1992, pp. 162-63). The researcher must be certain that the texts selected for analysis are in fact the most appropriate texts for answering the research questions posed (Frey et al., 1992, p. 164).

Second, once the type of text has been determined, the researcher selects a sample of this text type for analysis. Each story, or text, is approached only if it can be located within a larger grouping of stories or texts (e.g., films, newspaper stories about Hillary Clinton). This larger grouping of texts is commonly called the population from which a sample of stories or texts has been drawn (Frey et al., 1992, pp. 162-63). This population will be defined by time and place (e.g., all stories about Hillary Clinton in 1992 in the *New York Times* and the *New York Post*; see Detman, 1996).

According to the epistemological logics of positivism, this sample should be complete and accurate and be representative of the larger population of texts from which it is drawn. Incomplete or unrepresentative texts undermine the generalizability of the study (Frey et al., 1992, p. 163). On the basis of the analytic properties discovered in the sample of texts that have been analyzed, the analyst then generalizes to this larger population.

Next, the researcher must ensure that no bias has entered into the production of the text or into its analysis. The procedures used to produce the text must not "pose a threat to the validity of the data" (Frey et al., 1992, p. 164). Furthermore, the method of analysis brought to the text will presumably produce the same or a similar reading were another reader to analyze this body of work. That is, reliable interpretations can be produced (Silverman, 1993, p. 145). This means that a valid or accurate text has been created or secured for analysis, and the transcribed text equals the real text as heard or witnessed by the observer. Of course, as discussed in Chapter 4, this is an impossibility.

Fourth, multiple forms of narrative analysis can now be applied to this body of valid and reliable material (see Feldman, 1995, pp. 3-4; Reissman, 1993, pp. 4-5). Thus, for example, the semiotic approach to a text presumes that language is a sign system and meaning arises out of the relationship between signs (see Manning & Cullum-Swan, 1994, p. 466; Wiley, 1995, p. 13). The analyst dissects the various semiological or sign systems operating in a text, perhaps deploying some version of the semiotic square or uncovering the various binary oppositions and codes that operate in the text (e.g., male-female, nature-culture, etc.).[5]

A less sophisticated approach to language as a sign system is given in the method of content analysis. This approach involves the study of the manifest content of a message or text and its physical, syntactical, referential, and propositional units. Analysts make inferences about the characteristics of the receivers and producers of texts. Analysis is based on categories that are mutually exclusive, equivalent, and exhaustive. Analysis is validated by face, semantic, criterion-related, and construct validity (Frey et al., 1992, pp. 195-197; Krippendorf, 1980).

In contrast, various versions of narrative theory (Kozloff, 1992, p. 69) will go to great lengths to split a narrative into two parts: story (what happens to whom) and discourse (how the story is told). A time order will be imposed on the events in the story (beginning, middle, and end), and the reader may identify a hierarchy of character types (Propp, 1928/1968) within the story while making distinctions between real and implied authors, narrators, and readers (Kozloff, 1992, p. 77). Genre theory (Feuer, 1992, p. 145) extends narrative theory by examining types or genres of narrative (e.g., fiction, science, drama, comedy, tragedy, etc). The aesthetic, ritual, and ideological dimensions and functions of a narrative form are then studied. Particular genre types are seen as carrying different ideological messages (Feuer, 1992, p. 145; White, 1992, p. 173) that can be uncovered through audience-oriented, reader-response theories of reception (Allen, 1992). In practice, this approach often produces rather conventional ethnographies of communication (see below), which use content-based methods of analysis to uncover a text's ideological effects.

Alternatively, the analyst may employ a form of rhetorical criticism (historical, Neo-Aristotelian, generic, metaphoric, narrative, dramatic, or fantasy theme; [Frey et al., 1992, pp. 169-171]). This strategy involves the analysis of the persuasive impact of oral or written messages, giving special attention to speakers, messages, purposes, intended audience effects, cultural contexts, and the versions of reality created by a text (pp. 169-171). A dramaturgical analysis extends this rhetorical approach by treating a text as a communicative, dramatic event that can be studied in terms of a pentadic analysis, including act, purpose, agent, and scene (see Burke, 1969).

A discourse-based method is represented by conversation analysis (CA), which is the study of the social organization of everyday talk as given in transcribed texts. CA involves the description and analysis of the structures, machinery, organized practices, and formal procedures that produce order in a conversation (Psathas, 1995, p. 3). CA may also include the study of the categories or terms (membership categorization devices) persons use when they referentially (widow, mother, and teacher) locate themselves within ordinary talk (Silverman, 1993, p. 81).

Fifth, such methods will allow the writer to ascribe meaning to the messages contained within the text. This meaning is determined in one of four ways. First, the writer ascertains the intentions of the producer of the text, arguing that these intentions determine the meanings in the text.[6] Second, the analyst determines how receivers (readers) interpreted the text, often connecting the messages in the text to actions taken by receivers (e.g., voting for a particular political candidate).[7] Third, the meanings in the text are assessed structurally; that is, in terms of how the structural or functional units in the text work together to tell a particular story. Fourth, the researcher may apply a particular reading strategy (dominant, negotiated, or subversive readings) to determine the ideological content of a text or to critique the messages in the text in terms of their bias or persuasive power (see Fiske, 1994; Hall, 1980).[8]

Reading the Standard Narrative Model

These steps in and methods of narrative analysis suffer from the following problems. These problems are directly connected to the empiricist model outlined previously; that is, they reproduce an image of the positivist reader.

The standard narrative model works from within an interpretive structure that attempts to link five key terms: audience, text, structure, empirical inquiry, and lived experience. Audiences are turned into readers (see below). Texts are treated as narrative systems of meaning shaped by larger structural forces. The effects of a text are played out in the world of lived experience, experience being the behavioral referent for a text's effects. Empirical (narrative) inquiry thus connects audiences and experiences to the meanings in texts. The intertextual referents of a text are seldom examined. This allows the analyst to ignore how multiple authors and multiple readers circulate within the same work or within works that reinscribe a normative logic of sexual difference.

These methods of analysis risk reproducing the fallacy of objective reading. They typically (as noted previously) replace the reader's meanings with those of the analyst while using the responses of the reader as confirmation of the analyst's correct interpretation (Morris, 1990, p. 23). They capture the text, turning it into a vehicle for the display of the scholar's critical activity.

This framework presumes a fixed text with fixed meanings. These meanings can be dug out through rigorous content, semiotic, narrative or rhetorical analysis. Moreover, content-based methods of analysis, which break texts down into identifiable units, risk "destroying the very object they are supposed to be studying" (Kracauer, 1953, as quoted in Larsen, 1991, p. 122).[9] These methods fail to address language's radical indeterminacy, the slipperiness of signs and signifiers (Barthes, 1957/1972, 1982, 1985; Derrida, 1967/1978, 1974/1976), and the fact that language creates rather than mirrors reality. The hyperreality of the text is thereby ignored (Baudrillard, 1983).

These methods fail to examine the text as a meaningful whole. They presume a naive, transmission model of communication (Carey, 1989, p. 32); the text carries or transmits clear meanings to an ideal reader. This model ignores how audiences (readers) construct, apprehend, and bring meaning to and interact with the text in question (p. 32).

This empiricist (positivist) approach to narrative, like its realist-functional counterpart, treats audiences (readers) as market categories in which the text, as a site, becomes a place where media (textual) effects and needs are experienced. Thus, a unified, self-aware subject is presumed. Lived experience is recovered through measures of the text's effects on the audience members attitudes or interactional patterns.

Lived experience, however, is seldom examined, and of course the problems that surround the representation (and recovery) of lived experience (Chapter 1) are never examined. Hall (1985) reminds us, "When we contrast ideology to experience, or illusion to authentic truth, we are failing to recognize that there is no way of experiencing the 'real relations' of a particular society outside of its cultural and ideological categories" (p. 105; also quoted in White, 1992, p. 170).

This model then proceeds to conceptualize media structures as macroformations that produce stable (and overdetermined) effects on audiences. Media texts are viewed as either conduits for these messages or as commodities that reproduce dominant cultural ideologies. Thus, scholars engage in "scientific" studies that connect audiences (as formations) to media sites (TV shows), viewing cultural texts as carriers of ideology. These studies attempt to offer some totalizing, objective picture of the narrative processes at work in a particular social group. A Cartesian, ocular epistemology is perpetuated; the objective analyst as voyeur reads the effects of a text on its readers.

A normative epistemology organizes these practices. This epistemology assumes that the normal is what is most representative or most generalizable. This epistemology gives less attention to the nonrepresentative, marginal formations that can exist in a system of production (see Fiske, 1994, p. 196). Recall the discussion in Chapter 1 (Note 9) on sampling. This commitment to sample from a population of texts reproduces a positivist and empiricist conception of social structure and social life. It ignores the logic of what Psathas (1995, p. 50) calls the method of instances; that is, treating each instance of a phenomenon as an occurrence that evidences the operation of a set of cultural understandings currently available for use by cultural members. In the present context, the reader's task is to understand how this instance (this text) works; whether it occurs again is irrelevant. The question of sampling from a population is also not an issue because it is never possible to say in advance what an instance is a sample of (Psathas, 1995, p. 50). Nor is it safe to presume that the same reading will be produced a second time. Each interaction with the text produces a new interpretation.

In privileging lived experience, as the place where a reading is confirmed, this model reproduces the realist bias of ethnography in the traditional and modernist periods. This bias argued that ethnographers studied real people in the real world. Their task was clear: "Find out the typical ways of thinking and feeling, corresponding to the institutions and culture of a given community and formulate the results in the most convincing way" (Malinowski, 1922/1961, p. 3; also quoted in Van Maanen, 1995a, p. 6). "In the most convincing way" meant that the analyst had to show how culture and social structure were mapped into the cognitive and emotional structures of the natives or the persons studied. Individual beliefs, evidenced in attitudes and behaviors, directly corresponded to the institutions and culture of the group. Thus, the cultural transmission model is translated into realist ethnography. Students of narrative connect meanings (culture) to action in the real world.

As I have repeatedly stated, however, this is a flawed model. Humans are always already tangled up, as C. Wright Mills (1963) and Stuart Hall (1985) remind us, in a secondhand world of meanings and have no direct access to reality. Reality as it is known is lodged in these interpretive, narrative texts that ideologically mediate the real. In critically reading these texts, poststructuralists radically subvert the realist agenda because the real world is no longer the referent for analysis or experience. Ethnographies of communication or of group life must, accordingly, be directed to this world of ideology, this world of hyper-real narrativity, and its place in the dreams, fantasies, and interactions of everyday people. It is no longer appropriate to follow Malinowski's definition of ethnography.

The Storied, Performance
Approach to Narrative

It is necessary, then, to actively pursue the conjunctural, contextual, performance-based, "messy" approach to reading (and writing) outlined in Chapters 4 and 7. This approach embraces experimental, experiential, and critical readings that are always incomplete, personal, self-reflexive, and resistant to totalizing theories. It understands that readers and writers are coproducers of the text that is being written and read. This understanding requires a move away from the "scientific" postpositivist forms of narrative inquiry discussed previously. A text's meaning is best given in coperformances, when audience and readers-as-performers interact in and over the same text. This messy approach conceptualizes audiences (and readers) as processes that outlast any given media event (see Fiske, 1994, p. 196). It sees audiences as places where situated identities are negotiated in the face of cultural texts and institutional structures that attempt to create specific needs and gratifications. It sees structures as generative processes and cultural differences as instances of conflict and struggle.

A dialogical ethics of reading confronts the tensions that are involved in the analysis of culturally sensitive materials. The reader, to repeat, works to avoid those morally problematic ethical stances (custodian, curator, enthusiast, and skeptic) identified by Conquergood (1985a; Hill, 1995). Such readers, like the critics of poststructuralism (e.g., Farberman, 1991; Sanders, 1995), act like curators or exhibitors of exotic documents. This allows them to avoid the problem of entering and learning the cultural terrain where these exotic documents are given special meaning. At the same time, analysts must guard against what Meaghan Morris (1990) calls the production of the banal in cultural studies. This project, as noted previously, allows the researcher to produce circular subversive readings of any and all cultural texts.

Texts will not be read as just the carriers of ideological meanings or as just commodities; they will be seen as sites of political negotiation. Audience members will be taken up as empirical subjects (not textual constructions) who are in gendered-, class-, and racially specific relations with one another. Ethnographies will be empirical in the classical sense of the word based on the articulated experiences of people in concrete places. Ethnographies will not attempt to capture the totality of a group's way of life. The focus will be interpreted slices, glimpses, and specimens of interaction that display how cultural practices, connected to structural formations and narrative texts, are experienced at a particular time and place by interacting individuals.

The researcher strategically selects sites for interpretation that constitute the intersection of texts (stories) and interacting individuals. Interactional specimens are extracted from these sites, written off of the conversations and actions that occur within them. This model always works upward and outward from the concrete to the larger set of meanings that operate in a particular context. It offers glimpses of culture in practice, setting one set of practices and meanings off against others that may compete in the same situation (Fiske, 1994, p. 195).

The concept of structure is critical. In interpretive cultural studies, structure is a set of generative (often hegemonic), interactional and cultural practices that organize meanings at the local level. Critical academic inquiry guides this process: The researcher seeks to understand a subject (or class of subjects) within a given historical moment. Sartre's (1963, pp. 85-166) progressive-regressive method is employed. A variant on the pragmatic emphasis on the consequences of acts, this method looks forward to the conclusion of a set of acts. It then works back to the conditions, interpretations, and situations that shape this decision. By moving forward and backward in time, subjects and their projects are located within culture as a set of interpretive practices.

These interpretive practices are connected to systems of cultural discourse (medicine, law, education, religion, family, gender, cinema, television, sexuality, etc.) and to specific textual representations. Systems of discourse are structured by narrative history, woven through interpretations of the past and its representations (see Denzin, 1991a, pp. 238-239). This version of history establishes facts and fictions, agreed on truths, and locates experts who verify authentic accounts (readings). Any specific representation is part of a larger process that dialectically builds on itself and elaborates itself as it unfolds over time. Thus, the stories about Janet Cooke shifted and changed over time as new understandings were brought into the situation. This historical, narrative logic must be unraveled and connected to specific textual representations.

This will be a messy, multilevel, multimethod approach to narrative inquiry. The empirical thrust of this approach will be critically defined. That is, the scholar will seek to fit narrative methods to their historical moment and the structures that define this moment. At the same time, the intent will be to interrogate and criticize this moment and its narrative, storytelling practices. This approach will locate specific sites at which change can be produced and it will seek to employ participatory forms of critical inquiry that bring persons from the everyday world directly into the narrative, storytelling process (see Kincheloe & McLaren, 1994). This approach will always contextualize narrative methods, connecting them to specific cultural practices and social formations. At this site at which history, theory, method, and topic meet, the scholar produces messy, interpretive, performance texts. The goal is clear. As Trinh (1989, p. 141) observes, traditional, empiricist narrative methods represent an approach to storytelling that must be avoided. They turn the story told into a story analyzed. In so doing, they sacrifice meaning for analytic rigor. They privilege the analyst's listening ear. They only hear and read the story from within a set of predetermined structural categories. They do not hear the story as it was told. The goal is to recover these lost stories—to return to Grandma's stories and their tellings.

Notes

1. Here, I expand the concept of standpoint theory, going beyond the specific theories and theorists considered in Chapter 3.
2. In the analytic and storied approaches to narrative, narrative materials can be put to one of three uses. First, personal experience and self-stories can be collected and connected to the life story of a given individual. Second, self and personal experience stories from many different individuals can be collected and grouped around a common theme. Third, the researcher can offer a cross-case analysis of the materials that have been collected, examining processes and not persons per se (see Denzin, 1989b, p. 39).
3. Hill (1995, p. 313) expands Conquergood's (1985a) list of four pitfalls to include (a) the fetishization of the ritual form or turning it into a sham while appropriating its authority for self-serving purposes; and (b) ethnographic duplicity: believing that a Native American ritual, for example, can be duplicated in another context by a different set of cultural others.
4. This is a version of Polkinghorne's (1995) analytic use of narrative.
5. Jameson's (1990, 1992) well-known use of the semiotic square is an instance of this method, which has parallels to Propp's (1928/1968) structural analysis of the folktale and Levi-Strauss's (1962/1966) study of myth.
6. This reproduces the intentionalist fallacy discussed in Note 20 in Chapter 5.
7. Other attempts to validate and universalize one's findings include appeals to personal experience, the use of focus groups, citing the voices of informants, or appealing to the work of other scholars in the field (see Morris, 1990, p. 24).
8. Such readings may reproduce the kinds of "banal" interpretations Morris (1990, p. 21) attributes to certain versions of cultural studies (see Stabile, 1995).
9. A variant on this approach is given by computer-assisted models of data analysis (see Weitzman & Miles, 1995; see also Fielding & Lee, 1992; Miles & Huberman, 1994). These methods use content-based codes to break a fieldwork text down into manageable units. These methods presumably bring "rigor" and precision to qualitative inquiry.

CHAPTER 9

The Sixth Moment

Who must ethnographers be in postmodernity, when science is understood as a primary agency of power/knowledge and when computer simulation and the televisual, more than the novel or even film, give shape to the social?
—Clough (1995, p. 534)

Ethnography's future is the sixth moment (Lincoln, 1995a, p. 40). It remains to return to the beginning and to take up again the task of offering an interpretive framework for understanding ethnography's multiple places in the televisual societies of the twenty-first century. An emancipatory, critical interpretive interactionism, a cultural studies without guarantees (Hall, 1992, p. 282) seeks a proper place for ethnography, the most worldly of all our interpretive practices. This requires a framework that critically reads ethnography back through itself. This framework will show how our interpretive practices are complicitous with the cinematic apparatuses that reproduce the real for society and its members.

In returning to the beginning, it is now possible to reread the ethnographic experiments since 1986 (*Writing Culture* [Clifford & Marcus, 1986]) as more than the vagrant, self-indulgent efforts of a few who were challenging the borders and boundaries of traditional ethnography. Those who would dare to engage ethnopoetics, self-narratives, the New Journalism, performance and standpoint texts, and even poems, mysteries, and novels were threatening the established order and the very essence of science itself (see Clough, 1995; Prus, 1996, p. 227; Shelton, 1995b).

As the boundaries of the traditional realist ethnographic text were being challenged, counterforces were mobilized. The transgressors were policed, punished, mocked, even ridiculed. Resistances to the hegemonic order were marginalized and the deviants were labeled— some called them the new ethnographs (see Farberman, 1991, p. 475; see also Dawson & Prus, 1993, 1995; Farberman, 1992; Kleinman, 1993; Kunda, 1993; Lofland, 1993; Nader, 1993; Prus, 1996, p. 218; Sanders, 1995; Snow & Morrill, 1995a, 1995b). Under this reading, which emphasizes moves and countermoves, the hegemonic order is displaced, resisted by a new tribe of ethnographers who want to do things differently. Progress is at hand. Just as the transgressors are put back in their place, new spaces are opened up for new transgressions.

There is a danger in this model, however. Foregrounding resistance and subversion can lead to the optimistic belief that things are getting better (see Stabile, 1995, p. 406). Under this view, the old way of doing ethnography is being changed, and this is confirmed by the fact that innovative writing forms seem to be present everywhere. This position ignores the recuperative and conservative practices of the traditional, hegemonic ethnographic order—that order that insists on marginalizing the new, not treating it as a version of a new order of things, and always defining it as an aberrant variation on the traditional way of doing things (see Altheide, 1995).

Put bluntly, the verdict for many is in. The old, better than the new, can do the work of ethnography. Therefore, forget all this experimental stuff. There is more at issue, however, then different ways of writing. The material and ethical practices of an entire discipline are on the line.

In this conclusion, I offer preliminary observations on the many possible futures that lie in front of interpretive ethnography. I begin with the policing efforts and the critical reactions of the past decade to the new work. This will lead to a discussion of new models of truth, the ethics and epistemologies of a postpragmatist social criticism. A feminist (Ryan, 1995) communitarian moral ethic (Christians, 1995a, 1995b; Christians, Ferre, & Fackler, 1993; Craig, 1995; Rosen, 1994) will be sketched[1] and contrasted to the ethical systems that have traditionally structured ethnographic, interpretive practice. I will build on recent arguments calling for a public or civic journalism (Charity, 1995; Christians, 1995a; Fallows, 1996; Rosen, 1994). I will propose a civic or publicly responsible local ethnography that speaks to the central issues of self, society, and democracy. This project implements and extends critical ethnography (Carspecken, 1996). Ethnography in the sixth moment will embrace moral criticism. It will advocate a form of participatory democracy without necessarily advocating particular solutions to particular problems (Charity, 1995, p. 146).[2]

Letting the Old
Do the Work of the New

To repeat, many of the critics of the new writing presumed a universal ethnographic subject: the other who was not the ethnographer. These critics looked at society from the outside, contending that objective accounts of society could be given by objective observers (Smith, 1989, p. 44). This observer, as Smith (p. 44) argued, was able to write in a way that did not require the presence of a real subject in the world. Social experience and real people were irrelevant to the topic at hand. This lead to the production of an interpretive structure that said social phenomena could be interpreted as social facts (p. 45). This structure shifted arguments about agency, purpose, meaning, and intention from the subject to the phenomena being studied. It then transformed those phenomena into texts about society. The phenomena were then given a presence that rested in these textual descriptions (p. 45). Real live people entered the text as a part of discourse in the form of excerpts from field notes, the casual observations of the theorist, or as "ideal types" (p. 51). The scholars I have examined in this work wish to overturn this picture of social science writing.

This view of social science work has generated the by now familiar litany of criticisms of the new writing discussed in previous chapters. For the sake of convenience, I offer a summary of these criticisms, dividing them into two groups: those from the traditional realist, positivist camp and those from the poststructuralists. I also list the criteria of evaluation offered by the new writers (Table 9.1).

Table 9.1 Criticisms of the New Writing

Positivists	Poststructuralists	New Criteria
Fiction	The real	Emotion
Not objective	Values	Verisimilitude
Not valid or reliable	Gender	Dialogue
Biased texts	Voice	Construction
unrepresentative sample	Unified subject	of facts
Too literary	Narcissistic	Scenic method
No method of verification	Materialist neglect	Multiple points
How to read?	Oedipal biases	of view
Inconsequential topics	Realist bias	Language
Journalism	The unconscious	Narrative truth
Not science	Is science	Theory
No hard facts	Description	Praxis
Personal biases	Inscription	Emotion
		lived
		experience

The Realist-Positivist Attack

The realist-positivist critique focuses, as Table 9.1 indicates, on issues of method, truth, and verification. The positivist challenges the new writing because it fails to use agreed on methods of verification, including random samples, representative texts, and so-called unbiased methods of interpretation. The positivists reject the criteria of evaluation used by the new writers—namely, emotional intimacy, verisimilitude, shared experience, narrative truth, the figurative and self-reflective use of language, the use of the scenic method, multiple points of view, realistic dialogue, multiple voices, treating facts as social constructions, and minimal theory.

The positivist sees these new criteria as assaults on the pursuit of truth. These methods, these strategies of writing, and the persons who use them constitute grave threats to the social sciences. For some (Huber, 1995), the new writing and its "any thing goes" politics explain the dire straits that disciplines such as sociology now confront—namely, an apparent fragmentation of the field, the lack of a core body of knowledge, the underemployment of PhD's, the demise of select departments in the 1980s, and the challenges to others in the 1990s.

The new writing embodies certain self-destructive characteristics that, for observers such as Huber (1995), "increase the probability of attracting negative attention" (p. 200) for the disciplines, including a tendency to recruit reformists, a weak core, and some "affinity for antirationalist ideas" (p. 200). Huber offers four basic strategies to address these self-destructive practices: develop a central core of knowledge, silence the antirationalists,[3] collect solid facts about society that will make sociology useful to the welfare state, and follow a norm of civility. Huber's proposals cut to the core of the politics that are involved in the new writing.

The Irrationalists and Two Social Sciences

First, of the irrationalists, Huber (1995) states, "we should resist our admirable tendency to tolerate differences when it requires tolerance of perspectives that involve aggressive efforts to undermine everyone else" (p. 212). Not only are these people (the irrationalists) uncivil but they do not believe in truth or in the scientific method. She is clear on this: "An unknown proportion of sociologists feel that there are no standards of rationality, objectivity, or truth" (p. 204). Of course, this is a caricature, and there is good reason why Huber names no representative of this position: No one holds it.[4] This unknown, unnamed group is then compared to another sociological group—those who believe that sociology has a viable academic niche as a science (p. 204).

Thus, the field is divided into two camps—the irrationalists and the rationalists. This division creates another—those believing in science who also hold to a conception of a disciplinary core consisting of demography, social organization, and stratification (Huber, 1995, pp. 203-204).[5] Persons working in these three core areas (plus statistics; p. 210) also produce "replicable data most needed to understand how societies work" (p. 204); they "supply the knowledge needed to run welfare states" (p. 213).

The irrationalists resist this definition of a core (even perhaps of a society and its problems), and presumably contribute little to their understanding. Huber (1995) counters the irrationalists with her version of rationalism, arguing that sociology cannot be a science if it tolerates challenges to the belief in the "idea of the disinterested observer seeking objective truth with universal validity that is based on the notion of a reality independent of human thought and action" (p. 204).[6]

For Huber (1995), rationalism is presumably equated with logical empiricism, a belief system that distrusts philosophical and moral inquiry and believes in a disinterested social science observer who applies rational rules to research using methods to produce findings (Schwandt, 1996). Irrationalists question these rules and engage in moral inquiry. The chief rhetorical accomplishment of logical empiricism was its attempt to ideologically separate moral discourse from empirical inquiry (Schwandt, 1996). This is what Huber attempts.

This is a questionable strategy. It again divides the field into two camps, shutting down complex, subtle arguments in the process—for example, those between positivists, postpositivists, critical theorists, and constructivists (see Schwandt, 1996). At the same time, it valorizes one approach to truth and science, thereby ignoring the many criticisms that have been brought to this received approach to data collection, hypothesis testing, and theory construction. These criticisms include the problems of context stripping, the exclusion of meaning, the etic-emic dilemma, fitting general data to specific cases, emphasizing verification over discovery, ignoring the theory and value ladenness of facts, verification versus falsification, the interactive nature of the inquirer-inquired dyad, and a problematic ethical system (Cronbach, 1989; Guba & Lincoln, 1989, pp. 120-141, 1994, pp. 106-107; Rorty, 1991).

Other Interpretive Criteria

During the 1980s, mainstream American, but not European sociology (Giddens, Habermas, and Bordieu), turned its back on the methodological controversies surrounding positivism, postpositivism, critical theory, and constructivism that were sweeping across neighboring social science fields (Cronbach, 1989; Geertz, 1983; McCloskey, 1985; Rosaldo, 1989; Smith, Harre, & Van Langenhove, 1995). These controversies, as discussed in Chapters 1 and 2, challenged the presuppositions of objective social science as well as traditional ways of bringing authority to that research, including the use of terms such as reliability and validity. Many came to reject the ontological, epistemological, and methodological presuppositions Huber (1995) appears to endorse. Gone were beliefs in ontological realism, objectivist epistemologies, and the use of quantitative methods to verify hypotheses. The notion of knowledge as accumulation was replaced by a more relative, constructionist position (Guba & Lincoln, 1994, p. 114).

During the same time period, the so-called irrationalists developed complex criteria for evaluating interpretive work, including credibility, plausibility, context embeddedness, dependability, confirmability, authenticity, dialogue, narrative truth, emotional verisimilitude, and so on (see Altheide & Johnson, 1994; Lincoln, 1995b). Regrettably, Huber (1995) does not address this complex literature, except to dismiss it as another instance of irrationalism and relativisitc sociology (p. 205).

Indeed, Huber's stance effectively dismisses this literature and its contributions to this discourse. This leaves her open to the following questions (see Huber, 1973): Who is to police those who claim they have the correct view of knowledge, truth, or science and knowledge for whom? How can her perspective address the emergent methodological biases that adhere to positivism? How can she determine the truth of any assertion about the world when her methods are directly implicated in the way that world is created and examined? How can she guard against the emergent political or social biases reflected in her assumptions about the study of a so-called objective social world?

Value-Free Sociology

Under the guise of objective, nonpartisan, value-free social science, Huber (1995) would take democracy out of sociology. Her model is taken from ecology and it has Darwinian overtones: "Administrators . . . must choose . . . between a semistarvation diet for everyone, or the starving of weaker units in order to give stronger ones a chance to flourish" (p. 195). This stance leads to her criticisms of those partisans who advocate intellectual relativism, postmodernism, irrationalism, and the inclusion of students on administrative committees (pp. 201, 204-205, 207-209). These people and their ideas have brought "unclear standards, doubtful course rigor, a smorgasbord curriculum, and inappropriate graduate student participation" (p. 206) into sociology. The arguments of these people can no longer be tolerated.

The very people she wishes to quiet, those drawn to antirationalism, came into the field, she argues, in suspicious circumstances. They have given sociology the image of being partisan. If they cannot contribute to sociology's mission (Huber, 1995, p. 213), Huber wants them gone. These dissenters are calling for a pluralistic field that is broader than statistics, demography, social organization, and social stratification. They embrace alternative interpretive models of social science work, including the notion that science is a social institution that has values that often exclude or distort the perspectives of minorities, women, the poor, and the powerless.

These partisans suggest that a science must reflect multiple, interpretive perspectives, even, perhaps, a successor feminist science (Harding, 1991) or a science that embodies the interpretive and epistemological standpoints of different racial and ethnic groups (Collins, 1991; Smith, 1993). Acting as democratic communities, these new collectivities called for more American Sociological Association (ASA) sections that would represent particular standpoint interests. They also suggested that departmental affairs include input from graduate students. These proposals, Huber (1995) argues, had the effect of decentralizing sociology's core (p. 208).[7]

The partisans values make the field vulnerable to attack by administrators.[8] When have we ever been value free, however? Furthermore, how are we to admit new persons into field? Is there a new test that can be administered that will measure the degree to which a person adheres to Huber's values? In contesting these democratic moves, Huber seeks to reinscribe an organizational and disciplinary orthodoxy that will return the field to some historical moment when one view of sociology, its goals, and central interests held steady. This is nostalgia because when did that state ever exist?

It is not clear, however, how Huber's proposals would address, except through unilateral imposition, the core problems she identifies, including consistent standards of teaching and research, norms of civility, course rigor, an extreme ideology of democracy, and a central core in the field. Furthermore, it is not clear that the problems she identifies are the problems that others, who take a more pluralistic view, would locate in the field (Gamson, 1992). Indeed, Stinchcombe (1994, pp. 290-291) finds virtue in a disintegrated discipline, suggesting that it "represents the optimum state of affairs, both for the advance of knowledge and for the expansion of the minds of undergraduates."

Of course, pluralism in sociology is nothing new; openness and even radical dissent characterized the discipline in its most fruitful moments (the 1950s and 1960s). Ironically, there is even a radical pluralism within Huber's core that is embedded in the field's disciplinary history (Huber, 1995, p. 213), a minimalist canon of Weber and Marx (p. 213) that merges a qualified scientism (Weber's methodological writings) with Marx's radical reflexivity. These two paradigms have coexisted productively within the discipline throughout its history. Paradoxically, extremely narrow visions of sociology, such as Huber's, are new, and they can be seen as threatening the "traditional" pluralistic core of the discipline.

Sociology as an Interdisciplinary Project

It can be argued that Huber's (1995) version of sociology is what got us into this mess in the first place. Although no theory group dominated sociology during the decades she discusses (Wiley, 1995, p. 152), it is clear that mainstream, empirical, middle-range sociology held sway. The discipline divided itself into a series of subspecialities, including stratification, social organization, and demography. It is the work of these sociologists, not the irrationalists, that has drawn negative attention to the discipline (e.g., the two-sex life table; Huber, 1995, p. 202).[9] Huber engages in scapegoating by blaming the field's problems on the irrationalists. Indeed, her examples (pp. 202-203) of trivial research come from the mainstream and not the "radical" margins of the field.

Also, Huber's (1995) proposals stem from a period when departments and disciplines were exclusively "mission or generalist oriented," at which time their functions could be dictated by the needs of society as defined by a specific discipline. Over a period of decades, as disciplinary boundaries have blurred, departments and disciplines have become increasingly "domain oriented." This new emphasis reflects the more specific demands of a society increasingly dominated by and dependent on knowledge that can no longer be provided by a single discipline. The opening up of sociology to diverse interests and to interdisciplinary programs addresses this shift in focus.

This democratic, pluralistic model of science, which Huber (1995) objects to, explicitly addresses one of her central concerns. It creates the conditions for producing a wide range of empirical materials that bear on "nontrivial social problems" (p. 213). Such diverse materials can no longer be provided by a single discipline or a single paradigm within a discipline. Social problems-based interdisciplinary research has achieved wide acceptance in mainstream sociology (Clemens, Powell, McIlwaine, & Okamoto, 1995, pp. 483-484). This interdisciplinary model better describes the actual workings of the field in which "the advance of knowledge goes on with many different methods, many different theories, and with many different relations to ideological, granting agency, and theoretical objectives" (Stinchcombe, 1994, pp. 290-291).[10]

Dichotomous (science and antiscience) and stereotypical thinking will not solve sociology's institutional problems. Nor can sociology's long legacy of radical democracy be quieted. There is, however, too much at stake to allow Huber's voice and reading of the field to go unchallenged. Perhaps these new voices she fears will bring sociology back home to that vital core of concerns C. Wright Mills (1959) called the sociological imagination. It is hoped this will happen because it is clear that objections to the postmodern irrationalists involve more than disputes over epistemology or getting one's house in order. The material existence of an entire discipline is at stake.

The Interpretive Critics

There is a soft, interpretive version of Huber's (1995) realist, positivist critique. This is the version that turns postmodernism into a negative point of reference and then, using the method of guilt through association, criticizes the new writers for being postmodern. Like Huber, this position requires that the critic first define the enemy—in this case, postmodernism. This is done through a listing of names, usually Lyotard, Baudrillard, Foucault, Derrida, Nietzsche, Marx, Heidegger, Freud, and Wittgenstein (Farberman, 1991, pp. 475-476; Prus, 1996, p. 218). Then, the author says something such as these works "represent materials that could in themselves provide a lifetime of intellectual reading" (Prus, 1996, p. 218). Nonetheless, the critic offers a summary of these authors, suggesting that they are "highly cynical, completely relativist, pervasively despairing, intensely antiscientific" (Prus, 1996, p. 218). For those inclined to take such views, postmodernism and its so-called "anything goes" position offers "elements that are radical, fatalistic, absurd and nihilistic in the extreme" (Prus, 1996, p. 218), and perhaps it also "emits a faintly nativist aroma" (Farberman, 1991, p. 476).

The interpretive critic then locates himself in relation to this body of work, noting that postmodernism has "become one of the recent 'hot' realms of academic enterprise and debate" (Prus, 1996, p. 219). Although this fad may pass, it is incumbent on the interpretive critic to come to terms with it (p. 219).

Not surprisingly, the new-writing-as-postmodernism has many of the same flaws Huber brings to the new irrationalism. According to these critics, postmodernism simultaneously rejects the ideas of inter-subjectivity and the notion of an objectively located observer in the world.[11] For the postmodernists (according to the critics), this observer has no fixed (or intersubjectively constituted) place from which scientific truths can be launched (Prus, 1996, p. 223). In holding these beliefs, the postmodernists risk violating the "basic notions of an intersubjective/ethnographic social science" (p. 226). This happens when they follow Marxist agendas; use their ethnographies as a way to moralize; fail to respect the life worlds they study; ignore firsthand observations; use their texts to develop self-enchanting representations of the other; exploit ethnography to shock or entertain; use poems, pictures, or contrived fictional accounts to present the view of the other; disregard concepts central to the life world studied; and disavow researcher accountability concerning images conveyed by the ethnographic other to readers (p. 227).

Two key terms define these criticisms: lived experience and the criteria for judging the postmodern ethnographic representation (Lofland, 1995, p. 63; Snow & Morrill, 1995b, p. 360). For critics, such as Prus (1996), Farberman (1991, p. 475), and Snow and Morrill (1995a, 1995b), the so-called postmodern ethnographers reduce human lived experience either to textual reality (Prus, 1996, p. 245) or to self-narratives (Snow & Morrill, 1995a, p. 347). In both cases, everyday lived experience and its representations disappear. With this loss also go the usual criteria for evaluating a representation; that is, the use of theory, social facts, and the presence of the persons being studied, whose experience is given through quotes from interviews and conversations.

There are also other criteria as suggested in Table 9.1: those that are dangerously close to Huber's positivism, including hard facts, the absence of personal bias, and generic, processual analyses (Lofland, 1995; Prus, 1996, p. 253), and thick descriptions and new and true data based on the correct representation of the empirical facts in a situation (Lofland, 1995, p. 47). Because the postmodern ethnographers lack these kinds of criteria for evaluating their work, scholars are left in a situation in which anything goes. Fearful that others will not know how to handle this ambiguity, the critics then turn to their own criteria, offering the bewildered a way out of this postmodern madness.

Reading the Interpretive Critics

These critics refuse to accept the arguments concerning the crises of representation and legitimation outlined in Chapters 1 and 2. In rejecting the narrative turn in the human disciplines, these authors also reject the forms of textual experimentation that go with that turn. They nostalgically invoke an earlier, more pure historical moment when these arguments about narrative were not present. In that moment, ethnography's golden age, unfettered, theoretically sophisticated, conceptually dense qualitative inquiry took place.

This is the place of Huber's disinterested observer seeking objective truth about a stable reality—only a few words have changed. Reality is now obdurate (Prus, 1996, pp. 246-247), not objective, and the observer is intersubjectively involved with this world of study. Thus, practice and method are privileged, and the notion of objective, interpretive inquiry is maintained. There is no preoccupation with discourse as the material practice that constitutes representation and description, the two terms that are so central to the places of lived experience in the realist ethnographic text.

Therefore, not surprisingly, the realist critique reproduces Malinowski's conception of ethnography, the cultural transmission model that fits ways of thinking and feeling to institutional structures. This model gives value to lived experience as the site at which individual belief and action intersect with culture. Under this framework, texts are superfluous extensions of culture—mere entertainments. At the same time, these interpretive critics conflate the study of texts with a concern for language and meaning. Folding language into texts reifies language and divorces it, they contend, from the realm of "people, action, and the community in which language takes shape," (Prus, 1996, p. 245).

This is a strategic move because no poststructuralist would attempt to ignore language in use, nor would any poststructuralist fold language solely into texts. In so arguing, however, these critics are able to dispense with Mill's notion of a secondhand, text-mediated world of experience. The argument does not stop here. Texts are not worthy of analysis by sociologists. They have no place in the culture-action-individual ethnographic model.

This text-based criticism takes still another form. This is the critique of "such attenuation devices as poems, pictures, artifacts, and contrived or fictionalized accounts . . . and theatrical productions" (Prus, 1996, pp. 227-278; see also Farberman, 1991, p. 474; Snow & Morrill, 1995b, p. 361). People who do these things may be artistic or postmodern, but they are not social scientists and this is not ethnographic research (Prus, 1996, p. 227). More important, however (Snow & Morrill, 1995b),

> This performance turn, like the preoccupation with discourse and storytelling, will take us further from the field of social action and the real dramas of everyday life and thus signal the *death knell* of ethnography as an empirically grounded enterprise. (p. 361)

(Sadly, under this model there would be no place for Victor Turner or Dwight Conquergood or the work that routinely appears in *Text and Performance Quarterly*.)

The postmodern use of ethnography as a platform for moral, political, or social criticism is also challenged. Prus (1996, p. 227) will have none of this, and Snow & Morrill (1995b) are fearful of ethnographers using their ethnographies in moral ways:

> It is our view that there is little to be gained and much to be lost by making moral claims and engaging in moral posturing. It is far better to jettison such impulses and focus on the question of 'how best to describe and interpret the experiences of other people and other cultures.' (p. 362)

Thus, we have a value-free ethnography, which just tells it like it is. Politics must be kept out of our ethnographic practices. There is no place for Huber's irrationalists in ethnography today. Marxism, feminism, and cultural studies—these interpretive perspectives must be set aside because they bring values into this scientific project.

This move allows the critics to salvage a position of power for those who do ethnographic research. Farberman (1991, p. 477) is explicit: The ethnographs want to make the "competent professional investigator equal to the lay subject in the belief that this is an act of elite bashing that will oust a patriarchal establishment of white, male heterosexuals which will result in democratic redress." There are many reasons for taking what lay subjects say seriously, but this is not one of them. The so-called ethnographs are skeptical of social theory and complex conceptual frameworks because these frameworks impose one interpretive framework on another. Too often, the perspective of those studied gets lost in the analyst's complex grounded theory. This is why ethnographs listen to lay subjects.

Finally, the term postmodernism, as noted in previous chapters, refers to several things at the same time: a movement in the arts; new forms of social theory; historical transformations that have occurred since World War II; cultural life under late capitalism; life in a mass-mediated world in which the symbol of reality (hyperreality) has replaced the real; and a conservative historical moment characterized by a backlash against the political activities of many marginalized voices and communities (racial minorities, gays, elderly, and women).

For its critics, postmodernism carries all the negative implications outlined previously. It is as if postmodernism were a choice or an option. In discussing cultural studies and postmodernism, Grossberg (1992) states,

Cultural studies' interest in postmodernism is not a matter of accepting that the history of the modern has come to an end; it is rather that postmodernism poses a new project for cultural studies' own rearticulation; that it must critically examine and hopefully delink itself from some of the complexities with the modern. (p. 24)

We inhabit a cultural moment that has inherited (and been given) the name postmodern. A cultural studies and interpretive interactionism informed by poststructuralism, Marxism, feminism, and the standpoint epistemologies aims to make sense of this historical moment called the postmodern. In this sense, it is inappropriate to speak of a postmodern ethnography. The postmodern is our project. We seek, rather, an interpretive accounting of this historical moment—an accounting that examines the very features that make this moment so unique. At the same time, we desire to separate ourselves from the modernist ethnographic project. That project plays directly into the hands of those who would politically manage the postmodern, including giving such individuals words and arguments for attacking the new writing and all it stands for.

To summarize, six strategic moves are used by those who believe the old ways are better than the new. These moves allow those in power to marginalize the new writing forms.

1. The new writing is not scientific; therefore, it cannot be part of the ethnographic project.
2. The new writers are moralists, and moral judgments are not part of science.
3. The new writers have a faulty epistemology; they do not believe in disinterested observers who study a reality that is independent of human action.
4. The new writing uses fiction: This is not science. It is art.
5. The new writers do not study lived experience, which is the true province of ethnography. Hence, the new writers are not participant observers.
6. The new writers are postmodernists, and this is irrational because postmodernism is fatalistic, nativistic, radical, absurd, and nihilistic.

These six beliefs constitute complex discursive systems; separate literatures are attached to each. Taken together, they represent a formidable, yet dubious critique of the new writing. They make it clear that there are no problems with the old ways of doing ethnography. Indeed, the new ways create more problems than they solve. These beliefs serve to place the new writing outside ethnography, outside science, perhaps in the humanities or the arts. Some (Huber) would ban these persons from academia altogether. Others (Farberman and Prus) would merely exclude them from certain theory groups; that is, from symbolic interactionism or ethnographic, qualitative inquiry.

Whose Truth?

Two systems of truth are operating in this interaction that brings the new up against the old. The realist regime holds to the belief in firm and steady truths about the world. These truths are based on the ocular, visual model of verification discussed in Chapter 2. This model asserts that accurate representations of the world can be produced, and these representations truthfully map the worlds of real experience. The many problems with this model were detailed in Chapters 1 and 2, including beliefs in a stable world, a commitment to mimesis, confusions over lived experience and its representation, ignoring the parallax of discourses, and faith in the primacy of voice and vision; in summary, the failures of a ocular epistemology.

This epistemology produces information and knowledge but not understanding. It is suited to a modernist project that privileges one of the four visual regimes discussed in the previous chapter (Cartesian, Baconian, Baroque, and hysterical). These regimes use validity and reliability as marketing devices, obscuring the fact that the observer is not a neutral spectator; truth is always a function of the visual regime that is deployed.

Nor does this realist epistemology fit itself to some version of the seven-part thesis concerning ethnography's future outlined in the Introduction. Ethnography, as a gendered project, has changed because the world that ethnography confronts has changed. Ethnographers inhabit a postcolonial world—the age of multinational, electronic capitalism. This world is defined by difference and disjuncture and shifting borders and borderlines. Center and periphery intersect, making the local global, producing federations of exiles and refugees, and diasporas of twice-hyphenated Americans. Ethnographic texts as commodities and moral texts are grafted into this world. Despite the fact that ethnography is one of the principle moral discourses of the contemporary period, ethnographers do not have an undisputed warrant to study others; this right has been lost. Self-reflection is no longer an option, nor can it be presumed that objective accounts of another's situation can be easily given. Truth is also always personal and subjective. An evocative and not a representational epistemology is sought.

In contrast to the realist regime, the new writers seek a model of truth that is narrative, deeply ethical, open ended, and conflictual, performance, and audience based, and always personal, biographical, political, structural, and historical. Writing from a moving, unstable place, these experimentalists are neither insiders nor outsiders. They are on both sides of Trinh's and Anzaldua's hyphen, travelers in interconnected physical, social, moral, and sexual borderlands. They search for epiphanal stories that return to the beginning, the loss of innocence, science's seductions: a new way of writing—reflexive, transgressive, and simultaneously feminine and masculine (see Barone, 1995, p. 71).

One version of truth is constructed in the improvised performance, in the coproduced performance text, in mystories, and in storied, postmodern bodies, specularity undone—the truth of life's fictions in which experiences are evoked, not represented or explained. This performance truth involves audiences working with actors who are ethnographers, ethnographers who are performers, and performed texts as lived experience. This is ethnographic theater, Brecht's experiments with thinking audiences, challenges to text-centered ethnography, and dialogical performance art. Writers create texts that reclaim the stories a realist science has reduced to minor literature or to nonscience. Writers resist the efforts of those who would turn ethnography into stable, realist systems of meaning.

In dealing with the truth of life's fictions, the dividing line between fact and fiction is tested, and reality and text become one. Narrative, in its many storied, performance, and textual forms, is all that we have (see Benhabib, 1992, p. 14). Narrative, however, is configured in a specific way. The new writers deal with the facts of experience anchored in specific scenes or situations. Text and dialogue bring composite characters and persons-as-performers alive. Although the narrative advances by moving from scene to scene, multiple timelines and experiential frames overlap within the same scene or performance context (see Zeller, 1995, p. 82). A moral theory of self and society and of gender, sexuality, class, race, and ethnicity is presumed. This theory, as a minimal interpretive framework, provides a platform for performances that detail and criticize life in this postmodern society.

Multiple narrative styles are explored, including ethnographic poetics, narratives of the self, realist, phenomenological, exegetical, testimonial, and notional nonfiction texts. Understanding reality and image to be inseparably fused, the new writers reject the realist move that sees an underlying reality behind the images or symbols that seem to hold a group together. Where realists see facades to be penetrated, the new writers see worlds of experience held together by the most fragile of social and cultural logics. Situating themselves in the worlds studied, stirring it up, so to speak, the experimentalists are not passive observers bearing witness to transsituational, objective truths. There are no stories out there waiting to be told and no certain truths waiting to be recorded; there are only stories yet to be constructed.

The new writers question the "natural" relationship between narratives, truth, and reality—that relationship that sees the text mirroring the external world. The intent, instead, is to create a reflexive text. This text allows the reader to re-experience the events in question, coming to see the truth of the narrative that contains them. This truth is not based on mimesis, but rather it is grounded in the process of self-formation and self-understanding. It is not anchored in the so-called external world. The new writers create a new reader, a reader willing to suspend belief in the efficacy of the older narrative forms. (The critics of the new writing clearly resist this invitation.)

This new reader is willing to confront the unpresentable features of the postmodern world; capitalism's violence in its multiple forms: murder, rape, incest, child and spousal abuse, conspiracies, global genocide, state-sponsored murder, villains-victims-sleuths, corporate enemies, and the public at large as victim. This willingness to confront the unpresentable is based on more than a morbid desire to bear witness to or to be titillated by the Gothic, the decadent, the depraved, and the pornographically violent features of the culture. It reflects, as well, the desire to be informed, to be made aware of this postmodern world and its discontents, and to find in the violence a narrative or story line that will make sense. Also, that narrative repositions the self of the reader, giving the reader a safe hiding place out of the line of fire—a cozy story. Is this bad faith?

Morally tainted, flawed writers engage flawed readers, the walking wounded, in the coproduction of resistance texts, utopian and dystopian works that intervene in the world, making differences in the lives of real people. There is a constant search for a moral center and an ethics of practice in a world that is always moving. The text becomes the agent and the agency of self-discovery. In this way, writers and readers rediscover the truth of the old myths, folklore, the blues, the old stories, and shared moral journeys: Oedipal tales told over and over again (Edmunds & Dundes, 1983/1995)—somebody takes a trip and somebody stays home—and tiny moral tales about the the big picture.

There are now multiple forms of reflexivity, from the methodological and intertextual to standpoint, queer, feminist, and the postcolonial. These reflexive understandings of the new text unhinge science from within, bringing it closer to moral criticism. Now, the criticism is out in the open. The messy text becomes the place where ethnographers write for and not about the other. There is a conscious effort to avoid the telling of stories that reproduce the standard version of the knowing subject of contemporary ethnography. At the same time, writers make their ontologies and theories of existence explicit, connecting those formulations to their theories of the postmodern and its discontents. Constantly working against the sting of memory, the new writer uses personal troubles and lived biography as the starting place for critical ethnography.

Therefore, a performance-based, storytelling, listening, and hearing framework is privileged. Truth is fragile—a coproduction and an interactional experience lodged in the moment that connects the reader-as-audience-member and coperformer to a performance text. Truth is moral criticism—an ethical judgment that moves beyond the objective proclamations of positivism's scientific observer.

Positivism's Ethical Mandates

Not surprisingly, positivism's (and realism's) moral criticisms of the new writers privileged the critics as the morally proper entrepreneurs who were not only saving science for society but were also saving society through the use of science. This meant that the critics had to locate the new writers outside society and science. The new writers, the critics argued, followed nothing more than a hedonistic or politically correct moral ethic. They had suspended all foundational, evaluative criteria that could be brought to the observational and ethnographic project. Thus, the argument concerning "anything goes" simultaneously joined irrationalism with postmodernism, with the new writing, and with an antifoundational position that said there was no truth. The critics suggested that the persons who held these beliefs were new to the fields of the human sciences. As such, their arguments were based on and embodied an identity politics that was, in its standpoint epistemology versions, antiscience, antireason, anti-Enlightenment, and antitruth (Dickens, 1995, p. 538). In one fell swoop, politics, identity, and science were joined. Those who enacted an identity politics in and through their writing (and research) were no longer part of the scholarly community.

Having banned (or at least labeled) the dissidents, scientists were now free to pursue their modernist, Enlightenment aims in a solidified community that shared the same moral values, including the belief that facts and values should not be confused or intertwined (Sjoberg, Gill, Williams, & Kuh, 1995, p. 9). Central to this community was a set of ethical mandates that provided research guidelines for those who understood this distinction: students, scientists, journalists, universities, internal, institutional review boards (IRBs), granting agencies, journals, publishers, and even entire disciplines (Sieber, 1992; Timmermans, 1995).

These guidelines (Guba & Lincoln, 1989, pp. 120-141), based on a utilitarian view of human nature, shored up the modern positivist research agenda. They served to nullify the breaches and negative effects (invasions of privacy, denial of individual agency, and psychological and physical harm to human subjects including losses of personal dignity and self-esteem) that were produced by the informed consent model of science (see Lee, 1993, Chapter 10, 1995; Mitchell, 1993). Utilitarianism, with its emphasis on exchange and rational choice, implemented the belief that rational people will seek the same benefits and avoid the same costs in any situation (Sjoberg et al., 1995, p. 9).

This ethical model, with its informed consent forms, presumably protects subjects from deception, loss of privacy, and psychological or physical harm.[12] It makes science public because subjects agree to be studied. Hence, their privacy is not being invaded. Confidentiality of identifiable information must be maintained unless the subject gives permission to do otherwise.[13] These are ideals because, in practice, some scientists engage in fraudulent, unethical practices, including lying to their subjects and engaging in deceptions and misrepresentations concerning their research intentions (see Hilts, 1995).[14]

Under this model, three ethical principles (Sieber, 1992, p. 18) should guide research on human subjects—namely, (a) beneficence, or maximum benefits to science, humanity, and the research participants, while risks are kept to a minimum; (b) respect, including protecting the autonomy (and anonymity) of individuals; and (c) justice, involving reasonable, nonexploitive procedures.[15] These three principles generate six research norms concerning (a) the use of valid research designs by (b) competent researchers who (c) identify the possible negative consequences of the research while minimizing risks, maximizing benefits, and displaying respect for privacy and confidentiality. These researchers (d) randomly select representative subjects from a larger population. These subjects (e) voluntarily (freely) participate, giving informed consent, and are (f) compensated for injury (Sieber, 1992, p. 19).

If these norms and principles are followed, scientifically and ethically valid research is produced. Ethical practices are made to conform to scientific protocol (e.g., valid research designs, competent researchers, and random samples). In turn, scientific protocol defines ethical practice. An ideal subject (fully informed and reasonable person) is presumed, as is a fully competent, ethically conscientious researcher.

Exceptions to this system are allowed. Information can be withheld from subjects if full disclosure would invalidate the research. In addition, if any of the following conditions exist, research may be exempted from prior review: existing data, public documents, public officials and public service programs, normal educational practices (including the use of educational tests) are being analyzed; and hair and nail clippings, bodily excreta and external secretions, blood samples, voice recordings, dental records, and the recording of data from subjects 18 years or older, using noninvasive procedures, are being collected. This is a total science model; nothing is hidden. The scientist has full access to all the dark and hidden corners of human experience. This is the modernist project in full glory—a panoptic science for humankind.

Challenges to the
Traditional Ethical Model

This utilitarian, modernist model has, of course, been challenged. The modernist faith in a nonambiguous ethical code has failed (Dickens, 1995, p. 539). The twin banners of this code, universality and functionalism, are no longer accepted (Dickens, 1995, p. 539). Not only is the code blind to gender, race, class, and ethnicity (see Benhabib, 1992, p. 14) but no single, universally shared, rational choice model has been found to work. The code (Christians et al., 1993, pp. 193-194) rests on a cognitive model that privileges rational solutions to ethical dilemmas (the rationalist fallacy), and it presumes that humanity is a single subject (the distributive fallacy).

The model perpetuates a traditional, liberal conception of privacy and the public sphere (Benhabib, 1992, pp. 12, 104-105; Denzin, 1995a, pp. 206-207). This framework has excluded women and minorities from public discourse, defined the public good (justice) in masculine terms, and confined the public sphere to the polity and the economy, thus leaving the private sphere to the familial-domestic realm (Benhabib, 1992, p. 13). Under this traditional framework, privacy is defined in very limited terms to include the sphere of moral and religious conscience, the nonintervention of the state in free-market, economic transactions, or actions in the intimate sphere involving "the daily needs of life, of sexuality and reproduction, of care for the young, the sick and the elderly" (Benhabib, 1992, pp. 108-109).

Science inserts itself into this model in a very special way. Informed consent forms open the private to public inspection, allowing the participating citizen to contribute in the public good by being a scientific subject. Indeed, the citizen has a responsibility to participate in public science. In this way, justice is served. The state has now entered the private realm in the name of the public good, which is still defined in masculine terms. The participating scientist, as a competent researcher, embodies these liberal values that carry universal appeal to all parties.

This ethical code thus reinforces the concept of a private space in the postmodern society. This is a myth, however, because there are no longer (if there ever were) any private, sacred places. The scientific voyeur with his or her consent forms sustains the illusion that such spaces do exist. The twentieth-century histories of governmental surveillance and cinematic voyeurism indicate that this myth only operates for the benefit of the state (Denzin, 1995a, p. 207).

This code enforces a cloak, or veil of secrecy, which is supposed to protect the human subject. This veil surrounds the entire scientific project. Rights of privacy translate into procedures that ensure confidentiality. The citizen-as-scientific-subject is participating in a secret project; his or her attitudes, values, beliefs, and behaviors are private commodities. These are beliefs that define the core, sacred self. If made public, these beliefs could harm the person (and others). Extreme measures must be taken to keep these commodities private, including ensuring anonymity and the use of false names, codes, case numbers, and so on.[16] At the same time, science is a secretive (top secret) project.[17] In the commercial marketplace, scientific products compete for high monetary stakes. The science-as-secrecy model is incompatible with a communitarian view of ethnography as moral practice. This view is committed to a form of ethnographic practice that promotes universal solidarity (Christians et al., 1993, p. 14) while engaging in social critique and moral criticism. The science-as-secrecy model does not advance these aims.

Furthermore, this secrecy model is hierarchical (scientist-subject), noncontextual or nonsituational, logical, abstract, and assumes that a morally neutral, objective observer will get the facts right (Ryan, 1995, p. 144).[18] This system ignores the situatedness of power relations associated with gender, sexual orientation, class, ethnicity, race, and nationality (Ryan, 1995, p. 145). It glosses the ways in which the observer-ethnographer is implicated and embedded in the "ruling apparatus" (Smith, 1987, p. 107) of the society and the culture (Ryan, 1995, p. 144). That is, the powerful university-based scientist ventures out into some local community to do research, carrying the mantle of authority that comes with university sponsorship. Not surprisingly, the IRB guidelines that the researcher follows primarily protect the university from lawsuits should something go wrong. Consequently, the researcher is responsible for "balancing the many interests including interests within which he or she is vested" (Ryan, 1995, p. 144). The researcher is not morally neutral within this system. There were (and are) too many violations of the code—some of them quite monstrous (see Hilts, 1995).

This rights-, justice-, and acts-based system ignores the relational, dialogical nature of human interaction. It does not argue for a politics or ethics of the common good (Christians et al., 1993, p. 45). It seldom asks the researcher to step into the shoes of the persons being studied. A care-based ethical system does just this, asking the researcher to see other's situations as they feel and see them (Noddings, 1984, p. 24; Ryan, 1995, p. 148). The traditional model, in contrast, relegates emotionality and intuition to a secondary position in the ethical, decision-making process. It fails to develop an ethics of caring grounded in the concrete particularities of any given case (see Ryan, 1995, p. 147).

At the same time, this modernist image of inquiry is based on a voyeuristic, conflictual view of science and society. That is, the members of society must be persuaded to participate in the scientific project, and this participation will not always be in their best interest. This framework turns human beings into objects and gives scientists power over them. It does not encourage collaborative, reciprocal, trusting, nonoppressive relations between researchers and those studied (Ryan, 1995, p. 149). It enacts only one view of science—positivism's image of how science works. It does not give an explicit place to the kinds of inquiry explored in previous chapters—namely, a critical, interpretive, feminist, ethnographic project.

Finally, positivism's fact-value distinction is no longer allowed. Feminist (Ryan, 1995), standpoint (Smith, 1987), and postmodern (Benhabib, 1992) proponents challenge the position that accords a "privileged position [to] scientific knowledge " (Sjoberg et al., 1995, p. 9). With this challenge comes alternative moral and ethical guidelines. (Habermas [1990; see Benhabib, 1990, pp. 340-350], for example, has proposed a discourse-based ethical model much at odds with the natural science, rational choice model of positivism.) Communtarians question the concept of autonomous individuals. Human rights theorists challenge those who conceive of ethics and rights within a state- or community-based system (Sjoberg et al., 1995, p. 11). Feminists (Benhabib, 1992; Ryan, 1995) question the patriarchal biases of utilitarianism.

Feminist, Communitarian Ethical Model[19]

    I turn now to a feminist, communitarian moral ethic that extends the previous discussion. Table 9.2 summarizes the differences between the positivist and the feminist communitarian ethical systems (see Tong, 1993).

    After Christians et al. (1993, pp. 12-17, 194-195), the following assumptions organize this communitarian ethical system (see Lincoln, 1995b, pp. 280-281). It is based on an interactive, postpragmatist (Denzin, 1995a, pp. 215-217) approach to community, self, and inquiry in the cinematic, televisual age (see Schrum, 1995). This historical moment requires new conceptions of truth, the public, science, journalism, self, and community (Wiley, 1995). It breaks with classical liberal ethical models and their revisions that are flawed on two basic counts—the rationalist and distributive fallacies noted previously. It contends that community is ontologically and morally prior to persons, and that dialogical communication is the basis of the moral community. Civic transformation is taken to be the major goal of any ethical (and occupational) practice. This entails a commitment to the common good and to universal human solidarity. It calls for a sacred conception of science (Lincoln, 1995b), a conception that "honors the ecological as well as the human" (Lincoln, 1995b, p. 284), and stresses human dignity, care, justice, and interpersonal respect (Lincoln, 1995b, p. 284).

    A personally involved, politically committed ethnographer is presumed and not the morally neutral observer of positivism. Those studied are asked to be active participants in the collaborative research process. A new, local, and public ethnography joined with a public journalism is imagined. This new mode of discourse builds on and extends the innovative work of the literary (new) and investigative journalists (and private eyes) discussed in Chapters 5 and 6. In this framework, every moral act is a contingent accomplishment measured against the ideals of an feminist, interactive, and moral universalism (Benhabib, 1992, p. 6).

    By rejecting the rights-based model of positivist inquiry, the communitarian researcher also rejects positivism's three ethical principles (beneficence, anonymity, and justice). In turn, positivism's six research norms (valid designs, competent researchers, minimizing risks, random

Table 9.2 Two Ethical Systems

Positivism	*Communitarianism*
Autonomous individuals	Community
Utilitarianism	Communitarianism
Justice, respect	Solidarity, care
Beneficence	Love, mutuality
Privacy, secrecy	Public science
Gender blind	Moral identities
Contracts	Convenant
Hierarchical	Empowerment
Neutral observer	Morally involved observer
Subject as object	Subject as coparticipant
Facts	Narrative, dialogical,
Harm, exceptions	civic transformation

selection, informed consent, and compensation for injury) are also rejected.

The feminist, communitarian researcher does not invade the privacy of others, use informed consent forms, select subject's randomly, or measure research designs in terms of their validity. This framework presumes a researcher who builds collaborative, reciprocal, trusting, and friendly relations with those studied. This individual would not work in a situation in which the need for compensation from injury could be created. It is also understood that those studied have claims to ownership over any materials that are produced in the research process, including field notes (Lincoln, 1995a).

Feminist, communitarian research is judged by its authenticity, its fairness, and its ability to provoke transformations and changes in the public and private spheres of everyday life—transformations that speak to conditions of oppression (see Christians et al., 1993, pp. 194-195; Lincoln, 1995b, p. 277). This research values the connectedness that forms between researcher and researched. A friendly, cooperative relationality defines such inquiry. As Lincoln (1995b, p. 287) observes, "Relationality is the major characteristic of research that is neighborly." This research is rooted in "community, shared governance . . . and neighborliness" (Lincoln, 1995b, p. 287). This sense of neighborliness means this research serves the "community in which it is is carried out, rather than the community of knowledge producers and policymakers" (Lincoln, 1995b, p. 280).

In this way, the communitarian model sets itself off from the traditional, positivist academic community with its commitments to objectivity, contracts, neutral observers, and utilitarian notions of the greater good. The positivist concept of inquiry destroys community as the feminist communitarians understand that term.

Thus, the charge of ethical relativism, which the critics (Huber, 1995) simplistically bring to the new writing, is addressed (see Christians et al., 1993, p. 59). Indeed, the shoe is put on the other foot. The utilitarians are the relativists. In their system, value judgments are based on cost-benefit analyses, and no individual's analysis is privileged over another's (Christians et al., 1993, p. 57). Relativism must recognize lying and harm as justifiable means "to the greater happiness of the group" (Christians et al., 1993, p. 57). Thus, this is how the cost-benefit model work. It is no accident that it has an escape hatch concerning full disclosure when such would invalidate the research. If it is in the interest of the greater good, deception is warranted.

At the same time, utilitarian relativism is a morally conservative system, grounding its moral judgments in local community practice and in social consensus (Christians et al., 1993, p. 59). "An ethical relativist would have to accept the Nazi death camps . . . as logical extensions of the belief's, grounded in social and historical contexts, of those in control. 'Live and let live' becomes horribly ironic" (p. 59).

In contrast, the feminist, communitarian ethical system encourages moral decisions based on justifications derived from the moral terms listed previously and in column two in Table 9.2. This framework employs a communicative, care-based ethic that presumes a dialogical view of the self. In this model, the connectedness between people is recognized: People care for, are responsible for, and are accountable to one another (Ryan, 1995, p. 147). Extending Patricia Hill Collins's (1991, p. 215) work, this ethic of caring celebrates personal expressiveness, emotionality, and empathy. This feminist ethic values individual uniqueness and, after Collins, cherishes each person's invisible dignity, quiet grace, and unstated courage (Collins, 1991, p. 107), the mothering (and fathering) mind (Collins, 1991, p. 131), love, community, and justice (Collins, 1991, p. 197), and the expression of emotionality and caring in the text. This ethic of personal accountability makes individuals accountable for their values and the political consequences of their actions.

This model seeks to produce narratives that ennoble human experience while facilitating civic transformations in the public (and private) spheres. This ethic promotes universal human solidarity. It ratifies the dignity of the self and the value of human life. It is committed to human justice and the empowerment of groups of interacting individuals. It works to build covenant rather than contractual bonds within the local community (Christians et al., 1993, p. 14). In the workplace, "the mutuality principle . . . in contrast to contractarian individualism, insists that authority and decision making be allocated equitably" (p. 15).

This postpragmatist system situates the interactive moral self within the decisive contexts of gender, sexual orientation, race, class, ethnicity, religion, and nationality. It assumes the discursive power of individuals to articulate situated moral rules that are grounded in local community and group understandings. This is a conversational, interactional model. Moral and ethical reasoning occurs in the talk and interaction that goes on between self-aware, self-reflexive, and interacting individuals. Ethical talk (Benhabib, 1992, p. 9) moves forward because individuals are able to share one another's point of view in the social situation. Understanding, based on shared emotional experience (Denzin, 1984, p. 145) and not consensus, is the basis of this discourse, which takes as a given universal moral respect for every individual.

Public and Private Spheres of Experience

Individuals are participants in ongoing, pluralistic, moral communities. In these communities, the divisions between public and private intermingle. As discussed previously, in the contemporary period the distinctions between the public and the private, the civic and the civil, and the communal and the private have become hopelessly confused, if not erased. Accordingly, a new concept or set of terms is needed to describe the multiple moral and social spaces or spheres that exist within the local community. A single word will work: everyday life in the pluralistic, postsurveillance society. The engendered, everyday life world is entangled in the many social spheres that define the public and the private; public culture and private spaces can no longer be separated.

The postmodern, pluralistic, cinematic society, paraphrasing Christians et al. (1993, pp. 188-189), is characterized by multiple associations, a plurality of social structures (family, church, press, and school), and a plurality of ethnic, religious, and sacred cultures. The intermingling and protection of these multiple cultures and their sacred places and practices produces a "world-view pluralism [that is] the axis of communitarian democracy" (p. 189).

If the term public is confined to a narrow meaning—belonging to the people, or to the moral community—then all that is private (belonging to the person) is also public and part of the local and moral community. This distinction conceives of multiple spheres of social experience, from the many spheres of the private to the multiple spheres of the public (see Rosen, 1994, p. 380), including multiple arenas of public life (Charity, 1995, p. 10). Nothing is ever wholly private, and much of what occurs in public presumes confidential (private) understandings and agreements. Everyday life in this postsurveillance, moral community is deeply embedded in the mediated, hyperreal, televisual systems of meaning that bring the global village into the living room. The everyday life world is that moving moral space in which the dialogical self realizes itself in its so-called public and private narrative relations with others.

These relations are always immediate, phenomenologically real within the contours of the present. The moral, dialogical self is a narrative, storytelling production—a production that weaves its way through and into the storied lives of others. A narrative ethic (Frank, 1995, p. 157) that regards self-stories as moral acts is pursued. This ethic is judged by the sort of person it shapes (Frank, 1995, p. 157). This narrative ethic is grounded in the "historically contingent moral languages" (Christians et al., 1993, p. 187) that define everyday experience in the local community.

This moral discourse is ideally mediated by the norms of participatory democracy. These norms articulate free speech and moral respect for the other. This moral respect extends to those representative and participatory political structures that articulate the will and voice of the community. Individuals participate in these structures in three ways: as elected representatives (school board members), as professionals with specialized bodies of knowledge (teachers), and as participants in a communal, participatory system of interaction and governance (town hall meetings). Participatory politics in a democratic polity work to establish forms of communal solidarity and friendship that honor demands for justice, moral respect, and reciprocal care. With public journalism, the new ethnographies create the spaces in which these public (and private) moral demands can be heard.

Merging Ethnography
With Journalism

Now, a paradox is presented. The new or literary journalists opened up journalism (and ethnography) by using ethnographic procedures to write about important public issues. Readers read stories about real people who had real names. Writers, such as Wolfe, Mailer, Didion, Malcolm, and Capote, lifted the veil of secrecy that traditionally surrounds social science and ethnographic inquiry. These writers entered the many spheres of the private and the public that defined everyday life. They focused always on the epiphanal, the problematic, and the link between private troubles and larger, public issues: the what, who, where, when, why, and how of social life (Carey, 1986, pp. 166-167).

Gendered selves were connected to historical structures. Explanatory accounts of problematic social events were inevitably offered. Plunging always, as James Carey (1986, p. 149) argues, into journalism's invisible landscape, the dark continent of why and how, these explanations took one of four forms: "determining motives, elucidating causes, predicting consequences, or estimating significance" (p. 166). Of course, these writers had no agreed on objective method for assessing the evidence that would bear on motives, causes, consequences, or significance. Hence, explanation was (and is) always problematic and always moral and ideological (p. 166).

Like investigative journalists, the new journalists protected the public good. As watchdogs, they brought a sense of moral indignation to instances of corruption and betrayal of the public trust (Glasser & Ettema, 1989, p. 4). In so doing, these journalists objectified moral claims by making appeals to self-evident moral authorities, including the law, experts, formal codes, and everyday notions of common decency (Carey, 1986, p. 167). In these appeals, they created the grounds for the moral judgments that were stitched into their news stories (Carey, 1986, pp. 166-167).

Four nonnegotiable norms or principles guided this work: stories should be accurate (do not lie) and balanced, reporting should avoid harm (nonmaleficence), readers have the right to know certain information, and writers have as moral obligation to make public the course of action they favor (Christians et al., 1993, pp. 55-56). Truth telling (the need to know) must constantly be balanced against the principle of nonmaleficence, the amount of harm that will be done to an individual or an oppressed group. This often resolves into an assessment of the amount of harm that will be or has been done against or to an oppressed group in question (p. 55).

Writing Culture
in the Sixth Moment

In the present context, there are two normative, inscriptive systems—two ways of telling things about life in a democratic society, two ways of writing culture in the sixth moment. Journalism operates under the rule that the public has the right to know certain things and the First Amendment guarantees freedom of the press. Social science operates under another rule—the cloak of secrecy associated with a state-sponsored project that maintains the illusion of privacy within the postmodern world.

These two norms clash. They must be merged. Science's norms of silence, compliance, and complicity must be abandoned. Ethnography must move closer to a public or civic journalism (Christians, 1995a). Ethnographers must learn how to deploy the journalist's norms in the ethnographic context. A public, civic, or everyday life ethnography draws on the legacies of the new journalists. It borrows from the public journalists. It implements the writing culture project in the sixth moment. Like public journalism (Rosen, 1994, p. 376), it willingly breaks with old routines and evidences a desire to connect with people (citizens) and their concerns and biographical problems. It writes ethnographies that move people to action and works that promote serious discussion about democratic and personal politics. It makes readers actors and participants, not spectators, in the public dramas that define meaningful life in these twilight years of the twentieth century.

When modified then, journalism's norms open the door for a public or everyday life journalism (Carey, 1986, p. 195; Charity, 1995, p. 146)—local ethnographies of problematic democratic forms. This is a socially responsible ethnographic journalism that advocates democracy by creating a space for and giving a civic (public) voice to the biographically meaningful, epiphanal experiences that occur within the confines of the local moral community.[20]

This form of discourse transforms journalism's client, always the public, into something new (see Rosen, 1994, p. 370). Local, participatory, civic, journalistic ethnography answers to a new readership—the biographically situated reader who is a coparticipant in a public project that advocates democratic solutions to personal and public problems (Charity, 1995, p. 146).

Taken to the next level, transformed into public-journalism-as-ethnography, this writing answers to the following norms or goals. Public ethnography

- helps citizens make intelligent decisions about private troubles that have become public issues, including helping to get these decisions carried out (Charity, 1995, p. 2; Mills, 1959, p. 8);

- promotes interpretive works that raise public and private consciousness, which works help persons collectively work through the decision-making process and help isolate choices and core values, utilize expert and local systems of knowledge, and facilitate deliberative, civil discourse (Charity, 1995, pp. 4-8);

- rejects the classic, heroic model of those good, investigative journalists who "root out the inside story, tell the brave truth, face down the Joseph McCarthy's and Richard Nixons, expose corruption and go on crusades" (Charity, 1995, p. 9);

- seeks an ethnographer and a journalist who is an expert on public life, knows how to listen to the talk of citizens, to hear and present consensus when it emerges, is also a full-time citizen, and is committed to the belief that public life can be made to work (Charity, 1995, p. 10);

- sees the writer as a watchdog for the local community—a person who writes works that contribute to deliberative, participatory discourse, thereby maintaining the public's awareness of its own voice (Charity, 1995, pp. 104-105, 127);

- values writing that moves a public to meaningful judgment and meaningful action (Charity, 1995, p. 50), with a central goal being civic transformation (Christians et al., 1993, p. 14);
- exposes complacency, bigotry, and wishful thinking (Charity, 1995, p. 146) while "attempting to strengthen the political community's capacity to understand itself, converse well, and make choices (Rosen, 1994, p. 381);
- seeks dramatic stories and narratives that separate facts from stories, telling moving accounts that join private troubles with public issues (Charity, 1995, p. 72; Mills, 1959, p. 8);
- promotes a form of textuality that turns citizens into readers and readers into persons who take democratic action in the world (Charity, 1995, p. 19, 83-84).[21]

These are goals, ideals, and ways of merging critical ethnography (Carspecken, 1996), with applied action research (Reason, 1994), with the new public journalism, and with ethnography in the sixth moment. They presume the feminist, communitarian ethical model discussed previously.

These goals assume an ethnographer who functions and writes like a civic or public journalist. This means that ethnography as storytelling will be given greater emphasis. The ethnographer will also take a slightly different approach to interviewing, emphasizing a more aggressive, information-gathering mode of interaction and confronting persons with contradictions in their stories and accounts. This writer, as a watchdog for the local community, works outward from personal, biographical troubles to those public arenas that transform troubles into issues. A shared public consciousness is sought—a common awareness of troubles that have become issues in the public arena. This consciousness is shaped by a form of writing that merges the personal, the biographical, with the public. Janet Cooke's (1980) fictional story, "Jimmy's World," is an instance of such writing. Such stories expose complacency and bigotry in the public sphere.

Writing Norms

The feminist, communitarian ethical model produces a series of norms for the public ethnographic writing project.[22] These norms build on and elaborate the four nonnegotiable journalistic norms discussed previously (accuracy, nonmaleficence, the right to know, and making one's moral position public), The ethnographer's moral tales are not written to produce harm for the innocent (Christians, 1986, p. 124)—those who have been oppressed by the culture's systems of domination and repression (the principle of nonmaleficence). The identity of those written about should always be protected. These tales are factually and fictionally correct, organized under the rule that if something did not happen, it could have happened. When fiction is written or when composite cases are molded into a single story, the writer, having learned a lesson from Janet Cooke, is under an obligation to report this to the reader (see Christians et al., 1993, p. 55; Eason, 1986). Janet Malcolm (1990) reminds us that liberties should not be taken with the real words spoken by real persons.

The reader has the right to read what the ethnographer has learned, but this right to know should be balanced against the principle of nonmaleficence. Accounts should exhibit "interpretive sufficiency" (Christians et al., 1993, p. 120); that is, they should possess that amount of depth, detail, emotionality, nuance, and coherence that will permit a critical consciousness to be formed by the reader. Such texts should also exhibit representional adequacy, including the absence of racial, class, and gender stereotyping.[23]

The writer must be honest with the reader.[24] The text must be realistic and concrete with regard to character, setting, atmosphere, and dialogue. Extending the postmodern detectives (Chapter 6), this text provides a forum for the search for moral truths about the self. This forum explores the unpresentable in the culture; the discontents of postmodernism are documented and placed in narrative form. The new writer stirs up the world, objectivity is a fiction, and the writer's story (mystory) is part of the tale that is told. The writer has a theory about how the world works, and this theory is never far from the surface of the text. Self-reflexive readers are presumed—readers who seek honest but reflexive works that draw them into the many structures of verisimilitude that shape the story in question.

There remains the struggle to find a narrative voice that writes against a long tradition that favors autobiography and lived experience as the sites for reflexivity and selfhood (Clough, 1994, p. 157). As discussed in Chapter 7, this form of subjective reflexivity is a trap that too easily reproduces normative conceptions of self, agency, gender, desire, and sexuality. There is, to repeat, a pressing need to invent a reflexive form of writing that turns ethnography and experimental literary texts back "onto each other" (p. 162).

Always a skeptic, this new writer is suspicious of conspiracies, alignments of power and desire that turn segments of the public into victims. Therefore, these works trouble traditional, realist notions of truth and verification, asking always who stands to benefit by a particular version of the truth. The public ethnographer enacts an ethics of practice that privileges the client-public relationship. The ethnographer is a moral advocate for the public, although a personal moral code may lead individual researchers to work against the so-called best interests of a client or a particular segment of the public.

The ethnographer's tale is always allegorical, a symbolic tale, and a parable that is not just a record of human experience. This tale is a means of experience and a method of empowerment for the reader. It is a vehicle for readers to discover moral truths about themselves. More deeply, the ethnographic tale is a utopian tale of self and social redemption—a tale that brings a moral compass back into the readers (and the writer's) life. The ethnographer discovers the multiple "truths" that operate in the social world—the stories people tell one another about the things that matter to them (see Straley, 1992, p. 9). Like the public journalist, the ethnographer writes stories that create "pockets of critical consciousness . . . discourse[s] of cultural diversity" (Christians, 1996, p. 11). These stories move oppressed people to action, enabling transformations in the public and public spheres of everyday life.

In the End

I have argued throughout this book that American ethnography is deeply embedded in American culture. As that culture has gone postmodern and multinational, so too has ethnography. Difference and disjuncture define the contemporary, global, world cultural system that ethnography is mapped into. The twice- and thrice-hyphenated American (Asian-American-Japanese) defines the norm. In this world, reflexive ethnography is no longer an option, and the right to study anyone can no longer be presumed. Anthropology's foreign, strange lands have come home. Fragmented discourse and the vaguely unfamiliar familiar are now present everywhere. Magical realism, science fiction, comic book fantasies, and moral allegories define utiopian thought today.

Like American journalism, ethnography's "faults and triumphs are pretty much characteristics of the culture as a whole" (Carey, 1986, p. 194). The faults include obsessive voyeurism; a preoccupation with records, details, and statistics; overreliance on experts; the constant search for rational explanations of problematic conduct; naive realism; a preoccupation with the superficial; failed attempts to be objective; complicity with big business and with capitalism; and race, class, and gender biases.

The triumphs include a willingness to listen to ordinary people; a watchdog of cultural values; powerful stories about the underdog and the production of stories that move people to action; a celebration of, and love for, the concrete and the ordinary; an ability to eventually explain anything; an unwillingness to let go of the newsworthy; disrespect for the rich and the powerful; a voice of empowerment; and a commitment to democracy. Also, the forms of storytelling that ethnographers and journalists use are the same ones that are prized by the larger culture: narratives that draw from the scientific disciplines, popular culture itself (Carey, 1986, p. 194).

Recall the discussion in Chapter 5 concerning the historical relationship between journalism and the social sciences in the 1920s. Both professions were committed to producing factual, scientifically truthful statements about society. Both made distinctions between facts and fictions. Both were committed to the tenets of liberal democracy and to the belief that an informed citizenship was the key to a democratic society. Journalism and the ethnographically oriented social sciences were given the responsibility of producing and disseminating such information to the public at large and to students in the public school and college and university systems.

Recall the following from Robert E. Park (1950): "According to my earliest conception of a sociologist he was to be a kind of super-reporter" (pp. viii-ix). Together, the sociologist-as-reporter and the journalist made and told news—news that was local, timely, still under discussion, and relevant to the lives of community members (Park, 1950, p. 63). Such news addressed "the solid and unyielding structures of social life" (Carey, 1986, p. 195). This commitment kept a focus on ethnography and journalism as forms of democratic social practice (Carey, 1986, p. 195).

Things changed, however. At some point in this shared and collective history, journalism and ethnography became identified with and defined by either (in the case of journalism) the "breaking news, the news flash, the news bulletin" (Carey, 1986, p. 195), or, as with sociology, anthropology, and education, the hottest new theoretical, methodological, or political issue, which, to repeat, often had little relationship to the "solid and unyielding structures of social life" (p. 195). When this happened, "our understanding of journalism [and ethnography] as democratic social practices was impossibly narrowed" (p. 195).

As Carey (1986, pp. 195-196) observes, journalists started thinking of themselves as "being in the news business." The goal was to get the story first, not to dig deep and uncover the unknown. Ethnographers were in the business of making their practice respectable, confronting and living through crises and too often losing track of praxis and the politics of their trade. In the traditional and modern moments, ethnographers chased positivist science, produced monuments to timeless cultural truth, and believed in objectivity (Rosaldo, 1989, pp. 30-31). Recently, self-doubt born of intense reflexivity has produced a paralysis of form—a fear of the self and its place in the writer's text. We are past this moment, however.

Remember, however, Raymond Carver's (1989b) short story, *Intimacy*. This is a story about a writer who is accused of betraying those he has written about. The writer had some business out west and stops off in the little town where his former wife lives. It had been 4 years since they had seen each other. During that time, he started sending her copies of things he wrote as they appeared in print, even interviews and profiles. He thought she might be interested in his work and the recognition he was getting, although she never responded.

It is 9 a.m. and he has not called ahead. She takes him into the living room and offers him a cup of coffee. Then, she starts in, calling him names: a sick man with no principles, a slyboots, a ruthless, cold-hearted son of a bitch, and a man with a heart like a garbage pail. She charges him with being on a fishing expedition, with hunting for new material to write about. She suggests that he only remembers the low, shameful things, and that when he left it was like she had stopped living. "I loved you to the point of distraction . . . We were so *intimate*

. . . The memory of being that intimate with somebody" (Carver, 1989b, p. 446). He figuratively asks for her forgiveness and she gives it. Then he leaves.

In a proper world, this would be every writer's nightmare—being confronted by a former intimate about whom one has written and being told that a confidence was betrayed and that the wrong story was told. The list of writers who have broken promises and betrayed those they have have been intimate with is endless, and we do not live in a perfect world.

We are haunted by the lines quoted previously from Malcolm (1990, p. 4)—"Every journalist who is not too stupid or too full of himself to notice what is going on knows that what he is doing is morally indefensible"—and Didion (1968, p. xiv)—"People tend to forget that my presence runs counter to their best interest. . . . Writers are always selling somebody out."

This will not end, but the guilt quotient should be raised because it is no longer morally acceptable to do as we have done in the past.

Therefore, here at the end, at the beginning of the sixth moment, the promise of ethnography as a form of radical democratic social practice is re-engaged. Marx (1888/1983a, p. 158) reminds us that we are in the business of not just interpreting but of changing the world. A feminist, communitarian, public ethnography, working hand in hand with public journalism, is one way to forward this project.

The final rule: No text can do everything at once. The perfect ethnography cannot be written. Trinh, Raymond Chandler, and Raymond Carver would agree.

Notes

1. To repeat, this is a normative social ethics that stresses the dialogical, narrative foundations of self, community, and society, placing a premium on the values of human dignity, love, care, solidarity, and empowerment. A feminist, communitarianism seeks to " 'engender' the subject of moral reasoning" (Benhabib, 1992, pp. 10) through a narrative-based, interactive dialogic universalism that views every moral position as a contingent accomplishment. This communitarian ethic is grounded in a theory of community and the dialogic self that stands in sharp contrast to classic liberalism's ahistorical, atomistic conception of autonomous, isolated individuals in society (Benhabib, 1992, p. 70; Christians et al., 1991, 1993, p. 15). A communitarian ethic stresses human solidarity,

love, care, justice, stewardship, reciprocity, empowerment, the dialogic self, community, commitment, civic transformation, and mutuality (see Christians et al., 1993, p. 13). Drawing on the works of Taylor, Walzer, Sandel, and MacIntyre, this version of communitarianism is not to be confused with Amitai Etizioni's (1993) project (see Craig, 1995).

2. This is how Charity (1995, p. 146) defines public journalism.

3. For Huber (1995), the antirationalists are the humanists and those social scientists who have been drawn to the humanist's criticisms of positivistic science.

4. Even the most radical relativist holds to some set of criteria concerning truth and reason (see Schwandt, 1996, pp. 130-131).

5. Gamson (1992) suggests that the "core of sociology is political sociology, social psychology and sociology of culture" (p. 4), indicating that "the core of sociology is defined by the particular interests of the definers" (p. 4).

6. Even the most ardent logical empiricist rejects this belief. It is now understood that every observation is theory laden (Cronbach, 1989; Rorty, 1991).

7. During the decades in question, all the human disciplines experienced pressures from these same groups, which Huber (1995) contends helped to destroy sociology. One wonders, for example, why anthropology, a field that embraced these diverse theories and epistemologies, flourished during this period, whereas sociology languished.

8. Gamson (1992, p. 1) questions if this means that those "sociologists who are critical must either shut up or adapt the political line of administrators?"

9. A current example of this negative attention can be found in the media controversy surrounding the recent study of the sexual practices of Americans (see Laumann, Gagnon, Michael, & Michaels, 1994; Lewontin, 1995; Updike, 1995). This study has been criticized for its theories of human conduct and sexuality and its survey research methodology (see Chancer, 1995).

10. Consider, for example, the list of books nominated for the distinguished scholarly publication award of the ASA in 1989 (see Clemens et al., 1995, pp. 484-488).

11. Of course, no one rejects the concept of intersubjectivity, although since Husserl and Derrida no poststructuralist assumes that intersubjectivity is not easily accomplished. Of course, there is no objective place from which anything can be studied.

12. Some now argue that patient and consumer advocates should be members of IRBs, others suggest that advocates should be involved at earlier stages in research, including serving on the teams that draw up experimental protocols, and still others feel that third parties should interview subjects (patients) after they sign consent forms to ensure that "they understand the research and their choices" (Hilts, 1995). Some feel that consent forms have become like "rental car contracts" (Hilts, 1995).

13. The 1995 proposed Family Privacy Protection Act would require that parents must give written consent before their children can participate in nearly all types of federally funded research. Social scientists are objecting to this proposed legislation, arguing that it is a costly, ineffective procedure that will yield poorer quality research data that will ultimately harm children (American Sociological Association, 1995, pp. 1, 9).

14. For example, schizophrenic patients, uninformed of the risks, are allowed to relapse (stop taking their medication) so researchers can study this condition (Hilts, 1995).

15. Three types of at-risk subjects are recognized: children, newborns, and minors; prisoners, the mentally ill, and the mentally retarded; and pregnant women and the viable fetus.

16. Of course, the citizen may be coerced into participating in a scientific project, not knowing what public good will flow from this participation. The great Ivy League nude posture photo scandal is but another of many recent examples. From the 1940s through

the 1960s, undergraduates at Yale, Mount Holyoke, Vassar, Smith, and Princeton were routinely photographed in the nude for a scientific project (long since dismissed) conducted by W. H. Sheldon who believed body type could tell a great deal about intelligence, temperament, and moral worth (see Rosenbaum, 1995, p. 30). Hillary Rodham Clinton and George Bush were among those whose nude bodies were photographed and, until recently, available for public examination at the Smithsonian Institution ("Smithsonian Seals," 1995).

17. Thus, high-level scientific work is conducted behind locked doors, giving rise to industrial and scientific espionage of global proportion.

18. I borrow from Ryan (1995), who is speaking primarily about evaluation theory and practice. She seeks a feminine, morally based evaluation framework. Her evaluator is close to Carspecken's (1996) critical ethnographer and (in some ways) Charity's (1995) public journalist, a moral advocate and a social critic who examines "the everyday life of evaluands" (Ryan, 1995, p. 145) in a democratic society.

19. I thank Katherine E. Ryan and Clifford Christians for their assistance and critical comments on this section.

20. At the same time, it is understood that "participating in a citizen's initiative to clean up a polluted harbor is no less political than debating in cultural journals the pejorative presentation of certain groups in terms of stereotypical images" (Benhabib, 1992, p. 104).

21. I am involved, with Walter Feinberg and Belden Fields, in a study of one community's attempts to bring a form of radical democracy (site-based decision making) into the classroom. We are experimenting with these norms and goals in this project.

22. These are extensions of the norms Christians et al. (1993, pp. 55-57) see as operating for journalists.

23. I thank Clifford Christians for this principle (Christians, in press).

24. The rules in this paragraph plagiarize Raymond Chandler's (1995) "12 Notes on the Mystery Story" (pp. 1004-1011).

References

Agar, M. (1990). Exploring the excluded middle. *Journal of Contemporary Ethnography, 19,* 73-88.

Agee, J., & Evans, W. (1988). *Let us now praise famous men.* Boston: Houghton Mifflin. (Original work published 1944)

Agger, B. (1989). *Reading science.* Dix Hills, NY: General Hall.

Allen, R. C. (Ed.). (1992). Introduction to the second edition: More talk about TV. In R. C. Allen (Ed.), *Television and channels of discourse, reassembled: Contemporary criticism* (2nd ed., pp. 1-30). Chapel Hill: University of North Carolina Press.

Altheide, D. L. (1995). Horsing around with literary loops, or why postmodernism is fun. *Symbolic Interaction, 18,* 519-526.

Altheide, D. L., & Johnson, J. M. (1994). Criteria for evaluating qualitative research. In N. K. Denzin & Y. S. Lincoln (Eds.), *The handbook of qualitative research* (pp. 485-499). Thousand Oaks, CA: Sage.

Altrichter, H. (1993). The concept of quality in action research: Giving practitioners a voice in educational research. In M. Schratz (Ed.), *Qualitative voices in educational research: Social science and educational studies series 9* (pp. 40-55). London: Falmer.

American Sociological Association. (1995, December). *ASA testifies House bill harmful to nation, research* (Footnotes 1, 9). Washington, DC: Author.

Anderson, G. (1989). Critical ethnography in education: Origins, current status, and new directions. *Review of Educational Research, 59,* 249-270.

Anzaldua, G. (1981a). Speaking in tongues: A letter to third world writers. In C. Moraga & G. Anzaldua (Eds.), *This bridge called my back: Writings by radical women of color* (pp. 165-174). Watertown, MA: Peresephone Press.

Anzaldua, G. (1981b). La proeta. In C. Moraga & G. Anzaldua (Eds.), *This bridge called my back: Writings by radical women of color* (pp. 198-209). Watertown, MA: Peresephone Press.

Anzaldua, G. (1987). *Borderlands/la frontera.* San Francisco: Aunt Lute.

Appadurai, A. (1990). Disjuncture and difference in the global cultural economy. *Public Culture, 2*, 1-24.

Appadurai, A. (1993). Patriotism and its future. *Public Culture, 5*, 411-429.

Ashley, K., Gilmore, L., & Peters, G. (Eds.). (1994). *Autobiography & postmodernism.* Amherst: University of Massachusetts Press.

Ashmore, M. (1989). *The reflexive thesis: Wrighting sociology of scientific knowledge.* Chicago: University of Chicago Press.

Ashmore, M., Myers, G., & Potter, J. (1995). Discourse, rhetoric, reflexivity: Seven days in the library. In S. Jasanoff, G. E. Markle, J. C. Petersen, & T. Pinch (Eds.), *Handbook of science and technology studies* (pp. 321-343). London: Sage.

Atkinson, P. (1992). *Understanding ethnographic texts.* Newbury Park, CA: Sage.

Bacon, W. A. (1979). *The art of interpretation* (3rd ed.). New York: Holt, Rinehart & Winston.

Bacon, W. A. (1980). An aesthetics of performance. *Literature in Performance, 1*, 1-9.

Bakhtin, M. M. (1968). *Rabelais and his world.* Cambridge, MA: MIT Press.

Bakhtin, M. M. (1981). *The dialogical imagination.* Austin: University of Texas Press.

Bakhtin, M. M. (1986). *Speech genres and other late essays.* Austin: University of Texas Press.

Barone, T. (1995). Persuasive writings, vigilant readings, and reconstructed characters: The paradox of trust in educational storytelling. In J. A. Hatch & R. Wisniewski (Eds.), *Life history and narrative* (pp. 63-74). Washington, DC: Falmer.

Barthes, R. (1972). *Mythologies.* New York: Hill & Wang. (Original work published 1957)

Barthes, R. (1975). *The pleasure of the text.* New York: Hill & Wang.

Barthes, R. (1982). *A Barthes reader* (S. Sontag, Ed.). New York: Hill & Wang.

Barthes, R. (1985). *The grain of the voice: Interviews: 1962-1980* (L. Coverdale, Trans.). New York: Hill & Wang.

Bateson, G., & Mead, M. (1942). *Balinese character: A photographic essay.* New York: New York Academy of Sciences.

Baudrillard, J. (1983). *Simulations.* New York: Semiotext(e).

Baudrillard, J. (1988). *America.* London: Verso.

Bauman, B. (1995, February 4). The man who talked too much. *New York Times,* p. A15.

Bauman, R. (1986). *Story, performance, event: Contextual studies of oral narratives.* Cambridge, UK: Cambridge University Press.

Becker, H. S. (1966). Introduction. In C. R. Shaw (Ed.), *The jack-roller* (pp. v-xviii). Chicago: University of Chicago Press.

Becker, H. S., Geer, B., Hughes, E., Strauss, A. (1961). *Boys in White.* Chicago: University of Chicago Press.

Becker, H. S., McCall, M. M., & Morris, L. V. (1989). Theatres and communities: Three scenes. *Social Problems, 36*, 93-116.

Bellamy, J. D. (1982). Introduction. In T. Wolfe (Ed.), *The purple decades: A reader selected by Tom Wolfe* (pp. vii-xv). New York: Farrar, Straus, & Giroux.

Benhabib, S. (1990). Afterword: Communicative ethics and current controversies in practical philosophy. In S. Benhabib & F. Dallayr (Eds.), *The communicative ethics controversy* (pp. 330-369). Cambridge, MA: MIT Press.

Benhabib, S. (1992). *Situating the self: Gender, community and postmodernism in contemporary ethics.* New York: Routledge.

Benjamin, W. (1968). *Illuminations* (with an introduction by H. Arendt, Ed.; H. Zohn, Trans.). New York: Harcourt, Brace & World.

Benjamin, W. (1973). *Charles Baudelaire: A lyric poet in the era of high capitalism*. London: New Left Books.

Benson, P. (Ed.). (1993). *Anthropology and literature*. Urbana: University of Illinois Press.

Birringer, J. (1993). *Theatre, theory, postmodernism*. Bloomington: Indiana University Press.

Black, J. (1991). *The aesthetics of murder: A study in romantic literature and contemporary culture*. Baltimore, MD: Johns Hopkins University Press.

Bloch, E. (1988). A philosophical view of the detective novel (J. Zipes & F. Mecklenburg, Trans.). In E. Bloch (Ed.), *The utopian function of art and literature: Selected essays* (pp. 245-264). Cambridge, MA: MIT Press.

Boal, A. (1985). *Theatre of the oppressed*. New York: Theatre Communications Group. (Original work published 1979)

Boal, A. (1995). *The rainbow of desire: The Boal method of theatre and therapy* (A. Jackson, Trans.). New York: Routledge.

Bochner, A. P. (1994). Perspectives on inquiry II: Theories and stories. In M. Knapp & G. R. Miller (Eds.), *The handbook of interpersonal communication* (pp. 21-41). Thousand Oaks, CA: Sage.

Bochner, A. P., & Ellis, C. (1996). Taking ethnography into the twenty-first century. *Journal of Contemporary Ethnography, 25*, 3-5.

Bochner, A. P., & Waugh, J. B. (1995). Talking-with as a model for writing-about: Implications of Rortyean pragmatism. In L. Langsdorf & A. R. Smith (Eds.), *Recovering pragmatism's voice: The classical tradition, Rorty, and the philosophy of communication* (pp. 211-233). Albany: State University of New York Press.

Boelen, W. A. M. (1992). Street corner society: Cornerville revisited. *Journal of Contemporary Ethnography, 21*, 11-51.

Booth, W. C. (1983). *The rhetoric of fiction*. Chicago: University of Chicago Press. (Original work published 1961)

Bowman, M. S. (1988). Cultural critique as performance: The example of Walter Benjamin. *Literature in Performance, 8*, 4-11.

Boyers, J. S. (with Markle, G. E.) (1995). *Gophers, ghosts, and electronic dreams: A feminist critique of new literary forms*. Unpublished manuscript.

Brady, I. (Ed.). (1991a). *Anthropological poetics*. Savage, MD: Rowman & Littlefield.

Brady, I. (Ed.). (1991b). Introduction. In I. Brady (Ed.), *Anthropological poetics* (pp. 3-36). Savage, MD: Rowman & Littlefield.

Brady, I. (Ed.). (1991c). Preface. In I. Brady (Ed.), *Anthropological poetics* (pp. ix-xii). Savage, MD: Rowman & Littlefield.

Breen, J. L. (1994). The detective fiction of Tony Hillerman: A book-by-book guide. In M. Greenberg (Ed.), *The Tony Hillerman companion: A comprehensive guide to his life and work* (pp. 1-62). New York: HarperPaperbacks.

Brown, E. B. (1989). African-American women's quilting: A framework for conceptualizing and teaching African-American women's history. *Signs, 14*, 921-929.

Brown, R. H. (1987). *Society as text*. Chicago: University of Chicago Press.

Bruner, E. M. (1984). The opening up of anthropology. In E. M. Bruner (Ed.), *Text, play, and story: The construction and reconstruction of self and society* (pp. 1-18). Washington, DC: The American Ethnological Society.

Bruner, E. M. (1986). Experience and its expressions. In V. M. Turner & E. M. Bruner (Eds.), *The anthropology of experience* (pp. 3-30). Urbana: University of Illinois Press.

Bruner, E. M. (1993). Introduction: The ethnographic self and the personal self. In P. Benson (Ed.), *Anthropology and literature* (pp. 1-26). Urbana: University of Illinois Press.

Burch, N. (1990). *Life to those shadows*. Berkeley: University of California Press.

Burke, J. L. (1987). *The neon rain*. New York: Pocket Books.

Burke, J. L. (1988). *Heaven's prisoners*. New York: Pocket Books.

Burke, J. L. (1989). *Black cherry blues*. New York: Pocket Books.

Burke, J. L. (1990). *A morning for flamingoes*. New York: Avon.

Burke, J. L. (1992a). *A stained white radiance*. New York: Avon.

Burke, J. L. (1992b). Trouble in the Big Easy: Interview with James Lee Burke. *The Armchair Detective, 25,* 40-50.

Burke, J. L. (1993). *In the electric mist with confederate dead*. New York: Avon.

Burke, J. L. (1994). *Dixie City jam*. New York: Hyperion.

Burke, J. L. (1995). *Burning angel*. New York: Hyperion.

Burke, K. (1969). *Rhetoric of motives*. Berkeley: University of California Press.

Butler, J. (1990). *Gender trouble: Feminism and the subversion of identity*. New York: Routledge.

Caplan, P. (1988/1989). Engendering knowledge: The politics of ethnography. *Anthropology Today, 4*(5), 8-12; *4*(6), 14-17.

Capo, K. E. (1983). Performance of literature as social dialect. *Literature in Performance, 4,* 31-36.

Capo, K. E. (1988). Presence, aura, and memory: Implications of Walter Benjamin and the Frankfurt School for Performance Theory. *Literature in Performance, 8,* 28-34.

Capote, T. (1966). *In cold blood*. New York: Random House.

Carey, J. W. (1986). The dark continent of American journalism. In R. K. Manoff & M. Schudson (Eds.), *Reading the news* (pp. 146-196). New York: Pantheon.

Carey, J. W. (1989). *Communication as culture*. Boston: Unwin Hyman.

Carmody, D. (1993, May 30). Despite Malcolm trial, editors elsewhere vouch for accuracy of their work. *New York Times,* p. 126.

Carspecken, P. F. (1996). *Critical ethnography in educational research*. New York: Routledge.

Carspecken, P. F., & Apple, M. (1992). Critical research: Theory, methodology, and practice. In M. D. LeCompte, W. L. Millroy, & J. Preissel (Eds.), *The handbook of qualitative research in education* (pp. 507-554). New York: Academic Press.

Carter, D. (1992). Trouble in the Big Easy: Interview with James Lee Burke. *The Armchair Detective, 25,* 40-50.

Carvajal, D. (1995, February 6). Three words engulf Rutger's president. *New York Times,* p. A8.

Carver, R. (1989a). *Fires: Essays, poems, stories*. New York: Random House.

Carver, R. (1989b). Intimacy. In R. Carver (Ed.), *Where I'm calling from* (pp. 444-453). New York: Vintage.

Cawelti, J. G. (1976). *Adventure, mystery, and romance: Formula stories as art and popular culture*. Chicago: University of Chicago Press.

Chancer, L. (1995). Unintended intimacies: Sex and sociology: Review-essay: The social organization of sexuality: Sexual practices in the United States. *Contemporary Sociology, 24,* 298-302.

Chandler, R. (1972). *The simple art of murder*. New York: Ballantine.

Chandler, R. (1995). Twelve notes on the mystery story. In R. Chandler (Ed.), *Later novels & other writings* (pp. 1004-1011). New York: Penguin.

Chang, B. G. (1992). Empty intention. *Text and Performance Quarterly, 12,* 212-227.

Chappell, C. (1993). The forgotten tough guy novel. *The Armchair Detective, 26,*(3), 16-20.

Charity, A. (1995). *Doing public journalism.* New York: Guilford.

Charmaz, K. (1995). Between positivism and postmodernism: Implications for methods. *Studies in Symbolic Interaction, 17,* 43-72.

Cherryholmes, C. H. (1988). *Power and criticism: Poststructural investigations in education.* New York: Teacher's College Press.

Chessman, P. (1971). Production casebook. *New Theatre Quarterly, 1,* 1-6.

Chow, R. (1993). *Writing diaspora: Tactices of intervention in contemporary cultural studies.* Bloomington: Indiana University Press.

Christians, C. G. (1986). Reporting and the oppressed. In D. Elliot (Ed.), *Responsible journalism* (pp. 109-130). Beverly Hills, CA: Sage.

Christians, C. G. (1995a). *The common good in a global setting.* Paper presented to the Civic Journalism Interest Group at the Annual Meetings of the Association for Education in Journalism and Mass Communication, Washington, DC.

Christians, C. G. (1995b). The naturalistic fallacy in contemporary interactionist-interpretive research. *Studies in Symbolic Interaction, 19,* 125-130.

Christians, C. G. (in press). Social ethics and mass media practice. In J. Makau & R. Arnett (Eds.), *Communication ethics in an age of diversity.* Urbana: University of Illinois Press.

Christians, C. G., Ferre, J. P., & Fackler, P. M. (1993). *Good news: Social ethics and the press.* New York: Oxford University Press.

Christians, C. G., Rotzoll, K. B., & Fackler, M. (1991). *Media ethics: Cases and moral reasoning* (3rd ed.). New York: Longman.

Clandinin, D. J., & Connelly, F. M. (1994). Personal experience methods. In N. K. Denzin & Y. S. Lincoln (Eds.), *The handbook of qualitative research* (pp. 413-427). Thousand Oaks, CA: Sage.

Clark, K., & Holquist, M. (1984). *Mikhail Bakhtin.* Cambridge, MA: Belknap.

Clemens, E. S., Powell, W. W., McIlwaine, K., & Okamoto, D. (1995). Centennial essay: Careers in print: Books, journals, and scholarly reputations. *American Journal of Sociology, 101,* 433-494.

Clifford, J. (1986). Introduction: Partial truths. In J. Clifford & G. E. Marcus (Eds.), *Writing culture* (pp. 1-26). Berkeley: University of California Press.

Clifford, J. (1988). *The predicament of Culture.* Cambridge, MA: Harvard University Press.

Clifford, J., & Marcus, G. E. (Eds.). (1986). *Writing culture.* Berkeley: University of California Press.

Cline, E. (1989). The great debate. *The Armchair Detective, 22*(3), 317-322.

Clough, P. T. (1992). *The end(s) of ethnography.* Newbury Park, CA: Sage.

Clough, P. T. (1993a). On the brink of deconstructing sociology: Critical reading of Dorothy Smith's standpoint epistemology. *Sociological Quarterly, 34,* 169-182.

Clough, P. T. (1993b). Response to Smith's response. *Sociological Quarterly, 34,* 193-194.

Clough, P. T. (1994). *Feminist thought: Desire, power and academic discourse.* Cambridge, MA: Blackwell.

Clough, P. T. (1995). Beginning again at the end(s) of ethnography: Response to "The man at the end of the machine." *Symbolic Interaction, 18,* 527-534.

Coger, L. I., & White, M. R. (1973). *Readers theatre handbook.* Glenview, IL: Scott, Foresman.

Cohen, J. M. (1981, April 18). Letter to the editor. *Washington Post,* p. A12.

Cohn, R. (1988). Realism. In M. Banham (Ed.), *The Cambridge guide to theatre* (p. 815). Cambridge, UK: Cambridge University Press.

Coleridge, S. T. (1973). Biographia literaria. In W. Heath (Ed.), *Major British poets of the romantic period* (pp. 500-530). New York: Macmillan. (Original work published 1817)

Collins, P. H. (1986). Learning from the outsider within: The sociological significance of black feminist thought. *Social Problems, 33,* 14-32.

Collins, P. H. (1991). *Black feminist thought.* New York: Routledge.

Collins, P. H. (1992). Transforming the inner circle: Dorothy's Smith challenge to sociological theory. *Sociological Theory, 10,* 73-80.

Condit, C. M., & Selzer, J. A. (1985). The rhetoric of objectivity in the newspaper coverage of a murder trial. *Critical Studies in Mass Communication, 2,* 197-216.

Connell, R. W. (1992). A sober anarchism. *Sociological Theory, 10,* 80-87.

Connery, T. B. (Ed.). (1992). *A sourcebook of American literary journalism.* Westport, CT: Greenwood.

Conquergood, D. (1985a). Performing as a moral act: Ethical dimensions of the ethnography of performance. *Literature in Performance, 5,* 1-13.

Conquergood, D. (1985b). *Between two worlds: The Hmong Shaman in America* [Documentary Film]. Chicago: Siegel Productions.

Conquergood, D. (1986). Performing cultures: Ethnography, epistemology, and ethics. In E. Slembek (Ed.), *Miteinander sprechen and handeln: Festschrift fur Hellmut Geissner,* (pp. 55-147). Frankfurt: Scriptor.

Conquergood, D. (1989). Poetics, play, process and power: The performance turn in anthropology. *Text and Performance Quarterly, 9,* 82-88.

Conquergood, D. (1990). *The heart broken in half* [Documentary Film]. Chicago: Siegel Productions.

Conquergood, D. (1991). Rethinking ethnography: Towards a critical cultural politics. *Communication Monographs, 58,* 179-194.

Conquergood, D. (1992). Ethnography, rhetoric and performance. *Quarterly Journal of Speech, 78,* 80-97.

Cooke, J. (1980, September 28). Jimmy's world. *Washington Post,* p. A1.

Craig, D. A. (1995, August 9-12). *Communitarian journalism(s): Clearing the conceptual landscape.* Paper presented to the Qualitative Studies Division at the Annual Meetings of the Association for Education in Journalism and Mass Communication, Washington, DC.

Cramer, R. B. (1992). *What it takes: The way to the White House.* New York: Random House.

Cronbach, L. J. (1989). Construct validation after thirty years. In R. L. Linn (Ed.), *Intelligence, measurement, theory, and public policy* (pp. 147-171). Urbana: University of Illinois Press.

Dawson, L. L., & Prus, R. (1993). Interactionist ethnography and postmodernist discourse: Affinities and disjunctures in approaching human lived experience. *Studies in Symbolic Interaction, 15,* 147-177.

Dawson, L. L., & Prus, R. (1995). Postmodernism and linguistic reality versus symbolic interactionism and obdurate reality. *Studies in Symbolic Interaction, 17,* 67-99.

Debord, G. (1983). *Society of the spectacle.* Detroit: Black & Red.

de Certeau, M. (1984). *The practice of everyday life* (S. Rendall, Trans.). Berkeley: University of California Press.

de Lauretis, T. (1984). *Alice doesn't: Feminism, semiotics, cinema.* Bloomington: Indiana University Press.

Deleuze, G., & Guattari, F. (1987). *A thousand plateaus.* Minneapolis: University of Minnesota Press.

Denzin, N. K. (1984). *On understanding emotion*. San Francisco: Jossey-Bass.

Denzin, N. K. (1989a). *Interpretive biography*. Newbury Park, CA: Sage.

Denzin, N. K. (1989b). *Interpretive interactionalism*. Newbury Park, CA: Sage.

Denzin, N. K. (1991a). *Hollywood shot by shot: Alcoholism in American cinema*. Hawthorne, NY: Aldine.

Denzin, N. K. (1991b). Representing lived experience in ethnographic texts. *Studies in Symbolic Interaction, 12*, 59-70.

Denzin, N. K. (1991c). Back to Harold and Agnes. *Sociological Theory, 9*, 278-285.

Denzin, N. K. (1992a). *Symbolic interactionism and cultural studies*. Cambridge, MA: Blackwell.

Denzin, N. K. (1992b). Whose cornerville is it, anyway. *Journal of Contemporary Ethnography, 21*, 120-132.

Denzin, N. K. (1993). *The alcoholic society: Addiction & recovery of self*. New Brunswick, NJ: Transaction Publishing.

Denzin, N. K. (1994a). The art and politics of interpretation. In N. K. Denzin & Y. S. Lincoln (Eds.), *Handbook of qualitative research* (pp. 500-515). Thousand Oaks, CA: Sage.

Denzin, N. K. (1994b). Evaluating qualitative research in the poststructural moment: The lessons James Joyce teaches us. *Qualitative Studies in Education, 7*, 295-308.

Denzin, N. K. (1995a). *The cinematic society: The voyeur's gaze*. London: Sage.

Denzin, N. K. (1995b). The poststructural crisis in the social sciences. In R. H. Brown (Ed.), *Writing postmodernism* (pp. 38-59). Urbana: University of Illinois Press.

Denzin, N. K. (1995c). On hearing the voices of educational research: Review essay. *Curriculum Inquiry, 25*, 313-330.

Denzin, N. K. (1995d). The experimental text and the limits of visual understanding. *Educational Theory, 45*, 7-18.

Denzin, N. K. (1996a). Cultural studies, the New Journalism, and the narrative turn in ethnography. In C. A. Warren, M. Vavrus, & E. Munson (Eds.), *American cultural studies*. Minneapolis: University of Minnesota Press.

Denzin, N. K. (1996b). Institutional perspectives on sociology. *American Journal of Sociology, 102*.

Denzin, N. K. (in press-a). The standpoint epistemologies and social theory. *Current Perspectives in Social Theory, 19*.

Denzin, N. K. (in press-b). Performance texts. In W. Tierney & Y. S. Lincoln (Eds.), *Re-privileging voice: The poststructural turn in qualitative research*. Albany: State University of New York Press.

Denzin, N. K., & Lincoln, Y. S. (1994). Introduction: Entering the field of qualitative research. In N. K. Denzin & Y. S. Lincoln (Eds.), *The handbook of qualitative research* (pp. 1-18). Thousand Oaks, CA: Sage.

Derrida, J. (1976). *Of grammatology*. Baltimore, MD: Johns Hopkins University Press. (Original work published 1974)

Derrida, J. (1978). *Writing and difference*. Chicago: University of Chicago Press. (Original work published 1967)

Derrida, J. (1981). *Positions*. Chicago: University of Chicago Press.

Detman, L. A. (1996). *Tracing notions of women's places in society: An analysis of selected press coverage of Hillary Rodham Clinton*. Unpublished doctoral dissertation, University of Illinois, Department of Sociology, Urbana-Champaign.

Diamond, S. (1982). *Totems*. Barrytown, NY: Open Book/Station Hall.

Diamond, S. (1985a). Prosody. In J. I. Prattis (Ed.), *Reflections: The anthropological muse* (p. 264). Washington, DC: American Anthropological Association.

Diamond, S. (1985b). City night. In J. I. Prattis (Ed.), *Reflections: The anthropological muse* (p. 13). Washington, DC: American Anthropological Association.

Diamond, S. (1985c). Sunday in Biafra. In J. I. Prattis (Ed.), *Reflections: The anthropological Muse* (p. 32). Washington, DC: American Anthropological Association.

Diamond, S. (Ed.). (1986a). A special issue on poetry and anthropology. *Dialectical Anthropology, 11*, 2-4.

Diamond, S. (1986b). Preface. A special issue on poetry and anthropology. *Dialectical Anthropology, 11*, 2-4, 131-132.

Dickens, D. (1995). The ethical horizons of postmodernity. *Symbolic Interaction, 18*, 535-541.

Didion, J. (1968). *Slouching towards Bethlehem*. New York: Farrar.

Didion, J. (1979). *The white album*. New York: Simon & Schuster.

Didion, J. (1992). *After Henry*. New York: Simon & Schuster.

Donmoyer, R., & Yennie-Donmoyer, J. (1995). Data as drama: Reflections on the use of readers theatre as an artistic mode of data display. *Qualitative Inquiry, 1*(4), 402-428.

Dorst, J. D. (1989). *The written suburb: An ethnographic dilemma*. Philadelphia: University of Pennsylvania Press.

Downing, D. B. (1987). Deconstruction's scruples: The politics of enlightened critique. *Diacritics, 17*, 66-81.

Drotner, K. (1994). Ethnographic enigmas: "The everyday" in recent media studies. *Cultural Studies, 8*, 341-357.

Duff, W. (1985). Come seem with me. In J. I. Prattis (Ed.), *Reflections: The anthropological muse* (pp. 160-161). Washington, DC: American Anthropological Association.

Dufrenne, M. (1973). *The phenomenology of aesthetic experience*. Evanston, IL: Northwestern University Press.

Duranti, A., & Goodwin, C. (Eds.). (1992). *Rethinking context: Language as an interactive phenomenon*. Cambridge, UK: Cambridge University Press.

Eason, D. (1981). Telling stories and making sense. *Journal of Popular Culture, 15*, 125-129.

Eason, D. (1982). New journalism, metaphor and culture. *Journal of Popular Culture, 15*, 142-149.

Eason, D. (1984). The New Journalism and the image-world: Two modes of organizing experience. *Critical Studies in Mass Communication, 3*, 51-65.

Eason, D. (1986). On journalistic authority: The Janet Cooke scandal. *Critical Studies in Mass Communication, 3*, 429-447.

Edmunds, L., & Dundes, A. (Eds.). (1995). *Oedipus: A folklore casebook*. Madison: University of Wisconsin Press. (Original work published 1983 by Garland Publishing)

Eisenhart, M. A., & Howe, K. R. (1992). Validity in educational research. In M. D. LeCompte, W. L. Millroy, & J. Preissel (Eds.), *The handbook of qualitative research in education* (pp. 643-680). New York: Academic Press.

Eisner, E. W. (1991). *The enlightened eye: Qualitative inquiry and the enhancement of educational practice*. New York: Macmillan.

Eliot, T. S. (1952). The wasteland. In T. S. Eliot (Ed.), *The complete poems and plays, 1909-1950* (pp. 37-55). New York: Harcourt, Brace & World. (Original work published 1922)

Ellis, C. (1993). Telling a story of sudden death. *Sociological Quarterly, 34*, 711-773.

Ellis, C. (1994). Between social science and literature: What are our options? *Symbolic Interaction, 17*, 325-330.

Ellis, C. (1995a). *Final negotiations*. Philadelphia: Temple University Press.

Ellis, C. (1995b). Emotional and ethical quagmires in returning to the field. *Journal of Contemporary Ethnography, 24*, 68-98.

Ellis, C. (1995c). The other side of the fence: Seeing black and white in a small Southern town. *Qualitative Inquiry, 1*, 147-167.

Ellis, C. (1996). Evocative authoethnography: Writing emotionally about our lives. In Y. S. Lincoln & W. Tierney (Eds.), *Representation and the text: Reframing the narrative voice*. Albany: State University of New York Press.

Ellis, C., & Bochner, A. P. (1992). Telling and performing personal stories: The constraints of choice in abortion. In C. Ellis & M. G. Flaherty (Eds.), *Investigating subjectivity: Research on lived experience* (pp. 79-101). Newbury Park, CA: Sage.

Ellis, C., & Flaherty, M. G. (1992a). An agenda for the interpretation of lived experience. In C. Ellis & M. G. Flaherty (Eds.), *Investigating subjectivity: Research on lived experience* (pp. 1-16). Newbury Park, CA: Sage.

Ellis, C., & Flaherty, M. G. (Eds.). (1992b). *Investigating subjectivity: Research on lived experience*. Newbury Park, CA: Sage.

Etherton, M. (1988). Third World popular theatre. In M. Banham (Ed.), *The Cambridge guide to theatre* (pp. 991-992). Cambridge, UK: Cambridge University Press.

Etzioni, A. (1993). *The spirit of community: Rights, responsibilities, and the communitarian agenda*. New York: Crown.

Fallows, J. (1996). *Breaking the news: How the media undermine American democracy*. New York: Pantheon.

Farberman, H. A. (1991). Symbolic interactionism and postmodernism: Close encounters of a dubious kind. *Symbolic Interaction, 14*, 471-488.

Farberman, H. A. (1992). The grounds of critique: A choice among metaphysics, power, and communicative action: Reply to Fee and Clough. *Symbolic Interaction, 15*, 375-379.

Faulkner, W. (1967). Address upon receiving the Nobel Prize for literature. In M. Cowley (Ed.), *The portable Faulkner* (Expanded & Rev. ed., pp. 723-724). New York: Viking.

Fay, B. (1987). *Critical social science*. Ithaca, NY: Cornell University Press.

Feldman, M. (1995). *Strategies for interpreting qualitative data*. Thousand Oaks, CA: Sage.

Feuer, J. (1992). Genre study. In R. C. Allen (Ed.), *Television and channels of discourse, reassembled: Contemporary criticism* (2nd ed., pp. 138-160). Chapel Hill: University of North Carolina Press.

The fiction of truth [Editorial]. (1984, June 20). *New York Times*, p. 13.

Fiedler, L. A. (1982). *Love and death in the American novel* (Rev. ed.). New York: Stein & Day.

Fielding, N. G., & Lee, R. M. (Eds.). (1992). *Using computers in qualitative research* (Reprinted with updated resources section). Newbury Park, CA: Sage. (Original work published 1991)

Fine, G. A. (1993). Ten lies of ethnography. *Journal of Contemporary Ethnography, 22*, 267-294.

Fine, M. (1993). Working the hyphens: Reinventing self and other in qualitative research. In N. K. Denzin & Y. S. Lincoln (Eds.), *Handbook of qualitative research* (pp. 70-82). Thousand Oaks, CA: Sage.

Fischer, M. M. J. (1994). Autobiographical voices (1,2,3) and mosaic memory: Experimental sondages in the (post)modern world. In K. Ashley, L. Gilmore, & G. Peters

(Eds.), *Autobiography & postmodernism* (pp. 79-129). Amherst: University of Massachusetts Press.

Fish, S. (1980). *Is there a text in this class: The authority of interpretive communities.* Cambridge, MA: Harvard University Press.

Fishkin, S. F. (1985). *From fact to fiction: Journalism and imaginative writing in America.* Baltimore, MD: Johns Hopkins University Press.

Fiske, J. (1992). British cultural studies and television. In R. C. Allen (Ed.), *Television and channels of discourse, reassembled: Contemporary criticism* (2nd ed., pp. 284-326). Chapel Hill: University of North Carolina Press.

Fiske, J. (1994). Audiencing: Cultural practice and cultural studies. In N. K. Denzin & Y. S. Lincoln (Eds.), *The handbook of qualitative research* (pp. 189-198). Thousand Oaks, CA: Sage.

Fonow, M. M., & Cook, J. A. (1991). Back to the future: A look at the second wave of feminist epistemology and methodology. In M. M. Fonow & J. A. Cook (Eds.), *Beyond methodology: Feminist scholarship as lived research* (pp. 1-15). Bloomington: Indiana University Press.

Fontana, A. (1992). Paradoxes of postmodernism: Toward new expressive modes. *Studies in Symbolic Interaction, 13,* 29-37.

Foucault, M. (1984). What is enlightenment? In P. Rabinow (Ed.), *The Foucault reader* (pp. 32-50). New York: Pantheon.

Frank, A. (1991). *At the will of the body: Reflections on illness.* Boston: Houghton Mifflin.

Frank, A. (1995). *The wounded storyteller: Body, illness and ethics.* Chicago: University of Chicago Press.

Frey, L. R., Botan, C. H., Friedman, P. G., & Kreps, G. L. (1992). *Interpreting communication research: A case study approach.* Englewood Cliffs, NJ: Prentice Hall.

Friedrich, P. (1985). Industrial accident: Mexico. In J. I. Prattis (Ed.), *Reflections: The anthropological muse* (p. 102). Washington, DC: American Anthropological Association.

Frow, J., & Morris, M. (1993). Introduction. In J. Frow & M. Morris (Eds.), *Australian cultural studies: A reader* (pp. vii-xxxii). Urbana: University of Illinois Press.

Frus, P. (1994). *The politics and poetics of journalistic narrative.* New York: Cambridge University Press.

Fuss, D. (1989). *Essentially speaking: Feminism, nature & difference.* New York: Routledge.

Gamson, W. (1992, August). *Reactions to the TAGGE Report.* Washington, DC: American Sociological Association.

Ganguly, K. (1992). Accounting for others: Feminism and representation. In L. F. Rakow (Ed.), *Women making meaning: New feminist directions in communication* (pp. 60-79). New York: Routledge.

Gans, H. (1980). *Deciding what's news.* New York: Vintage.

Geertz, C. (1973). *The interpretation of culture.* New York: Basic Books.

Geertz, C. (1983). *Local knowledge.* New York: Basic Books.

Geertz, C. (1988). *Words and lives.* Stanford, CA: Stanford University Press.

Geertz, C. (1995). *After the fact.* Cambridge, MA: Harvard University Press.

Giroux, H. A. (1994). *Disturbing pleasures.* New York: Routledge.

Glaser, B., & Strauss, A. (1967). *The discovery of grounded theory.* Chicago: Aldine.

Glasser, T. L., & Ettema, J. S. (1989). Investigative journalism and the moral order. *Critical Studies in Mass Communication, 6,* 1-20.

Glover, D., & Kaplan, C. (1992). Guns in the house of culture? Crime fiction and the politics of the popular. In L. Grossberg, C. Nelson, & P. Treichler (Eds.), *Cultural studies* (pp. 213-226). New York: Routledge.

Goffman, E. (1959). *The presentation of self in everyday life*. New York: Doubleday.

Goodson, I. (1995). The story so far: Personal knowledge and the political. In J. A. Hatch & R. Wisniewski (Eds.), *Life history and narrative* (pp. 89-98). Washington, DC: Falmer.

Gottlieb, A., & Graham, P. (1993). *Parallel worlds: An anthropologist and a writer encounter Africa*. Chicago: University of Chicago Press.

Green, B. (1981, April 19). Janet's world: The story of a child who never existed—How and why it came to be published. *Washington Post*, pp. A12-A14.

Greenfield, M. (1981, April 21). Reality is good enough. *Washington Post*, p. A19.

Grindal, B. T., & Shephard, W. H. (1993). Redneck girl: From experience to performance. In P. Benson (Ed.), *Anthropology and literature* (pp. 151-172). Urbana: University of Illinois Press.

Gross, J. (1993a, July 3). U.S. judge weighs retrial of New Yorker libel case. *New York Times*, p. 145.

Gross, J. (1993b, June 23). Jurors decide for psychoanalyst. *New York Times*, pp. Al, A21.

Gross, J. (1993c, May 21). Shawn has a say in New Yorker trial. *New York Times*, p. A10.

Gross, J. (1993d, May 12). Tough questioning of libel plaintiff. *New York Times*, p. A13.

Gross, J. (1993e, May 11). In New Yorker libel trial the analyst is examined. *New York Times*, p. A12.

Grossberg, L. (1988). Wandering audiences, nomadic critics. *Cultural Studies, 3*, 377-391.

Grossberg, L. (1992). *We gotta get out of this place*. New York: Routledge.

Grossberg, L. (1993). Can cultural studies find true happiness in communication? *Journal of Communication, 43*, 89-97.

Guba, E. G. (1990). The alternative paradigm dialog. In E. G. Guba (Ed.), *The paradigm dialog* (pp. 17-30). Newbury Park, CA: Sage.

Guba, E., & Lincoln, Y. S. (1989). *Fourth generation evaluation*. Newbury Park, CA: Sage.

Guba, E. G., & Lincoln, Y. S. (1994). Competing paradigms in qualitative research. In N. K. Denzin & Y. S. Lincoln (Eds.), *The handbook of qualitative research* (pp. 105-117). Thousand Oaks, CA: Sage.

Habermas, J. (1990). *Moral consciousness and communicative action*. Cambridge, MA: MIT Press. (Original work published 1983)

Hall, S. (1980). Encoding/decoding. In S. Hall, D. Hobson, A. Lowe, & P. Willis (Eds.), *Culture, media, language* (pp. 128-138). London: Hutchinson.

Hall, S. (1982). The rediscovery of "Ideology": Return of the repressed in media studies. In M. Gurevitch, T. Bennett, J. Curran, & J. Woollacott (Eds.), *Culture, society and the media* (pp. 56-90). London: Methuen.

Hall, S. (1985). Signification, representation, ideology: Althusser and the post-structuralist debates. *Critical Studies in Mass Communication, 2*, 91-114.

Hall, S. (1986). On postmodernism and articulation: An interview with Stuart Hall (L. Grossberg, Ed.). *Journal of Communication Inquiry, 10*, 45-60.

Hall, S. (1992). Cultural studies and its theoretical legacies. In L. Grossberg, C. Nelson, & P. Treichler (Eds.), *Cultural studies* (pp. 277-294). New York: Routledge.

Hamera, J. (1986). Postmodern performance, postmodern criticism. *Literature in Performance, 7*, 13-20.

Hammersley, M. (1992). *What's wrong with ethnography?* London: Routledge.

Hammett, D. (1980). *Five complete novels*. New York: Avenel.

Hansberry, L. (1969). *To be young, gifted and black.* New York: Signet.

Haraway, D. (1985). A manifesto for cyborgs: Science, technology and socialist feminism in the 1980s. *Socialist Review, 80,* 65-107.

Haraway, D. (1988). Situated knowledge: The science question in feminism and the privilege of partial perspective. *Feminist Studies, 14,* 575-599.

Harding, S. (1991). *Whose science? Whose knowledge: Thinking from women's lives.* Ithaca, NY: Cornell University Press.

Harper, D. (1994). On the authority of the image: Visual methods at the crossroads. In N. K. Denzin & Y. S. Lincoln (Eds.), *The handbook of qualitative research* (pp. 403-412). Thousand Oaks, CA: Sage.

Hartsock, N. M. (1983). The feminist standpoint: Developing the ground for a specifically feminist historical materialism. In S. Harding & M. Hintikka (Eds.), *Discovering reality* (pp. 283-310). Boston: Reidel.

Hatch, J. A., & Wisniewski, R. (Eds.). (1995). *Life history and narrative.* Washington, DC: Falmer.

Hay, J. (1992). Afterword. In R. C. Allen (Ed.), *Television and channels of discourse, reassembled: Contemporary criticism* (2nd ed., pp. 354-385). Chapel Hill: University of North Carolina Press.

Hayano, D. M. (1979). Auto-ethnography. *Human Organization, 38,* 99-104.

Hayano, D. M. (1982). *Poker faces.* Berkeley: University of California Press.

Haycraft, H. (1972). *Murder for pleasure: The life and times of the detective story.* New York: Biblo & Tannen.

Hersey, J. (1980). The legend on the license. *Yale Review, 70,* 1-25.

Hertz, R. (1996). Editor's introduction: Ethics, reflexivity and voice. *Qualitative Sociology, 19*(Special methods issue: Ethics, reflexivity and voice), 3-10.

Heyne, E. (1987). Toward a theory of literary nonfiction. *Modern Fiction Studies, 33,* 479-490.

Hilbert, R. A. (1990). The efficacy of performance science: Comment on McCall and Becker. *Social Problems, 37,* 133-135.

Hill, R. T. (1995). The Nakwa Powamu ceremony as rehearsal: Authority ethics and ritual appropriation. *Text and Performance Quarterly, 15,* 301-320.

Hilts, P. J. (1995, January 15). Conference is unable to agree on ethical limits of research. *New York Times,* p. A12.

Hollowell, J. (1977). *Fact and fiction: The New Journalism and the nonfiction novel.* Chapel Hill: University of North Carolina Press.

Holquist, M. (1983). Whodunit and other questions: Metaphysical detective stories in postwar fiction. In G. W. Most & W. M. Stowe (Eds.), *Poetics of murder* (pp. 149-174). New York: Harcourt Brace Jovanovich.

hooks, b. (1989). *Talking black, thinking feminist, thinking black.* Boston: South End.

hooks, b. (1990). *Yearning: Race, gender, and cultural politics.* Boston: South End.

Huber, J. (1973). Reply to Blumer: But who will scrutinize the scrutinizers? *American Sociological Review, 38,* 798-800.

Huber, J. (1995). Centennial essay: Institutional perspectives on sociology. *American Journal of Sociology, 101,* 194-216.

Hymes, D. (1985). Foreword. In J. I. Prattis (Ed.), *Reflections: The anthropological muse* (pp. 11-13). Washington, DC: American Anthropological Association.

Irigaray, L. (1985). *Speculum of the other woman* (G. G. Gill, Trans.). Ithaca, NY: Cornell University Press.

Iser, W. (1978). *The act of reading: A theory of aesthetic response.* Baltimore, MD: Johns Hopkins University Press.

Jackson, M. (1989). *Paths toward a clearing: Radical empiricism and ethnographic inquiry.* Bloomington: Indiana University Press.

Jackson, S. (1993). Ethnography and the audition: Performance as ideological critique. *Text and Performance Quarterly, 13,* 21-43.

Jameson, F. (1983). On Raymond Chandler. In G. V. Most & W. W. Stowe (Eds.), *The poetics of murder: Detective fiction and literary theory* (pp. 122-148). New York: Harcourt Brace Jovanovich.

Jameson, F. (1990). *Signatures of the visible.* New York: Routledge.

Jameson, F. (1991). *Postmodernism, or, the cultural logic of late capitalism.* Durham, NC: Duke University Press.

Jameson, F. (1992). *The geopolitical aesthetic: Cinema and space in the world system.* Bloomington: Indiana University Press.

Jay, M. (1988). Scopic regimes of modernity. In H. Foster (Ed.), *Vision and visuality* (pp. 3-23). Seattle: Bay Press.

Jay, M. (1993). *Downcast eyes: The denigration of vision in twentieth-century French thought.* Berkeley: University of California Press.

"Jimmy" story brings suit. (1981, August 7). *Washington Post,* p. A2.

Johnson, J. (1976). *Doing field research.* New York: Free Press.

Jones, C. (1981, December 20). In the land of the Khmer Rouge. *New York Times Magazine,* pp. 70-80, 86-87.

Jordan, J. (1985). *On call.* Boston: South End.

Joyce, J. (1964a). *Dubliners.* New York: Viking. (Original work published 1914)

Joyce, J. (1964b). *A portrait of the artist as a young man.* New York: Viking. (Original work published 1916)

Joyce, J. (1968a). *Ulysses.* New York: Viking. (Original work published 1922)

Joyce, J. (1968b). *Finnegans wake.* New York: Viking. (Original work published 1939)

Joyce, J. (1978). *The portable James Joyce* (with an introduction and notes by Harry Levin). New York: Viking.

Kapferer, B. (1986). Performance, and the structuring of meaning and experience. In V. M. Turner & E. M. Bruner (Eds.), *The anthropology of experience* (pp. 188-203). Urbana: University of Illinois Press.

Kawin, B. F. (1978). *Mindscreen: Bergman, Goddard, and first-person film.* Princeton, NJ: Princeton University Press.

Kiberd, D. (1992, January 3). Bloom the liberator [Literary Supplement]. *New York Times,* pp. 3-6.

Kincheloe, J. L., & McLaren, P. L. (1994). Rethinking critical theory and qualitative research. In N. K. Denzin & Y. S. Lincoln (Eds.), *The handbook of qualitative research* (pp. 138-157). Thousand Oaks, CA: Sage.

Kirk, J., & Miller, M. L. (1986). *Reliability and validity in qualitative research.* Beverly Hills, CA: Sage.

Kleinman, S. (1993). The textual turn. *Contemporary Sociology, 22,* 11-13.

Knight, S. (1980). *Form and ideology in crime fiction.* Bloomington: Indiana University Press.

Kohn, N. (1994). Glancing off a postmodern wall: A visit to the making of Zulu Dawn. *Studies in Symbolic Interaction, 16,* 85-106.

Kozloff, S. (1992). Narrative theory and television. In R. C. Allen (Ed.), *Television and channels of discourse, reassembled: Contemporary criticism* (2nd ed., pp. 67-100). Chapel Hill: University of North Carolina Press.

Kracauer, S. (1953). The challenge to qualitative content analysis. *Public Opinion Quarterly, 16,* 631-642.

Krieger, S. (1983). *The mirror dance: Identity in a woman's community.* Philadelphia: Temple University Press.

Krieger, S. (1991). *Social science & the self: Personal essays as an art form.* New Brunswick, NJ: Rutgers University Press.

Krieger, S. (1992). Addendum to Mitchell Stevens's "lessons of a deficient sociology." *Studies in Symbolic Interaction, 13,* 101-103.

Krippendorf, K. (1980). *Content analysis.* Beverly Hills, CA: Sage.

Krupat, A. (1994). Introduction. In A. Krupat (Ed.), *Native American autobiography: An anthology* (pp. 3-18). Madison: University of Wisconsin Press.

Kunda, G. (1993). Writing about reading: Review-essay: Reading ethnographic research by Martyn Hammersley, and reading ethnography by David Johnson. *Contemporary Sociology, 22,* 13-15.

Kurosawa, A. (Director). (1950). *Rashomon* [Film].

Langellier, K. M. (1983). A phenomenological approach to audience. *Literature in Performance, 3,* 34-39.

Larsen, P. (1991). Textual analysis of fictional media content. In K. B. Jensen & N. W. Jankowski (Eds.), *A handbook of qualitative methodologies for communication research* (pp. 121-134). New York: Routledge.

Lather, P. (1986). Issues of validity in openly ideological research: Between a rock and a soft place. *Interchange, 17,* 63-84.

Lather, P. (1991). *Getting smart.* New York: Routledge.

Lather, P. (1993). Fertile obsession: Validity after poststructuralism. *Sociological Quarterly, 34,* 673-694.

Laumann, E. O., Gagnon, J. H., Michael, R. T., & Michaels, S. (1994). *The social organization of sexuality: Sexual practices in the United States.* Chicago: University of Chicago Press.

Lavie, S., Narayan, K., & Rosaldo, R. (Eds.). (1993). *Creativity/anthropology.* Ithaca, NY: Cornell University Press.

Lee, R. L. M., & Ackerman, S. E. (1994). Farewell to ethnography? Global embourgeoisement and the dispriviliging of the narrative. *Critique of Anthropology, 14,* 339-354.

Lee, R. M. (1993). *Doing research on sensitive topics.* Newbury Park, CA: Sage.

Lee, R. M. (1995). *Dangerous fieldwork.* Thousand Oaks, CA: Sage.

Lemert, C. (1992). Subjectivity's limit: The unsolved riddle of the standpoint. *Sociological Theory, 10,* 63-72.

Lentricchia, F. (1990). In place of an afterword—Someone reading. In F. Lentricchia & T. McLaughglin (Eds.), *Critical terms for literary study* (pp. 321-338). Chicago: University of Chicago Press.

Levin, H. (1978). Editor's introduction. In *The portable James Joyce* (with an introduction and notes by H. Levin; pp. 1-16). New York: Viking.

Lévi-Strauss, C. (1966). *The savage mind.* Chicago: University of Chicago Press. (Original work published 1962)

Lewis, A. (1995, August 25). Stranger than fiction. *New York Times,* p. A15.

Lewis, O. (1966). *La Vida.* New York: Random House.

Lewontin, R. C. (1995, April 20). Sex, lies and social science. *New York Review of Books,* 42(7), 24-29.

Liggett, C. E. (1970). *The theatre student: Concert theatre.* New York: Rosen Press.

Lincoln, Y. (1995a). The sixth moment: Emerging problems in qualitative research. *Studies in Symbolic Interaction, 19,* 37-55.

Lincoln, Y. (1995b). Emerging criteria for quality in qualitative and interpretive inquiry. *Qualitative Inquiry, 1,* 275-289.

Lincoln, Y. S., & Denzin, N. K. (1994). The fifth moment. In N. K. Denzin & Y. S. Lincoln (Eds.), *The handbook of qualitative research* (pp. 575-586). Thousand Oaks, CA: Sage.

Lincoln, Y. S., & Guba, E. G. (1985). *Naturalistic inquiry.* Beverly Hills, CA: Sage.

Lipman, J. (1984, June 18). At the New Yorker, editor and writer differ on the facts. *Wall Street Journal,* p. 1.

Lofland, J. (1995). Analytic ethnography: Features, failings, and futures. *Journal of Contemporary Ethnography, 24,* 30-67.

Lofland, J., & Lofland, L. H. (1995). *Analyzing social settings* (3rd ed.). Belmont, CA: Wadsworth.

Lofland, L. H. (1993). Fighting the good fight—Again. *Contemporary Ethnography, 22,* 1-3.

Lonergan, B. (1977). Consciousness and the Trinity. In W. J. Ong (Ed.), *Interfaces of the word* (pp. 121-122). Ithaca, NY: Cornell University Press. (Reprinted from speech given at the 1963 North American College in Rome)

Lorde, A. (1984). *Sister outsider.* Trumansburg, NY: Crossing Press. (Original work published 1963)

Loseke, D. R. (1995). *Homelessness and involuntary commitment: Constructing persons, writing rights.* Presented at the 1995 Annual Meetings of the Midwest Sociological Society, Chicago.

Lottman, J. M. (1979, Autumn). The origin of plot in the light of typology. *Poetics Today, 1*(1-2), 161-184.[1]

Loxley, R. B. (1983). Roles of the audience: Aesthetic and social dimensions of the performance event. *Literature in Performance, 3,* 40-44.

Lyman, S. (1990). *Civilization: Contents, discontents, malcontents and other essays in social theory.* Fayetteville: University of Arkansas Press.

Lyotard, J.-F. (1984). *The postmodern condition.* Minneapolis: University of Minnesota Press.

Macdonald, R. (1970). Introduction. In R. Macdonald (Ed.), *Archer at large* (pp. vii-xi). New York: Knopf.

MacKinnon, C. (1982). Feminism, Marxism, method and the state: An agenda for theory. *Signs, 7,* 515-544.

Maclay, J. H. (1971). *Readers theatre: Toward a grammar of practice.* New York: Random House.

Mai, T. V. (1983). *Vietnam: Un peuple, des voix.* Paris: Pierre Horay.

Mailer, N. (1966). *The armies of the night: History as a novel, the novel as history.* New York: New American Library.

Mailer, N. (1979). *The executioner's song: A true life novel.* New York: Warner Books.

Mailer, N. (1995). *Oswald's tale: An American mystery.* New York: Random House.

Maines, D. R. (1993). Narrative's moment and sociology's phenomena: Toward a narrative sociology. *Sociological Quarterly, 34,* 17-38.

Malcolm, J. (1984). *In the freud archives.* New York: Knopf.

Malcolm, J. (1990). *The journalist and the murderer.* New York: Vintage.

Malcolm, J. (1992). *The purloined clinic: Selected writings.* New York: Knopf.

Malinowski, B. (1961). *Argonauts of the Western Pacific*. New York: E. P. Dutton. (Original work published 1922)

Malraux, A. (1930). *The royal way*. New York: Smith & Haas.

Mann, J. (1981, April 17). The respect for truth deeper than we thought. *Washington Post*, pp. B1, B3.

Manning, P. K., & Cullum-Swan, B. (1994). Narrative, content, and semiotic analysis. In N. K. Denzin & Y. S. Lincoln (Eds.), *The handbook of qualitative research*. (pp. 463-477). Thousand Oaks, CA: Sage.

Maraniss, D. A. (1981, April 16). Post reporter's Pulitzer prize is withdrawn. *Washington Post*, pp. A1, A25-A27.

March 14 retrial set in case against a New Yorker writer. (1993, October 14). *New York Times*, p. A18.

Marcus, G., & Fischer, M. (1986). *Anthropology as cultural critique*. Chicago: University of Chicago Press.

Marcus, G. E. (1994). What comes (just) after "Post"? The case of ethnography. In N. K. Denzin & Y. S. Lincoln (Eds.), *The handbook of qualitative research* (pp. 563-574). Thousand Oaks, CA: Sage.

Martin, B. (1992). *Matrix and line: Derrida and the possibilities of postmodern social theory*. Albany: State University of New York.

Marx, K. (1983a). Theses on Feuerbach. In E. Kamenka (Ed.), *The portable Karl Marx* (pp. 155-158). New York: Penguin. (Original work published 1888)

Marx, K. (1983b). From the eighteenth brumaire of Louis Bonaparte. In E. Kamenka (Ed.), *The portable Karl Marx* (pp. 287-324). New York: Penguin. (Original work published 1852)

Mascia-Lees, F. E., Sharpe, P., & Cohen, C. B. (1993). The postmodern turn in anthropology: Cautions from a feminist perspective. In P. Benson (Ed.), *Anthropology and literature* (pp. 225-248). Urbana: University of Illinois Press.

Mayne, J. (1990). *The woman at the keyhole: Feminism and women's cinema*. Bloomington: Indiana University Press.

McCall, M., & Becker, H. S. (1990). Performance science. *Social Problems, 32*, 117-132.

McCloskey, D. (1985). *The rhetoric of economics*. Madison: University of Wisconsin Press.

McHale, B. (1992). *Constructing postmodernism*. New York: Routledge.

McKeon, M. (1987). *The origins of the English novel: 1600-1740*. Baltimore, MD: Johns Hopkins University Press.

McMillen, L. (1994, November 30). A shakeup in anthropology: New editors dramatically revise a staid journal. *Chronical of Higher Education*, A10-A11, A17.

Mead, M., & Bateson, G. (1978). Margaret Mead and Gregory Bateson on the use of the camera in anthropology. *Studies in Visual Communication, 4*, 78-80.

Michener, J. A. (1981, May 4). On integrity in journalism. *U.S. News & World Report*, pp. 79-80.

Mienczakowski, J. (1992). *Synching out loud: A journey into illness*. Brisbane, Australia: Griffth University, Reprographics.

Mienczakowski, J. (1994). Reading and writing research. *NADIE Journal, 18*(International research issue), 45-54.

Mienczakowski, J. (1995). The theatre of ethnography: The reconstruction of ethnography into theatre with emancipatory potential. *Qualitative Inquiry, 1*(3), 360-375.

Mienczakowski, J., & Morgan, S. (1993). *Busting: The challenge of the drought spirit*. Brisbane, Australia: Griffth University, Reprographics.

Miles, M. B., & Huberman, A. M. (1994). *Qualitative data analysis* (2nd ed.). Thousand Oaks, CA: Sage.

Miller, J. H. (1990). Narrative. In F. Lentricchia & T. McLaughglin (Eds.), *Critical terms for literary study* (pp. 66-79). Chicago: University of Chicago Press.

Mills, C. W. (1959). *The sociological imagination.* New York: Oxford.

Mills, C. W. (1963). *Power, politics, and people: The collected essays of C. Wright Mills* (edited with an introduction by Irving Louis Horowitz). New York: Ballantine.

Mishler, E. G. (1990). Validation in inquiry-guided research: The role of exemplars in narrative studies. *Harvard Educational Review, 60,* 415-441.

Mitchell, R. G., Jr. (1993). *Secrecy and fieldwork.* Newbury Park, CA: Sage.

Mitchell, R. G., Jr., & Charmaz, K. (1995). Telling tales, writing stories. *Journal of Contemporary Ethnography, 25,* 144-166.

Mitchell, W. J. T. (Ed.). (1981). *On narrative.* Chicago: University of Chicago Press.

Morris, M. (1988). *The pirate's fiancee: Feminism, reading, postmodernism.* London: Verso.

Morris, M. (1990). Banality in cultural studies. In P. Mellencamp (Ed.), *Logics of television: Essays in cultural criticism* (pp. 14-43). Bloomington: Indiana University Press.

Morris, M. (1993). At Henry Parkes Motel. In J. Frow & M. Morris (Eds.), *Australian cultural studies: A reader* (pp. 241-275). Urbana: University of Illinois Press.

Morrison, T. (1974). *Sula.* New York: Random House.

Mulkay, M. J. (1985). *The word, and the world: Explorations in the form of sociological analysis.* London: Allen and Unwin.

Nader, L. (1993). Paradigm busting and vertical linkage. *Contemporary Sociology, 22,* 6-7.

Nelson, R. K. (1983). *Make prayers to the raven: A Koyukon view of the northern forest.* Chicago: University of Chicago Press.

Nelson, R. K. (1989). *The island within.* New York: Vantage.

Noddings, N. (1984). *Caring: A feminine approach to ethics and moral education.* Berkeley: University of California Press.

Northcott, A. (1995). *New woman.* Unpublished song, University of Illinois, Institute of Communications Research, Urbana.

Okely, J., & Callaway, H. (Eds.). (1992). *Anthropology and autobiography.* New York: Routledge.

Olesen, V. (1994). Feminist models of qualitative research. In N. K. Denzin & Y. S. Lincoln (Eds.), *The handbook of qualitative research* (pp. 158-174). Thousand Oaks, CA: Sage.

Ong, W. J. (1977). *Interfaces of the world.* Ithaca, NY: Cornell University Press.

Pace, P. (1987). Language poetry: The radical writing project. *Literature in Performance, 7,* 23-33.

Page, B. (1995). *Parkland College instructor mom/student son co-performance text.* Performance text, University of Illinois, Department of Special Education, Urbana.

Paget, D. (1987). Verbatim theatre: Oral history and documentary techniques. *New Theatre Quarterly, 12,* 317-336.

Paget, M. A. (1990a). Performing the text. *Journal of Contemporary Ethnography, 9,* 136-155.

Paget, M. A. (1990b). Life mirrors work mirrors text mirrors life. . . . *Social Problems, 37,* 137-148.

Paget, M. A. (1993). *A complex sorrow* (M. L. DeVault, Ed). Philadelphia: Temple University Press.

Park, R. E. (1950). An autobiographical note. In R. E. Park (Ed.), *Race and culture: Essays in the sociology of contemporary man* (pp. v-ix). New York: Free Press.

Park-Fuller, L. M. (1986). Voices: Bakhtin's heterglossia and polyphony, and the performance of narrative literature. *Literature in Performance, 7,* 1-12.

Paul, R. S. (1992, Fall). The soul of mystery. *The Armchair Detective, 25,* 450-454.

Pauly, J. J. (1990). The politics of the New Journalism. In N. Sims (Ed.), *Literary journalism in the twentieth century* (pp. 110-129). New York: Oxford University Press.

Peirce, C. S. (1905, April). What pragmatism is. *The Monist, 15,* 161-181.

Penzler, O. (1995). Collecting mystery fiction: Dashiell Hammett. *The Armchair Detective, 28,* 404-412.

Peterson, E. E. (1983). Symposium: The audience in interpretation theory: Introduction. *Literature in Performance, 3,* 33.

Pfohl, S. (1992). *Death at the Parasite Cafe: Social science (fictions) and the postmodern.* New York: St. Martin's.

Pickering, J. V. (1975). *Readers theatre.* Belmont, CA: Dickenson.

Poe, E. A. (1966). *Complete stories and poems of Edgar Allan Poe.* New York: Doubleday.

Polkinghorne, D. E. (1988). *Narrative knowing in the human sciences.* Albany: State University of New York Press.

Polkinghorne, D. E. (1995). Narrative configuration in qualitative analysis. In J. A. Hatch & R. Wisniewski (Eds.), *Life history and narrative* (pp. 5-23). Washington, DC: Falmer.

Pollock, D. (1988). Aesthetic negation after WWII: Mediating Bertolt Brecht and Theodor Adorno. *Literature in Performance, 8,* 12-20.

Porter, D. (1981). *The pursuit of crime: Art and ideology in detective fiction.* New Haven, CT: Yale University Press.

Prattis, J. I. (Ed.). (1985a). *Reflections: The anthropological muse.* Washington, DC: American Anthropological Association.

Prattis, J. I. (1985b). Dialectics and experience in fieldwork: The poetic dimension. In J. I. Prattis (Ed.), *Reflections: The anthropological muse* (pp. 266-283). Washington, DC: American Anthropological Association.

Prattis, J. I. (1985c). The bear—On the birth of my son. In J. I. Prattis (Ed.), *Reflections: The anthropological muse* (pp. 81-82). Washington, DC: American Anthropological Association.

Press group asks return of "Jimmy" award. (1981, April 23). *Washington Post,* p. B2.

Price, D. (1985). Preface to my thesis. In J. I. Prattis (Ed.), *Reflections: The anthropological muse* (pp. 220). Washington, DC: American Anthropological Association.

Probyn, E. (1993). *Sexing the self: Gendered positions in cultural studies.* London: Routledge.

Pronzini, B., & Greenberg, M. H. (Eds.). (1985a). *The ethnic detectives: Masterpieces of mystery fiction.* New York: Dodd, Mead.

Pronzini, B., & Greenberg, M. H. (1985b). Introduction. In B. Pronzini & M. H. Greenberg (Eds.), *The ethnic detectives: Masterpieces of mystery fiction* (pp. ix-xii). New York: Dodd, Mead.

Propp, V. (1968). *The morphology of the folktale* (L. Scott, Trans.) (Rev. ed.). Austin: University of Texas Press. (Original work published 1928)

Prus, R. (1996). *Symbolic interaction and ethnographic research.* Albany: State University of New York Press.

Psathas, G. (1995). *Conversation analysis: The study of talk-in-interaction.* Thousand Oaks, CA: Sage.

Quantz, R. A. (1992). On critical ethnography (with some postmodern consideration). In M. D. LeCompte, W. L. Millroy, & J. Preissel (Eds.), *The handbook of qualitative research in education* (pp. 447-506). New York: Academic Press.

Rabinow, P. (Ed.). (1984). *The Foucault reader.* New York: Pantheon.

Racevskis, K. (1983). *Michel Foucault and the subversion of intellect.* Ithaca, NY: Cornell University Press.

Radway, J. (1988). Reception study: Ethnography and the problems of dispersed audiences and nomadic subjects. *Cultural Studies, 3*, 359-376.

Ramos, M. (1993). *The ballad of Rocky Ruiz.* New York: St. Martin's.

Ramos, M. (1994). *The ballad of Gato Guerrero.* New York: St. Martin's.

Reason, P. (1994). Three approaches to participative inquiry. In N. K. Denzin & Y. S. Lincoln (Eds.), *The handbook of qualitative research* (pp. 324-339). Thousand Oaks, CA: Sage.

Reevell, P. (1995). Review of Robert C. Allen to be continued . . . soap operas around the world. *Media, Culture & Society, 17*, 701-704.

Reese, S. D. (1990). The news paradigm and the ideology of objectivity: A socialist at the Wall Street Journal. *Critical Studies in Mass Communication, 7*, 390-409.

Reid, A. (1982, February 22). Notes from a Spanish village. *New Yorker*, pp. 30-45.

Reissman, C. A. (1993). *Narrative analysis.* Newbury Park, CA: Sage.

Richardson, L. (1991). Postmodern social theory. *Sociological Theory, 9*, 173-179.

Richardson, L. (1992). The consequences of poetic representation: Writing the other, rewriting the self. In C. Ellis & M. G. Flaherty (Eds.), *Investigating subjectivity: Research on lived experience* (pp. 125-137). Newbury Park, CA: Sage.

Richardson, L. (1993). Poetic representation, ethnographic representation and transgressive validity: The case of the skipped line. *Sociological Quarterly, 34*, 695-710.

Richardson, L. (1994a). Writing as a method of inquiry. In N. K. Denzin & Y. S. Lincoln (Eds.), *The handbook of qualitative research* (pp. 516-529). Thousand Oaks, CA: Sage.

Richardson, L. (1994b). Nine poems: Marriage and the family. *Journal of Contemporary Ethnography, 23*, 3-14.

Richardson, L. (1995). Writing-stories: Co-authoring "The Sea Monster," a writing story. *Qualitative Inquiry, 1*, 189-203.

Richardson, L. (in press). But is it sociology? *Journal of Contemporary Ethnography.*

Richardson, L., & Lockridge, E. (1991). The sea monster: An ethnographic drama. *Symbolic Interaction, 14*, 335-340.

Riley, T. J. (1995, January 20). Letter to the editor: Controversial editorship at anthropology journal. *Chronical of Higher Education*, A20.

Rinehart, R. (1994). Warp speed in Barcelona: Olympism, ideology and experience. *Studies in Symbolic Interaction, 16*, 123-159.

Roman, L. (1992). The political significance of other ways of narrating ethnography: A feminist materialist approach. In M. D. Le Compte, W. L. Millroy, & J. Preissle (Eds.), *The handbook of qualitative research in education* (pp. 555-594). New York: Academic Press.

Ronai, C. R. (1992). The reflexive self through narrative: A night in the life of an erotic dancer/researcher. In C. Ellis & M. G. Flaherty (Eds.), *Investigating subjectivity: Research on lived experience* (pp. 102-124). Newbury Park, CA: Sage.

Ronai, C. R. (1995). Multiple reflections of child sex abuse: An argument for a layered account. *Journal of Contemporary Ethnography, 23*, 395-426.

Rorty, R. (1980). *Philosophy and the mirror of nature.* Princeton, NJ: Princeton University Press.

Rorty, R. (1989). *Contingency, irony, and solidarity.* Cambridge, UK: Cambridge University Press.

Rorty, R. (1991). *Objectivity, relativism, and truth.* New York: Cambridge University Press.

Rosaldo, R. (1989). *Culture & truth.* Boston: Beacon.

Rose, D. (1990). *Living the ethnographic life* (Qualitative Research Series, Vol. 23). Newbury Park, CA: Sage.

Rose, D. (1991). In search of experience: The anthropological poetics of Stanley Diamond. In I. Brady (Ed.), *Anthropological poetics* (pp. 219-233). Savage, MD: Rowman & Littlefield.

Rose, E. (1995). The wearld. *Studies in Symbolic Interaction, 17*, 110-135.

Rosen, J. (1994). Making things more public: On the political responsibility of the media intellectual. *Critical Studies in Mass Communication, 11*, 362-388.

Rosenbaum, R. (1995, January 15). The great Ivy League nude posture photo scandal. *New York Times Magazine*, pp. 26-31, 40, 46, 55-56.

Ross, A. (1988). The new sentence and the commodity form: Recent American writing. In C. Nelson & L. Grossberg (Eds.), *Marxism and the interpretation of culture* (pp. 361-380). Urbana: University of Illinois Press.

Ryan, K. E. (1995). Evaluation ethics and issues of social justice: Contributions from female moral thinking. In N. K. Denzin (Ed.), *Studies in symbolic interaction: A research annual* (Vol. 19, pp. 143-151). Greenwich, CT: JAI.

Sanders, C. R. (1995). Stranger than fiction: Insights and pitfalls in post-modern ethnography. *Studies in Symbolic Interaction, 17*, 89-104.

Sanmiguel, L. M. (1995). *Re-defining endometriosis/re-defining me.* Unpublished play, University of Illinois, Institute of Communications Research, Urbana.

Sartre, J.-P. (1963). *Search for a method.* New York: Knopf.

Sayre, H. (1990). Performance. In F. Lentricchia & T. McLaughglin (Eds.), *Critical terms for literary study* (pp. 91-104). Chicago: University of Chicago Press.

Schechner, R. (1986). Magnitudes of performance. In V. M. Turner & E. M. Bruner (Eds.), *The anthropology of experience* (pp. 344-369). Urbana: University of Illinois Press.

Scheurich, J. J. (1992). *The paradigmatic transgressions of validity.* Unpublished manuscript.

Schmitt, R. L. (1993). Cornerville as obdurate reality: Retooling the research act through postmodernism. *Studies in Symbolic Interaction, 15*, 121-145.

Schneider, J. W. (1991). Troubles with textual authority in sociology. *Symbolic Interaction, 14*, 295-319.

Schopen, B. (1989). *The big silence.* New York: Mysterious Press.

Schopen, B. (1990). *The desert look.* New York: Mysterious Press.

Schratz, M. (1993a). Voices in educational research: An introduction. In M. Schratz (Ed.), *Qualitative voices in educational research: Social science and educational studies series 9* (pp. 1-7). London: Falmer.

Schratz, M. (1993b). An epilogue: Putting voices together. In M. Schratz (Ed.), *Qualitative voices in educational research: Social science and educational studies series 9* (pp. 179-184). London: Falmer.

Schratz, M. (Ed.) (1993c). *Qualitative voices in educational research: Social science and educational studies series 9.* London: Falmer.

Schrum, L. (1995). Framing the debate: Ethical research in the information age. *Qualitative Inquiry, 1*, 311-326.

Schudson, M. (1978). *Discovering the news: A social history of American newspapers.* New York: Basic Books.

Schwandt, T. A. (1996). Farewell to criteriology. *Qualitative Inquiry, 2*(1), 58-72.

Schwarz, B. (1994). Where is cultural studies? *Cultural Studies, 8*, 377-393.

Sedgwick, E. K. (1987). A poem is being written. *Representations, 17*, 110-119.

Sedgwick, E. K. (1990). *Epistemology of the closet.* Berkeley: University of California Press.

Seidman, S. (1991). The end of sociological theory: The postmodern hope. *Sociological Theory, 9,* 131-146.

Seidman, S. (1994). Symposium: Queer theory/sociology: A dialogue. *Sociological Theory, 12,* 166-177.

Sharpe, J. (1993). *Allegories of empire: The figure of woman in the colonial text.* Minneapolis: University of Minnesota Press.

Sheehy, G. (1973). *Hustling: Prostitution in our wide-open society.* New York: Dell.

Shelton, A. (1994). My bloody valentine. *Studies in Symbolic Interaction, 16,* 191-211.

Shelton, A. (1995a). Foucault's madonna: The secret life of Carolyn Ellis. *Symbolic Interaction, 18,* 83-87.

Shelton, A. (1995b). The man at the end of the machine. *Symbolic Interaction, 18,* 505-518.

Shi, D. E. (1995). *Facing facts: Realism in American thought and culture, 1850-1920.* New York: Oxford University Press.

Sieber, J. E. (1992). *Planning ethically responsible research: A guide for students and internal review boards.* Newbury Park, CA: Sage.

Silet, C. P. (1993, Fall). A little class on murder: An interview with Carolyn G. Hart. *The Armchair Detective, 26,* 46-49.

Silverman, D. (1993). *Interpreting qualitative data: Methods for analyzing talk, text and interaction.* Newbury Park, CA: Sage.

Silverman, K. (1988). *The acoustic mirror: The female voice in psychoanalysis and cinema.* Bloomington: Indiana University Press.

Sims, N. (Ed.). (1984). *The literary journalists.* New York: Ballantine.

Sims, N. (Ed.). (1990). *Literary journalism in the twentieth century.* New York: Oxford University Press.

Sjoberg, G., Gill, E., Williams, N., & Kuhn, K. E. (1995). Ethics, human rights and sociological inquiry: Genocide, politicide and other issues of organizational power. *American Sociologist, 26,* 8-19.

Smith, D. E. (1987). *The everyday world as problematic: A feminist sociology.* Boston: Northwestern University Press.

Smith, D. E. (1989). Sociological theory: Methods of writing patriarchy. In R. A. Wallace (Ed.), *Feminism and sociological theory* (pp. 34-64). Newbury Park, CA: Sage.

Smith, D. E. (1990a). *The conceptual practices of power: A feminist sociology of knowledge.* Boston: Northeastern University Press.

Smith, D. E. (1990b). *Texts, facts, and femininity: Exploring the relations of ruling.* New York: Routledge.

Smith, D. E. (1992). Sociology from women's perspective: A reaffirmation. *Sociological Theory, 10,* 88-97.

Smith, D. E. (1993). High noon in textland: A critique of Clough. *Sociological Quarterly, 34,* 183-192.

Smith, G. W. (1990). Political activist as ethnographer. *Social Problems, 37,* 629-648.

Smith, J., Harre, R., & Van Langenhove, L. (Eds.). (1995). *Rethinking psychology, Vol. 1: Conceptual foundations.* London: Sage.

Smith, J. K. (1984). The problem of criteria for judging interpretive inquiry. *Educational Evaluation and Policy Analysis, 6,* 379-391.

Smith, L. (1995, October 8). Review, southern exposure by Alice Adams [Book Review]. *New York Times,* p. 7.

Smithsonian seals off nude photos. (1995, January 21). *New York Times,* p. A9.

Snow, D., & Morrill, C. (1993). Reflections on anthropology's ethnographic crisis of faith: Review essay: Culture and anomie by Christopher Herbert, The Savage Witches by Henrika Kuklick, Romantic Motives by George Stocking, Jr., and Colonial Situations by George Stocking, Jr. *Contemporary Sociology, 22,* 8-11.

Snow, D., & Morrill, C. (1995a). A revolution? Review-essay, Handbook of Qualitative Research, co-editors, N. Denzin and Y. S. Lincoln. *Journal of Contemporary Ethnography, 22,* 341-349.

Snow, D., & Morrill, C. (1995b). Ironies, puzzles, and contradictions in Denzin and Lincoln's vision of qualitative research. *Journal of Contemporary Ethnography, 22,* 358-362.

Snyder, G. (1990). *The practice of the wild: Essays by Gary Snyder.* New York: North Point Press.

Special issue: Street corner society revisited. (1992). *Journal of Contemporary Ethnography, 21*(1), entire issue.

Spender, S. (1984). Introduction. In M. Lowery (Ed.), *Under the volcano* (pp. xii-xxiii). New York: New American Library. (Original work published 1947)

Spindler, G., & Spindler, L. (1992a). Cultural process and ethnography: An anthropological perspective. In M. D. LeCompte, W. L. Millroy, & J. Preissle (Eds.), *The handbook of qualitative research in education* (pp. 53-92). New York: Academic Press.

Spindler, G., & Spindler, L. (1992b). Crosscultural, comparative, reflective interviewing in Schonhausen and Roseville. In M. Schratz (Ed.), *Qualitative voices in educational research: Social science and educational studies series 9* (pp. 106-125). London: Falmer.

Spivak, G. C. (1988). Can the subaltern speak? In C. Nelson & L. Grossberg (Eds.), *Marxism and the interpretation of cultures* (pp. 271-313). Urbana: University of Illinois Press.

Spivak, G. C. (1990). *The post-colonial critic: Interviews, strategies, dialogues* (S. Harasym, Ed.). New York: Routledge.

Springer, C. (1991). Comprehension and crisis: Reporter films and the Third World. In L. D. Friedman (Ed.), *Unspeakable images: Ethnicity and the American cinema* (pp. 167-189). Urbana: University of Illinois Press.

Stabile, C. A. (1995). Resistance, recuperation, and reflexity: The limits of a paradigm. *Critical Studies in Mass Communication, 12,* 403-422.

Stacey, J. (1994). *Star gazing: Hollywood cinema and female spectatorship.* New York: Routledge.

Stake, R. (1994). Case studies. In N. K. Denzin & Y. S. Lincoln (Eds.), *The handbook of qualitative research* (pp. 236-247). Thousand Oaks, CA: Sage.

Stern, C. S., & Henderson, B. (1993). *Performance texts and contexts.* New York: Longman.

Stevens, M. (1992). Susan Krieger's The Mirror Dance: Lessons of a deficient sociology. *Studies in Symbolic Interaction, 13,* 83-100.

Stewart, J. (1989). *Drinkers, drummers, and decent folk: Ethnographic narratives of village trinidad.* Albany: State University of New York Press.

Stinchcombe, A. L. (1994). The disintegrated disciplines and the future of sociology. *Sociological Forum, 9,* 279-291.

Stoller, P., & Olkes, C. (1987). *In sorcery's shadow.* Chicago: University of Chicago Press.

Stout, D. (1995, August 30). A child at play and Malcolm's missing notes. *New York Times,* pp. B1, B4.

Straley, J. (1992). *The woman who married a bear.* New York: Signet.

Straley, J. (1993). *The curious eat themselves.* New York: Bantam Books.

Straley, J. (1996). *The music of what happens.* New York: Bantam Books.

Strauss, A., & Corbin, J. (1990). *Basics of qualitative research.* Newbury Park, CA: Sage.

Strine, M. S. (1988). Response: Negotiating the tensions between art and everyday life. *Literature in Performance, 8,* 35-38.

Strine, M. S., Long, B., & Hopkins, M. F. (1990). Research in interpretation and performance studies. In G. M. Phillips & J. T. Wood (Eds.), *Speech communication: Essays to commemorate the seventy-fifth anniversary of the Speech Communication Association.* Carbondale: Southern Illinois University Press.

Stucky, N. (1993). Toward an aesthetics of natural performance. *Text and Performance Quarterly, 13,* 168-180.

Symons, J. (1985). *Bloody murder: From the detective story to the crime novel.* London: Viking.

Talese, G. (1972). *Honor thy father.* New York: Fawcett.

Tallant, C. (1988). Editor's introduction: Symposium: Performance and critical theory—The Frankfurt School. *Literature in Performance, 8,* 1-3.

Taussig, M. (1993). *Mimesis and alterity.* New York: Routledge.

Tedlock, D. (1983). *The spoken word and the word of interpretation.* Philadelphia: University of Pennsylvania Press.

Terry, J. (1991). Theorizing deviant historiography. *Differences, 3,* 55-74.

Thompson, H. S. (1967). *Hell's Angels: A strange and terrible saga.* New York: Ballantine.

Thompson, H. S. (1973). *Fear and loathing: On the campaign trail of '72.* San Francisco: Straight Arrow.

Thompson, H. S. (1979). *The great shark hunt.* New York: Summit.

Thompson, J. (1993). *Fiction, crime, and empire.* Urbana: University of Illinois Press.

Timmermans, S. (1994). Sociological poetics. *Studies in Symbolic Interaction, 16,* 79-83.

Timmermans, S. (1995). Cui bono? Institutional review board ethics and ethnographic research. Studies in Symbolic Interaction, 19, 155-173.

Todorov, T. (1977). *The poetics of prose.* Ithaca, NY: Cornell University Press.

Tong, R. (1993). *Feminine and feminist ethics.* Belmont, CA: Wadsworth.

Travisano, R. V. (1994). Lobstering out of Narrow River: Minding one's grasp. *Studies in Symbolic Interaction, 16,* 161-190.

Trinh, T. M-ha. (1989). *Woman, native, other: Writing postcoloniality and feminism.* Bloomington: Indiana University Press.

Trinh, T. M-ha. (1991). *When the moon waxes red: Representation, gender and cultural politics.* New York: Routledge.

Trinh, T. M-ha. (1992). *Framer framed.* New York: Routledge.

Turner, E. (1993). Experience and poetics in anthropological writing. In P. Benson (Ed.), *Anthropology and literature* (pp. 27-47). Urbana: University of Illinois Press.

Turner, V. (1981). Social dramas and stories about them. In W. Mitchell (Ed.), *On narrative* (pp. 141-168). Chicago: University of Chicago Press.

Turner, V. (1982). *From ritual to theatre.* New York: Performing Arts Journal Publications.

Turner, V. (1986a). Dewey, Dilthey, and drama: An essay in the anthropology of experience. In V. M. Turner & E. M. Bruner (Eds.), The anthropology of experience (pp. 33-44). Urbana: University of Illinois Press.

Turner, V. (1986b). *The anthropology of performance.* New York: Performing Arts Journal Publications.

Turner, V., & Bruner, E. (Eds.). (1986). *The anthropology of experience.* Urbana: University of Illinois Press.

Turner, V. (with Turner, E.). (1982). Performing ethnography. *Drama Review, 26,* 33-50.

Tyler, P. E., & Simons, L. M. (1981, April 17). "Jimmy" episode evokes outrage, sadness. *Washington Post,* p. A3.

Tyler, S. A. (1986). Post-modern ethnography: From document of the occult to occult document. In J. Clifford & G. E. Marcus (Eds.), *Writing culture* (pp. 122-140). Berkeley: University of California Press.

Ulmer, G. (1989). *Teletheory*. New York: Routledge.

Ulmer, G. L. (1994). *Heuretics: The logic of invention*. Baltimore, MD: Johns Hopkins University Press.

Updike, J. (1995, August 10). Hopper's polluted silence. *New York Review of Books, 42*(13), pp. 19-21.

Van Maanen, J. (1988). *Tales of the field*. Chicago: University of Chicago Press.

Van Maanen, J. (Ed.). (1995a). *Representation in ethnography*. Thousand Oaks, CA: Sage.

Van Maanen, J. (1995b). An end to innocence: The ethnography of ethnography. In J. Van Maanen (Ed.), *Representation in ethnography* (pp. 1-35). Thousand Oaks, CA: Sage.

Van Oosting, J. (1981). Some observations upon the common aesthetics of story writing and the solo performance of prose fiction. *Literature in Performance, 2*, 66-75.

Vidich, A. J., & Lyman, S. M. (1994). Qualitative methods: Their history in sociology and anthropology. In N. K. Denzin & Y. S. Lincoln (Eds.), *The handbook of qualitative research* (pp. 23-59). Thousand Oaks, CA: Sage.

Walker, A. (1983). *In search of our mothers' gardens*. New York: Harcourt Brace Jovanovich.

Walsh, E. (1981, April 23). "Jimmy's World" is a dominant topic as nation's newspaper editors meet. *Washington Post*, p. A3.

Walstrom, M. (1996). "Mystory" of anorexia nervosa: New discourses for change and recovery. *Cultural Studies: A Research Annual, 1*, 67-99.

Warren, R. P. (1946). *All the king's men*. New York: Harcourt Brace.

Webster, S. (1982). Dialogue and fiction in ethnography. *Dialectical Anthropology, 7*, 91-114.

Weitzman, E. A., & Miles, M. B. (1995). *A software sourcebook: Computer programs for qualitative data analysis*. Thousand Oaks, CA: Sage.

Westerman, F. (1985). Here come the anthros. In J. I. Prattis (Ed.), *Reflections: The anthropological muse* (pp. 237-238). Washington, DC: American Anthropological Association.

White, H. V. (1973). *Metahistory*. Baltimore, MD: Johns Hopkins University Press.

White, M. (1992). Ideological analysis. In R. C. Allen (Ed.), *Television and channels of discourse, reassembled: Contemporary criticism (2nd ed., pp. 161-202)*. Chapel Hill: University of North Carolina Press.

Whyte, W. F. (1943). *Street corner society*. Chicago: University of Chicago Press.

Whyte, W. F. (1955). *Street corner society* (2nd ed.). Chicago: University of Chicago Press.

Whyte, W. F. (1981). *Street corner society* (3rd ed.). Chicago: University of Chicago Press.

Whyte, W. F. (1992). In defense of street corner society. *Journal of Contemporary Ethnography, 21*, 52-68.

Whyte, W. F. (1993). *Street corner society* (4th ed.). Chicago: University of Chicago Press.

Wiley, N. (1995). *The semiotic self*. Chicago: University of Chicago Press.

Wilson, E. (1946). Who killed Roger Ackroyd? In H. Haycraft (Ed.), *The art of the mystery story* (pp. 390-397). New York: Simon & Schuster.

Wimsatt, W. K., & Beardsley, M. C. (1954). The intentional fallacy. In D. Newton-de Molina (Ed.), *On literary intention* (pp. 1-13). Edinburgh, UK: Edinburgh University Press.

Wolcott, H. F. (1992). Posturing in qualitative research. In M. D. LeCompte, W. L. Millroy, & J. Preissle (Eds.), *The handbook of qualitative research in education* (pp. 3-52). New York: Academic Press.

Wolcott, H. F. (1994). *Transforming qualitative data: Description, analysis and interpretation.* Thousand Oaks, CA: Sage.

Wolcott, J. (1995, September 25). Raymond Chandler's smoking gun. *The New Yorker,* pp. 99-104.

Wolfe, M. (1992). *A thrice-told tale: Feminism, postmodernism, and ethnographic responsibility.* Stanford, CA: Stanford University Press.

Wolfe, T. (1969). *The electric Kool-Aid acid test.* New York: Bantam.

Wolfe, T. (1973). The New Journalism. In T. Wolfe & E. W. Johnson (Eds.), *The New Journalism: An anthology* (pp. ix-52). New York: Harper & Row.

Wolfe, T. (1982). *Tom Wolfe: The purple decades: A reader selected by Tom Wolfe.* New York: Farrar, Straus, & Giroux.

Wolfe, T. (1987). *The bonfire of the vanities.* New York: Farrar.

Wolfe, T., & Johnson, E. W. (Eds.). (1973). *The New Journalism: An anthology.* New York: Harper & Row.

Zavarzadeh, M. (1976). *The mythopoeic reality: The postwar American nonfiction novel.* Urbana: University of Illinois Press.

Zelizer, B. (1992). *Covering the body: The Kennedy assassination, the media, and the shaping of collective memory.* Chicago: University of Chicago Press.

Zelizer, B. (1993). Journalists as interpretive communities. *Critical Studies in Mass Communications, 10,* 291-237.

Zelizer, B. (1995). Journalism's "last" stand: Wirephoto and the discourse of resistance. *Journal of Communication, 45,* 78-92.

Zeller, N. (1995). Narrative strategies for case reports. In J. A. Hatch & R. Wisniewski (Eds.), *Life history and narrative* (pp. 75-88). Washington, DC: Falmer.

Zeman, B. T., & Zeman, A. (1992, Fall). The cornerstones of crime. *The Armchair Detective, 25,* 434-444.

Zola, I. K. (1982). *Missing pieces: A chronicle of living with a disability.* Philadelphia: Temple University Press.

Note

1. I thank Patricia T. Clough for this reference.

Index

315

and intertextual reflexivity, 220
Turner, Victor:
  liminal experiences, 92, 123
  and performance, 91-92, 103
Tyler, Stephen, 163, 164, 167, 173

Ulmer, Gregory:
  and interpretive reading,
    239-40
  see also Mystory and Teletheory

Validity:
  and critical poststructuralism,
    6-7,9
  and journalism, 132
  as legitimization, 13-14
  in Malcolm/Masson story, 152-56
  in new writing, 253-54
  and poetic texts, 210, 216-17
  and politics, 9
  and postpositivism, 6
  and power, 6
  and verisimilitude, 10-13
Van Maanen, John, 205
Verbal Texts, 31-36, 40-48:
  inscription of, 41-45
Verisimilitude:
  deconstructive, 13
  levels of, 10
  multiple forms of, 20
Voyeurism:
  and cinema, 18-19, 45

White, Hayden, 132-33
Whyte, William Foote, 12-13, 128-29
Wolfe, Marjorie:
  on methodological reflexivity, 219, 221
Wolfe, Thomas:
  as detective, 166
  and new journalist epistemology, 130,
    133-35
  and social realism, 139
  writing approach of, 137-38
Writing:
  and autoethnography, 26
  crime, 163-95
  experimental ethnographic, 48n.3,
    126-28, 138-39
  as inscription, 25-26
  L. Grossberg models of, 88n.8
  J. Joyce on, 21-27
  and lived experience, 26
  and modernist inscription, 33
  new forms of, 45-48
  and narrative, 158n.1
  and queer theory, 83
  seven points of, 131
  social science versus journalism, 129
  and standpoint theory, 85-87
Woman, Native, Other, (Trinh), 72
Writing Culture, (Clifford and Marcus),
    xv-xvi, xvii, 27, 250-51
Writing culture:
  journalism and ethnography, 280-87

Zavarzadeh, Musud, 136-37, 138

About the Author

Norman K. Denzin is Distinguished Professor of Communications, College of Communications scholar, and Professor of Sociology and Humanities at the University of Illinois, Urbana-Champaign. He is author of numerous books, including *The Cinematic Society, Images of Postmodern Society, The Research Act, Interpretive Interactionism, Hollywood Shot by Shot, Symbolic Interactionism and Cultural Studies, The Recovering Alcoholic,* and *The Alcoholic Self,* which won the Cooley Award from the Society for the Study of Symbolic Interaction in 1988. He is editor of *Studies in Symbolic Interaction: A Research Annual, Cultural Studies,* and *The Sociological Quarterly.* He is coeditor of the Sage publication, *Handbook of Qualitative Research,* and coeditor of *Qualitative Inquiry.*